Contingency, Hegemony, Universality

PHRONESIS

A series from Verso edited by
Ernesto Laclau and Chantal Mouffe

Since 1989, when the first Phronesis book was published, many events of fundamental importance to the series have taken place. Some of them initially brought the hope that great possibilities were opening up for the extension and deepening of democracy, one of the main points of focus in our reflections. Disenchantment, however, came quickly and what we witnessed instead was the reinforcement and generalization of the neoliberal hegemony. Today, the left-wing project is in an even deeper crisis than it was ten years ago. An increasing number of social-democratic parties, under the pretence of 'modernizing' themselves, are discarding their Left identity. According to the advocates of the 'third way', and with the advent of globalization, the time has come to abandon the old dogmas of Left and Right and promote a new entrepreneurial spirit at all levels of society.

Phronesis's objective is to establish a dialogue among all those who assert the need to redefine the Left/Right distinction – which constitutes the crucial dynamic of modern democracy – instead of relinquishing it. Our original concern, which was to bring together left-wing politics and the theoretical developments around the critique of essentialism, is more pertinent than ever. Indeed, we still believe that the most important trends in contemporary theory – deconstruction, psychoanalysis, the philosophy of language as initiated by the later Wittgenstein and post-Heideggerian hermeneutics – are the necessary conditions for understanding the widening of social struggles characteristic of the present stage of democratic politics, and for formulating a new vision for the Left in terms of radical and plural democracy.

Contingency, Hegemony, Universality

Contemporary Dialogues on the Left

JUDITH BUTLER, ERNESTO LACLAU
and SLAVOJ ŽIŽEK

VERSO

London • New York

First published by Verso 2000
© Judith Butler, Ernesto Laclau, Slavoj Žižek 2000
All rights reserved

The moral rights of the authors have been asserted

5   7   9   10   8   6   4

Verso
UK: 6 Meard Street, London W1F 0EG
US: 180 Varick Street, New York, NY 10014–4606

Verso is the imprint of New Left Books

ISBN 1-85984-757–9
ISBN 1–85984–278–X (pbk)

British Library Cataloguing in Publication Data
A catalogue record for this book is available from the British Library

Library of Congress Cataloging-in-Publication Data
A catalog record for this book is available from the Library of Congress

Typeset by M Rules
Printed by Biddles Ltd, www.biddles.co.uk

Contents

Introduction

The three of us conferred for a few years on how to put together a volume that seeks both to establish the common trajectory of our thought and to stage in a productive way the different intellectual commitments that we have. We started this process by producing the three questionnaires which appear at the beginning of the volume. The result that you have before you thus represents the culmination of several conversations, of several written reviews and exchanges, and, in the case of Slavoj Žižek and Ernesto Laclau, a collaboration that dates back to 1985, the year that Chantal Mouffe and Ernesto Laclau published *Hegemony and Socialist Strategy*. In fact, that book provides the background for this dialogue, not only because it established a new direction to Antonio Gramsci's notion of hegemony, but also because it represented a turn to poststructuralist theory within Marxism, one that took the problem of language to be essential to the formulation of an antitotalitarian, radical democratic project.

There are arguments in that book which are reconsidered through different theoretical lenses in the present one, and there are also arguments made against that text which are implicitly taken up in the written exchange that follows. One argument in the book took the following form: new social movements often rely on identity-claims, but 'identity' itself is never fully constituted; in fact, since identification is not reducible to identity, it is important to consider the incommensurability or gap between them. It does not follow that the failure of identity to achieve complete determination undermines the social movements at issue; on the contrary, that incompleteness is essential to the project of hegemony itself. No social movement can, in fact, enjoy its status as an open-ended, democratic political articulation without presuming and operationalizing the negativity at the heart of identity.

The theoretical category which attempted to understand this failure, negativity, gap or incompleteness was that of 'antagonism' as formulated in that earlier work. Subsequently Laclau, who continues to situate himself in the Gramscian tradition, elaborated the category of 'dislocation', drawing his tools from an intellectual spectrum from Derrida and Lacan to Wittgenstein. Whereas Žižek most emphatically makes use of Lacanian theory to address this issue, especially through recourse to 'the Real', he also makes use of Hegel, and offers reasons for eschewing the Derridan framework. Butler may be said to make use of a different Hegel, emphasizing the possibilities of negation in his work, along with Foucault and some Derrida, to consider what remains unrealizable in the discursive constitution of the subject.

There are significant differences among us on the question of the 'subject', and this comes through as we each attempt to take account of what constitutes or conditions the failure of any claim to identity to achieve final or full determination. What remains true, however, is that we each value this 'failure' as a condition of democratic contestation itself. Where we differ is how to conceive of the subject – whether it is foundational, Cartesian; whether it is structured by sexual difference, and through what means the definition of that sexual difference is secured. We also disagree on whether to understand the failure of identity as a structural or necessary feature of all identity-constitution, and how to take account of that structure and necessity. Whereas Butler is aligned with a historically variable account of subject-constitution (a Foucauldian line), Žižek bases his claims about the founding negativity of identity in the work of Lacan and Laclau in an approach which, without being strictly Lacanian, has several points of convergence with the Lacanian Real.

One of the arguments made against *Hegemony and Socialist Strategy* – and, indeed, against structuralist and poststructuralist interventions in political theory – is that it either fails to take account of the concept of universality or erodes its force by questioning its foundational status. All three of us, however, maintain that universality is not a static presumption, not an a priori given, and that it ought instead to be understood as a process or condition irreducible to any of its determinate modes of appearance. Whereas we sometimes differ on how the emphasis is to be made, we each offer accounts of universality which assume that the negative condition of all political articulation is 'universal' (Žižek), that the contestatory process determines forms of universality which are brought into a productive and ultimately irresolvable conflict with each other (Laclau), or that there is a process of translation by which the repudiated within universality is readmitted into the term in the process of remaking it (Butler).

Along the way, we each consider different ideological deployments of universality, and caution against both substantial and procedural approaches to the question. We thus differentiate ourselves (already internally differentiated) from the Habermasian effort to discover or conjure a pre-established universality as the presupposition of the speech act, a universality which is said to pertain to a rational feature of 'man', a substantive conception of universality which equates it with a knowable and predictable determination, and a procedural form which presumes that the political field is constituted by rational actors.

Of importance throughout these essays is the strategic question of hegemony: of how the political field is constituted, of what possibilities emerge from an approach to the political field that inquires into conditions of its possibility and articulation. Significantly, Laclau detects a movement of Marxist theory from the postulation of a 'universal class' which would ultimately eliminate political mediation and relations of representation, to a 'hegemonic' universality which makes the political constitutive of the social link. The poststructuralism of his approach is thus aligned with the critique of totalitarianism and, specifically, the trope of a 'knowing' vanguard subject who 'is' all the social relations he articulates and mobilizes. Whereas Laclau associates Hegel with the metaphysics of closure, Žižek understands him as a theorist of reflexivity in confrontation with the Real, and Butler makes use of him to inquire into the necessary limits of formalism in any account of sociality. Laclau makes clear the anti-totalitarianism of a logical and linguistic

approach to the problem of representation that insists upon the irre-
ducibility of difference. Žižek reminds us that global capital cannot be
excluded from the 'postmodern' analysis of language and culture, and
continues to expose the obscene underside of power. Butler raises the
question of how new social movements rearticulate the problem of
hegemony, considering the challenge of recent sexual politics to the
theory of sexual difference, and proposes a counter-imperialist conception of translation.

We are all three committed to radical forms of democracy that seek
to understand the processes of representation by which political articulation proceeds, the problem of identification – and its necessary
failures – by which political mobilization takes place, the question of the
future as it emerges for theoretical frameworks that insist upon the productive force of the negative. Although we do not self-consciously reflect
upon the place of the intellectual on the Left, perhaps this text will
operate as a certain kind of placement, one that recasts (and retrieves)
philosophy as a critical mode of inquiry that belongs – antagonisti-
cally – to the sphere of politics.

During the course of our debates, we quote extensively from one
another's contributions. Such cross-references are identified by the
writer's initials, followed by the relevant page number.

This volume was written mainly in the spring and summer of 1999,
co-ordinated by editors Jane Hindle and Sebastian Budgen at Verso. We
have them to thank for keeping us on track. Judith Butler also thanks
Stuart Murray for his indispensable assistance with the manuscript.

J.B., E.L., S.Ž., September 1999

Questions

These are the questions each author wanted to address to the others; they form the basis of the dialogues in the book.

QUESTIONS FROM JUDITH BUTLER

1. I would like to know more precisely whether the Lacanian view on the constitution of the subject is compatible with the notion of hegemony. I understand that the notion of the uncompleted subject or the barred subject appears to guarantee a certain incompletion of interpellation, but does it not do this by way of installing a bar as the condition and structure of all subject-constitution? Is the incompleteness of subject-formation that hegemony requires one in which the subject-in-process is incomplete precisely because it is constituted through exclusions that are politically salient, not structurally static? In other words, isn't the incompletion of subject-formation linked to the democratic process of the contestation over signifiers? Can the ahistorical recourse to the Lacanian bar be reconciled with the strategic question that hegemony poses, or does it stand as a quasi-transcendental limitation on all possible subject-formation and, hence, as indifferent to politics?

2. What constitutes a viable theory of agency for contemporary political life? Does the Derridan notion of 'decision' suffice to explain the

kinds of negotiations that political agency requires? Is 'decision' an ethical or existential category and, if so, how is it to be related to the sphere of the political?

3.   What is the status of 'logic' in describing social and political process and in the description of subject-formation? Does a logic that invariably results in aporias produce a kind of status that is inimical to the project of hegemony? (This question is a subsidiary to Question 1.) Are such logics incarnated in social practice? What is the relation between logic and social practice?

4.   What is the relation between psychoanalytic versions of identification and forms of political identification? Does psychoanalysis provide the theory for politics? And which psychoanalysis?

5.   Is it possible to talk about 'the metaphysical logic of identity' as if it were singular?

6.   What does it mean performatively to assume a subject-position, and is that ever simple?

7.   If sexual difference is a deadlock, does that mean that feminism is a dead end? If sexual difference is 'real' in the Lacanian sense, does that mean that it has no place in hegemonic struggles? Or is it the quasi-transcendental limit to all such struggle, and hence frozen in place as the pre- or ahistorical?

8.   Is the recent effort to divide critical theories into universalisms and historicisms part of a failed and blinded dialectic that refuses to discriminate among nuanced positions? Does this have to do with the place of Kant in resurgent forms of deconstruction and Lacanianism? Is there also a Lacanian doxa that prevents a heterodox appropriation of Lacan for the thinking of hegemony?

8a.   Are we all still agreed that hegemony is a useful category for describing our political dispositions? Would clarifying this be a good place to start?

9.   Does a serious consideration of Hegel lead us to rethink the Kantian oppositions between form and content, between quasi-transcendental

claims and the historical examples that are invoked to illustrate their truth?

10. In what does the critical authority of the critical theorist consist? Are our own claims subject to an autocritique, and how does that appear at the level of rhetoric?

QUESTIONS FROM ERNESTO LACLAU

1. In many contemporary debates, universalism is presented as opposed to the plurality of social actors which proliferate in the contemporary world. There is, however, in this question of the relationship universalism versus particularism, a certain polysemy regarding the two poles. Is multiculturalism, for instance, reducible to a particularistic logic which denies any right to the 'universal'? Also: is the notion of 'pluralism' – which evokes a variety of subject-positions of the same social actor – directly assimilable to 'multiculturalism', which involves reference to integral cultural/social communities which do not, however, overlap with the global national community? Conversely, is it true that the only conceivable form of universalism is linked to a foundationalist or essentialist grounding?

2. One of the many consequences of the increasing fragmentation of contemporary societies is that communitarian values – contextualized in so far as we are always dealing with *specific* communities – are supplemented by discourses of *rights* (such as, for instance, the rights of peoples or cultural minorities to self-determination) which are asserted as valid independently of any context. Are these two movements – assertion of universal rights and assertion of communitarian specificity – *ultimately* compatible? And if they are not, is not this incompatibility positive, as it opens the terrain for a variety of negotiations and a plurality of language games which are necessary for the constitution of public spaces in the societies in which we live?

3. Classical theories of emancipation postulated the ultimate homogeneity of the social agents to be emancipated – in Marxism, for

instance, the condition for the proletariat to be the agent of a global emancipation was that it had no particular interests to defend, because it had become the expression of pure human essence. In the same way, in some forms of classical democratic politics – Jacobinism would be the clearest example – the *unity* of the will of the people is the precondition for any democratic transformation. Today, on the contrary, we tend to speak of emancipation*s* (in the plural), which start from a diversity of social demands, and to identify democratic practice with the negotiated consensus among a plurality of social actors. What notion of social agency is compatible with this transformed approach?

4. The theory of hegemony presupposes, on the one hand, that the 'universal' is an object both impossible and necessary – always requiring, as a result, the presence of an ineradicable remainder of particularity – and, on the other, that the relation between power and emancipation is not one of exclusion but, on the contrary, one of mutual – albeit contradictory – implication. Is the hegemonic relation, conceived in this way, constitutive of the political link? And if so, what are the strategic games it is possible to play starting from its internal tensions?

5. The category of *difference*, in one way or the other, is at the root of the most important theoretical approaches of the last thirty years. Nomadic identities in Deleuze and Guattari, micro-physics of power in Foucault, *différance* in Derrida, the logic of the signifier in Lacan, are alternative ways of dealing with the constitutive character of 'difference'. Are they incompatible with each other and, if so, where do those incompatibilities lie? How can we assess their respective productivity for political analysis?

6. The question of transcendentality has been haunting contemporary theory for a long while. What, for instance, is the status of psychoanalytic categories such as the Oedipus or castration complex? Are they historical products or, rather, the a priori conditions of any possible society? There is the widespread feeling that neither a radical historicism nor a fully fledged transcendentalism would constitute appropriate answers, and some kind of solution which avoids the pitfalls of the two extremes – such as the notion of *quasi*-transcendentalism – has been

postulated. The status of this 'quasi' is, however, so far insufficiently explored. What would be the preconditions for a theoretical advance in this field, and what would be the consequences of the latter for historical analysis?

QUESTIONS FROM SLAVOJ ŽIŽEK

1. *The Real and historicity*: is the Lacanian Real the ultimate bedrock, the firm referent of the symbolic process, or does it stand for its totally non-substantial inherent limit, point of failure, which maintains the very gap between reality and its symbolization, and thus sets in motion the contingent process of historicization – symbolization?

2. *Lack and repetition*: is the movement of repetition grounded in some primordial lack, or does the notion of a primordial, founding lack necessarily involve the reinscription of the process of repetition into the metaphysical logic of identity?

3. *The social logic of (dis)identification*: is disidentification necessarily subversive of the existing order, or is a certain mode of disidentification, of 'maintaining a distance' towards one's symbolic identity, consubstantial with effective participation in social life? What are the different modes of disidentification?

4. *Subject, subjectivization, subject-positions*: is the 'subject' simply the result of the process of subjectivization, of interpellation, of performatively assuming some 'fixed subject-position', or does the Lacanian notion of the 'barred subject' (and the German Idealist notion of subject as self-relating negativity) also pose an alternative to traditional identitarian-substantialist metaphysics?

5. *The status of sexual difference*: again, does sexual difference simply stand for 'man' and 'woman' as two subject-positions individuals assume through repetitive performative acquisition, or is sexual difference 'real' in the Lacanian sense – that is, a deadlock – so that every attempt at translating it into fixed subject-positions fails?

6.   *Phallic signifier*: is the notion of phallus in Lacan 'phallogocentrist' – that is, the notion of a central signifier which, as a kind of transcendental point of reference, structures the field of sexuality – or does the fact that, for Lacan, phallus as signifier is a *'prosthetic' supplement* to the subject's lack, change something?

7.   *The Universal and historicism*: is it enough, today, to follow the Jamesonian advice 'Historicize!'? What are the limits of the historicist criticism of false universals? Is it not much more productive, for inherent theoretical as well as for political reasons, to maintain the paradoxical notion of the Universal as simultaneously impossible and necessary?

8.   *Hegel*: is Hegel simply the metaphysician *par excellence*, so that every attempt to assert the post-metaphysical complex of temporality–contingency–finitude is by definition anti-Hegelian, or is the very post-metaphysical hostility against Hegel a kind of index of its own theoretical limitation, so that one should, rather, focus on bringing to the light of day 'another Hegel' which does not fit the doxa of 'panlogicism'?

9.   *Lacan and deconstruction*: is it theoretically correct to conceive of Lacan as one in the series of deconstructionists, or does the fact that a whole set of features distinguish Lacan from the deconstructionist doxa (maintaining the notion of the subject as *cogito*, etc.) point towards an incommensurability between the two fields?

10.   *The political question*: should we accept the 'postmodern' notion of the plurality of (mostly ethnic, sexual or lifestyle) struggles for recognition, or does the recent resurgence of right-wing populism compel us to rethink the standard co-ordinates of 'postmodern' radical politics, and to revive the tradition of the 'critique of political economy'? How does all this affect the notions of hegemony and totality?

Restaging the Universal:
Hegemony and the Limits of Formalism

Judith Butler

Ernesto Laclau, Slavoj Žižek and I have had several conversations over recent years pertaining to poststructuralism, the political project of hegemony, and the status of psychoanalysis. We have all, I believe, worked at the theoretical margins of a Left political project, and have various degrees of continuing affinity with Marxism as a critical social theory and movement. Certain key concepts of progressive social theory have received new and varying articulations in our work, and we are all commonly concerned with the status and formation of the subject, the implications of a theory of the subject for the thinking of democracy, the articulation of 'universality' within a theory of hegemony. Where we differ, to my mind, is perhaps first and foremost in our approaches to the theory of the subject in a consideration of hegemony, and in the status of a 'logical' or 'structural' analysis of political formations in relation to their specific cultural and social articulations.

My understanding of the view of hegemony established by Ernesto Laclau and Chantal Mouffe in *Hegemony and Socialist Strategy* (1985)[1] is that democratic polities are constituted through exclusions that return to haunt the polities predicated upon their absence. That haunting becomes politically effective precisely in so far as the return of the excluded forces an expansion and rearticulation of the basic premises of democracy itself. One claim that Laclau and Žižek make in their subsequent writings is that the formation of any democratic polity – or, indeed, any particular subject-position within that polity – is necessarily incomplete. There are, however, divergent ways of understanding that incompletion. I understood the 'incompletion' of the subject-position in the following ways: (1) as the failure of any particular articulation to describe the population it represents; (2) that every subject is constituted differentially, and that what is produced as the 'constitutive outside' of the subject can never become fully inside or immanent. I take this last point to establish the fundamental difference between the Althusserian-inflected work of Laclau and Mouffe and a more Hegelian theory of the subject in which all external relations are – at least ideally – transformable into internal ones.

One other way of explaining this 'incompletion' of the subject is to establish its 'necessity' through recourse to a Lacanian psychoanalytic account of it. Žižek has suggested – and Laclau has partially agreed – that the Lacanian 'Real' is but another name for this 'incompletion', and that every subject, regardless of its social and historical conditions, is liable to the same postulate of inconclusiveness. The subject which comes into existence through the 'bar' is one whose prehistory is necessarily foreclosed to its experience of itself as a subject. That founding and defining limit thus founds the subject at a necessary and irreversible distance from the conditions of its own traumatic emergence.

I have indicated to both Žižek and Laclau that I would like to know more precisely whether the Lacanian view on the constitution of the subject is finally compatible with the notion of hegemony. I understand that the notion of the uncompleted or barred subject appears to guarantee a certain incompletion of interpellation: 'You call me this, but what I am eludes the semantic reach of any such linguistic effort to capture me.' Is this eluding of the call of the other accomplished through the installation of a bar as the condition and structure of all subject-constitution? Is the incompleteness of subject-formation that hegemony requires one in which the subject-in-process is incomplete precisely because it is constituted through exclusions that are politically salient, not structurally static or foundational? And if this distinction is wrong-headed, how are we to think those constituting exclusions that are structural and foundational together with those we take to be politically salient to the movement of hegemony? In other words, should not the incompletion of subject-formation be linked to the democratic contestation over signifiers? Can the ahistorical recourse to the Lacanian bar be reconciled with the strategic question that hegemony poses, or does it stand as a quasi-transcendental limitation on all possible subject-formations and strategies and, hence, as fundamentally indifferent to the political field it is said to condition?

If the subject always meets its limit in the selfsame place, then the subject is fundamentally exterior to the history in which it finds itself: there is no historicity to the subject, its limits, its articulability. Moreover, if we accept the notion that all historical struggle is nothing other than a vain effort to displace a founding limit that is structural in status, do we then commit ourselves to a distinction between the historical and the structural domains that subsequently excludes the historical domain from the understanding of opposition?

This problem of a structural approach to the founding limits of the subject becomes important when we consider possible forms of opposition. If hegemony denotes the historical possibilities for articulation that emerge within a given political horizon, then it will make a significant difference whether we understand that field as historically revisable and transformable, or whether it is given as a field whose integrity is secured by certain structurally identifiable limits and exclusions. If the terms of both dominance and opposition are constrained by such a field of articulability, the very possibility of expanding the possible sites of articulation for justice, equality, universality will be determined in part by whether we understand this field as subject to change through time. My understanding of hegemony is that its normative and optimistic moment consists precisely in the possibilities for expanding the democratic possibilities for the key terms of liberalism, rendering them more inclusive, more dynamic and more concrete. If the possibility for such change is precluded by a theoretical overdetermination of the structural constraints on the field of political articulability, then it becomes necessary to reconsider the relation between history and structure to preserve the political project of hegemony. I believe that however else we may disagree, Laclau, Žižek and I do agree on the project of radical democracy and on the continuing political promise of the Gramscian notion of hegemony. Distinct from a view that casts the operation of power in the political field exclusively in terms of discrete blocs which

vie with one another for control of policy questions, hegemony emphasizes the ways in which power operates to form our everyday
understanding of social relations, and to orchestrate the ways in which
we consent to (and reproduce) those tacit and covert relations of power.
Power is not stable or static, but is remade at various junctures within
everyday life; it constitutes our tenuous sense of common sense, and is
ensconced as the prevailing epistemes of a culture. Moreover, social
transformation occurs not merely by rallying mass numbers in favour of
a cause, but precisely through the ways in which daily social relations are
rearticulated, and new conceptual horizons opened up by anomalous or
subversive practices.

The theory of performativity is not far from the theory of hegemony
in this respect: both emphasize the way in which the social world is
made – and new social possibilities emerge – at various levels of social
action through a collaborative relation with power.

I plan to approach these questions through two different routes. The
first will be to consider the problem of constitutive exclusion from within
a Hegelian perspective by focusing on the 'Terror' and its relation to postulates of universality in *The Phenomenology of Spirit*. The second will be to
illustrate how the notion of universality, as elaborated by Laclau, might
be further restaged in terms of cultural translation. I hope to be able to
clarify further, in my subsequent contributions to this volume, how I
understand the relationship between psychoanalysis, social theory, and
the project of hegemony. Although I am critical of certain appropria-
tions of psychoanalysis for thinking about the limits of political
self-identification, I will hope to make clear in my next contribution the
centrality of psychoanalysis to any project that seeks to understand
emancipatory projects in both their psychic and social dimensions.

I focus on the topic of universality because it is one of the most contested topics within recent social theory. Indeed, many have voiced the
fear that constructivist and poststructuralist accounts of universality fail
to offer a strong substantive or procedural account of what is common
to all citizen-subjects within the domain of political representation.
There are still some political theorists who want to know what politically
relevant features of human beings might be extended to all human
beings (desire, speech, deliberation, dependency), and then to base their

normative views of what a political order ought to be on that universal description. Seyla Benhabib has shown us how both Rawls and Habermas, in different ways, offer an account of universality which eschews the question of human nature and a substantive account of universalizable features in favour of a procedural method which establishes universalizability as a criterion for justifying the normative claims of any social and political programme.[2] Although the procedural method purports to make no substantive claims about what human beings are, it does implicitly call upon a certain rational capacity, and attributes to that rational capacity an inherent relation to universalizability. The Kantian presumption that when 'I' reason I participate in a rationality that is transpersonal culminates in the claim that my reasoning presupposes the universalizability of my claims. Thus the procedural approach presupposes the priority of such a rationality, and also presupposes the suspect character of ostensibly non-rational features of human conduct in the domain of politics.

The question of universality has emerged perhaps most critically in those Left discourses which have noted the use of the doctrine of universality in the service of colonialism and imperialism. The fear, of course, is that what is named as universal is the parochial property of dominant culture, and that 'universalizability' is indissociable from imperial expansion. The proceduralist view seeks to sidestep this problem by insisting that it makes no substantive claims about human nature, but its exclusive reliance on rationality to make its claim belies this very assertion. The viability of the proceduralist solution relies in part on the status of formal claims and, indeed, whether one can establish a purely formal method for adjudicating political claims. Here the Hegelian critique of Kantian formalism is worth reconsidering, mainly because Hegel called into question whether such formalisms are ever really as formal as they purport to be.

In Hegel's Lesser Logic, Part One of his *Encyclopaedia of the Philosophical Sciences* (1830),[3] he links the reformulation of universality with his critique of formalism. When he introduces the identification of universality with abstract thought in the section entitled 'Preliminary Conception' (paras 19–83), he proceeds by way of several revisions of the notion of universality itself. At first he refers to the product, the

form, and the character of thought together as 'universal', which he renders as equivalent to 'the abstract'. He then proceeds to disaggregate
and revise his definition, noting that '*thinking*, as an *activity*, is the *active*
universal', and the deed, its product, 'what is brought forth, is precisely
the universal' (para. 20). Thus he offers three different names for a universality that he simultaneously identifies as singular and insists upon as
various. He adds to this set of revisions the notion that the subject,
which operates through the pronominal 'I', is also the universal, so that 'I'
is but another synonym and specification of universality itself.

At this point, it is unclear whether we have arrived at the last in a
series of revisions, or whether this most recently proffered definition
will lead to yet another. It becomes clear in the subsequent paragraphs
that Hegel is inhabiting a Kantian voice, when he finally begins his par-
aphrase of the Kantian view explicitly: 'Kant employed the awkward
expression, that I "accompany" all my representations – and my sensations, desires, actions, etc., too. "I" is the universal in and for itself, and
communality is one more form – although an external one – of universality' (para. 20). It seems important to ask what Hegel means here by
'external' form, since it appears that he will soon invoke an 'internal'
one, and that the internal will be precisely the one that Kant overrides.
The meaning of 'internal form' is, however, on its way:

> taken abstractly as such, 'I' is pure relation to itself, in which abstraction
> is made from representation and sensation, from every state as well as
> from every peculiarity of nature, of talent, of experience, and so on. To
> this extent, 'I' is the existence of the entirely *abstract* universality, the
> abstractly *free*. (para. 20)

Whatever the 'internal form' of universality will prove to be, it will
doubtless be related to the concrete form of universality as well. Hegel
then begins to object overtly to the bifurcation of the person that the
abstraction of universality requires: ' "I" is *thinking* as the *subject*, and
since I am at the same time in all my sensations, notions, states, etc.,
thought is present everywhere and pervades all these determinations as
[their] category' (para. 20; brackets in translation). The positing of the
universal 'I' thus requires the exclusion of what is specific and living

from the self for its definition. Universality in its abstract form thus requires cutting the person off from qualities which he or she may well share with others, but which do not rise to the level of abstraction required for the term 'universality'.

What is universal is therefore what pertains to every person, but it is not everything that pertains to every person. Indeed, if we can say that conceptions, states of consciousness, feelings, what is specific and living, also pertain to every person, we have apparently identified a universal feature which does not fit under the rubric of universality. Thus, the abstract requirement on universality produces a situation in which universality itself becomes doubled: in the first instance it is abstract; in the second it is concrete.

Hegel pursues this line in relation to empirical and moral judgements, showing how, in each instance when the universal is conceived as a feature of thought, it is by definition separated from the world it seeks to know. Thought is understood to have within itself the rules it needs in order to know things, or to know how to act in relation to them. The things themselves are not germane to the problem of knowledge, and thinking becomes not only abstract but self-referential. To the extent that the universality of thought guarantees freedom, freedom is defined precisely over and against all exterior influence. Hegel once again inhabits the Kantian position, only to mark his departure from it as the exposition unfolds:

> Thinking immediately involves *freedom*, because it is the activity of the universal, a self-relating that is therefore abstract, a being-with-itself that is undetermined in respect of subjectivity, and which in respect of its *content* is, at the same time, only in the *matter* [itself] and in its determinations. (para. 23; brackets in translation)

Hegel then proceeds to associate this conception of abstract freedom intrinsic to the act of thought with a certain hubris – a will to mastery, we might add, that must be countered by 'humility' and 'modesty'. '[W]ith respect to its content,' he writes:

> thinking is only genuine . . . insofar as it is immersed in the *matter* [*in die* Sache *vertieft ist*], and with respect to its form insofar as it is not a *particular*

being or doing of the subject, but consists precisely in this, that consciousness conducts itself as an abstract 'I', as *freed* from *all particularity*
[*Partikularität*] of features, states, etc., and does only what is universal, in
which it is identical with all individuals. (para. 23)

Hegel does not make clear in what this 'universal action' consists, but he
does stipulate that it is not 'the act of the subject' [*nicht ein besonderes Sein
oder Tun des Subjekts*], and that it is something like the reverse of any
such act. His universal action is only ambiguously active: it immerses
itself in the facts or the 'matter'. '[T]o consider ourselves as *worthy* of
conduct of this sort', he writes, 'consists precisely in the giving up
[*fahrenzulassen*] of our *particular* opinions and beliefs and in allowing the
matter [itself] to hold sway over us [*in sich walten zu lassen*]' (para. 23).

Thus, Hegel objects to the formulation of abstract universality by
claiming that it is solipsistic and that it denies the fundamental sociabil-
ity of humans: 'for that is just what freedom is: being at home with
oneself in one's other, depending upon oneself, and being one's own
determinant . . .. Freedom [in this abstract sense] is only present where
there is no other for me that is not myself' (para. 24, *Zusatz* 2). This, is
in Hegel's view, a merely 'formal' freedom. For freedom to become concrete, thought must 'immerse itself in the *matter*'. Subsequently, he will
caution against forms of empiricism which hold that one contributes
nothing to the object, but merely traces the immanent features that it
displays. Hegel will conclude that not only is the thinking self fundamentally related to what it seeks to know, but the formal self loses its
'formalism' once it is understood that the production and exclusion of
the 'concrete' is a necessary precondition for the fabrication of the
formal. Conversely, the concrete cannot be 'had' on its own, and it is
equally vain to disavow the act of cognition that delivers the concrete to
the human mind as an object of knowledge.

Hegel's brief criticism of Kantian formalism underscores a number
of points that are useful to us as we consider whether Hegel's own philosophy can be delivered as a formalist schema – something Žižek tends
to do – and whether universality can be understood in terms of a theoretical formalism – something Žižek, Laclau and I have all come close to
doing. In the first instance, it seems crucial to see that formalism is not

a method that comes from nowhere and is variously applied to concrete situations or illustrated through specific examples. On the contrary, formalism is itself a product of abstraction, and this abstraction requires its separation from the concrete, one that leaves the trace or remainder of this separation in the very working of abstraction itself. In other words, abstraction cannot remain rigorously abstract without exhibiting something of what it must exclude in order to constitute itself as abstraction.

Hegel writes that categories of thought which are considered subjective, as Kant's are, produce the objective, 'and are permanently in antithesis to the objective [*den bleibenden Gegensatz am Objektiven haben*]' (para. 25). Abstraction is thus contaminated precisely by the concretion from which it seeks to differentiate itself. Secondly, the very possibility of illustrating an abstract point by a concrete example presupposes the separation of the abstract and the concrete – indeed, presupposes the production of an epistemic field defined by that binary opposition. If the abstract is itself produced through separating off and denying the concrete, and the concrete clings to the abstract as its necessary contamination, exposing the failure of its formalism to remain rigorously itself, then it follows that the abstract is fundamentally dependent on the concrete, and 'is' that concrete other in a way which is systematically elided by the posterior appearance of the concrete as an illustrative example of an abstract formalism.

In the Greater Logic,[4] Hegel gives the example of the person who thinks that he might learn how to swim by learning what is required before entering the water. The person does not realize that one learns to swim only by entering the water and practising one's strokes in the midst of the activity itself. Hegel implicitly likens the Kantian to one who seeks to know how to swim before actually swimming, and he counters this model of a self-possessed cognition with one that gives itself over to the activity itself, a form of knowing that is given over to the world it seeks to know. Although Hegel is often dubbed a philosopher of 'mastery', we can see here – and in Nancy's trenchant book on Hegel's 'inquietude' – that the ek-static disposition of the self towards its world undoes cognitive mastery.[5] Hegel's own persistent references to 'losing oneself' and 'giving oneself over' only confirm the point that the knowing subject cannot be understood as one who imposes ready-made

categories on a pregiven world. The categories are shaped by the world
it seeks to know, just as the world is not known without the prior action
of those categories. And just as Hegel insists on revising several times his
very definition of 'universality', so he makes plain that the categories by
which the world becomes available to us are continually remade by the
encounter with the world that they facilitate. We do not remain the
same, and neither do our cognitive categories, as we enter into a knowing encounter with the world. Both the knowing subject and the world
are undone and redone by the act of knowledge.

In the section of *The Phenomenology of Spirit*[6] called 'Reason', Hegel
makes it clear that universality is not a feature of a subjective cognitive
capacity, but linked to the problem of reciprocal recognition. Moreover,
recognition itself is dependent on custom or *Sittlichkeit*: 'in the universal
Substance, the individual has this *form* of subsistence not only for his
activity as such, but no less also for the *content* of that activity; what he
does *is* the skill and customary practice of all' (para. 351). Recognition
is not possible apart from the customary practices in which it takes
place, and so no formal conditions of recognition will suffice. Similarly,
to the extent that what Hegel calls the 'universal Substance' is essentially
conditioned by customary practice, the individual instantiates and reproduces that custom. In Hegel's words: 'the individual in his *individual*
work already *unconsciously* performs a *universal* work . . .' (ibid.).

The implication of this view is that any effort to establish universality
as transcendent of cultural norms seems to be impossible. Although
Hegel clearly understands customary practice, the ethical order and the
nation as simple unities, it does not follow that the universality which
crosses cultures or emerges out of culturally heterogeneous nations must
therefore transcend culture itself. In fact, if Hegel's notion of universality is to prove good under conditions of hybrid cultures and vacillating
national boundaries, it will have to become a universality forged through
the work of cultural translation. And it will not be possible to set the
boundaries of the cultures in question, as if one culture's notion of universality could be translated into another's. Cultures are not bounded
entities; the mode of their exchange is, in fact, constitutive of their identity.[7] If we are to begin to rethink universality in terms of this constitutive
act of cultural translation, which is something I hope to make clear later

on in my remarks, then neither a presumption of linguistic or cognitive commonness nor a teleological postulate of an ultimate fusion of all cultural horizons will be a possible route for the universal claim.

What implications does this critique of formalism have for the thinking of universality in political terms? It is important to remember that for Hegel, the key terms of his philosophical vocabulary are rehearsed several times, and that nearly every time they are uttered they accrue a different meaning or reverse a prior one. This is especially true of words such as 'universality' and 'act', but also of 'consciousness' and 'self-consciousness'. The section entitled 'Absolute Freedom and Terror' in *The Phenomenology of Spirit* draws upon prior conceptions of the deed as it considers precisely what an individual can do under conditions of state terror. Drawing on the French Revolution, Hegel understands the individual as incapable of action which (a) acts upon an object, and (b) offers a reflection to that individual of his own activity. This was the norm of action that governed Hegel's previous discussion of work in the 'Lordship and Bondage' section. Under conditions of state terror, no individual works, for no individual is able to externalize an object which carries his signature: consciousness has lost its capacity for mediated self-expression, and 'it lets nothing break loose to become a *free object* standing over against it' (para. 588).

Although the individual works and lives under a regime which calls itself 'universality' and 'absolute freedom', the individual cannot find himself in the universal work of absolute freedom. Indeed, this failure of the individual to find a place in this absolute system (a critique of the Terror that anticipates Kierkegaard's critique of Hegel himself) exposes the limits to this notion of universality, and hence belies its claim to absoluteness. In Hegel's view, to perform a deed one must become individuated; universal freedom, deindividuated, cannot perform a deed. All it can do is to vent its fury, the fury of destruction. Thus, within the condition of absolute terror, actual self-consciousness becomes the opposite to universal freedom, and the universal is exposed as qualified, which is to say that the universal proves to be a false universal. Because there is no room for self-consciousness or the individual under these conditions, and because no deed can be performed that conforms with the norm of mediated self-expression, any 'deed' that does appear is radically disfigured and disfiguring. For Hegel, the only deed that can appear is an anti-deed, destruction itself, a nothingness that comes of a nothingness. In his view, the sole work and deed of universal freedom is therefore death (para. 360).

Not only is the individual nullified and, therefore, dead, but this death has both literal and metaphorical meanings. That individuals were easily killed under the Reign of Terror for the sake of 'absolute freedom' is well-documented. Moreover, there were individuals who survived, but they are not 'individuals' in any normative sense. Deprived of recognition and of the power to externalize themselves through deeds, such individuals become nullities whose sole act is to nullify the world that has nullified them. If we are to ask: What kind of freedom is this?, the answer Hegel offers is that it is 'the empty point of the absolutely free self', 'the coldest and meanest of all deaths', no more significant than 'cutting off a head of cabbage or swallowing a mouthful of water' (para. 590).

Hegel is clearly exposing what happens when a faction sets itself up as the universal and claims to represent the general will, where the general will supersedes the individual wills of which it is composed and, in fact, exists at their expense. The 'will' that is officially represented by the government is thus haunted by a 'will' that is excluded from the representative function. Thus the government is established on the basis of a paranoid economy in which it must repeatedly establish its one claim to universality by erasing all remnants of those wills it excludes from the domain of representation. Those whose wills are not officially represented or recognized constitute 'an unreal pure will' (para. 591), and since that will is not known, it is incessantly conjectured and suspected. In an apparently paranoid fit, universality thus displays and enacts the violent separations of its own founding. Absolute freedom becomes this abstract self-consciousness which understands annihilation to be its work, and effaces (annihilates) all trace of the alterity that clings to it.

At this stage of Hegel's exposition, the figure of an annihilating universality that assumes an animated form parallels the 'Lord' of the 'Lordship and Bondage' section. As its annihilation becomes objective to it, this 'universality', figured as a sentient being, is said to feel the terror of death: 'the terror of death is the vision of this negative nature of itself' (para. 592). Not only does universality see itself as negative, and thus as the opposite of what it thought it was; it also undergoes the pure transition from one extreme to the other, and so comes to know itself as transition – that is, as that which has negation as its essential activity, and is itself also subject to negation.

Although universality at first denoted that which is self-identical to all human beings, it loses that self-identity as a consequence of its refusal to accommodate all humans within its purview. It becomes not only split between an official and a spectral universality, but it becomes dismembered into an estate system which reflects the divided character of the will and the discontinuities inherent in this version of universality. Those who are dispossessed or remain radically unrepresented by the general will or the universal do not rise to the level of the recognizably human within its terms. The 'human' who is outside that general will is subject to annihilation by it, but this is not an annihilation from which meaning can be derived: its annihilation is nihilism. In Hegel's terms: 'its negation is the death that is without meaning, the sheer terror of the negative that contains nothing positive . . .' (para. 594).

Hegel describes the nihilistic consequences of formal notions of universality in graphic terms. To the extent that universality fails to embrace all particularity and, on the contrary, is built upon a fundamental hostility to particularity, it continues to be and to animate the very hostility by which it is founded. The universal can be the universal only to the extent that it remains untainted by what is particular, concrete, and individual. Thus it requires the constant and meaningless vanishing of the individual, which is dramatically displayed by the Reign of Terror. For Hegel, this abstract universality not only requires that vanishing, and enacts that negation, but it is so fundamentally dependent upon that vanishing that without that vanishing it would be nothing. Without that vanishing immediacy, we might say, universality itself would vanish. But either way, universality is nothing without its vanishing which means, in Hegelian terms, that it 'is' that very vanishing. Once the transience of individual life is understood as crucial to the operation of abstract universality, universality itself vanishes as a concept which is said to include all such life: 'this vanished immediacy is the universal will itself' (para. 594).

Although it may seem that Hegel is working towards a true and all-inclusive universality, this is not the case. Rather, what he offers is a view of universality that is inseparable from its founding negations. The all-encompassing trajectory of the term is necessarily undone by the exclusion of particularity on which it rests. There is no way to bring the excluded particularity into the universal without first negating that particularity. And that negation would only confirm once again that universality cannot proceed without destroying that which it purports to include. Moreover, the assimilation of the particular into the universal leaves its trace, an unassimilable remainder, which renders universality ghostly to itself.

The reading I have been offering here presupposes that Hegel's ideas cannot be read apart from his text. In other words, it is not possible to cull 'the theory of universality' from his text and offer it in discrete and plain propositions, because the notion is developed through a reiterative textual strategy. Not only does universality undergo revision in time, but its successive revisions and dissolutions are essential to what it 'is'. The propositional sense of the copula must be replaced with the speculative one.

It may seem that such a temporalized conception of universality has little to do with the region of politics, but consider the political risks of maintaining a static conception, one that fails to accommodate challenge, one that refuses to respond to its own constitutive exclusions.

Thus we can come to some preliminary conclusions about Hegel's procedure here: (1) universality is a name which undergoes significant accruals and reversals of meaning, and cannot be reduced to any of its constitutive 'moments'; (2) it is inevitably haunted by the trace of the particular thing to which it is opposed, and this takes the form (a) of a spectral doubling of universality, and (b) a clinging of that particular thing to universality itself, exposing the formalism of its claim as necessarily impure; (3) the relation of universality to its cultural articulation is insuperable; this means that any transcultural notion of the universal will be spectralized and stained by the cultural norms it purports to transcend; and (4) no notion of universality can rest easily within the notion of a single 'culture', since the very concept of universality compels an understanding of culture as a relation of exchange and a task of translation. In terms which we might call Hegelian – but which Hegel himself did not use – it becomes necessary to see the notion of a discrete and entitative 'culture' as essentially other to itself, in a definitional relationship with alterity.[8] And here we are not referring to *one* culture which defines itself over and against *another*, for that formulation preserves the notion of 'culture' as a wholism. On the contrary, we are seeking to approach the notion of culture in terms of a defining problem of translation, one which is significantly related to the problem of cross-cultural translation that the concept of universality has become.

This juncture of my argument is one place where my differences with Laclau and Žižek might be most clearly understood. One difference that is doubtless apparent is that my approach to Hegel draws upon a certain set of literary and rhetorical presumptions about how meaning is generated in his text. I therefore oppose the effort to construe Hegel in formal terms or, indeed, to render him compatible with a Kantian formalism, which is something Žižek has done on occasion.[9] Any effort to reduce Hegel's own text to a formal schematism will become subject to the very same critique that Hegel has offered of all such formalisms, and subject to the same founderings.

Reading 'Hegel's "Logic of Essence"',[10] Žižek considers the Hegelian paradox that whatever a thing 'is' is determined by its external conditions, that is, the historical conditions of its emergence, from which it acquires its specific attributes: 'after we decompose an object into its ingredients, we look in vain in them for some specific feature which holds together this multitude and makes of it a unique, self-identical thing' (p. 148). This effort to find the defining feature internal to the object is thwarted, however, by the recognition – noted above – that a thing is conditioned by its external circumstances. What happens, according to Žižek, is that a 'purely symbolic, tautological gesture . . . posit[s] these external conditions as the conditions–components of the thing' (ibid.). In other words, conditions that are external to the thing are posited as internal and immanent to the thing. Furthermore, at the same time that external and arbitrary conditions are rendered as immanent and necessary features of the thing, the thing is also grounded and unified by this performative act of definition. This is what Žižek refers to as 'the tautological "return of the thing to itself"' (ibid.). This 'positing' is a sleight of hand, no doubt, but it is a founding and necessary one, and for Žižek it takes the form of a universal feature of all selfhood.

Žižek continues his exposition by suggesting a parallel between this Hegelian moment and what Lacan calls the '*point de capiton*', where an arbitrary sign not only appears essential to what it signifies, but actively organizes the thing under the sign itself. With characteristic humour and bravado, Žižek then suggests that this Lacanian notion can be easily illustrated by the killer shark in Spielberg's *Jaws*, which 'provides a common "container" for . . . free-floating, inconsistent fears' (p. 149), social in nature, such as the intrusions of government and big business, immigration, political instability. The *point de capiton* or 'container' 'anchors' and 'reifies' this unruly set of social meanings, and 'block[s] any further inquiry into the social meaning' (ibid.).

What interests me in this exposition is the formal and transposable character of the performative act that Žižek so deftly identifies. Is the act of tautological positing by which an external condition comes to appear as immanent the same as the *point de capiton*, and can the instance of popular culture be used to illustrate this formal point which is, as it were, already true, prior to its exemplification? Hegel's point against Kant was precisely that we cannot identify such structures first and then apply them to their examples, for in the instance of their 'application' they become something other than what they were. The link between theoretical formalism and a technological approach to the example becomes explicit here: theory is applied to its examples, and its relation to its example is an 'external' one, in Hegelian terms. The theory is articulated on its self-sufficiency, and then shifts register only for the pedagogical purpose of illustrating an already accomplished truth.

Although I do have objections to a technological approach to theory, and to the link between formalism and technology that leaves its object outside, my stronger concern has to do with how we read the moment of arbitrariness and how we approach the problem of the remainder. Žižek offers us a tool which we can use in a great variety of contexts to see how a transexemplary identity-constituting function works. A set of fears and anxieties emerges, a name is retroactively and arbitrarily attached to those fears and anxieties: suddenly, that bundle of fears and anxieties becomes a single thing, and that thing comes to function as a cause or ground of whatever is disturbing. What first appeared as a disorganized field of social anxiety is transformed by a certain performative operation into an ordered universe with an identifiable cause. No doubt there is great analytic power to this formulation, and its brilliance no doubt accounts for Žižek's well-earned reputation as a searing social critic.

But what is the place and time of this performative operation? Does it happen in all places and times? Is it an invariant feature of human culture, of language, of the name, or is it restricted to the powers of nominalism within modernity? As a tool that can be transposed from any and every context on to any and every object, it operates precisely as a theoretical fetish that disavows the conditions of its own emergence.

Žižek makes it clear that this tautological gesture by which an object is formed and defined and subsequently animated as a cause, is always and only tenuous. The contingency that the name seeks to subdue returns precisely as the spectre of the thing's dissolution. The relation between that contingency and the conferral of necessity is dialectical, in Žižek's view, since the one term can easily turn into the other. Moreover, the act is one that can be found in both Kant and Hegel. For Hegel, 'it is only the subject's free act of "dotting the i" which retroactively installs necessity' (p. 150). Further along, Žižek argues: 'the same tautological gesture is already at work in Kant's analytic of pure reason: the synthesis of the multitude of sensations in the representation of the object . . . [involves the] positing of an X as the unknown substratum of the perceived phenomenal sensations' (ibid.). That 'X' is posited, but it is precisely empty, without content, an 'act of pure formal conversion' which instates unity, and constitutes the act of symbolization that Žižek finds equally instantiated in the work of Hegel and Kant.

What is necessary for this act of symbolization to take place is a certain linguistic function of positing, which retroactively confers necessity on the object (signified) through the name (signifier) that it uses. One might speculate: the act of symbolization breaks apart when it finds that it cannot maintain the unity that it produces, when the social forces it seeks to quell and unify break through the domesticating veneer of the name. Interestingly, though, Žižek does not consider the social disruption of this act of symbolization, but centres instead on the 'surplus' that is produced by this act of positing. There is an expectation of a meaning, a substance, that is at once produced and thwarted by the formal act of positing. The identity that the name confers turns out to be empty, and this insight into its emptiness produces a critical position on the naturalizing effects of this naming process. The emperor has no clothes, and we are somehow relieved of the prejudicial and phobic logics that establish the 'Jews' or another ethnic minority as the 'cause' of an array of social anxieties. For Žižek, the critical moment emerges when we are able to see this structure fall apart, and when the substantial and causative force attributed to a single thing through the name is exposed as arbitrarily attributed.

Similarly, this happens when we think we have found a point of opposition to domination, and then realize that that very point of opposition is the instrument through which domination works, and that we have unwittingly enforced the powers of domination through our participation in its opposition. Dominance appears most effectively precisely as its 'Other'. The collapse of the dialectic gives us a new perspective because it shows us that the very schema by which dominance and opposition are distinguished dissimulates the instrumental use that the former makes of the latter.

In these and numerous other instances, Žižek gives us a critical perspective that involves rethinking the way in which necessity, contingency and opposition are thought within everyday life. But where does one go from here? Does the exposition of an aporia, even a constitutive aporia at the level of the linguistic performative, work in the service of a counter-hegemonic project? What is the relation of this formal exposure of false substance and false contradiction to the project of hegemony? If these are some of the tricks that hegemony uses, some of the ways in which we come to order the social world against its contingency, then it is indubitably insightful. But if we cannot see how something new might come of such invariant structures, does it help us to see how new social and political articulations can be wrought from the subversion of the natural attitude within which we live?

Moreover, there is a difference here between a structural and a cultural account of performativity, understood as the positing function of language. Žižek shows how this positing creates the appearance of its necessary ground and causality, and this is surely not unlike the account of gender performativity I have offered in *Gender Trouble*[11] and else-where. There I suggested that the performance of gender creates the illusion of a prior substantiality – a core gendered self – and construes the effects of the performative ritual of gender as necessary emana-tions or causal consequences of that prior substance. But where Žižek isolates the structural features of linguistic positing and offers cultural examples to illustrate this structural truth, I am, I believe, more con-cerned to rethink performativity as cultural ritual, as the reiteration of cultural norms, as the habitus of the body in which structural and social dimensions of meaning are not finally separable.

It seems important to remember that 'hegemony' – as defined by Antonio Gramsci and elaborated by both Chantal Mouffe and Ernesto Laclau in *Hegemony and Socialist Strategy* – centrally involved the possibil-ity of new articulations of political formations. What Žižek offers us is an insight into invariant aporetic and metaleptic structures that afflict all performativity within politics. The incommensurability between the generalized formulation and its illustrative examples confirms that the context for the reversals he identifies is extraneous to their structure. Hegemony did involve a critical interrogation of consent as well, and it seems to me that Žižek continues this tradition by showing us how power compels us to consent to that which constrains us, and how our very sense of freedom or resistance can be the dissimulated instrument of dominance. But what remains less clear to me is how one moves beyond such a dialectical reversal or impasse to something new. How would the new be produced from an analysis of the social field that remains restricted to inversions, aporias and reversals that work regardless of time and place? Do these reversals produce something other than their own structurally identical repetitions?

The other aspect of hegemony, however, which is concerned with new political articulations of the social field, structures Laclau's recent work. As I have suggested elsewhere,[12] I have some doubts over whether the Lacanian thesis in Laclau's work, which emphasizes the Real as the limit-point of all subject-formation, is compatible with the social and political analysis he provides. No doubt it makes a difference whether one understands the invariable incompleteness of the subject in terms of the limits designated by the Real, considered as the point where self-representation founders and fails, or as the inability of the social category to capture the mobility and complexity of persons (see Denise Riley's recent work[13]). In any case, that is not my main concern here. Although Laclau offers us a dynamic notion of hegemony which seeks to find social locations for the politically new, I have some difficulty with his way of casting the problem of particular and universal. I propose, then, to turn to some of his recent formulations of that problem, and to return to a consideration of the problem of universality and hegemony towards the end of this discussion.

In his edited volume *The Making of Political Identities*,[14] Laclau draws attention to a 'double movement' in the politicization of identities at the end of the twentieth century:

> There is a decline both of the great historical actors and of those central public spaces where decisions meaningful for society as a whole had been taken in the past. But, at the same time, there is a politicization of vast areas of social life that opens the way for a proliferation of particularistic identities. (p. 4)

Concerned with the challenges posed by 'the emergence of a plurality of new subjects that have escaped the classical frameworks' (ibid.), Laclau proceeds to reflect on the challenge that these particularisms pose to the Enlightenment schema in which the universal claims of the subject are a prerequisite for politics in the proper sense.[15]

Laclau's most sustained discussion of universality in relation to the present political demands of particularism takes place in *Emancipation(s)* (1996),[16] where he seeks to derive a conception of universality from the chain of equivalence, a concept that is central to *Hegemony and Socialist Strategy*, published a decade earlier. In *Emancipation(s)*, Laclau attempts to show that each and every particular identity is never complete in its effort to achieve self-determination. A particular identity is understood to be one that is tied to a specific content, such as gender, race or ethnicity. The structural feature that all these identities are said to share is a constitutive incompleteness. A particular identity becomes an identity by virtue of its relative location in an open system of differential relations. In other words, an identity is constituted through its difference from a limitless set of other identities. That difference is specified in the course of Laclau's exposition as a relation of *exclusion* and/or *antagonism*. Laclau's point of reference here is Saussure rather than Hegel, and this implies that the differences which constitute (and invariably limit) the positing of identity are not binary in character, and that they belong to a field of operation that lacks totality. One might profitably argue against the trope of Hegel's philosophy as 'totalizing',[17] and one might also note that Laclau offers a poststructuralist revision of Saussure in this discussion, but such debates on the status of totality, while they are important, take us in another direction. In any case, we are, I believe, in agreement that the field of differential relations from which any and all particular identities emerge must be limitless. Moreover, the 'incompleteness' of each and every identity is a direct result of its differential emergence: no particular identity can emerge without presuming and enacting the exclusion of others, and this constitutive exclusion or antagonism is the shared and equal condition of all identity-constitution.

What becomes interesting is the role that this limitless field of differentially based definitions plays for Laclau in the theorization of universality. When the chain of equivalence is operationalized as a political category, it requires that particular identities acknowledge that they share with other such identities the situation of a necessarily incomplete determination. They are fundamentally the set of differences by which they emerge, and this set of differences constitutes the structural features of the domain of political sociality. If any such particular identity seeks to universalize its own situation without recognizing that other such identities are in an identical structural situation, it will fail to achieve an alliance with other emergent identities, and will mistakenly identify the meaning and place of universality itself. The universalization of the particular seeks to elevate a specific content to a global condition, making an empire of its local meaning. Where universality is to be found, according to Laclau, it is as an 'empty but ineradicable place' (p. 58). It is not a presumed or a priori condition that might be discovered and articulated, and it is not the ideal of achieving a complete list of any and all particularisms which would be unified by a shared content. Paradoxically, it is the absence of any such shared content that constitutes the promise of universality:

> if the place of the universal is an empty one and there is no *a priori* reason for it not to be filled by *any* content, if the forces which fill that place are constitutively split between the concrete politics that they advocate and the ability of those politics to fill the empty place, the political language of any society whose degree of institutionalization has, to some extent, been shaken or undermined, will also be split. (p. 60)

Thus Laclau identifies a condition common to all politicization, but it is precisely not a condition with a content: it is, rather, the condition by which any specific content fails fully to constitute an identity, a condition of necessary failure which not only pertains universally, but *is* the 'empty and ineradicable place' of universality itself. A certain necessary tension emerges within any political formation inasmuch as it seeks to fill that place and finds that it cannot. This failure to fill the place, however, is precisely the futural promise of universality, its status as a limitless and unconditional feature of all political articulation.

Inevitable as it is that a political organization will posit the possible filling of that place as an ideal, it is equally inevitable that it will fail to do so. Much as this failure cannot be directly pursued as the 'aim' of politics, it does produce a value – indeed, the value of universality that no politics can do without. Thus the aim of politics must then change, it seems, in order to accommodate precisely this failure as a structural source of its alliance with other such political movements. What is identical to all terms in an

> equivalential chain . . . can only be the pure, abstract, absent fullness of the community, which lacks . . . any direct form of representation and expresses itself through the equivalence of the differential terms . . . it is essential that the chain of equivalences remain open: otherwise its closure could only be the result of one more difference specifiable in its particularity and we would not be confronted with the fullness of the community as an absence. (p. 57)

Linda Zerilli explains Laclau's conception of the universal in these terms: 'This universalism is not One: it is not a preexisting something (essence or form) to which individuals accede, but, rather, the fragile, shifting, and always incomplete achievement of political action; it is not the container of a presence but the placeholder of an absence.'[18] Zerilli deftly shows that – *pace* Žižek – 'incompleteness' of identity in Laclau's political theory cannot be reduced to the Lacanian Real, and suggests that the universal will not be founded in a linguistic or psychic condition of the subject. Moreover, it will not be found as a regulative ideal, a utopian postulation, which transcends the particular, but will always be 'politically articulated relations of difference' (p. 15). Emphasizing what Laclau terms the 'parasitic attachment' of the universal to some particular, Zerilli argues that the universal will be found only *in* the chain of particulars itself.

As part of her point, Zerilli cites the work of Joan Wallach Scott, whose recent examination of French feminism in post-revolutionary France provides an implicit reformulation of Laclau's position. Zerilli explains that Scott traces the 'need both to accept and to refuse "sexual difference" as a condition of inclusion in the universal' (p. 16). In *Only Paradoxes to Offer*, Scott argues that French feminists in the eighteenth and nineteenth centuries had to make rights claims on the basis of their difference, but also had to argue that their claims were a logical extension of universal enfranchisement. Reconciling sexual difference with universality took many tactical and paradoxical forms, but rarely were these positions able to overcome a certain dissonant formulation of the problem. To argue in favour of sexual difference could mean arguing in favour of particularism, but it could also be – if one accepts the foundational status of sexual difference to all humanity – appealing directly to the universal. Zerilli understands Scott to be offering a reverse, but complementary, formulation to Laclau's. Whereas Laclau shows that the structural incompleteness of every particular claim is implicated in a universal, Scott shows that there is no possibility of extricating the universal claim from the particular. I would add to this discussion only by suggesting that Scott highlights the sometimes undecidable coincidence of particular and universal, showing that the very same term, 'sexual difference', can denote the particular in one political context and the universal in another. Her work seems to me to provoke the following question: do we always know whether a claim is particular or universal, and what happens when the semantics of the claim, governed by political context, renders the distinction undecidable?

I would like to raise two questions about the exposition above: one takes us back to Hegel and the relation between particular and universal, the other takes us forward to the question of cultural translation, mentioned briefly above. First: what precisely does it mean to find the universal both in the relation among particulars and inseparable from that relation? Second: must the relation among particulars that Laclau and Zerilli examine become one of cultural translation if the universal is to become an active and operating concept in political life?

The first question requires us to consider the status of this structural incompletion of identity. What is the structural level that guarantees this incompletion? Laclau's argument is based on the Saussurean model of language and its early appropriation by Foucault in *The Archaeology of Knowledge*,[19] one that has surely influenced my work and that of Žižek also. The notion that all identity is posited in a field of differential relations is clear enough, but if these relations are pre-social, or if they constitute a structural level of differentiation which conditions and structures the social but is distinct from it, we have located the universal in yet another domain: in the structural features of any and all languages. Is this significantly different from identifying the universal in the structural presuppositions of the speech act, in so far as both projects elaborate a universal account of some characteristics of language?

Such an approach separates the formal analysis of language from its cultural and social syntax and semantics, and this further suggests that what is said about language is said about all language-users, and that its particular social and political formations will be but instances of a more generalized and non-contextual truth about language itself. Moreover, if we conceive of universality as an 'empty' place, one that is 'filled' by specific contents, and further understand political meanings to be the contents with which the empty place is filled, then we posit an exteriority of politics to language that seems to undo the very concept of political performativity that Laclau espouses. Why should we conceive of universality as an empty 'place' which awaits its content in an anterior and subsequent event? Is it empty only because it has already disavowed or suppressed the content from which it emerges, and where is the trace of the disavowed in the formal structure that emerges?

The claim to universality always takes place in a given syntax, through a certain set of cultural conventions in a recognizable venue. Indeed, the claim cannot be made without the claim being recognized as a claim. But what orchestrates what will and will not become recognizable as a claim? Clearly, there is an establishing rhetoric for the assertion of universality and a set of norms that are invoked in the recognition of such claims. Moreover, there is no cultural consensus on an international level about what ought and ought not to be a claim to universality, who may make it, and what form it ought to take. Thus, for the claim to work, for it to compel consensus, and for the claim, performatively, to enact the very universality it enunciates, it must undergo a set of translations into the various rhetorical and cultural contexts in which the meaning and force of universal claims are made. Significantly, this means that no assertion of universality takes place apart from a cultural norm, and, given the array of contesting norms that constitute the international field, no assertion can be made without at once requiring a cultural translation. Without translation, the very concept of universality cannot cross the linguistic borders it claims, in principle, to be able to cross. Or we might put it another way: without translation, the only way the assertion of universality can cross a border is through a colonial and expansionist logic.

A recent resurgence of Anglo-feminism in the academy has sought to restate the importance of making universal claims about the conditions and rights of women (Okin, Nussbaum) without regard to the prevailing norms in local cultures, and without taking up the task of cultural translation. This effort to override the problem that local cultures pose for international feminism does not understand the parochial character of its own norms, and does not consider the way in which feminism works in full complicity with US colonial aims in imposing its norms of civility through an effacement and a decimation of local Second and Third World cultures. Of course, translation by itself can also work in full complicity with the logic of colonial expansion, when translation becomes the instrument through which dominant values are transposed into the language of the subordinated, and the subordinated run the risk of coming to know and understand them as tokens of their 'liberation'.

But this is a limited view of colonialism, one which assumes that the colonized emerges as a subject according to norms that are recognizably Eurocentric. According to Gayatri Chakravorty Spivak, 'universalism' as well as 'internationalism' come to dominate a politics centred on the subject of rights, thereby occluding the force of global capital and its differential forms of exploitation from the theorization of subordinated peoples. In Spivak's terms, we have yet to think that form of impoverished life which cannot be articulated by the Eurocentric category of the subject. The narrative of political self-representation is itself part of a certain dominant Leftism, in her view, but it does not provide all that constitutes the site of hegemonic resistance. In 'Can the Subaltern Speak?',[20] Spivak remarks: 'it is impossible for the French intellectuals [referring mainly to Deleuze and Foucault] to imagine the power and desire that would inhabit the unnamed subject of the Other of Europe' (p. 280). The exclusion of the subordinated other of Europe is so central to the production of European epistemic regimes 'that the subaltern cannot speak'. Spivak does not mean by this claim that the subaltern does not express her desires, form political alliances, or make culturally and politically significant effects, but that within the dominant conceptualization of agency, her agency remains illegible. The point would not be to extend a violent regime to include the subaltern as one of its members: she is, indeed, already included there, and it is precisely the means of her inclusion that effects the violence of her effacement. There is no one 'other' there, at the site of the subaltern, but an array of peoples who cannot be homogenized, or whose homogenization is the effect of the epistemic violence itself. The First World intellectual cannot refrain from 'representing' the subaltern, but the task of representation will not be easy, especially when it concerns an existence that requires a translation, because translation always runs the risk of appropriation. In her essay, Spivak both counsels and enacts a self-limiting practice of cultural translation on the part of First World intellectuals.

At once refusing the 'romanticization of the tribal' and the ruse of the transparency that is the instrument of colonial 'reason', Spivak offers cultural translation as both a theory and practice of political responsibility.[21] She refers to Mahasweta Devi, whose feminist fiction she translated, as a subaltern who speaks. But here we ought not to think that we know what 'speaking' is, for what becomes clear in these stories

is that Devi's writing is less a synthesis of available discourses than a certain 'violent shuttling' between discourses that shows the sharp edges of
all available discourses of collectivity. Can we read for hegemony without knowing how to read for the mobility of this kind of exclusion,
without assuming in advance that the translator's point will be to bring
this writing into forms of agency legible to an Anglo-European audi-
ence? In this sense, the task of the postcolonial translator, we might say,
is precisely to bring into relief the non-convergence of discourses so that
one might know through the very ruptures of narrativity the founding
violences of an episteme.

Translation can have its counter-colonialist possibility, for it also
exposes the limits of what the dominant language can handle. It is not
always the case that the dominant term as it is translated into the language (the idioms, the discursive and institutional norms) of a
subordinated culture remains the same upon the occasion of translation.
Indeed, the very figure of the dominant term can alter as it is mimed
and redeployed in that context of subordination. Thus, Homi Bhabha's
emphasis on the splitting of the signifier in the colonial context seeks to
show that the master – to use Hegelian parlance – loses some of his
claim to priority and originality precisely by being taken up by a mimetic
double. Mimesis can effect a displacement of the first term or, indeed,
reveal that the term is nothing other than a series of displacements that
diminish any claim to primary and authentic meaning. There is, of
course, no such translation without contamination, but there is no
mimetic displacement of the original without an appropriation of the
term that separates it from its putative authority.

By emphasizing the cultural location of the enunciation of universality, one sees not only that there can be no operative notion of
universality that does not assume the risks of translation, but that the
very claim of universality is bound to various syntactic stagings within
culture which make it impossible to separate the formal from the cultural
features of any universalist claim. Both the form and the content of
universality are highly contested, and cannot be articulated outside the
scene of their embattlement. Using Foucault's language of genealogy, we
might insist that universality is an 'emergence' [*Entstehung*] or a 'non-
place', 'a pure distance, which indicates that the adversaries do not

belong to a common space. Consequently, no one is responsible for an emergence: no one can glory in it, since it always occurs in the interstice.'[22] Maintaining that universality is a 'site of contest' has become something of an academic truism, but considering the meaning and promise of that contest has not.

On the one hand – as Laclau and Žižek know very well, and Étienne Balibar has made very clear[23] – universality has been used to extend certain colonialist and racist understandings of civilized 'man', to exclude certain populations from the domain of the human, and to produce itself as a false and suspect category. When we begin the critique of such notions of universality, it may seem to some – especially to the Habermasians – that we operate with another concept of universality in mind, one which would be truly all-encompassing. Laclau has argued persuasively that no concept of universality can ever be all-encompassing, and that were it to enclose all possible contents, it would not only close the concept of time, but ruin the political efficacy of universality itself. Universality belongs to an open-ended hegemonic struggle.

But what does happen, then, when a disenfranchised group proceeds to claim 'universality', to claim that they ought properly to be included within its purview? Does that claim presuppose a broader, more fundamental notion of universality, or is it that the claim is performative, producing a notion of universality which exercises, in Žižek's terms, a retroactive necessity upon the conditions of its emergence? Does the new universality appear as if it has been true all along? This last formulation does not concede that it exists as a prior concept, but that, as a consequence of having been posited, it assumes the present quality of having always been so. But here, we must be cautious: the positing of new forms of universality does not produce this effect for everyone, and many of the current struggles over national sovereignty and the proper limits for extending group rights affirm that the performative effects of such claims are hardly uniform.

The assertion of universality by those who have conventionally been excluded by the term often produces a performative contradiction of a certain sort. But this contradiction, in Hegelian fashion, is not self-cancelling, but exposes the spectral doubling of the concept itself. And it prompts a set of antagonistic speculations on what the proper venue for the claim of universality ought to be. Who may speak it? And how ought it to be spoken? The fact that we do not know the answers to these questions confirms that the question of universality has not been settled. As I have argued elsewhere,[24] to claim that the universal has not yet been articulated is to insist that the 'not yet' is proper to an understanding of the universal itself: that which remains 'unrealized' by the universal constitutes it essentially. The universal announces, as it were, its 'non-place', its fundamentally temporal modality, precisely when challenges to its *existing* formulation emerge from those who are not covered by it, who have no entitlement to occupy the place of the 'who', but nevertheless demand that the universal as such ought to be inclusive of them. At stake here is the exclusionary function of certain *norms* of universality which, in a way, transcend the cultural locations from which they emerge. Although they often appear as transcultural or formal criteria by which existing cultural conventions are to be judged, they are precisely cultural conventions which have, through a process of abstraction, come to appear as post-conventional principles. The task, then, is to refer these formal conceptions of universality back to the contaminating trace of their 'content', to eschew the form/content distinction as it furthers that ideological obfuscation, and to consider the cultural form that this struggle over the meaning and scope of norms takes.

When one has no right to speak under the auspices of the universal, and speaks none the less, laying claim to universal rights, and doing so in a way that preserves the particularity of one's struggle, one speaks in a way that may be readily dismissed as nonsensical or impossible. When we hear about 'lesbian and gay human rights', or even 'women's human rights', we are confronted with a strange neighbouring of the universal and the particular which neither synthesizes the two, nor keeps them apart. The nouns function adjectivally, and although they are identities and grammatical 'substances', they are also in the act of qualifying and being qualified by one another. Clearly, however, the 'human' as previously defined has not readily included lesbians, gays and women, and the current mobilization seeks to expose the conventional limitations of the human, the term that sets the limits on the universal reach of international law. But the exclusionary character of those conventional norms of universality does not preclude further recourse to the term, although it does mean entering into that situation in which the conventional meaning becomes unconventional (or catachrestic). This does not mean that we have a priori recourse to a truer criterion of universality. It does suggest, however, that conventional and exclusionary norms of universality can, through perverse reiterations, produce unconventional formulations of universality that expose the limited and exclusionary features of the former one at the same time that they mobilize a new set of demands.

This point is made in a significant way by Paul Gilroy who, in *The Black Atlantic*,[25] takes issue with forms of contemporary scepticism that lead to a full-scale rejection of the key terms of modernity, including 'universality'. Gilroy also, however, takes his distance from Habermas, noting that Habermas fails to take into account the centrality of slavery to the 'project of modernity'. Habermas's failure, he notes, can be attributed to his preference for Kant over Hegel(!): 'Habermas does not follow Hegel in arguing that slavery is itself a modernizing force in that it leads both master and servant first to self-consciousness and then to disillusion, forcing both to confront the unhappy realization that the true, the good, and the beautiful do not have a shared origin' (p. 50). Gilroy accepts the notion that the very terms of modernity, however, may be radically reappropriated by those who have been excluded from those terms.

The main terms of modernity are subject to an innovative reuse – what some might call a 'misuse' – precisely because they are spoken by those who are not authorized in advance to make use of them. And what emerges is a kind of political claim which, I would argue, is neither exclusively universal nor exclusively particular; where, indeed, the particular interests that inhere in certain cultural formulations of universality are exposed, and no universal is freed from its contamination by the particular contexts from which it emerges and in which it travels. Slave uprisings that insist upon the universal authorization for emancipation nevertheless borrow from a discourse that runs at least a double risk: the emancipated slave may be liberated into a new mode of subjection[26] that the doctrine of citizenship has in store, and that doctrine may find itself rendered conceptually riven precisely by the emancipatory claims it has made possible. There is no way to predict what will happen in such instances when the universal is wielded precisely by those who signify its contamination, but the purification of the universal into a new formalism will only reinitiate the dialectic that produces its split and spectral condition.

'Seeking recourse' to an established discourse may, at the same time, be the act of 'making a new claim,' and this is not necessarily to extend an old logic or to enter into a mechanism by which the claimant is assimilated into an existing regime. The established discourse remains established only by being perpetually re-established, so it risks itself in the very repetition it requires. Moreover, the former discourse is reiterated precisely through a speech act that shows something it may not say: that the discourse 'works' through its effective moment in the present, and is fundamentally dependent for its maintenance on that contemporary instance. The reiterative speech act thus offers the possibility – though not the necessity – of depriving the past of the established discourse of its exclusive control over defining the parameters of the universal within politics. This form of political performativity does not retroactively absolutize its own claim, but recites and restages a set of cultural norms that displace legitimacy from a presumed authority to the mechanism of its renewal. Such a shift renders more ambiguous – and more open to reformulation – the mobility of legitimation in discourse. Indeed, such claims do not return us to a wisdom we already have, but provoke a set of questions that show how profound our sense of not-knowing is and must be as we lay claim to the norms of political principle. What, then, is a right? What ought universality to be? How do we understand what it is to be a 'human'? The point – as Laclau, Žižek and I would certainly all agree – is not then to answer these questions, but to permit them an opening, to provoke a political discourse that sustains the questions and shows how unknowing any democracy must be about its future. That universality is not speakable outside of a cultural language, but its articulation does not imply that an adequate language is available. It means only that when we speak its name, we do not escape our language, although we can – and must – push the limits.

Notes

1. Ernesto Laclau and Chantal Mouffe, *Hegemony and Socialist Strategy: Towards a Radical Democratic Politics*, London and New York: Verso 1985.

2. Seyla Benhabib, *Critique, Norm, and Utopia: A Study of the Foundations of Critical Theory* (New York: Columbia University Press 1986, pp. 279–354.

3. G.W.F. Hegel, *The Encyclopaedia Logic: Part I of the Encyclopaedia of Philosophical Sciences with the Zusätze*, trans. T.F. Geraets, W.A. Suchting and H.S. Harris, Indianapolis, IN: Hackett 1991.

4. G.W.F. Hegel, *Hegel's Science of Logic*, trans. A.V. Miller, New York: Humanities Press 1976.

5. See Jean-Luc Nancy, *L'Inquiétude du négatif*, Paris: Hachette 1997.

6. G.W.F. Hegel, *Hegel's Phenomenology of Spirit*, trans. A.V. Miller, Oxford: Oxford University Press 1977.

7. See Homi Bhabha, *The Location of Culture*, New York: Routledge 1996.

8. On this point of definition, see Johannes Fabian, *Time and the Other: How Anthropology Makes its Object*, New York: Columbia University Press 1983.

9. See Slavoj Žižek, *Tarrying with the Negative: Kant, Hegel, and the Critique of Ideology*, Durham, NC: Duke University Press 1993.

10. Ibid.

11. See Judith Butler, *Gender Trouble: Feminism and the Subversion of Identity*, New York: Routledge 1990.

12. See the exchange between Ernesto Laclau and Judith Butler in the jointly authored dialogue 'Uses of Equality', *Diacritics* 27.1, Spring 1997.

13. Denise Riley, *The Words of Selves: Identification, Solidarity, Irony*, Stanford, CA: Stanford University Press, forthcoming.

14. Ernesto Laclau, ed., *The Making of Political Identities*, London and New York: Verso 1994.

15. Joan Wallach Scott, *Only Paradoxes to Offer: French Feminists and the Rights of Man* (Cambridge, MA: Harvard University Press 1996) shows how feminist claims in the French Revolution were invariably double, and not always internally reconciled: both a specific claim made about the rights of women and a universal claim about their personhood. Indeed, it seems to me that most minority rights struggles employ both particularist and universalist strategies at once, producing a political discourse that sustains an ambiguous relation to Enlightenment notions of universality. See Paul Gilroy, *The Black Atlantic: Modernity and Double Consciousness* (Cambridge, MA: Harvard University Press 1993) for another strong formulation of this paradoxical coincidence of particular and universal claims.

16. Ernesto Laclau, *Emancipation(s)*, London and New York: Verso 1996.

17. See the new Preface to Judith Butler, *Subjects of Desire: Hegelian Reflections in Twentieth-Century France* [1987], New York: Columbia University Press 1999.

18. Linda M.G. Zerilli, 'The Universalism Which is Not One', *Diacritics* 28.2, Summer 1998: 15. See in particular her cogent critique of Naomi Schor.

19. Michel Foucault, *The Archaeology of Knowledge & The Discourse on Language*, trans. Alan Sheridan, New York: Pantheon Books 1972.

20. Gayatri Chakravorty Spivak, 'Can the Subaltern Speak?', in *Marxism and the Interpretation of Culture*, ed. Cary Nelson and Lawrence Grossberg, Urbana: University of Illinois Press 1988.

21. Gayatri Chakravorty Spivak, 'A Translator's Preface' and 'Afterword' to Mahasweta Devi, 'Imaginary Maps', in *The Spivak Reader*, ed. Donna Landry and Gerald MacLean, New York: Routledge 1996, p. 275.

22. Michel Foucault, 'Nietzsche, Genealogy, History', in *Language, Counter-memory, Practice*, ed. Donald F. Bouchard, Ithaca, NY: Cornell University Press 1977, p. 150.

23. Étienne Balibar, 'Ambiguous Universality', *Differences* 7.1, Spring 1995.

24. See Judith Butler *Excitable Speech: A Politics of the Performative*, New York: Routledge 1997.

25. Paul Gilroy, *The Black Atlantic*.

26. Saidiya Hartman, *Scenes of Subjection*, New York: Oxford University Press 1998.

Identity and Hegemony:
The Role of Universality in the
Constitution of Political Logics

Ernesto Laclau

I   Hegemony: what's in a name?

I will take as my starting point Judith Butler's Question 8a: 'Are we all still agreed that hegemony is a useful category for describing our political dispositions?' My answer is certainly affirmative, and I would add only that 'hegemony' is more than a useful category: it defines the very terrain in which a political relation is actually constituted. To ground this assertion, however, requires throwing some light on what is specific in a hegemonic logic. I will attempt to do this through a consideration of the conceptual displacements that a hegemonic approach introduced in the basic categories of classical political theory.

Let us start by quoting a passage from Marx which could be considered as the zero-degree of hegemony:

> The proletariat is coming into being in Germany only as a result of the rising *industrial* development. For it is not the *naturally arising* poor but the *artificially impoverished*, not the human masses mechanically oppressed by the gravity of society but the masses resulting from the *drastic dissolution* of society, mainly of the middle estate, that form the proletariat . . . By proclaiming the *dissolution of the hitherto world order* the proletariat merely states the *secret of its own existence*, for it *is in fact* the dissolution of that world order. By demanding the *negation of private property*, the proletariat simply raises to the rank of a *principle of society* what society has made the

principle of the *proletariat*, what, without its own cooperation, is already incorporated in *it* as the negative result of society. . . . As philosophy finds its *material* weapons in the proletariat, so the proletariat finds its *spiritual* weapons in philosophy. And once the lightning of thought has squarely struck the ingenuous soil of the people the emancipation of the *Germans* into *human beings* will take place.[1]

Let us now compare this passage with the following one from the same essay:

On what is a partial, a merely political revolution based? On the fact that *part of civil society* emancipates itself and attains *general* domination; on the fact that a definite class, proceeding from its *particular situation*, undertakes the general emancipation of society. . . . For the *revolution of a nation* and the *emancipation of a particular class of civil society to coincide*, for *one* estate to be acknowledged as the state of the whole society, all the defects of society must conversely be concentrated in another class, a particular estate must be looked upon as the *notorious crime* of the whole of society, so that liberation from that sphere appears as general self-liberation. For *one* estate to be *par excellence* the estate of liberation, another estate must conversely be the obvious estate of oppression.[2]

If we compare these two passages, we are confronted with several quite remarkable differences. In the first case, emancipation results from a 'drastic dissolution of society', while in the second it comes about as a consequence of a partial section of civil society achieving '*general* domination'. That is, while all particularity dissolves in the first case, in the second a passage through particularity is the condition of emergence of any universalizing effects. We know very well the sociologico-teleological hypothesis on which the first case rests: the logic of capitalist development would lead to a proletarianization of the middle classes and the peasantry so that, in the end, a homogeneous proletarian mass will become the vast majority of the population in its final showdown with the bourgeoisie. That is to say that – the proletariat having embodied the universality of the community – the state, as a separate instance, loses any reason to exist, and its withering away is the unavoidable consequence of the emergence of a community for which the division state/civil society has become superfluous. In the second case, on the contrary, no such given, unmediated universality can be asserted: something which does not cease to be particular has to demonstrate its rights to identify its own particular aims with the universal emancipatory aims of the community. Moreover, while in the first case power becomes superfluous, inasmuch as the actual being of civil society realizes universality in and for itself, in the second case, any potential universalizing effect depends on the antagonistic exclusion of an oppressive sector – which means that power and political mediation are inherent to any universal emancipatory identity. Thirdly, emancipation, in the first case, leads to an unmediated fullness, the retrieval of an essence which does not require anything external to itself to be what it is. In the second case, on the contrary, two mediations are needed in order to constitute the emancipatory discourse: first, the transformation of the particularistic interests of the rising dominant sector in the emancipatory discourse of the whole of society; secondly, the presence of an oppressive regime which is the very condition of that transformation. So in this case emancipation, the very possibility of a universal discourse addressing the community as a whole, depends not on a collapse of all particularities, but on a paradoxical interaction between them.

For Marx, of course, only full, non-mediated reconciliation constitutes a true emancipation. The other alternative is just the partial or spurious universality which is compatible with a class society. The attainment of full emancipation and universality depends, however, on the verification of his basic hypothesis: the simplification of class structure under capitalism. It is sufficient that the logic of capital does not move in that direction for the realm of particularism to be prolonged *sine die* (a particularism which, as we have seen, is not incompatible with a plurality of universalizing effects). Now, were emancipation and universalization to be restricted to this model, two consequences for the logic of our argument would follow. First, the political mediation, far from withering away, would become the very condition of universality and emancipation in society. As, however, this mediation arises from the actions of a limited historical actor within society, it cannot be attributed to a pure and separate sphere, as can the Hegelian universal class.

It is a partial and pragmatic universality. But, secondly, the very possibility of domination is made dependent on the ability of a limited historical actor to present its own 'partial' emancipation as equivalent to the emancipation of society as a whole. As this 'holistic' dimension cannot be reduced to the particularity which assumes its representation, its very possibility involves an autonomization of the sphere of ideological representations *vis-à-vis* the apparatuses of straight domination. Ideas, in the words of Marx, become material forces. If domination involves political subordination, the latter in turn can be achieved only through processes of universalization which make all domination unstable. With this we have all the dimensions of the political and theoretical situation which make possible the 'hegemonic' turn in emancipatory politics.

Let us start by considering the theoretical displacements that the 'hegemonic' intervention of Gramsci introduces in relation to both Marx's and Hegel's political thought. As Norberto Bobbio asserts in a classic essay on Gramsci's conception of civil society: '*Civil society in Gramsci does not belong to the structural moment, but to the superstructural one.*'[3] In Gramsci's own terms:

> What we can do, for the moment, is to fix two major superstructural 'levels': the one that can be called 'civil society', that is the ensemble of organisms commonly called 'private', and the 'political society' or 'the State'. These two levels correspond on the one hand to the function of 'hegemony' which the dominant group exercises throughout society and on the other hand to that of 'direct domination' or command exercised through the 'State' and 'juridical' government'.[4]

The typical example of civil society's hegemony given by Gramsci is the Church during the Middle Ages.

Both Marx and Gramsci privilege, against Hegel, civil society over the state, but while Marx's reversal of Hegel involves the subordination of the superstructure to the structure, for Gramsci the reversal takes place entirely within the superstructure. The matter is further complicated by the fact that Gramsci's concept of civil society is openly derived from Hegel, but it is still considered as a superstructural one. This is possible, according to Bobbio, only if Gramsci is referring not to Hegel's notion of a 'system of needs' but to that other moment of civil society which involves a rudimentary form of organization (corporation and police). That is, even when he privileges civil society as against the state conceived as domination (force), there is in Gramsci an emphasis on organization – on something depending on the intervention of a *will*. It is this emphasis that Bobbio stresses. As he points out, there are in the *Prison Notebooks* three dichotomies – economic moment/ethico – political moment; necessity/freedom; objective/subjective – in which the second term always plays the primary and subordinating role. The dichotomy base/superstructure would be the source of Gramsci's polemic against economism and his privileging of the political dimension crystallized in the *party*. The dichotomy institution/ideology within the superstructure leads, on the other hand, to his notion that subordinated classes have to win their battle, first, on the level of civil society. From this derives the centrality given by Gramsci to the category of *hegemony*.

There is no doubt that Gramsci, on the whole, opposes civil society to the state conceived as domination. What should we do, however, with passages such as the following: 'But what does that signify if not that by 'State' should be understood not only the apparatus of government, but also the 'private' apparatus of 'hegemony' or civil society?'[5] 'In politics the error occurs as a result of an inaccurate understanding of what the State (in its integral meaning: dictatorship + hegemony) really is.'[6] We could also add his analysis of 'statolatry', in which he refers to 'the two forms in which the State presents itself in the language and culture of specific epochs, i.e. as civil society and as political society'.[7] I think we have to inscribe these apparent (or perhaps real) textual hesitations within the context of a wider question: to what extent does a 'collective will' belong to the state or to civil society, to the pre-political or to the political sphere? Let us consider Bobbio's assertion that for Gramsci the ethico-political is the moment of freedom conceived as consciousness of necessity. This assimilation – whether we can attribute it to Gramsci or not – is clearly too hasty. The notion of freedom as consciousness of necessity is a Spinozean–Hegelian notion which explicitly excludes an active subject of history who could operate in a contingent or instrumental way over given material conditions. In its Hegelian version, it involves the idea of freedom as self-determination, and this presupposes the abolition of the subject/object distinction and the necessary determination by a whole which has nothing external to itself and cannot operate instrumentally in relation to anything. Now, if the Gramscian subject is in a *contingent* relation to its own material conditions, two necessary consequences follow:

1. There is no longer any question of an objectivity which necessarily imposes its own diktats, for the contingent interventions of the social actors partially determine such a structural objectivity. The most we can have is the transient objectivity of a 'historical bloc' which partially stabilizes the social flux, but there is no 'necessity' whose consciousness exhausts our subjectivity – political or otherwise;

2. In the same way, on the side of the 'active subject of history' we find only ultimate contingency. But the problem then arises: *where* and how is that subject constituted? What are the places and logics of its constitution which make the actions that subject is supposed to perform compatible with the contingent character of this intervention? As Bobbio has indicated, those movements presuppose: a) the active construction of the primacy of the moment of the *party* (not in the usual sociological sense, but as another name for the primacy of the superstructure over the structure); (b) the primacy of the moment of *hegemony* (which is equivalent to the prevalence of the ideological over the institutional).

These two primacies combined exclude a set of places of constitution of the 'active subject of history'. First, if hegemony involves a series of universalizing effects, that place of constitution cannot be the 'system of needs', in the Hegelian sense, which is a realm of pure particularity. But, secondly, it cannot be the realm of the universal class – the state as an ethico-political sphere – because the irradiation over society of those universalizing effects prevents them from being relegated to a single sphere. Thirdly, and for the same reasons, civil society cannot be constituted as a truly separate instance, for its functions both anticipate and extend the state's role. The state would be the name or the hypostasis of a function which far exceeds its institutional frontiers.

Perhaps the ambiguities of Gramsci *vis-à-vis* the frontiers state/civil society lie not so much in Gramsci's thought but in social reality itself. If the state, defined as the ethico-political moment of society, does not constitute an instance within a topography, then it is impossible simply to identify it with the public sphere. If civil society, conceived as a site of private organizations, is itself the locus of ethico-political effects, its relation with the state as a public instance becomes blurred. Finally, the level of the 'structure' is not simply such a level if its principles of organization are themselves contaminated by the hegemonic effects deriving from the other 'levels'. Thus, we are left with a horizon of intelligibility of the social which is grounded not in *topographies* but in *logics*. These are the logics of 'party' and 'hegemony', which are ultimately identical, as both presuppose non-dialectical articulations which cannot be reduced to any system of topographical locations. The slippery Gramscian terminology reflects – while at the same time it conceals – this impossible overlapping between logics and topography. A final example of this impossible overlapping can be found in the intriguing primacy granted by Gramsci to ideology over the institutional apparatus. Does not this primacy fly in the face of the importance he gives to institutional organization in achieving hegemony? Only in appearance. If the hegemonic *universalizing* effects are going to irradiate from a *particular* sector in society, they cannot be reduced to the organization of that particularity around its own interests, which will necessarily be corporative. If the hegemony of a *particular* social sector depends for its success on presenting its own aims as those realizing the *universal* aims of the community, it is clear that this identification is not the simple prolongation of an institutional system of domination but that, on the contrary, all expansion of the latter presupposes the success of that articulation between universality and particularity (i.e. a hegemonic victory). No model in which the economic (the structure) determines a first institutional level (politics, institutions) to be followed by an epiphenomenal world of ideas will do the trick, given that society is configured as an ethico-political space, and that the latter presupposes *contingent articulations*. The centrality of the intellectual (= ideological) function in grounding the social link necessarily follows from this.

At this point the various displacements that Gramsci makes, in relation to Hegel and Marx, become fully intelligible. With Marx and against Hegel, Gramsci moves the centre of gravity of social analysis from state to civil society – any 'universal class' arises from the latter, not from a separate sphere constituted *above* civil society. But with Hegel against Marx, he will conceive this moment of universality as a *political* moment, and not as a reconciliation of society with its own essence. For Gramsci, however, the only universality that society can achieve is a *hegemonic* universality – a universality contaminated by particularity. So, if on the one hand he undermines the separateness of the Hegelian state by extending the area of ethico-political effects to a multitude of organizations belonging to civil society, on the other this very extension involves, to a large extent, that civil society is constituted as a political space. This explains the hesitations, in Gramsci's texts, about the frontiers between state and civil society to which we have referred above, and also explains why he had to emphasize the moment of 'corporation' in the Hegelian analysis of civil society: the construction of the apparatuses of hegemony had to cut across the distinction between public and private.

Let us try now to put together the various threads of our argument. The two texts from Marx with which we started deal with universal human emancipation, but do so in a fundamentally different way: in the first, universality means *direct* reconciliation of society with its own essence – the universal is expressed without needing any mediation. In the second case, universal emancipation is achieved only through its transient identification with the aims of a particular social sector – which means that it is a *contingent* universality constitutively requiring political mediation and relations of representation. It is the deepening of this second view of emancipation and its generalization to the whole of politics in the modern age that constitutes Gramsci's achievement. Its result, as we have seen, was the elaboration of the theoretical framework which gave its centrality to the category of 'hegemony'. We now have to ask about the historical conditions of its generalization as a tool of political analysis, and the structural dimensions it involves.

Gramsci was writing at a time when it was already clear that mature capitalism was not advancing in the direction of an increasing homogenization of the social structure but, on the contrary, towards an ever greater social and institutional complexity. The notion of 'organized capitalism' had been proposed in the years immediately preceding and succeeding the First World War, and this tendency was accentuated with the slump of the 1930s. In this new historical situation it was clear that any 'universal class' was going to be the effect of a laborious political construction, not of the automatic and necessary movements of any infrastructure.

The specificity of Gramsci's theoretical turn can be seen more clearly if we inscribe it within the system of politico-intellectual alternatives elaborated by Marxism since the beginning of the century. Let us take Sorel and Trotsky as two thinkers who were at least partially aware of the problems Gramsci was addressing. Sorel understood that the main trends of capitalist development were not leading in the direction predicted by Marxism but were generating, on the contrary, an increasing social complexity incompatible with the emergence in civil society of any 'universal class'. That is why the purity of the proletarian will had to be maintained, according to Sorel, through artificial means: the myth of the general strike had, as its main function, the protection of the *separate* identity of the working class. While this increasing social complexity led Gramsci to assert the need to expand the moment of political mediation, it led Sorel to a total repudiation of politics. As much as in Marx, true emancipation meant for Sorel a fully reconciled society, but while for Marx emancipation would be the result of the objective laws of capitalist development, for Sorel it was to be the consequence of an autonomous intervention of the will. And, as this will tended to reinforce the isolation of the proletarian identity, any hegemonic articulation was excluded as a matter of principle.

Something similar happens in the case of Trotsky. His thought starts with the realization that the relation between global emancipation and its possible agents is unstable: the Russian bourgeoisie is too weak to carry out its democratic revolution, and the democratic tasks have to be carried out under the leadership of the proletariat – this is what he called 'permanent revolution'. But while for Gramsci this hegemonic transference led to the construction of a complex collective will, for Trotsky it was simply the strategic occasion for the working class to carry out its own *class* revolution. The hegemonic task does not affect the identity of the hegemonic agent. The whole approach does not go beyond the Leninist conception of 'class alliances'.

It is in these two precise points – where Gramsci parts company with Sorel and Trotsky – that we find the possibility of expanding and radicalizing a theory of hegemony. Against Sorel, emancipatory struggle requires articulation and political mediation; against Trotsky, the transference of the democratic tasks from one class to another changes not only the nature of the tasks but also the identity of the agents (who cease to be merely 'class' agents). A political dimension becomes constitutive of *all* social identity, and this leads to a further blurring of the line of demarcation state/civil society. It is precisely this further blurring that we find in contemporary society in a more accentuated way than in Gramsci's time. The globalization of the economy, the reduction of the functions and powers of nation-states, the proliferation of international quasi-state organizations – everything points in the direction of complex processes of decision-making which could be approached in terms of hegemonic logics, but certainly not on the basis of any simple distinction public/private. The only thing to add is that Gramsci was still thinking within a world in which both subjects and institutions were relatively stable – which means that most of his categories have to be redefined and radicalized if they are to be adapted to the present circumstances.

This further refinement and radicalization require us to engage in a very precise task: to move from a purely sociologistic and descriptive account of the *concrete* agents involved in hegemonic operations to a *formal* analysis of the logics involved in the latter.[8] We gain very little, once identities are conceived as complexly articulated collective wills, by referring to them through simple designations such as classes, ethnic groups, and so on, which are at best names for transient points of stabilization. The really important task is to understand the logics of their constitution and dissolution, as well as the formal determinations of the spaces in which they interrelate. It is to the question of these formal determinations that I will devote the rest of this section.

Let us now return to our text by Marx on *political* emancipation, and consider the logical structure of its different moments. We have, in the first place, the identification of the aims of a particular group with the emancipatory aims of the whole community. How is this identification possible? Are we dealing with a process of *alienation* of the community, which abandons its true aims to embrace those of one of its component parts? Or with an act of demagogic manipulation by the latter, which succeeds in rallying the vast majority of society under its own banners? Not at all. The reason for that identification is that this particular sector is the one which is able to bring about the downfall of an estate which is perceived as a '*general* crime'. Now, if the 'crime' is a *general* one and, however, only a *particular* sector or constellation of sectors – rather than the 'people' as a whole – is able to overthrow it, this can only mean that the distribution of power within the 'popular' pole is essentially uneven. While in our first quotation from Marx universality of the content and formal universality exactly overlapped in the body of the proletariat, we have in the so-called political emancipation a split between the particularism of the contents and the formal universalization deriving from their irradiation over the whole of society. This split is, as we have seen, the effect of the universality of the crime combined with the particularity of the power capable of abolishing it. *Thus we see a first dimension of the hegemonic relation: unevenness of power is constitutive of it.* We can easily see the difference with a theory like Hobbes's. For Hobbes, in the state of nature power is evenly distributed among individuals, and, as each tends towards conflicting aims, society becomes impossible. So the covenant which surrenders total power to the Leviathan is an essentially non-political act in that it totally excludes the interaction between antagonistic wills. A power which is total is no power at all. If, on the contrary, we have an originally uneven distribution of power, the possibility of ensuring social order can result from that very unevenness and not from any surrender of total power into the hands of the sovereign. In that case, however, the claim of a sector to rule will depend on its ability to present its own particular aims as the ones which are compatible with the actual functioning of the community – which is, precisely, what is intrinsic to the hegemonic operation.

This, however, is not enough. For if the generalized acceptance of the hegemony of the force carrying out political emancipation depended only on its ability to overthrow a repressive regime, the support it would get would be strictly limited to such an act of overthrowing, and there would be no 'coincidence' between the 'revolution of the nation' and the 'emancipation' of a particular class of civil society. So, what can bring about this coincidence? I think that the answer is to be found in Marx's assertion that 'a particular estate must be looked upon as the *notorious crime* of the whole of society, so that liberation from that sphere appears as general self-liberation'. For this to be possible, several displacements become necessary, all of which point towards an increasing complexity in the relation between universality and particularity. In the first place, a system of domination is always, ontically speaking, a particular one, but if it is to be seen as 'the *notorious* crime of the whole of society', its own particularity has in turn to be seen as a symbol of something different and incommensurable with it: the obstacle which prevents society from coinciding with itself, from reaching its fullness. There is no concept, of course, which would correspond to that fullness and, as a result, no concept corresponding to a *universal* object blocking it, but an impossible object, to which no concept corresponds, can still have a name: it borrows it from the particularity of the oppressive regime – which thus becomes partially universalized. In the second place, if there is a *general* crime, there should be a *general* victim. Society, however, is a plurality of particularistic groups and demands. So if there is going to be the subject of a certain global emancipation, the subject antagonized by the general crime, it can be *politically constructed* only through the *equivalence* of a plurality of demands. As a result, these particularities are also split: through their equivalence they do not simply remain themselves, but also constitute an area of universalizing effects – not exactly Rousseau's general will, but a pragmatic and contingent version of it. Finally, what about that impossible object, the fullness of society, against which the 'notorious crime' sins, and which emancipation tries to reach? It obviously lacks any form of direct expression, and can accede to the level of representation, as in the two previous cases, only by a passage through the particular. This particular is given, in the present case, by the aims of that sector whose ability to overthrow the oppressive regime opens the way to political emancipation – to which we have to add only that, in this process, the particularity of the aims does not remain as mere particularity: it is contaminated by the chain of equivalences it comes to represent. We can, in this way, point to a second dimension of the hegemonic relation: *there is hegemony only if the dichotomy universality/particularity is superseded; universality exists only incarnated in – and subverting – some particularity but, conversely, no particularity can become political without becoming the locus of universalizing effects.*

This second dimension leads us, however, to a new problem. What is inherent in the hegemonic relation, if the universal and the particular reject each other but nevertheless require each other, is *the representation of an impossibility*. Fullness of society and its correlate, total 'crime', are *necessary* objects if the 'coincidence' between particular and general aims is going to take place at all. If the passage through the particular is required, however, it is because universality cannot be represented in a *direct* way – there is no concept corresponding to the object. This means that the object, in spite of its necessity, is also impossible. If its necessity requires access to the level of representation, its impossibility means that it is always going to be a distorted representation – that the means of representation are going to be *constitutively* inadequate.[9] We already know what these means of representation are: particularities which, without ceasing to be particularities, assume a function of universal representation. This is what is at the root of hegemonic relations.

What is the ontological possibility of relations by which particular identities take up the representation of something different from themselves? We said earlier that something to which no *concept* corresponds (a *that* without a *what*) can still have a *name* – assuming that a function of universal representation consists, in this sense, of widening the gap between the order of naming and that of what can be conceptually grasped. We are, in some way, in a comparable situation to the one described by Derrida in *Speech and Phenomena* apropos of Husserl: 'meaning' and 'knowledge' do not overlap. We can say that, as a result of this constitutive gap: (1) the more extended the chain of equivalences that a particular sector comes to represent and the more its aims become a *name* for global emancipation, the looser will be the links between that name and its original particular meaning, and the more it will approach the status of an empty signifier;[10] (2) as this total coincidence of the universal with the particular is, however, ultimately impossible – given the constitutive inadequacy of the means of representation – a remainder of particularity cannot be eliminated. The process of naming itself, as it is not constrained by any a priori conceptual limits, is the one that will retroactively determine – depending on contingent hegemonic articulations – what is actually named. This means that the transition from Marx's *political* emancipation to *total* emancipation can never arrive. This shows us a third dimension of the hegemonic relation: *it requires the production of tendentially empty signifiers which, while maintaining the incommensurability between universal and particulars, enables the latter to take up the representation of the former.*

Finally, a corollary of our previous conclusions is that 'representation' is constitutive of the hegemonic relation. The elimination of all representation is the illusion accompanying the notion of a *total* emancipation. But, in so far as the universality of the community is achievable only through the mediation of a particularity, the relation of representation becomes constitutive. We have, as inherent to the representative link, the same dialectic between name and concept that we have just mentioned. If the representation was total – if the representative moment was entirely transparent to what it represents – the 'concept' would have an unchallenged primacy over the 'name' (in Saussurean terms: the signified would entirely subordinate to itself the order of the signifier). But in that case there would be no hegemony, for its very requisite, which is the production of tendentially empty signifiers, would not obtain. In order to have hegemony we need the sectorial aims of a group to operate as the name for a universality transcending them – this is the synecdoche constitutive of the hegemonic link. But if the name (the signifier) is so attached to the concept (signified) that no displacement in the relation between the two is possible, we cannot have any hegemonic rearticulation. The idea of a totally emancipated and transparent society, from which all tropological movement between its constitutive parts would have been eliminated, involves the end of all hegemonic relation (and also, as we will see later, of all democratic politics). Here we have a fourth dimension of 'hegemony': *the terrain in which it expands is that of the generalization of the relations of representation as condition of the constitution of a social order.* This explains why the hegemonic form of politics tends to become general in our contemporary, globalized world: as the decentring of the structures of power tends to increase, any centrality requires that its agents are constitutively overdetermined – that is, that they always represent *something more* than their mere particularistic identity.

To conclude, I would like to make two remarks. First: in so far as this complex dialectic between particularity and universality, between ontic content and ontological dimension, structures social reality itself, it also structures the identity of the social agents. As I will try to argue later, it is the very lack within the structure that is at the origin of the subject. This means that we do not simply have subject positions within the structure, but also the subject as an attempt to fill these structural gaps. That is why we do not have just *identities* but, rather, *identification*. If identification is required, however, there is going to be a basic ambiguity at the heart of all identity. This is the way I would approach the question of *disidentification* raised by Žižek.

As for the question concerning historicism, my perspective coincides entirely with Žižek's. I think that radical historicism is a self-defeating enterprise. It does not recognize the ways in which the universal enters into the constitution of all particular identities. From a theoretical point of view, the very notion of particularity presupposes that of totality (even total *separation* cannot escape the fact that separation is still a type of relation between entities – the monads require a 'pre-established harmony' as a condition of their non-interaction). And, politically speaking, the right of particular groups of agents – ethnic, national or sexual minorities, for instance – can be formulated only as *universal* rights. The appeal to the universal is unavoidable once, on the one hand, no agent can claim to speak *directly* for the 'totality' while, on the other, reference to the latter remains an essential component of the hegemonico-discursive operation. *The universal is an empty place, a void which can be filled only by the particular, but which, through its very emptiness, produces a series of crucial effects in the structuration/destructuration of social relations*. It is in this sense that it is both an impossible and a necessary object. In a recent work, Žižek has described quite accurately my own approach to the question of the universal. After referring to a first conception of universality – the Cartesian *cogito*, for which the universal has a positive and neutral content, indifferent to particularities – and a second – the Marxist one, for which the universal is the distorted expression of a particular identity – he adds:

There is, however, a third version, elaborated in detail by Ernesto Laclau: the Universal is empty, yet precisely as such always-already filled in, that is, hegemonized by some contingent, particular content that acts as its stand-in – in short, each Universal is the battleground on which the multitude of particular contents fight for hegemony . . . The distinction between this third version and the first is that the third version allows for no content of the Universal which would be effectively neutral and, as such, common to all its species . . . all positive content of the Universal is the contingent result of hegemonic struggle – in itself, the Universal is absolutely empty.[11]

Having reached this point, however, we have to deal in more detail with this peculiar logic by which an object, through its very impossibility, still produces a variety of effects shown in the universalization of the relations of representation – which, as we have seen, is the condition of possibility of the hegemonic link. What is the ontological structure of such a link? We will start tackling this problem through the consideration of two authors to whom our questionnaire makes repeated reference: Hegel and Lacan.

II   Hegel

Let us start by considering an objection Žižek makes to my reading of Hegel, for it shows clearly what are, in my view, the limitations of Hegelian dialectic as a candidate for rendering the hegemonic relation intelligible. Žižek asserts:

The only thing to add to Laclau's formulation is that his anti-Hegelian twist is, perhaps, all too sudden:

We are not dealing here with 'determinate negation' in the Hegelian sense: while the latter comes out of the apparent positivity of the concrete and 'circulates' through contents that are always determinate, our notion of negativity depends on the failure in the constitution of all determination. (*Emancipation(s)*, p. 14)

What, however, if the infamous 'Hegelian determinate negation' aims precisely at the fact that every particular formation involves a gap between the Universal and the Particular – or, in Hegelese, that a particular formation never coincides with its (universal) notion – and that it is this very gap that brings about its dialectical dissolution?[12]

Žižek gives the example of the state: it is not that positive actual states imperfectly approach their notion, but that the very notion of the state *qua* rational totality cannot be actualized. 'Hegel's point here is not that the State which would fully fit its notion is impossible – it is possible; the catch is, rather, that *it is no longer a* state, *but a religious community*.'[13]

I would like to make two points to Žižek. The first is that he is entirely right in asserting that, for Hegel, no particular formation ever coincides with its own notion, simply because the notion itself is internally split, and brings about its own dialectical dissolution. I never put this into doubt. But, secondly, the dialectical pattern of this dissolution requires it to be a pattern made of necessary transitions: it is – to take the example – a religious community *and nothing else* that results from the non-coincidence of the state with its notion. The important question is this: accepting entirely that the Absolute Spirit has no positive content of its own, and is just the succession of all dialectical transitions, of its impossibility of establishing a final overlapping between the universal and the particular – are these transitions *contingent* or *necessary*? If the latter, the characterization of the whole Hegelian *project* (as opposed to what he actually did) as panlogicist can hardly be avoided.

From this point of view, the evidence is overwhelming. Let me just stress a few points:

1. As in most post-Kantian Idealist systems, Hegel aspires to a presuppositionless philosophy. This means that the irrational – and ultimately contradictory – moment of the thing in itself has to be eliminated. Furthermore, if Reason is going to be its own grounding, the Hegelian list of categories cannot be a catalogue, as in Aristotle or Kant – the categories have to deduce themselves from each other in an orderly fashion. This means that all determinations are going to be *logical* determinations. Even if something is

irrational, it has to be retrieved as such by the system of Reason.

2. If the system is going to be grounded on no presupposition, the method and the content to which it is applied cannot be external to each other.

> For this reason, Hegel's account of the method can come only at the end of the *Logic*, not at the beginning. The Absolute Idea, whose 'form' is said to be the method, is visible only at the culmination: 'the Idea is thought itself . . . as the self-determining totality of its own determinations and laws, which it gives to itself rather than having them already and finding them within itself' (E: 19A).[14]

3. The Absolute Idea as the system of all determinations is a closed totality: beyond it, no further advance is possible. The dialectical movement from one category to the next excludes all contingency (although Hegel was far from being consistent in this respect, as is shown in his famous remarks on Krug's pen). It is difficult to avoid the conclusion that Hegel's panlogicism is the highest point of modern rationalism. This shows us why the hegemonic relation cannot be assimilated to a dialectical transition: for although one of the prerequisites of conceptually grasping the hegemonic link – the incommensurability between Particular and Universal – is met by a dialectical logic, the other – the contingent character of the link between the two – does not obtain.

This, however, is not the whole story. I cannot simply dismiss Žižek's reading of Hegel, for two reasons. First, that I agree with most of what he does *out of* Hegel's texts. Second, that I do not think that he is projecting into those texts a series of considerations extraneous to the texts themselves. They clearly apply to them. So how do I deal with this apparent contradiction on my part? I am certainly not prepared to concede anything concerning the panlogistic nature of Hegel's intellectual *project*. However, we should not take the word for the deed. As the highest point of modern rationalism, Hegel claimed, for Reason, a role the latter had never claimed for itself in the past: to rethink, in terms of its own logical transitions, the totality of the ontological distinctions that the philosophical tradition had discerned within the real. This gives

way to a double movement: if Reason, on the one hand, has hegemonized the whole realm of differences, the latter, on the other, could not
avoid contaminating the former. So many dialectical transitions are *spurious* logical transitions. Since the nineteenth century, criticism of Hegel
has taken the form of asserting that many of his deductions derive their
apparent acceptability from illegitimate empirical assumptions smuggled
into the argument (Trendelenburg, for instance). This was the main line
of Schelling's criticism of Hegel: he attempted to show that, apart from
many inconsistent deductions in his *Logic*, the whole project of a presuppositionless philosophy was flawed, for it could not even start without
accepting the laws of logic and a rationalist approach to concepts (as
innate ideas), a dogmatic metaphysical realism which starts from 'Being'
as a lifeless objectivity, and language as a pre-constituted medium.[15]
Against this vision, Schelling asserts that Philosophy cannot be presuppositionless, and that human existence is a starting point more primary
than the concept. Feuerbach, Kierkegaard and Engels – all of whom
attended Schelling's courses – accepted his basic criticism, and developed their own particular approaches, giving priority to 'existence' over
'reason'. In some sense, it has to be accepted that Hegel represents the
closure of the metaphysical tradition which started with Plato.
Schelling's 'positive philosophy' is a new beginning, in which the whole
of contemporary thought was to engulf itself.

   Now, I want to stress that, in my departure from dialectics, I *do not*
take the Schellingian road. The 'discourse' approach that I take in relation to the 'social construction of reality' prevents me from accepting
any sharp distinction between existence and consciousness. This does
not mean, however, that I believe that a system of conceptually necessary transitions is the only alternative to an opaque empiricity. The
main difficulty that stands in the way of a purely speculative dialectics is,
in my view, the role of ordinary language in the dialectical transitions.
Let us quote in full the passage, in Hegel's *Logic*, where he tries to tackle
this problem:

> Philosophy has the right to select from the language of common life
> which is made for the world of pictorial thinking, such expressions as *seem
> to approximate* to the determinations of the Notion. There cannot be any

question of *demonstrating* for a word selected from the language of common life that in common life, too, one associates with it the same Notion for which philosophy employs it; for common life has no Notions, but only pictorial thoughts and general ideas, and to recognize the Notion in what is else a general idea is philosophy itself. It must suffice therefore if pictorial thinking, in the use of its expressions that are employed for philosophical determinations, has before it some vague idea of their distinctive meaning; just as it may be the case that in these expressions one recognizes nuances of pictorial thought that are more closely related to the corresponding Notions.[16]

This passage is crucial, for the problem at stake here is the precise role of the 'pictorial thinking' in the dialectical transitions. If the images associated with pictorial thought are indifferent names given to entities constituted entirely outside them, the names would be entirely arbitrary and logically irrelevant; if, on the contrary, the transition depends on a verisimilitude deriving from the intuitive meaning of the name *before* its inscription in that transition, *in that case the transition cannot be a logical one.* Now, dialectical logic presupposes that you cannot dissociate form and content, that the content actually *named* is an integral part of the whole logical movement of the concept. But if the name gets its meaning from a language *pre-existing* that logical movement, the movement itself becomes something quite different from a logical deduction: it becomes a *tropological* movement by which a name fills, as a metaphor, a gap opened in a chain of reasoning. So the pictorial image is not, as Hegel claims, a vague or imprecise version of a determination made fully explicit by Philosophy, but, on the contrary, vagueness and imprecision *as such* are fully constitutive of the philosophical argument. We have to conclude that dialectical logic is the terrain of a generalized rhetoric. The richness of Hegel's texts lies not so much in their attempt strictly to derive concepts out of a presuppositionless starting point – a rule they violate on every page – but in the implicit rhetoric which governs their transitions. This is what, I think, lends its credentials to many of Žižek's *démarches*. We should not forget, however, that panlogicism is still there, operating as a strait-jacket limiting the effects of the rhetorical displacements.

This also explains my reaction to Butler's Question 9. For the reasons that I have just presented, no sharp distinction can be maintained, in a Hegelian perspective, between form and content – they mediate each other. But also, in a perspective like mine, which approaches hegemonic transitions in terms of rhetorical displacements, it is impossible conceptually to grasp form independently from content (although not for logical reasons). As for the question of the quasi-transcendentals, it poses problems of its own to which I will return later. The only remark I would like to make to Butler is that the opposition form/content is not the same as the opposition between quasi-transcendentals and examples. For an example *is not* a content. A content is an integral part of a concept, while something, in order to be an example, should add nothing to what it is an example of, and should be substitutable by an indefinite number of other examples. If I say: 'Jews are responsible for the national decline', 'Communists are defenders of the interests of the masses', or 'Women are exploited in a patriarchal society', it is evident that all three can be examples of the agreement between subject and verb in a sentence, without the grammatical rule being altered by the semantical content of the examples. It is always, of course, possible that, through a set of discursive devices, something that in a particular discourse *appears* as an example determines the conceptual content in some way, but to establish this requires the study of particular discursive instances.

To conclude: Hegelian dialectics gives us only partially adequate ontological tools to determine the logic of the hegemonic link. The contingent dimension of politics cannot be thought within a Hegelian mould. When we move from Hegel to Lacan, however, we find an entirely different scenario.

III   Lacan

Let me say, to start with, that I would not establish the opposition between 'orthodox Lacanian doxa' and 'heterodox appropriation of Lacan for the thinking of hegemony' in the sharp terms in which Butler does. Any appropriation of a theoretical approach will be more or less orthodox, depending on the degree of identification that one finds with the 'appropriated' author. But if by orthodox doxa one understands philological obsession and mechanical repetition of the same categories without 'developing' them as required by new contexts, it is clear that any intellectual intervention worth the name will be 'heterodox'.

So: let us fully engage in a heterodox game. Judith Butler is essentially concerned with the question of whether Lacan's 'barred subject' imposes or does not impose structural limitations to the strategic movements required by a hegemonic logic. The kernel of her scepticism about the potential fruitfulness of a Lacanian approach to politics is neatly stated: 'Can the ahistorical recourse to the Lacanian bar be reconciled with the strategic question that hegemony poses, or does it stand as a quasi-transcendental limitation on all possible subject-formation and, hence, as indifferent to politics?' (Question 1). Now, to some extent Žižek hints to what would be my own answer to Butler's question when he refers to the Lacanian Real as 'its [the symbolic's] totally non-substantial inherent limit, point of failure, which maintains the very gap between reality and its symbolization and thus sets in motion the contingent process of historicization–symbolization?' (Question 1).

Let us consider the matter carefully. What is involved in constructing a quasi-transcendental category as (1) 'a limitation on all possible subject-formation', and (2) a limitation which is 'indifferent to politics'? In my view, it involves the introduction of two contradictory requirements because 'limitation' seems to imply that some political identities are excluded as a result of the quasi-transcendental limit. If, however, what results from the latter is an indifference to politics, one should apparently conclude that the limit is no limit at all – and, as a corollary, that the only way of superseding such indifference would be some kind of *positive* transcendental grounding, which is precisely what the first requirement was attempting to undermine. In order to go beyond this blind alley, one should perhaps ask oneself a different question: *Is it a bar whose function consists in showing the ultimate impossibility of full representation, a limit on what can be represented, or, rather, does it expand the relation of representation (as a failed representation, of course) beyond all limitation? If this were the case, it would open the way to a more radical historicism than anything that could be grounded in either a system of positive transcendental categories or in an appeal to a 'concrete' which lives in the ignorance of its own conditions of possibility.* Hegemony requires, as we have seen, a generalization of the relations of representation, but in such a way that the process of representation itself creates retroactively the entity to be represented. The non-transparency of the representative to the represented, the irreducible autonomy of the signifier *vis-à-vis* the signified, is the condition of a hegemony which structures the social from its very ground and is not the epiphenomenal expression of a transcendental signified which would submit the signifier to its own predetermined movements. This 'liberation' of the signifier *vis-à-vis* the signified – the very precondition of hegemony – is what the Lacanian bar attempts to express. The other side of the coin, the contingent imposition of limits or partial fixations – without which we would be living in a psychotic universe – is what the notion of 'point de capiton' brings about.[17]

The representation of the unrepresentable constitutes the terms of the paradox within which hegemony is constructed – or, in the terms we used earlier, we are dealing with an object which is at the same time impossible and necessary. This is not far from the terrain of the Lacanian notion of a 'real' which resists symbolization. At this point, however, Butler raises an objection: 'to claim that the real resists symbolization is still to symbolize the real as a kind of resistance. The former claim (the real resists symbolization) can only be true if the latter claim ('the real resists symbolization' is a symbolization) is true, but if the second claim is true, the first is necessarily false.'[18]

Butler presents her argument in terms of Russell's paradox ('the class of all classes which are not members of themselves, is it a member of itself?', etc.), but the very way she formulates it evokes, quite easily, the standard Idealist criticism of Kant's 'thing in itself' (if categories apply only to phenomena, I cannot say that the thing is the external *cause* of my sensations, that it *exists*, etc.). Now, if her assertion was of this last type, she would be advocating *total* representability, pure transparency of thought to itself, and in that case unrepresentability could be conceived only as radical unawareness – but to admit even the *possibility* of existence of something of which we are *essentially* unaware (that is, not even potentially mediated by thought) would break the link between representability and actuality. As Hegel said in the *Encyclopaedia*:

> Only when we discern that the content – the particular, is not self-subsistent, but derivative from something else, are its finitude and untruth shown in their proper light. . . . The only content which can be held to be the truth is one not mediated with something else, not limited by other things: or, otherwise expressed, it is one mediated by itself, where mediation and immediate reference-to-self coincide. . . . Abstract thought (the scientific form used by 'reflective' metaphysic) and abstract intuition (the form used by immediate knowledge) are one and the same.[19]

But perhaps Butler is not advocating total representability – although it is difficult to see how the sublation of any 'non-representable' within the field of representation could lead to any different reading. Perhaps what she intends to point to is not a contradiction *sensu stricto* but a paradox – in that case she would be referring to an *aporia* of thought, and we would be back to the terms of Russell's dilemma. The question there would be: what can we do when we are confronted with a discursive space organized around logically unanswerable aporias? We can do several things, but there is one especially that I want to stress, given its centrality for what I have to say later on: we can initiate a tropological (rhetorical) movement between the categories establishing the terms of the aporia. Let us consider, as an example, the analysis made by Paul de Man of the role of the 'zero' in 'Pascal's Allegory of Persuasion'.[20] Pascal was confronted with the objection to his principle of infinite smallness: that – if the postulate of a homogeneity between space and number was to be maintained – it would be possible to conceive of an extension composed of parts that are not extended, given that we have numbers made of units which are devoid of number (the one). Pascal's answer consists of two movements: on the one hand he tried to dissociate the order of number from the order of space – by showing that if the *one* is, strictly speaking, not a number, for it is exempt from plurality, it still belongs to the order of number because, through reiterated multiplication, all other numbers are obtained from, made of units which include, the *one*. On the other hand, however, if the homology between number, time and motion is to be maintained, the equivalent of 'instant' or 'stasis' has to be found in the order of number. Pascal finds it in the 'zero'. Now, as to the difference with the *one*, the zero is radically heterogeneous with the order of number and, moreover, crucial if there is going to be an order of number at all. In De Man's words: 'There can be no *one* without zero, but the zero always appears in the guise of a *one*, of a (some)thing. The name is the trope of the zero. The zero is *always* called a one, when the zero is actually nameless, "*innommable*".[21] So we have a situation in which: (1) a systemic totality cannot be constituted without appealing to something radically heterogeneous *vis-à-vis* what is representable within it; (2) this something has, anyway, to be somehow represented if there is to be a system at all; (3) as this will, however, be the representation of something which is *not* representable within the system – even more: the representation of the radical impossibility of representing the latter – that representation can take place only through tropological substitution.

This is the point Butler's argument is really missing: if the representation of the Real was a representation of something entirely *outside* the symbolic, this representation of the unrepresentable *as unrepresentable* would amount, indeed, to full inclusion – this was, for instance, the way in which Hegel was able to include the 'contingent' within his logical system. But if what is represented is an *internal* limit of the process of representation as such, the relationship between internality and externality is subverted: the Real becomes a name for the very failure of the Symbolic in achieving its own fullness. The Real would be, in that sense, a retroactive effect of the failure of the Symbolic. Its name would be both the name of an empty place and the attempt to fill it through that very naming of what, in De Man's words, is nameless, *innommable*. This means that the presence of that name within the system has the status of a suturing *tropos*. Bruce Fink has shown that there are, in Lacan, 'two different orders of the real: (1) a real before the letter, that is, a presymbolic real, which, in the final analysis, is but our own hypothesis (R_1), and (2) a real after the letter which is characterized by impasses and impossibilities due to the relations among elements of the symbolic order itself (R_2), that is, which is generated by the symbolic'.[22]

Thus we can start seeing how the hegemonic operation involves both the presence of a Real which subverts signification and the representation of Real through tropological substitution. The bar in the relation $\frac{S}{s}$ is the

very precondition of a primacy of the signifier without which hegemonic displacements would be inconceivable. There are, however, two
concomitant aspects that I want to stress because they have capital
importance in understanding the workings of the hegemonic logic. The
first concerns the break of the isomorphism postulated by Saussure
between the order of the signifier and the order of the signified. It was
very quickly realized that such an isomorphism led to a contradiction
with the principle that language is form, and not substance, which was
the cornerstone of Saussurean linguistics. For if there was total isomorphism between the order of the signifier and the order of the
signified, it was impossible to distinguish one from the other in purely
formal terms, so that the only alternatives were either to maintain a strict
formalism which would necessarily lead to the collapse of the distinction
between signifier and signified (and the dissolution of the category of
sign) or to smuggle – inconsistently – the substances (phonic and conceptual) into linguistic analysis. It was at this point that the decisive
advance was made by Hjelmslev and the Copenhagen School, who
broke with the principle of isomorphism and constructed the difference
between the two orders – signifier and signified – in purely formal terms.
Now, this change is decisive from a psychoanalytic perspective, for it
allows the exploration of the unconscious to detach itself from the
search for an ultimate meaning. In Lacan's words, the psychoanalytic
process is concerned not with *meaning* but with *truth*. To mention just one
example that I take from Fink: Freud's 'Rat Man', through 'verbal
bridges', constructed a 'rat complex', partly through meaningful associations – for example, rat = penis, for rats spread diseases such as syphilis,
and so on – but partly also through purely verbal associations which
have nothing to do with meaning – '*Raten* means instalments, and leads
to the equation of rats and florins; *Spielratte* means gambler, and the Rat
Man's father, having incurred a debt gambling, becomes drawn into the
rat complex.'[23] The importance of this dissociation of truth from meaning for hegemonic analysis is that it enables us to break with the
dependence on the signified to which a rationalist conception of politics
would have otherwise confined us. What is crucial is not to conceive the
hegemonic process as one in which empty places in the structure would
be simply filled by preconstituted hegemonic forces.[24] There is a process

of contamination of the empty signifiers by the particularities which carry out the hegemonic sutures, but this is a process of *mutual* contamination; it does operate in both directions. For that reason it leads to an autonomization of the signifier which is decisive to the understanding of the political efficacy of certain symbols. To give just one example: without this autonomization it would be impossible to understand the eruptions of xenophobia in former Yugoslavia over the last ten years.

This leads me, however, to stress a second point which goes, to some extent, in the opposite direction from the first. There have been certain forms of argumentation, in Lacanian circles, which tend to emphasize what has been called the 'materiality of the signifier'. Now, if by 'materiality' one refers to the bar which breaks the transparency of the process of signification (the isomorphism we referred to above), this notion would be unobjectionable. But what is important is not to confuse 'materiality' conceived in this sense with the phonic substance as such, because in that case we would be reintroducing substance into the analysis, and we would fall back into the inconsistent Saussurean position discussed above.[25] As has recently been argued, the primacy of the signifier should be asserted, but with the proviso that signifiers, signifieds and signs should all be conceived of as signifiers.[26] To go back to the example of the 'rat complex': the fact that the association of 'rat' with 'penis' involves a passage through the signified, while the association with 'instalment' takes place through a merely verbal bridge, constitutes a perfectly secondary distinction: in both cases there is a displacement of signification determined by a system of structural positions in which each element (conceptual or phonic) functions as a signifier – that is, it acquires its value only through its reference to the whole system of signifiers within which it is inscribed. This point is important for political analysis, because some rationalistic attempts to 'domesticate' the theory of hegemony assert that it is a remainder *at the level of the signified* which provides a necessary anchoring point to what would otherwise be a limitless flux, unable to signify anything. The problem, however, does not actually pose itself in those terms. There is, certainly, an anchoring role played by certain privileged discursive elements – this is what the notion of *point de capiton* or 'Master-Signifier' involves – but this anchoring function does not consist in an ultimate remainder of conceptual substance which would persist through all processes of discursive variation. To give an example: the fact that in some political contexts – South Africa, for example – 'black' can operate as a Master-Signifier organizing a whole set of discursive positions does not mean that 'black' has an ultimate signified independent of all discursive articulation. It functions, rather, as a pure signifier, in the sense that its signifying function would depend on its position within a signifying chain – a position which will be determined partly through 'meaningful' associations (as in the case of 'rat' and 'penis') and partly through verbal bridges, in Freud's sense. The relatively stable set of all these positions is what constitutes a 'hegemonic formation'. So we will understand by 'materiality of the signifier' not the phonic substance as such but the inability of *any* linguistic element – whether phonic or conceptual – to refer *directly* to a signified. This means the priority of value over signification, and what Lacan called the permanent sliding of the signified under the signifier.

The ultimate point which makes an exchange between Lacanian theory and the hegemonic approach to politics possible and fruitful is that in both cases, any kind of unfixity, tropic displacement, and so on, is organized around an original lack which, while it imposes an extra duty on all processes of representation – they have to represent not just a determinate ontic content but equally the principle of representability as such – also, as this dual task cannot but ultimately fail in achieving the suture it attempts, opens the way to a series of indefinite substitutions which are the very ground of a radical historicism. The examples chosen by Žižek in his questions are very relevant to illustrate the point. If repetition is made possible/impossible by a primordial lack, no ontic content can ultimately monopolize the ontological function of representing representability as such (in the same way that, as I have tried to show,[27] the function of *ordering*, in Hobbes, cannot be the special privilege of any *concrete social order* – it is not an attribute of a *good* society, as in Plato, but an ontological dimension whose connection with particular ontic arrangements is, of its own nature, contingent). So there is no possibility of 'reinscription of the process of repetition in the metaphysical logic of identity'. For the same reason the 'barred subject', which prevents the process of interpellation from chaining the 'individual' entirely to a subject position, introduces an area of indeterminacy which makes possible, among other things, Butler's parodic performances. The same can be said of the status of sexual difference, which – as Žižek has convincingly shown – is linked not to particular sexual roles but to a real/impossible kernel which can enter the field of representation only through tropological displacements/incarnations.[28] (In terms of the theory of hegemony, this presents a strict homology with the notion of 'antagonism' as a real kernel preventing the closure of the symbolic order. As we have repeatedly argued, antagonisms are not objective relations but the point where the limit of all objectivity is shown. Something at least comparable is involved in Lacan's assertion that there is no such thing as a sexual relationship.) Finally, I want to add that I agree entirely with Žižek that the notion of 'phallus' in Lacan does not have any necessary phallogocentric implications. 'Phallus', as the signifier of desire, has largely been replaced in Lacan's later teaching by the '*objet petit a*', and this makes possible, even more clearly, the study of its whole range of effects on the structuration of the field of representation.

I would like to conclude this section by referring to Butler's question about the relation between politics and psychoanalysis. Let me just say that a theoretical intervention, when it really makes a difference, is never restricted to the field of its initial formulation. It always produces some kind of restructuration of the ontological horizon within which knowledge had moved so far. Mentioning some examples of which Althusser was fond, we can say that behind Platonic philosophy is Greek mathematics; behind seventeenth-century rationalisms, Galileo's mathematization of nature, and behind Kantianism, Newton's physics. We can similarly say that we are still living in the century of Freud, and I would go as far as to say that most of what is fruitful and innovative in contemporary philosophy is, to a large extent, an attempt to come to terms with Freud's discovery of the unconscious. This transformation, however, should not be conceived so much as the incorporation, for philosophical consideration, of a new *regional field* but, rather, as the opening of a new transcendental horizon within which the whole field of objectivity has to be thought again – as a widening, on the ontological level, of the kind of relations between objects which it is possible to think about. What, for instance, involves asserting that an object is impossible and, at the same time, necessary? What effects would such an object have in the restructuration of the whole field of representation? Seen from this perspective, Lacanian theory should be considered a radicalization and development of what was *in nuce* contained in the Freudian discovery. But, considered from this angle, psychoanalysis is not alone: it is, rather, the epicentre of a wider transformation embracing contemporary thought as a whole. It is to this aspect of our discussion that I now want to move.

IV Objectivity and rhetoric

In his work, Žižek has tried, forcefully and repeatedly, to present the image of a Lacan entirely outside the field of a poststructuralism that he identifies mainly with deconstruction. The frontier between the two traditions turns, for him, around the Lacanian maintenance of the *cogito*. How valid is this thesis? In his latest book[29] – a work that I deeply admire – Žižek starts by asserting that a 'spectre is haunting Western academia', which is none other than 'the spectre of the Cartesian subject'.[30] We are, however, a bit perplexed when, after this spectacular beginning of what announces itself as a Cartesian manifesto, we read on the following page that ' [t]he point, of course, is not to return to the *cogito* in the guise in which this notion has dominated modern thought (the self-transparent thinking subject), but to bring to light its forgotten obverse, the excessive, unacknowledged kernel of the *cogito*, which is far from the pacifying image of the transparent Self'.[31] Now, one has to recognize that this is a *most* peculiar way of being Cartesian. It is like calling oneself a fully fledged Platonist while rejecting the theory of forms; or proclaiming *urbi et orbi* that one is a Kantian – with just the small qualification that one denies that categories are transcendental conditions of understanding. It is evident that if Descartes had come to terms with the obverse side to which Žižek refers, he would have considered that his intellectual project had utterly failed. And it is also clear to me that one cannot relate Lacan to philosophers such as Hegel or Descartes, in the way Žižek wants, without emptying them of what constitutes the kernel of their theoretical projects.

So I want to offer a different outline concerning the saga of twentieth-century intellectual thought. The main aspects would be the following. The century started with three illusions of immediacy, of the possibility of an immediate access to the 'things themselves'. These illusions were the referent, the phenomenon, and the sign, and they were the starting point of the three traditions of Analytic Philosophy, Phenomenology and Structuralism. Since then, the history of these three traditions has been remarkably similar: at some stage, in all three, the illusion of immediacy disintegrates and gives way to one or other form of thought in which discursive mediation becomes primary and constitutive. This is what happens to Analytic Philosophy after Wittgenstein's *Philosophical Investigations*, to phenomenology after Heidegger's existential analytic, and to Structuralism after the poststructuralist critique of the sign. (And, I would argue, to Marxism after Gramsci.) Within this historical framework, it is clear to me that one of the most important moments in the critique of the transparency of the linguistic sign is to be found in Lacan's *linguisteries*, in his notion of the primacy of the signifier to which we referred earlier. So Lacan is not only, for me, a poststructuralist, but also one of the two crucial moments in the emergence of a poststructuralist theoretical terrain. The other is deconstruction, of course, which I see as extending the field of the undecidable quasi-infrastructures[32] and, as a result, expanding the field of what are for Lacan the 'kinks in the symbolic order'[33] – in a more rigorous fashion, in some respects, than anything to be found in Lacanianism.

The way which I am proposing of establishing the dominant break governing the emergence of a thought that we can properly call 'contemporary' is clearly very different from that suggested by Žižek and it explains our partially divergent intellectual allegiances. This does not mean, however, that I reject *in toto* the criterion Žižek uses in drawing his intellectual frontiers. The criterion is valid, but I would deny that one can establish, on this basis, a *dominant* frontier in the way Žižek does. Žižek's frontier is established by asserting the need – in Lacanian theory – for an object which is simultaneously *impossible* and *necessary*. The deduction of its possibility from its necessity – the non-acknowledgement of its obverse, obscene side, to use Žižek's words – would be the inner limitation of modernity's logic of transparency;

while the opposite move, the denial of its necessity out of its impossibility, would be the stigma of postmodernity and poststructuralism (a rather forced assimilation, for it can hardly be claimed of, for instance, Derrida). Now, with the need to assert both sides – necessity and impossibility – I could hardly be in disagreement, for it is the cornerstone of my own approach to hegemonic logics – the latter not involving a flat rejection of categories of classical political theory such as 'sovereignty', 'representation', 'interest', and so on, but conceiving of them, instead, as objects *presupposed* by hegemonic articulatory logics but, however, always ultimately unachievable by them. I am a Gramscian, not a Baudrillardian.

This double condition of necessity and impossibility makes possible, among other things, three endeavours: (1) to understand the logics by which each of the two dimensions subverts the other; (2) to look at the political productivity of this mutual subversion – that is, what it makes possible to understand about the workings of our societies which goes beyond what is achievable by unilateralizing either of the two poles; 3) to trace the genealogy of this undecidable logic, the way it was *already* subverting the central texts of our political and philosophical tradition. An always open intertextuality is the ultimately undecidable terrain in which hegemonic logics operate. Žižek, however, has constructed his discourse through a different intellectual strategy: he has privileged the moment of necessity, and on the basis of that he has constructed a genealogy which locates Lacan within the rationalist tradition of the Enlightenment, weakening in this way his links with the whole intellectual revolution of the twentieth century, to which he really belongs. As, however, the moment of impossibility is really working in the Lacanian texts – and Žižek would be the last to deny it – he has Lacanianized the tradition of modernity, most visibly in the case of Hegel,[34] in a way which I see as hardly legitimate. Instead of exploring the logics of what follows from the relationship necessity/impossibility, we are confronted with an – in my view – arbitrary decision of privileging one pole of this dichotomy, while the effects of the other are severely limited from the outset by this initial privilege. This is not without some consequences for Žižek's discourse concerning politics – as we will see later. Indulging for once in one of those jokes Žižek is so fond of, I would say that I am an intellectual bigamist trying to exploit this ambiguity by drawing on its best strategic possibilities, while Žižek is a staunch monogamist (Lacanian) in theory, who, however, makes all kinds of practical concessions – this is his obverse, obscene side – to his never publicly recognized mistress (deconstruction).

With this conclusion in mind, we can now move to some more general matters concerning social knowledge. Let us refer, first, to the question of the status of the transcendental. I would argue that the transcendental dimension is unavoidable but that transcendentality, in the full sense of the term, is impossible (that is why that we can speak of quasi-transcendentals).[35] Why this impossibility? Because full transcendentality would require, to start with, a neat demarcatory frontier from the empirical, which is not available. There is no object without conditions of possibility transcending it (this is the unavoidable transcendental horizon), but, as this horizon consists of undecidable infrastructures – iteration, supplementarity, re-mark, and so on – the empirical moment of the decision is in a complex relation internality/externality to the transcendental horizon. The category of 'difference' has undergone a considerable process of inflation in contemporary thought, but, of its many uses, there is one which I think is particularly fruitful: the one which sees it as what closes a structure while remaining utterly heterogeneous *vis-a-vis* it. This is why my answer to Butler's question concerning the unicity or plurality of 'the metaphysical logic of identity' would be that, irrespective of its many variations, a hard nucleus of meaning remains in all of them, which is the denial of the constitutive character of difference, the assertion of the possibility of a closure of the structure through its own internal resources.

We can now move to Butler's various questions concerning social logics and their relation to social practices. What, in the first place, is a social logic? We are not, of course, talking about formal logic, or even about a general dialectical logic, but about the notion which is implicit in expressions such as 'the logic of kinship', 'the logic of the market', and so forth. I would characterize it as a rarefied system of objects, as a 'grammar' or cluster of rules which make some combinations and substitutions possible and exclude others. It is what, in our work, we have called 'discourse',[36] which broadly coincides with what in Lacanian theory is called the 'symbolic'. Now, if the symbolic was all there was in social life, social logics and social practices would exactly overlap. But we know there is more in social practices than the enactment of the symbolic through institutionalized performances. There is, in our analysis, the moment of antagonism, which – as we pointed out above – is not part of social objectivity but the limit of objectivity (of the symbolic) in constituting itself. Although our analysis of antagonism is not derivative from Lacanian theory, it can overlap to a large extent with Lacan's notion of the Real as an ultimate core which resists symbolization – as Žižek perceived very early, in his review of *Hegemony and Socialist Strategy* published in 1985, almost immediately after the publication of our book.[37]

This subversion of the Symbolic by the Real has to take place, however, with the only raw materials available: the different structural locations shaping the symbolic space. This system of structural locations (or distinctions) has, like any linguistic structure, only two properties: their relations of combination and substitution – what in strictly linguistic terms would be the syntagmatic and paradigmatic relations. In terms of broader social analysis, these would correspond to the distinction that we have established between logics of difference (of differential institutionalization) and logics of equivalence (which construct antagonisms on the basis of the dichotomization of the social space via substitutions).

What happens when we move from the purely linguistic side of social practices to their performative dimension, in which Butler is especially interested? When we make this move we are not, strictly speaking, outside the linguistic, because if – as we stated above – language is form, not substance, the fact that we are dealing with words in one case and with actions in the other is something that we can keep fully within a unified grammar as long as the principle of differentiality is strictly maintained. But the performative dimension helps to make more visible an aspect of any meaningful action that a purely logicist notion of language could otherwise have kept in the dark: it is the fact that a strict enactment of a rule via an instititionalized performance is ultimately impossible. The application of a rule already involves its own subversion. Let us think of Derrida's notion of iteration: something, in order to be repeatable, has to be different from itself. Or Wittgenstein's conception of applying a rule: I need a second rule to know how to apply the first, a third one to know how to apply the second, and so on . . . so that the only possible conclusion is that the instance of application is internal to the rule itself, and constantly displaces the latter. The importance of this notion of a continuity operating through partial discontinuities is obvious for the theory of hegemony.

But this reflection makes fully visible one of Butler's potentially most original contributions to social theory, her notion of 'parodic performance'. Butler has applied her notion only to very precise examples, and has not gone far enough in the direction of universalizing her own notion, but my optimistic reading of her texts is that this generalization, if it is fully developed, can tell us something really important concerning the structuration of social life. My argument would be as follows: if a parodic performance means the creation of a distance between the action actually being performed and the rule being enacted, and if the instance of application of the rule is internal to the rule itself, parody is constitutive of any social action. Of course the word 'parody' has a playful ring to it, but this is not essential. One can think of very tragic parodies of universal dimensions, like the one of Greeks and Romans enacted in the course of the French Revolution. In actual fact, *any* political action – a strike, a speech in an election, the assertion of its right by an oppressed group – has a parodic component, as far as a certain meaning which was fixated within the horizon of an ensemble of institutionalized practices is displaced towards new uses which subvert its literality. This movement is *tropological* inasmuch as the displacement is not governed by any necessary logic dictated by what is being displaced, and *catachrestical* inasmuch as the entities constituted through the displacement do not have any literal meaning outside the very displacements from which they emerge. This is why I prefer to speak not of *parody* but of the social organized as a rhetorical space – not only because in that way we can avoid misunderstanding based on the playful connotations of the term parody, but also because the latter unduly restricts the *tropoi* which could be constitutive of social identities.

I would argue that the space of this tropological movement subverting the symbolic order is the place of emergence of the Subject. In *New*

Reflections on the Revolution of Our Time,[38] I maintained that the Subject is the distance between the undecidability of the structure and the decision. If what emerges from the tropological displacement was pre-announced by what is being displaced – or if the logic of the displacement was governed by an a priori specifiable norm – the tropological dimension could not be constitutive of the social (it would simply be an adornment of the expression – as in ancient rhetoric – easily substitutable by a literal formulation). If, on the contrary, the tropological movement is essentially catachrestical, it is constitutive, and the moment of the decision does not recognize a principle of grounding external to itself. As Kierkegaard – quoted by Derrida – said: 'the moment of the decision is the moment of madness'. And as I would add (which Derrida wouldn't): this is the moment of the subject before subjectivation.

This point is crucial because it shows us the basic distinction on which, I think, all political – and, finally, social – analysis is grounded. If we conceive of the decision in the terms just presented, all decision is internally split: it is, on the one hand, *this* decision (a precise ontic content) but it is, on the other hand, *a* decision (it has the ontological function of bringing a certain closure to what was structurally open). The crucial point is that the ontic content cannot be derived from the ontological function, and so the former will be only a transient incarnation of the latter. The fullness of society is an impossible object which successive contingent contents try to impersonate through catachrestical displacements. This is exactly what hegemony means. And it is also the source of whatever freedom can exist in society: no such freedom would be possible if the 'fullness' of society had reached its 'true' ontic form – the good society, as in Plato – and the tropological movement would have been replaced by a fully fledged literality.[39]

This is the point of introducing a short remark on Ethics. I have been confronted many times with one or other version of the following question: if hegemony involves a decision taken in a radically contingent terrain, what are the grounds for deciding one way or the other? Žižek, for instance, observes: 'Laclau's notion of hegemony describes the universal mechanism of ideological "cement" which binds any social body together, a notion that can analyse all possible sociopolitical orders,

from Fascism to liberal democracy; on the other hand, Laclau none the
less advocates a determinate political option, "radical democracy".[40] I
do not think this is a valid objection. It is grounded in a strict distinction
between the descriptive and the normative which is ultimately derivative
from the Kantian separation between pure and practical Reason. But
this is, precisely, a distinction which should be eroded: there is no such
strict separation between fact and value. A value-orientated practical
activity will be confronted with problems, facilities, resistances, and so
on, which it will discursively construct as 'facts' – facts, however, which
could have emerged in their facticity only from within such activity. A
theory of hegemony is not, in that sense, a neutral description of what
is going on in the world, but a description whose very condition of possibility is a normative element governing, from the very beginning,
whatever apprehension of 'facts' as facts there could be.

That being said, the problem remains of how these two dimensions,
even if they cannot be entirely separated, can actually be articulated. Let
us consider Marx's postulate of a society in which the free development
of each is the condition for the free development of all. Is this an ethical postulate or a descriptive statement? It is clear that it is both, for it is,
on the one hand, a description of the final, necessary movement of
History and, on the other, an aim with which we are asked to identify. If
freedom is conceived as self-determination, the very distinction between
freedom and necessity collapses. The link between the two aspects is so
close that we can hardly speak of articulation. For that reason, it is
wrong to present classical Marxism as a purely descriptive science, purified of all ethical commitment. What it does not have is a *separate* ethical
argument, for the objective process it recognizes *already* has a normative
dimension. It was only later, when the faith in the necessary laws of historical development was put into question, that the need for an ethical
grounding of socialism was experienced, and it led to a return to
Kantian dualisms, as happened with Bernstein and Austro-Marxism.

So what about hegemony? A hegemonic approach would fully accept
that the moment of the ethical is the moment of the universality of the
community, the moment in which, beyond any particularism, the universal speaks by itself. The other side of it, however, is that society
consists only of particularities, and that in this sense, all universality

will have to be incarnated in something that is utterly incommensurable with it. This point is crucial: there is no logical transition from an unavoidable ethical moment, in which the fullness of society manifests itself as an empty symbol, to any particular normative order. There is an ethical *investment* in particular normative orders, but no normative order which is, in and for itself, ethical. So – the true question of a contemporary ethics is not the old-fashioned debate on the articulation between the descriptive and the normative, but the much more fundamental question of the relationship between the *ethical* (as the moment of madness in which the fullness of society shows itself as both impossible and necessary) and the *descriptive/normative complexes* which are the ontic raw materials incarnating, in a transient way, that universality – that elusive fullness. Hegemony is, in this sense, the name for this unstable relation between the *ethical* and the *normative*, our way of addressing this infinite process of investments which draws its dignity from its very failure. The object being invested is an essentially ethical object. I would go even further: it is the *only* ethical object. (I think Emmanuel Levinas progressed to some extent towards this distinction between the ethical and the normative, through his differentiation between ethics and morality. He did not, however, resist the temptation to give some sort of content to ethics, which considerably diminished the radicalism of his undeniable breakthrough.) So, going back to our original question, I would say that 'hegemony' is a theoretical approach which depends on the essentially ethical decision to accept, as the horizon of any possible intelligibility, the incommensurability between the ethical and the normative (the latter including the descriptive). It is this incommensurability which is the source of the unevenness between discourses, of a moment of *investment* which is not dictated by the nature of its object and which, as a result, redefines the terms of the relationship between what *is* and what *ought* to be (between ontology and ethics): ontology is ethical through and through, inasmuch as any description depends on the presence (through its absence) of a fullness which, while it is the condition of any description, makes any *pure* description utterly impossible. But if, with these considerations, we have displaced the terms of the debate from the normative/descriptive distinction to one grounded in the incommensurability between ethics and the normative order, we have said very little about the ways in which this incommensurability is negotiated. So we have to start speaking about politics.

V Politics and the negotiation of universality

If the moment of the ethical is the moment of a radical investment (in the sense that there is nothing in the ontic characteristics of the object receiving the investment that predetermines that it, rather than other objects, should be such a recipient), two important conclusions follow. First, only that aspect of a decision which is not predetermined by an existing normative framework is, properly speaking, ethical. Second, any normative order is nothing but the sedimented form of an initial ethical event. This explains why I reject two polarly opposed approaches which tend to universalize the conditions of the decision. The first consists of the different variants of a universalistic ethics which attempt to reintroduce some normative content in the ethical moment, and to subordinate the decision to such a content, however minimal it could be (Rawls, Habermas, etc.). The second is pure decisionism, the notion of the decision as an original *fiat* which, because it has no *aprioristic* limits, is conceived as having no limits at all. So what are those limits which are other than aprioristic? The answer is: the ensemble of sedimented practices constituting the normative framework of a certain society. This framework can experience deep dislocations requiring drastic recompositions, but it never disappears to the point of requiring an act of *total* refoundation. There is no place for Lycurguses of the social order.

This leads to other aspects which require consideration. First, that if the radical ethical investment looks, on one side, like a *pure* decision, on the other it has to be collectively accepted. From this point of view it operates as a surface for the inscription of something external to itself – as a principle of *articulation*. To give just one example: Antonio Conselheiro, a millenarian preacher, had wandered for decades in the Brazilian *sertão*, at the end of the nineteenth century, without recruiting too many followers. Everything changed with the transition from the Empire to the republic, and the many administrative and economic changes it brought about – which, in various ways, dislocated traditional life in the rural areas. One day Conselheiro arrived in a village where people were rioting against the tax collectors, and pronounced the words which were to become the key equivalence of his prophetic discourse: 'The Republic is the Antichrist'. From that point onwards his discourse provided a surface of inscription for all forms of rural discontent, and became the starting point of a mass rebellion which took several years for the government to defeat. We see here the articulation between the two dimensions mentioned above: (1) the transformation of the signifiers of Good and Evil in those of the opposition Empire/Republic is something which was not predetermined by anything inherent in the two pairs of categories – it was a contingent equivalence and, in that sense, a radical decision. People accepted it because it was the only available discourse addressing their plight. (2) But if that discourse had clashed with important unshakeable beliefs of the rural masses, it would have had no effectivity at all. This is the way in which I would establish distances with 'decisionism': the subject who takes the decision is only *partially* a subject; he is also a background of sedimented practices organizing a normative framework which operates as a limitation on the horizon of options. But if this background persists through the contamination of the moment of the decision, I would also say that the decision persists through the subversion of the background. This means that the construction of a communitarian normative background (which is a political and in no way a merely ethical operation) takes place through the limitation of the ethical by the normative and the subversion of the normative by the ethical. Isn't this one more way of stating what hegemony is about?

So inscription means an investment not based on any preceding rationality. It is constitutive. But could we not say that the opposite move, an investment which is always-already contaminated by normative particularity, is also operating from the outset? For what *has to be* invested, in order to have actual historical effectivity, subverts the object of the investment as much as it needs the latter for that process of subversion to take place. Let us give another historical example to illustrate the point: Sorel's notion of the constitution of the historical will through the myth of the 'general strike'.[41] That myth has all the characteristics of an ethical principle: in order to function as a proper myth, it has to be an object devoid of any particular determination – an empty signifier. But in order to be empty, it has to signify *emptiness* as such; it has to be like a body which can show *nakedness* only by the very *absence* of dress.[42] Let us assume that I participate in a demonstration for *particular* aims, in a strike for a rise in wages, in a factory occupation for improvements in working conditions. All these demands can be seen as aiming at particular targets which, once achieved, put an end to the movement. But they can be seen in a different way: what the demands aim for is not actually their *concretely* specified targets: these are only the contingent occasion of achieving (in a partial way) something that utterly transcends them: the fullness of society as an impossible object which – through its very impossibility – becomes thoroughly ethical. The ethical dimension is what *persists* in a chain of successive events in so far as the latter are seen as something which is split from their own particularity from the very beginning. Only if I live an action as incarnating an impossible fullness transcending it does the investment become an *ethical* investment; but only if the materiality of the investment is not fully absorbed by the *act* of investment as such – if the distance between the ontic and the onto-logical, between *investing* (the ethical) and that in which one invests (the normative order) is never filled – can we have hegemony and politics (but, I would argue, also ethics).[43]

Let us now recapitulate our main conclusions.

1. The ethical substance of the community – the moment of its totalization or universalization – represents an object which is simultaneously impossible and necessary. As impossible, it is incommensurable with any normative order; as necessary, it has to have access to the field of representation, which is possible only if the ethical substance is invested in some form of normative order.

2. This investment, as it shows no inner connection between what is invested and the social norms which receive the investment, depends on the central category of *decision*, conceived as an act of articulation grounded on no a priori principle external to the decision itself.

3. Since the subject constituted through that decision is no pure sub-ject, but always the partial result of sedimented practices, its

decision will never be *ex nihilo* but a displacement – within existing social norms – of the impossible object of the ethical investment (the alternative ways of naming it).

4. All decision is internally split: as required by a dislocated situation, it is *a* decision; but it is also *this* decision, this particular ontic content. This is the distinction between *ordering* and *order*, between *changing* and *change*, between the *ontological* and the *ontic* – oppositions which are only contingently articulated through the investment of the first of the terms into the second. This investment is the cornerstone of the operation called hegemony, which has within it, as we have seen, an ethical component. The description of the *facts* of social life and the normative orders on which those facts are based, which is compatible with a hegemonic approach, is different from those approaches which start by identifying the ethical with a hard normative core, and with those which postulate total decisionism.

5. So the question: 'If the decision is contingent, what are the grounds for choosing this option rather than a different one?', is not relevant. If decisions are contingent displacements within contextual communitarian orders, they can show their verisimilitude to people living inside those orders, but not to somebody conceived as a pure mind outside *any* order. This radical contextualization of the normative/descriptive order has, however, been possible only because of the radical decontextualization introduced by the ethical moment.

I now want to state a corollary of my analysis which will be crucial for the argument I intend to present in the second round of this exchange. If the ethical moment is essentially linked to the presence of empty symbols in the community, the community requires the constant production of those symbols in order for an ethical life to be possible. If the community, on top of that, is to be a democratic one, everything turns around the possibility of keeping always open and ultimately undecided the moment of articulation between the particularity of the normative order and the universality of the ethical moment. Any kind of full absorption of the latter by the former can lead only either to totalitarian

unification or to the implosion of the community through a proliferation
of purely particularistic identities. (This is, frequently, the atomistic version of the totalitarian dream. The secret link between both is often
provided by the defence of religious or ethnic fundamentalisms in terms
of the right to cultural diversity.) The only democratic society is one
which permanently shows the contingency of its own foundations – in
our terms, permanently keeps open the gap between the ethical moment
and the normative order.

This, in my view, is the main political question confronting us at this
end of the century: what is the destiny of the universal in our societies?
Is a proliferation of particularisms – or their correlative side: authori-
tarian unification – the only alternative in a world in which dreams of a
global human emancipation are rapidly fading away? Or can we think
of the possibility of relaunching new emancipatory projects which are
compatible with the complex multiplicity of differences shaping the
fabric of present-day societies? It is on these questions that my next
intervention in this discussion will be centred.

Notes

1. Karl Marx, 'Contribution to the Critique of Hegel's Philosophy of Law.
Introduction', in Karl Marx and Frederick Engels, *Collected Works*, vol. 3, London:
Lawrence & Wishart 1975, pp. 186–7; original emphasis.

2. Ibid., pp. 184–5.

3. Norberto Bobbio, 'Gramsci and the concept of civil society', in Chantal Mouffe,
ed., *Gramsci and Marxist Theory*, London: Routledge 1979, p. 30; original emphasis.

4. Antonio Gramsci, *Selections from the Prison Notebooks*, ed. and trans. Quintin Hoare
and Geoffrey Nowell Smith, London: Lawrence & Wishart 1971, p. 12.

5. Ibid., p. 261.

6. Ibid., p. 239.

7. Ibid., p. 268.

8. Formal analysis and abstraction are essential for the study of concrete historical
processes – not only because the theoretical construction of the object is the requirement of any intellectual practice worthy of the name, but also because social reality
itself generates abstractions which organize its own principles of functioning. Thus
Marx, for instance, showed how the *formal* and *abstract* laws of commodity production
are at the core of the actual concrete workings of capitalist societies. In the same way,
when we try to explain the structuration of political fields through categories such as

'logic of equivalence', 'logic of difference' and 'production of empty signifiers', we are attempting to construct a theoretical horizon whose abstractions are not merely analytical but *real* abstractions on which the constitution of identities and political articulations depends. This, of course, is not understood by a certain empiricism, very widespread in some approaches within the social sciences, which confuses analysis of the concrete with purely factual and journalistic accounts. For a particularly crude example of this misconception (together with several others), see Anna Marie Smith, *Laclau and Mouffe. The Radical Democratic Imaginary*, London and New York: Routledge 1998.

9. See Ernesto Laclau, 'Power and Representation' *Emancipation(s),* London and New York: Verso 1996, pp. 84–104.

10. See my essay 'Why Do Empty Signifiers Matter to Politics?' in Ibid., pp. 34–46.

11. Slavoj Žižek, *The Ticklish Subject: The Absent Centre of Political Ontology*, London and New York: Verso 1999, pp. 100–101.

12. Ibid., pp. 176–7.

13. Ibid., pp. 177; original emphasis.

14. Alan White, *Absolute Knowledge: Hegel and the Problem of Metaphysics*, Athens, OH and London: Ohio University Press 1983, pp. 51.

15. Behind this problem there is, of course, the one of determining whether Hegel's philosophy should be conceived as a metaphysico-theological doctrine or as a transcendental ontology. On this question, see White, (*passim*); and Klaus Hartmann, 'Hegel: A Non-Metaphysical View', in Alastair MacIntyre, ed., Hegel. *A Collection of Critical Essays*, Garden City, Anchor 1972.

16. *Hegel's Science of Logic*, trans. by A.V. Miller, Atlantic Highlands, NJ: Humanities Press International Inc 1993, p. 708.

17. For a clear and rigorous discussion of the various dimensions of this matter, see Yannis Stavrakakis, *Lacan and the Political*, London: Routledge 1999.

18. Judith Butler, *Bodies that Matter*, New York: Routledge 1993, p. 207.

19. *The Logic of Hegel*, trans. from *The Encyclopedia of the Philosophical Sciences* by W. Wallace, Oxford: Clarendon Press 1892, p. 137.

20. Paul de Man, 'Pascal's Allegory of Persuasion', in *Aesthetic Ideology*, Minneapolis and London: University of Minnesota Press 1996, pp. 51–69.

21. Ibid. p. 59.

22. Bruce Fink, *The Lacanian Subject*, Princeton, NJ: Princeton University Press 1995, p. 27.

23. Ibid. p. 22.

24. This tendency is found in a great deal of the literature on Gramsci.

25. It has to be said that Lacan's position on this issue is rather ambivalent and fluctuating.

26. The point has been cogently made by Jason Glynos in an unpublished paper, 'Of Signifiers, Signifieds and Remainders of Particularity: from Signifying Dissemination to Real Fixity', presented in the Ideology and Discourse Analysis seminar, University of Essex, 25 February 1998.

27. See Ernesto Laclau, 'Subject of Politics. Politics of the Subject', in *Emancipation(s)*, pp. 47–65.

28. Žižek, *The Ticklish Subject*, ch. 6.

29. *The Ticklish Subject*.

30. Ibid. p. 1.

31. Ibid. p. 2.

32. See the systematization of the Derridan 'infrastructures' presented by Rodolphe Gasché in *The Tain of the Mirror. Derrida and the Philosophy of Reflection*, Cambridge, MA and London: Harvard University Press 1986, Part Two.

33. Fink, *The Lacanian Subject*, pp. 30–31.

34. Let us be precise. Žižek's work on the Hegelian texts is always insightful and worth taking into consideration. As I said above, my disagreement starts only when he conceives of his own findings as the only logic shaping Hegel's intellectual project, without realizing that panlogicism is still very much part of the latter, and it limits the effects of the rhetorical moves that Žižek is pointing out.

35. See Gasché, *The Tain of the Mirror*.

36. See Ernesto Laclau, entry on 'Discourse', in *A Companion to Contemporary Political Philosophy* ed. by Robert A. Goodin and Philip Pettit, Oxford: Basil Blackwell, 1993, pp. 431–7.

37. Slavoj Žižek, 'La société n'existe pas', *L'Âne, magazine du Champ Freudien*: 17 (Winter 1986): 33.

38. Ernesto Laclau, *New Reflections on the Revolution of Our Time*, London and New York: Verso 1990, pp. 60–68.

39. It is precisely because I fully appreciate the potentialities of the notion of 'parodic performances' for a theory of hegemony, that I find some of Butler's questions rather perplexing. She asks: 'If sexual difference is "real" in the Lacanian sense, does that mean that it has no place in hegemonic struggles?' I would argue that exactly *because* sexual difference is real and not symbolic, because it is not necessarily linked to any aprioristic pattern of symbolic positions, that the way is open to the kind of historicist variation that Butler asserts – and that a hegemonic game becomes possible. The same goes for some of Butler's other questions: 'Does a logic that invariably results in aporias produce a kind of stasis that is inimical to the project of hegemony?' If there were no aporia, there would be no possiblity of hegemony, for a necessary logic inimical to hegemonic variations would impose itself, entirely unchallenged. We have here the same mutually subverting relationship between necessity and impossibility to which we have been referring from the beginning.

40. Žižek, *The Ticklish Subject*, p. 174.

41. I have presented this argument concerning Sorel in various essays. See especially 'The Death and Resurrection of the Theory of Ideology', *Journal of Political Ideologies* 1.3 (1996): 201–20; and 'The Politics of Rhetoric', paper presented at the conference on 'Culture and Materiality', which took place at the University of California, Davis, 23–25 April 1998 (forthcoming 2000).

42. In Art History the distinction is often made between *the nude* (a body represented

as it is, without reference to dress, as in Ancient sculpture) and the *naked* (where the absence of dress is fully visible, as in Northern painting of the late Middle Ages and early Renaissance).

43. The same argument that I have made about Sorel could be made about the dialectic between representability/unrepresentability in mystical discourse. See Ernesto Laclau, 'On the Names of God', in Sue Golding, ed., *The Eight Technologies of Otherness*, London: Routledge 1997, pp. 253–64.

Class Struggle or Postmodernism? Yes, please!

Slavoj Žižek

> The realization of the world as global market, the undivided reign of great financial conglomerates, etc., all this is an indisputable reality and one that conforms, essentially, to Marx's analysis. The question is, where does politics fit in with all this? What kind of politics is *really* heterogeneous to what capital demands? – that is today's question.
>
> (*Alain Badiou*)

In a well-known Marx Brothers joke Groucho answers the standard question 'Tea or coffee?' with 'Yes, please!' – a refusal of choice. The basic underlying idea of this essay is that one should answer in the same way the false alternative today's critical theory seems to impose on us: either 'class struggle' (the outdated problematic of class antagonism, commodity production, etc.) or 'postmodernism' (the new world of dispersed multiple identities, of radical contingency, of an irreducible ludic plurality of struggles). Here, at least, we can have our cake and eat it – how?

To begin with, I would like to emphasize my closeness to both my partners in this endeavour: in both Judith Butler's and Ernesto Laclau's work, there is a central notion (or, rather, two aspects of the same central notion) that I fully endorse, finding it extraordinarily productive. In Judith Butler's work, this notion is that of the fundamental *reflexivity* of human desire,[1] and the notion (concomitant to the first one, although developed later) of 'passionate attachments', of traumatic fixations that are unavoidable and, simultaneously, inadmissible – in order to remain operative, they have to be repressed; in Laclau, it is, of course, the notion of *antagonism* as fundamentally different from the logic of symbolic/structural difference, and the concomitant notion of the hegemonic struggle for filling out the empty place of universality as necessary/impossible. In both cases, we are thus dealing with a term (universality, 'passionate attachment') which is simultaneously impossible and necessary, disavowed and unavoidable. So where is my difference with the two of them? To define it is more difficult than it may appear: any direct attempt to formulate it via a comparison between our respective positions somehow misses the point.[2] I have dealt in more detail with the task of providing the 'cognitive mapping' for tracing these differences in my latest book;[3] so, to avoid repetition, this essay is conceived as a supplement to that book, focusing on a specific topic: that of universality, historicity and the Real.

Another introductory remark: it is quite probable that a counterclaim could sometimes be made that in my dialogue with Butler and Laclau I am not actually arguing against their position but against a watered-down popular version which they would also oppose. In such cases I plead guilty in advance, emphasizing two points: first – probably to a much greater degree than I am aware – my dialogue with them relies on shared presuppositions, so that my critical remarks are rather to be perceived as desperate attempts to clarify *my own* position via its clear delimitation; secondly, my aim – and, as I am sure, the aim of all three of us – is not to score narcissistic points against others, but – to risk an old-fashioned expression – to struggle with the Thing itself which is at stake, namely, the (im)possibilities of radical political thought and practice today.

I

Let me begin with Laclau's concept of *hegemony*, which provides an exemplary matrix of the relationship between universality, historical contingency and the limit of an impossible Real – one should always bear in mind that we are dealing here with a distinct concept whose specificity is often missed (or reduced to some vague proto-Gramscian generality) by those who refer to it. The key feature of the concept of hegemony lies in the contingent connection between intrasocial differences (elements *within* the social space) and the limit that separates society itself from non-society (chaos, utter decadence, dissolution of all social links) – the limit between the social and its exteriority, the non-social, can articulate itself only in the guise of a difference (by mapping itself on to a difference) between elements of social space. In other words, radical antagonism can be represented only in a distorted way, through the particular differences internal to the system.[4] Laclau's point is thus that external differences are always-already also internal and, furthermore, that the link between the two is ultimately contingent, the result of political struggle for hegemony, not inscribed into the very social Being of agents.

In the history of Marxism, the tension that defines the concept of hegemony is best exemplified by its oscillation between the radical revolutionary logic of equivalence (Us against Them, Progress against Reaction, Freedom against Tyranny, Society against Decadence), which had to have recourse to different contingent groups to realize the universal task of global social transformation (from working class to colonized peasants; see also Sorel's oscillation from Leftist Syndicalism to Fascism), and the 'revisionist' reduction of the progressive agenda to a series of particular social problems to be resolved gradually via compromises. More generally, we are suspended between a pure corporate vision of society as a Body with each part occupying its proper place, and the radical revolutionary vision of antagonism between society and antisocial forces ('the people is split into friends and enemies of the people') – and, as Laclau emphasizes, both these extremes ultimately coincide: a pure corporate vision has to eject forces that oppose its organic notion of the social Body into pure externality (the Jewish plot, etc.), thus reasserting radical antagonism between the social Body and the external force of Decadence; while radical revolutionary practice has to rely on a *particular* element (class) which embodies universality (from Marxist proletariat to Pol Pot's peasants). The only solution to this deadlock seems to be to accept it as such – to accept that we are condemned to the unending struggle between particular elements to stand in for the impossible totality:

> If hegemony means the representation, by a particular social sector, of an impossible totality with which it is incommensurable, then it is enough that we make the space of tropological substitutions fully visible, to enable the hegemonic logic to operate freely. If the fullness of society is unachievable, the attempts at reaching it will necessarily fail, although they will be able, in the search for that impossible object, to solve a variety of partial problems.[5]

Here, however, a series of questions arises from my perspective. Does not this solution involve the Kantian logic of the infinite approach to the impossible Fullness as a kind of 'regulative Idea'? Does it not involve the resigned/cynical stance of 'although we know we will fail, we should persist in our search' – of an agent which knows that the global Goal towards which it is striving is impossible, that its ultimate effort will necessarily fail, but which none the less accepts the need for this global Spectre as a necessary lure to give it the energy to engage in solving partial problems? Furthermore (and this is just another aspect of the same problem), is not this alternative – the alternative between achieving 'fullness of society' and solving 'a variety of partial problems' – too limited? Is it not that – here, at least – there *is* a Third Way, although definitely not in the sense of the Risk Society theorists? What about changing the very fundamental *structural principle* of society, as happened with the emergence of the 'democratic invention'? The passage from feudal monarchy to capitalist democracy, while it failed to reach the 'impossible fullness of society', certainly did more than just 'solve a variety of partial problems'.

A possible counter-argument would be that the radical break of the 'democratic invention' consists in the very fact that what was previously considered an *obstacle* to the 'normal' functioning of power (the 'empty place' of power, the gap between this place and the one who actually exerts power, the ultimate indeterminacy of power) now becomes its positive *condition*: what was previously experienced as a threat (the struggle between more subjects-agents to fill in the place of power) now becomes the very condition of the legitimate exercise of power. The extraordinary character of 'democratic invention' thus consists in the fact that – to put it in Hegelian terms – the contingency of power, the gap between power *qua* place and its place-holder, is no longer only 'in itself', but becomes 'for itself', is acknowledged explicitly 'as such', reflected in the very structure of power.[6] What this means is that – to put it in the well-known Derridan terms – the condition of impossibility of the exercise of power becomes its condition of possibility: just as the ultimate failure of communication is what compels us to talk all the time (if we could say what we want to say directly, we would very soon stop talking and shut up for ever), so the ultimate uncertainty and precariousness of the exercise of power is the only guarantee that we are dealing with a legitimate democratic power.

The first thing to add here, however, is that we are dealing with a *series* of breaks: within the history of modernity itself, one should distinguish between the break of the 'first modernity' ('democratic invention': the French Revolution, the introduction of the notion of the sovereignty of the people, of democracy, of human rights . . .) and the contemporary break of what Beck, Giddens and others call the 'second modernity' (the thorough reflexivization of society).[7] Furthermore, is not already the 'first modernity' already characterized by the inherent tension between the 'people's democracy' (People-as-One, General Will) with its potentially 'totalitarian' outcome, and the liberal notion of individual freedom, reducing state to a 'night watchman' of civil society.

So the point is that, again, we are dealing with the multitude of configurations of the democratic society, and these configurations form a kind of Hegelian 'concrete universality' – that is to say, we are not dealing simply with different subspecies of the genus of Democracy, but with a series of breaks which affect the very universal notion of Democracy: these subspecies (early Lockeian liberal democracy, 'totalitarian' democracy . . .) in a way explicate ('posit', are generated by) the inherent tension of the very universal notion of political Democracy. Furthermore, this tension is not simply internal/inherent to the notion of Democracy, but is defined by the way Democracy relates to its Other: not only its political Other – non-Democracy in its various guises – but primarily that which the very definition of *political* democracy tends to exclude as 'non-political' (private life and economy in classical liberal-ism, etc.). While I fully endorse the well-known thesis that the very gesture of drawing a clear line of distinction between the Political and the non-Political, of positing some domains (economy, private intimacy, art . . .) as 'apolitical', is a political gesture *par excellence*, I am also tempted to turn it around: what if the political gesture *par excellence*, at its purest, *is* precisely the gesture of separating the Political from the non-Political, of excluding some domains from the Political?

II

Let me, then, take a closer look at Laclau's narrative which runs from Marxist essentialism (the proletariat as the universal class whose revolu-tionary mission is inscribed into its very social being and thus discernible via 'objective' scientific analysis) to the 'postmodern' recognition of the contingent, tropological, metaphorico-metonymic, link between a social agent and its 'task'. Once this contingency is acknowledged, one has to accept that there is no direct, 'natural' correlation between an agent's social position and its tasks in the political struggle, no norm of devel-opment by which to measure exceptions – say, because of the weak political subjectivity of the bourgeoisie in Russia around 1900, the work-ing class had to accomplish the bourgeois-democratic revolution itself . . .[8] My first observation here is that while this standard post-modern Leftist narrative of the passage from 'essentialist' Marxism, with the proletariat as the unique Historical Subject, the privileging of economic class struggle, and so on, to the postmodern irreducible plu-rality of struggles undoubtedly describes an actual historical process, its proponents, as a rule, leave out the resignation at its heart – the accept-ance of capitalism as 'the only game in town', the renunciation of any real attempt to overcome the existing capitalist liberal regime.[9] This point was already made very precisely in Wendy Brown's perspicuous observation that 'the political purchase of contemporary American identity politics would seem to be achieved in part *through* a certain renaturalization of capitalism'.[10] The crucial question to be asked is thus:

to what extent a critique of capitalism is foreclosed by the current configuration of oppositional politics, and not simply by the 'loss of the
socialist alternative' or the ostensible 'triumph of liberalism' in the global
order. In contrast with the Marxist critique of a social whole and Marxist
vision of total transformation, to what extent do identity politics require
a standard internal to existing society against which to pitch their claims,
a standard that not only preserves capitalism from critique, but sustains
the invisibility and inarticulateness of class – not incidentally, but endem-
ically? Could we have stumbled upon one reason why class is invariably
named but rarely theorized or developed in the multiculturalist mantra,
'race, class, gender, sexuality'?[11]

One can describe in very precise terms this reduction of class to an
entity 'named but rarely theorized': one of the great and permanent
results of the so-called 'Western Marxism' first formulated by the young
Lukács is that the class-and-commodity structure of capitalism is not
just a phenomenon limited to the particular 'domain' of economy, but
the structuring principle that overdetermines the social totality, from
politics to art and religion. *This* global dimension of capitalism is suspended in today's multiculturalist progressive politics: its
'anti-capitalism' is reduced to the level of how today's capitalism breeds
sexist/racist oppression, and so on. Marx claimed that in the series
production–distribution–exchange–consumption, the term 'production'
is doubly inscribed: it is simultaneously one of the terms in the series and
the structuring principle of the entire series. In production as one of the
terms of the series, production (as the structuring principle) 'encounters
itself in its oppositional determination',[12] as Marx put it, using the precise Hegelian term. And the same goes for the postmodern political
series class–gender–race . . .: in class as one of the terms in the series of
particular struggles, class *qua* structuring principle of the social totality
'encounters itself in its oppositional determination'.[13] In so far as postmodern politics promotes, in effect, a kind of 'politicization of the
economy', is not this politicization similar to the way our supermarkets –
which fundamentally exclude from their field of visibility the actual
production process (the way vegetables and fruit are harvested and
packed by immigrant workers, the genetic and other manipulations in

their production and display, etc.) – stage within the field of the displayed goods, as a kind of ersatz, the spectacle of a pseudo-production
(meals prepared in full view in 'food courts', fruit juices freshly squeezed
before the customers' eyes, etc.)?[14] An authentic Leftist should therefore
ask the postmodern politicians the new version of the old Freudian
question put to the perplexed Jew: 'Why are you saying that one should
politicize the economy, when one should in fact politicize the
economy?'[15]

So: in so far as postmodern politics involves a '[t]heoretical retreat
from the problem of domination within capitalism',[16] it is *here*, in this
silent suspension of class analysis, that we are dealing with an exemplary
case of the mechanism of ideological *displacement*: when class antagonism
is disavowed, when its key structuring role is suspended, 'other markers
of social difference may come to bear an inordinate weight; indeed,
they may bear all the weight of the sufferings produced by capitalism in
addition to that attributable to the explicitly politicized marking'[17]. In
other words, this displacement accounts for the somewhat 'excessive'
way the discourse of postmodern identity politics insists on the horrors
of sexism, racism, and so on – this 'excess' comes from the fact that these
other '-isms' have to bear the surplus-investment from the class struggle
whose extent is not acknowledged.[18]

Of course, the postmodernists' answer would be that I am 'essential-
izing' class struggle: there is, in today's society, a series of particular
political struggles (economic, human rights, ecology, racism, sexism,
religious . . .), and no struggle can claim to be the 'true' one, the key to
all the others . . . . Usually, Laclau's development itself (from his first
breakthrough work, *Politics and Ideology in Marxist Theory*, to his standard
classic, co-authored with Chantal Mouffe, *Hegemony and Socialist Strategy*)
is presented as the gradual process of getting rid of the 'last remnants of
essentialism':[19] in the first book – following the classic Marxist tradition – the economy (the relations of production and economic laws)
still serves as a kind of 'ontological anchorage point' for the otherwise
contingent struggles for hegemony (i.e. in a Gramscian way, the struggle
for hegemony is ultimately the struggle between the two great classes for
which of them will occupy-hegemonize a series of other 'historical
tasks' – national liberation, cultural struggle, etc.); it is only in the second

book that Laclau definitely renounces the old Marxist problematic of infra- and superstructure, that is, the objective grounding of the 'super-structural' hegemonic struggle in the economic 'infrastructure' – economy itself is always-already 'political', a discursive site (one of the sites) of political struggles, of power and resistance, 'a field penetrated by pre-ontological undecidability of irrevocable dilemmas and aporias'.[20]

In their *Hegemony* book, Laclau and Mouffe clearly privilege the *political struggle for democracy*, – that is to say, they accept Claude Lefort's thesis that the key moment in modern political history was the 'democratic invention' and all other struggles are ultimately the 'application' of the principle of democratic invention to other domains: race (why should other races not also be equal?), sex, religion, the economy . . . . In short, when we are dealing with a series of particular struggles, is there not always one struggle which, although it appears to function as one in the series, effectively provides the horizon of the series as such? Is this not also one of the consequences of the notion of hegemony? So, in so far as we conceive radical plural democracy as 'the promise that plural democracy, and the struggles for freedom and equality it engenders, should be deepened and extended to all spheres of society',[21] is it possible simply to extend it to the economy as another new terrain? When Brown emphasizes that 'if Marxism had any analytical value for *political* theory, was it not in the insistence that the problem of freedom was contained in the social relations implicitly declared "unpolitical" – that is, naturalized – in liberal discourse',[22] it would be too easy to accept the counter-argument that postmodern politics, of course, endorses the need to denaturalize/repoliticize the economy, and that its point is precisely that one should also denaturalize/repoliticize a series of other domains (relations between the sexes, language, etc.) left 'undeconstructed' by Marx. Postmodern politics definitely has the great merit that it 'repoliticizes' a series of domains previously considered 'apolitical' or 'private'; the fact remains, however, that it does *not* in fact repoliticize capitalism, because *the very notion and form of the 'political' within which it operates is grounded in the 'depoliticization' of the economy*. If we are to play the postmodern game of plurality of political subjectivizations, it is formally necessary that we do *not* ask certain questions (about how to subvert capitalism as such, about the constitutive limits of political democracy and/or the democratic state as such . . .). So, again, apropos of Laclau's obvious counter-argument that the Political, for him, is not a specific social domain but the very set of contingent decisions that ground the Social, I would answer that the postmodern emergence of new multiple political subjectivities certainly does *not* reach this radical level of the political act proper.

What I am tempted to do here is to apply the lesson of Hegelian 'concrete universality' to 'radical democracy': Laclau's notion of hegemony is in fact close to the Hegelian notion of 'concrete universality', in which the specific difference overlaps with the difference constitutive of the genus itself; as in Laclau's hegemony, in which the antagonistic gap between society and its external limit, non-society (the dissolution of social links), is mapped on to an intra-social structural difference. But what about the infamous Hegelian 'reconciliation' between Universal and Particular rejected by Laclau on account of the gap that forever separates the empty/impossible Universal from the contingent particular content that hegemonizes it?[23] If we take a closer look at Hegel, we see that – in so far as every particular species of a genus does not 'fit' its universal genus – when we finally arrive at a particular species that fully fits its notion, *the very universal notion is transformed into another notion.* No existing historical shape of state fully fits the notion of State – the necessity of dialectical passage from State ('objective spirit', history) into Religion ('Absolute Spirit') involves the fact that the only existing state that effectively fits its notion is a *religious community* – which, precisely, is *no longer a state.* Here we encounter the properly dialectical paradox of 'concrete universality' *qua* historicity: in the relationship between a genus and its subspecies, one of these subspecies will always be the element that negates the very universal feature of the genus. Different nations have different versions of soccer; Americans do not have soccer, because 'baseball *is* their soccer'. This is analogous to Hegel's famous claim that modern people do not pray in the morning, because reading the newspaper *is* their morning prayer. In the same way, in disintegrating socialism, writers' and other cultural clubs did act as political parties. Perhaps, in the history of cinema, the best example is the relationship between Western and sci-fi space operas: today, we no longer have 'substantial' Westerns, because space operas *have taken their place*, that is, *space operas* are *today's Westerns*. So, in the classification of Westerns, we would have to supplement the standard subspecies with space opera as today's non-Western stand-in for the Western. Crucial here is this intersection of different genuses, this partial overlapping of two universals: the Western and space opera are not simply two different genres, they *intersect* – that is, in a certain epoch, space opera becomes a subspecies of the Western (or, the Western is 'sublated' in the space opera). . . . In the same way, 'woman' becomes one of the subspecies of man, Heideggerian *Daseinsanalyse* one of the subspecies of phenomenology, 'sublating' the preceding universality; and – back to a 'radical democracy' – in the same way, 'radical democracy' that was actually 'radical' in the sense of politicizing the sphere of economy *would, precisely, no longer be a '(political) democracy'*.[24] (This, of course, does not mean that the 'impossible fullness' of Society would in fact be actualized: it simply means that the limit of the impossible would be transposed on to another level.) And what if the Political itself (the radically contingent struggle for hegemony) is also split/barred in its very notion? What if *it can be operative only in so far as it 'represses' its radically contingent nature, in so far as it undergoes a minimum of 'naturalization'?* What if the essentialist lure is irreducible: we are never dealing with the Political 'at the level of its notion', with political agents who fully endorse their contingency – and the way out of this deadlock via notions like 'strategic essentialism' is definitely condemned to fail?

My conclusion would thus be to emphasize that the impossibility at work in Laclau's notion of antagonism is *double*: not only does 'radical antagonism' mean that it is impossible adequately to represent/articulate the *fullness* of Society – on an even more radical level, *it is also impossible adequately to represent/articulate this very antagonism/negativity that prevents Society from achieving its full ontological realization*. This means that ideological fantasy is not simply the fantasy of the impossible fullness of Society: not only is Society impossible, this impossibility itself is distortedly represented–positivized within an ideological field – *that* is the role of ideological fantasy (say, of the Jewish plot).[25] When this very *impossibility* is represented in a positive element, inherent impossibility is changed into an external obstacle. 'Ideology' is also the name for the guarantee that *the negativity which prevents Society from achieving its fullness does actually exist*, that it has a positive existence in the guise of a big Other who pulls the strings of social life, like the Jews in the anti-Semitic notion of the 'Jewish plot'. In short, the basic operation of ideology is not only the dehistoricizing gesture of transforming an empirical obstacle into the eternal condition (women, Blacks . . . are by nature subordinated, etc.), but also the *opposite* gesture of transposing the a priori closure/impossibility of a field into an empirical obstacle. Laclau is well aware of this paradox when he denounces as ideological the very notion that after the successful revolution, a non-antagonistic self-transparent society will come about. However, this justified rejection of the fullness of post-revolutionary Society does *not* justify the conclusion that we have to renounce any project of a global social transformation, and limit ourselves to partial problems to be solved: the jump from a critique of the 'metaphysics of presence' to anti-utopian 'reformist' gradualist politics is an illegitimate short circuit.

III

Like Laclau's notion of universality as impossible/necessary, Butler's elaboration of universality is much more refined than the standard historicist denouncing of each universality as 'false', that is, secretly privileging some particular content, while repressing or excluding another. She is well aware that universality is unavoidable, and her point is that – while, of course, each determinate historical figure of universality involves a set of inclusions/exclusions – universality simultaneously opens up and sustains the space for questioning these inclusions/exclusions, for 'renegotiating' the limits of inclusion/exclusion as part of the ongoing ideologico-political struggle for hegemony. The predominant notion of 'universal human rights', for instance, precludes – or, at least, reduces to a secondary status – a set of sexual practices and orientations; and it would be too simplistic to accept the standard liberal game of simply insisting that one should redefine and broaden our notion of human rights to include also all these 'aberrant' practices – what standard liberal humanism underestimates is the extent to which such exclusions are *constitutive* of the 'neutral' universality of human rights, so that their actual inclusion in 'human rights' would radically rearticulate, even undermine, our notion of what 'humanity' in 'human rights' means. None the less, the inclusions/exclusions involved in the hegemonic notion of universal human rights are not fixed and simply consubstantial with this universality but the stake of the continuous ideologico-political struggle, something that can be renegotiated and redefined, and the reference to universality can serve precisely as a tool that stimulates such questioning and renegotiation ('If you assert universal human rights, why are we [gays, Blacks . . .] not also part of it?').

So when we criticize the hidden bias and exclusion of universality, we should never forget that we are already doing so *within* the terrain opened up by universality: the proper critique of 'false universality' does not call it into question from the standpoint of pre-universal particularism, it mobilizes the tension inherent to universality itself, the tension between the open negativity, the disruptive power, of what Kierkegaard would have called 'universality-in-becoming', and the fixed form of established universality. Or – if I may interpret Butler in Hegelian terms – we have, on the one hand, the 'dead', 'abstract' universality of an ideological notion with fixed inclusions/exclusions and, on the other, 'living', 'concrete' universality as the permanent process of the questioning and renegotiation of its own 'official' content. Universality becomes 'actual' precisely and only by rendering thematic the exclusions on which it is grounded, by continuously questioning, renegotiating, displacing them, that is, by assuming the gap between its own form and content, by conceiving itself as unaccomplished in its very notion. This is what Butler's notion of the politically salient use of 'performative contradiction' is driving at: if the ruling ideology performatively 'cheats' by undermining – in its actual discursive practice and the set of exclusions on which this practice relies – its own officially asserted universality, progressive politics should precisely openly practise performative contradiction, asserting on behalf of the given universality the very content this universality (in its hegemonic form) excludes.

Here I should just like to emphasize two further points:

the exclusionary logic is always redoubled in itself: not only is the subordinated Other (homosexuals, non-white races . . .) excluded/ repressed, but hegemonic universality itself also relies on a disavowed 'obscene' particular content of its own (say, the exercise of power that legitimizes itself as legal, tolerant, Christian . . . relies on a set of publicly disavowed obscene rituals of violent humiliation of the subordinated[26]). More generally, we are dealing here with what one is tempted to call the *ideological practice of disidentification*. That is to say, one should turn around the standard notion of ideology as providing a firm identification to its subjects, constraining them to their 'social roles': what if, on a different – but no less irrevocable and structurally necessary – level, ideology is effective precisely by constructing a space of *false disidentification*, of false distance towards the actual co-ordinates of those subjects' social existence?[27] Is not this logic of disidentification discernible from the most elementary case of 'I am not only an American (husband, worker, democrat, gay . . .), but, beneath all these roles and masks, a human being, a complex unique personality' (where the very distance towards the symbolic feature that determines my social place guarantees the efficiency of this determination), up to the more complex case of cyberspace playing with one's multiple identities? The mystification operative in the perverse 'just playing' of cyberspace is therefore double: not only are the games we are playing in it more serious than we tend to assume (is it not that, in the guise of a fiction, of 'it's just a game', a subject can articulate and stage features of his symbolic identity – sadistic, 'perverse', and so on – which he would never be able to admit in his 'real' intersubjective contacts?), but the opposite also holds, that is, the much-celebrated playing with multiple, shifting personas (freely constructed identities) tends to obfuscate (and thus falsely liberate us from) the constraints of social space in which our existence is trapped. Let me evoke another example: why did Christa Wolf's *The Quest for Christa T.* exert such a tremendous impact on the GDR public in the 1960s? Because it is precisely a novel about the failure – or, at least, the vacillation – of ideological interpellation, about the failure of fully recognizing oneself in one's socio-ideological identity:

> When her name was called: 'Christa T.!' – she stood up and went and did what was expected of her; was there anyone to whom she

could say that hearing her name called gave her much to think about: Is it really me who's meant? Or is it only my name that's being used? Counted in with other names, industriously added up in front of the equals sign? And might I just as well have been absent, would anyone have noticed?'[28]

Is not this gesture of 'Am I that name?', this probing into one's symbolic identification so well expressed by Johannes R. Becher's quote which Wolf put at the very beginning of the novel: 'This coming-to-oneself – what is it?', hysterical provocation at its purest? And my point is that such a self-probing attitude, far from effectively threatening the predominant ideological regime, is what ultimately makes it 'livable' – this is why her West German detractors were in a way paradoxically right when, after the fall of the Wall, they claimed that Christa Wolf, by expressing the subjective complexities, inner doubts and oscillations of the GDR subject, actually provided a realistic literary equivalent of the ideal GDR subject, and was as such much more successful in her task of securing political conformity than the open naive propagandist fiction depicting ideal subjects sacrificing themselves for the Communist Cause.[29]

The theoretical task is not only to unmask the particular content of inclusions/exclusions involved in the game, but to account for the enigmatic emergence of the space of universality itself. Furthermore – and more precisely – the real task is to explore the fundamental shifts in the very logic of the way universality works in the socio-symbolic space: premodern, modern and today's 'postmodern' notion and ideological practice of universality do not, for example, differ only with regard to the particular contents that are included/excluded in universal notions – somehow, on a more radical level, the very underlying notion of universality functions in a different way in each of these epochs. 'Universality' *as such* does not mean the same thing since the establishment of bourgeois market society in which individuals participate in the social order not on behalf of their particular place within the global social edifice but *immediately*, as 'abstract' human beings.

Let me return to the notion of universal human rights. The

Marxist symptomal reading can convincingly demonstrate the particular content that gives the specific bourgeois ideological spin to the notion of human rights: 'universal human rights are in effect the right of white male property owners to exchange freely on the market, exploit workers and women, and exert political domination . . .'. This identification of the particular content that hegemonizes the universal form is, however, only half the story; its other, crucial half consists in asking a much more difficult supplementary question about the *emergence of the very form of universality*: how, in what specific historical conditions, does abstract universality itself become a 'fact of (social) life'? In what conditions do individuals experience themselves as subjects of universal human rights? That is the point of Marx's analysis of 'commodity fetishism': in a society in which commodity exchange predominates, individuals themselves, in their daily lives, relate to themselves, as well as to the objects they encounter, as to contingent embodiments of abstract-universal notions. What I am, my concrete social or cultural background, is experienced as contingent, since what ultimately defines me is the 'abstract' universal capacity to think and/or to work. Or: any object that can satisfy my desire is experienced as contingent, since my desire is conceived as an 'abstract' formal capacity, indifferent towards the multitude of particular objects that may – but never fully do – satisfy it. Or take the already-mentioned example of 'profession': the modern notion of profession implies that I experience myself as an individual who is not directly 'born into' his social role – what I will become depends on the interplay between contingent social circumstances and my free choice; in this sense, today's individual has the profession of electrician or professor or waiter, while it is meaningless to claim that a medieval serf was a peasant by profession. The crucial point here is, again, that in certain specific social conditions (of commodity exchange and a global market economy), 'abstraction' becomes a direct feature of actual social life, the way concrete individuals behave and relate to their fate and to their social surroundings. Here Marx shares Hegel's insight into how universality becomes 'for itself' only in so far as individuals no

longer fully identify the kernel of their being with their particular
social situation, only in so far as they experience themselves as forever 'out of joint' with regard to this situation: the concrete,
effective existence of the universality is the individual without a
proper place in the global edifice – in a given social structure,
Universality becomes 'for itself' only in those individuals who lack
a proper place in it. The mode of appearance of an abstract universality, its entering into actual existence, is thus an extremely
violent move of disrupting the preceding organic balance.

My claim is thus that when Butler speaks of the unending political
process of renegotiating the inclusions/exclusions of the predominant
ideological universal notions, or when Laclau proposes his model of the
unending struggle for hegemony, *the 'universal' status of this very model is
problematic*: are they providing the *formal* co-ordinates of *every* ideologico-
political process, or are they simply elaborating the notional structure of
today's ('postmodern') *specific* political practice which is emerging after the
retreat of the classical Left?[30] They (more often than not, in their explicit
formulations) *appear* to do the first (for Laclau, say, the logic of hegemony
is somewhat unambiguously articulated as a kind of Heideggerian *existential structure* of social life), although one can also argue that they are
merely theorizing a very specific historical moment of the 'postmodern'
Left. . . .[31] In other words, the problem for me is *how to historicize historicism itself*. The passage from 'essentialist' Marxism to postmodern
contingent politics (in Laclau), or the passage from sexual essentialism to
contingent gender-formation (in Butler), or – a further example – the
passage from metaphysician to ironist in Richard Rorty, is not a simple
epistemological progress but part of the global change in the very nature
of capitalist society. It is not that before, people were 'stupid essentialists'
and believed in naturalized sexuality, while now they know that genders
are performatively enacted; one needs a kind of metanarrative that
explains this very passage from essentialism to the awareness of contingency: the Heideggerian notion of the epochs of Being, or the
Foucauldian notion of the shift in the predominant *épistème*, or the standard sociological notion of modernization, or a more Marxist account
in which this passage follows the dynamic of capitalism.

IV

So, again, crucial in Laclau's theoretical edifice is the paradigmatically Kantian co-dependency between the 'timeless' existential a priori of the logic of hegemony and the *historical narrative* of the gradual passage from the 'essentialist' traditional Marxist class politics to the full assertion of the contingency of the struggle for hegemony – just as the Kantian transcendental a priori is co-dependent with his anthropologico-political evolutionary narrative of humanity's gradual progression towards enlightened maturity. The role of this evolutionary narrative is precisely to resolve the above-mentioned ambiguity of the formal universal frame (of the logic of hegemony) – implicitly to answer the question: is this frame really a non-historical universal, or simply the formal structure of the specific ideologico-political constellation of Western late capitalism? The evolutionary narrative mediates between these two options, telling the story of how the universal frame was 'posited as such', became the explicit structuring principle of ideologico-political life. The question none the less persists: is this evolutionary passage a simple passage from error to true insight? Is it that each stance fits its own epoch, so that in Marx's time 'class essentialism' was adequate, while today we need the assertion of contingency? Or should we combine the two in a proto-Hegelian way, so that the very passage from the essentialist 'error' to 'true' insight into radical contingency is historically conditioned (in Marx's time, the 'essentialist illusion' was 'objectively necessary', while our epoch enables the insight into contingency)? This proto-Hegelian solution would allow us to combine the 'universal' scope or 'validity' of the concept of hegemony with the obvious fact that its recent emergence is clearly linked to today's specific social constellation: although socio-political life and its structure were always-already the outcome of hegemonic struggles, it is none the less only today, in our specific historical constellation – that is to say, in the 'postmodern' universe of globalized contingency – that the radically contingent-hegemonic nature of the political processes is finally allowed to 'come/return to itself', to free itself of the 'essentialist' baggage. . . .

This solution, however, is problematic for at least two reasons. First, Laclau would probably reject it as relying on the Hegelian notion of the necessary historical development that conditions and anchors political struggles. Second, from my perspective, today's postmodern politics of multiple subjectivities is precisely not political enough, in so far as it silently presupposes a non-thematized, 'naturalized' framework of economic relations. Against the postmodern political theory which tends increasingly to prohibit the very reference to capitalism as 'essentialist', one should assert that the plural contingency of postmodern political struggles and the totality of Capital are not opposed, with Capital somehow 'limiting' the free drift of hegemonic displacements – today's capitalism, rather, provides *the very background and terrain for the emergence of shifting–dispersed–contingent–ironic–and so on, political subjectivities*. Was it not Deleuze who in a way made this point when he emphasized how capitalism is a force of 'deterritorialization'? And was he not following Marx's old thesis on how, with capitalism, 'all that is solid melts into air'?

So, ultimately, my key point apropos of Butler and Laclau is the same in both cases: the need to distinguish more explicitly between contingency/substitutability *within* a certain historical horizon and the more fundamental exclusion/foreclosure that *grounds this very horizon*. When Laclau claims that 'if the fullness of society is unachievable, the attempts at reaching it will necessarily fail, although they will be able, in the search for that impossible object, to solve a variety of partial problems', does he not – potentially, at least – conflate two levels, the struggle for hegemony *within* a certain horizon and the more fundamental exclusion that sustains this very horizon? And when Butler claims, against the Lacanian notion of constitutive bar or lack, that 'the subject-in-process is incomplete precisely because it is constituted through exclusions that are politically salient, not structurally static', does she also not – potentially, at least – conflate two levels, the endless political struggle of/for inclusions/exclusions *within* a given field (say, of today's late capitalist society) and a more fundamental exclusion which sustains this very field?

This, finally, enables me to approach directly the main deconstructionist criticism of Lacan adopted by Butler: that Lacan gets stuck in a negative-transcendental gesture. That is to say: while Butler acknowledges that, for Lacan, the subject never achieves full identity, that the process of subject-formation is always incomplete, condemned to ultimate failure, her criticism is that Lacan elevates the very obstacle that prevents the subject's complete realization into a transcendental a priori 'bar' (of 'symbolic castration'). So, instead of acknowledging the thorough contingency and openness of the historical process, Lacan posits it under the sign of a fundamental, ahistorical Bar or Prohibition. Underlying Butler's criticism, therefore is the thesis that Lacanian theory, at least in its predominant 'orthodox' form, limits radical historical contingency: it underpins the historical process by evoking some quasi-transcendental limitation, some quasi-transcendental a priori that is not itself caught in the contingent historical process. Lacanian theory thus ultimately leads to the Kantian distinction between some formal a priori framework and its contingent shifting historical examples. She evokes the Lacanian notion of the 'barred subject': while she recognizes that this notion implies the constitutive, necessary, unavoidable incompletion and ultimate failure of every process of interpellation, identification, subject-constitution, she none the less claims that Lacan elevates the bar into an ahistorical a priori Prohibition or Limitation which circumscribes every political struggle in advance. . . .

My first, almost automatic reaction to this is: is Butler herself relying here on a silent proto-Kantian distinction between form and content? In so far as she claims that 'the subject-in-process is incomplete precisely because it is constituted through exclusions that are politically salient, not structurally static', is not her criticism of Lacan that Lacan ultimately confounds the *form* of exclusion (there will always be exclusions; some form of exclusion is the necessary condition of subjective identity . . .) with some particular, specific *content* that is excluded? Butler's reproach to Lacan is thus, rather, that he is not 'formalist' enough: his 'bar' is too obviously branded by the particular historical content – in an illegitimate short circuit, he elevates into a quasi-transcendental a priori a certain 'bar' that emerged only within specific, ultimately contingent historical conditions (the Oedipus complex, sexual difference). This is especially clear apropos of sexual difference: Butler reads Lacan's thesis that sexual difference is 'real' as the assertion that it is an ahistorical, frozen opposition, fixed as a non-negotiable framework that has no place in hegemonic struggles.

I claim that this criticism of Lacan involves a misrepresentation of his position, which here is much closer to Hegel. That is to say: the crucial point is that the very *form*, in its universality, is always rooted, like an umbilical cord, in a particular content – not only in the sense of hegemony (universality is never empty; it is always coloured by some particular content), but in the more radical sense that the very *form* of universality emerges through a radical dislocation, through some more radical impossibility or 'primordial repression'. The ultimate question is not which particular content hegemonizes the empty universality (and thus, in the struggle for hegemony, excludes other particular contents); the ultimate question is: which specific content has to be excluded so that the very *empty form* of universality emerges as the 'battlefield' for hegemony? Let us take the notion of 'democracy': of course the content of this notion is not predetermined – what 'democracy' will mean, what this term will include and what it will exclude (that is, the extent to which and the way women, gays, minorities, non-white races, etc., are included/excluded), is always the result of contingent hegemonic struggle. However, this very open struggle presupposes not some fixed content as its ultimate referent, but *its very terrain*, delimited by the 'empty signifier' that designates it ('democracy', in this case). Of course, in the democratic struggle for hegemony, each position accuses the other of being 'not really democratic': for a conservative liberal, social democratic interventionism is already potentially 'totalitarian'; for a social democrat, the traditional liberal's neglect of social solidarity is non-democratic . . . so each position tries to impose its own logic of inclusion/exclusion, and all these exclusions are 'politically salient, not structurally static'; in order for this very struggle to take place, however, its *terrain* must constitute itself by means of a more fundamental exclusion ('primordial repression') that is not simply historical–contingent, a stake in the present constellation of the hegemonic struggle, since it *sustains the very terrain of historicity*.

Take the case of sexual difference itself: Lacan's claim that sexual difference is 'real–impossible' is strictly synonymous with his claim that 'there is no such thing as a sexual relationship'. For Lacan, sexual difference is not a firm set of 'static' symbolic oppositions and inclusions/exclusions (heterosexual normativity which relegates homosexuality and other 'perversions' to some secondary role), but the name of a deadlock, of a trauma, of an open question, of something that *resists* every attempt at its symbolization. Every translation of sexual difference into a set of symbolic opposition(s) is doomed to fail, and it is this very 'impossibility' that opens up the terrain of the hegemonic struggle for what 'sexual difference' will mean. What is barred is *not* what is excluded under the present hegemonic regime.[32]

The political struggle for hegemony whose outcome is contingent, and the 'non-historical' bar or impossibility are thus strictly correlative: there is a struggle for hegemony precisely *because* some preceding 'bar' of impossibility sustains the void at stake in the hegemonic struggle. So Lacan is the very opposite of Kantian formalism (if by this we understand the imposition of some formal frame that serves as the a priori of its contingent content): Lacan forces us to make thematic the exclusion of some traumatic 'content' that is constitutive of the empty universal form. There is historical space only in so far as this space is sustained by some more radical exclusion (or, as Lacan would have put it, *forclusion*). So one should distinguish between two levels: the hegemonic struggle for which particular content will hegemonize the empty universal notion; and the more fundamental impossibility that renders the Universal empty, and thus a terrain for hegemonic struggle.

So, with regard to the criticism of Kantianism, my answer is that it is Butler and Laclau who are secret Kantians:[33] they both propose an abstract a priori formal model (of hegemony, of gender performativity . . .) which allows, within its frame, for the full contingency (no guarantee of what the outcome of the fight for hegemony will be, no last reference to the sexual constitution . . .); they both involve a logic of 'spurious infinity': no final resolution, just the endless process of complex partial displacements. Is not Laclau's theory of hegemony 'formalist' in the sense of proffering a certain a priori formal matrix of social space? There will always be some hegemonic empty signifier; it is only its content that shifts. . . . My ultimate point is thus that Kantian formalism and radical historicism are not really opposites, but two sides of the same coin: every version of historicism relies on a minimal 'ahistorical' formal framework defining the terrain within which the open and endless game of contingent inclusions/exclusions, substitutions, renegotiations, displacements, and so on, takes place. The truly radical assertion of historical contingency has to include the dialectical tension between the domain of historical change itself and its traumatic 'ahistorical' kernel *qua* its condition of (im)possibility. Here we have the difference between historicity proper and historicism: *historicism* deals with the endless play of substitutions within the same fundamental field of (im)possibility, while *historicity* proper makes thematic different structural principles of this very (im)possibility. In other words, the historicist theme of the endless open play of substitutions is the very form of ahistorical ideological closure: by focusing on the simple dyad essentialism–contingency, on the passage from the one to the other, it obfuscates concrete historicity *qua* the change of the very global structuring principle of the Social.

How, then, are we to conceive this 'ahistorical' status of sexual difference? Perhaps an analogy with Claude Lévi-Strauss's notion of the 'zero-institution' could be of some help here. I am referring to Lévi-Strauss's exemplary analysis, from *Structural Anthropology*, of the spatial disposition of buildings in the Winnebago, one of the Great Lakes tribes. The tribe is divided into two subgroups ('moieties'), 'those who are from above' and 'those who are from below'; when we ask an individual to draw on a piece of paper, or on sand, the ground plan of his or her village (the spatial disposition of cottages), we obtain two quite different answers, depending on his or her membership of one or the other subgroup. Both perceive the village as a circle, but for one subgroup there is within this circle another circle of central houses, so that we have two concentric circles; while for the other subgroup the circle is split into two by a clear dividing line. In other words, a member of the first subgroup (let us call it 'conservative-corporatist') perceives the ground plan of the village as a ring of houses more or less symmetrically disposed around the central temple; whereas a member of the second ('revolutionary-antagonistic') subgroup perceives his or her village as two distinct heaps of houses separated by an invisible frontier. . . .[34] Lévi-Strauss's central point is that this example should in no way entice us into cultural relativism, according to which the perception of social space depends on the observer's group membership: the very splitting into the two 'relative' perceptions implies a hidden reference to a constant – not the objective, 'actual' disposition of buildings but a traumatic kernel, a fundamental antagonism the inhabitants of the village were unable to symbolize, to account for, to 'internalize', to come to terms with – an imbalance in social relations that prevented the community from stabilizing itself into a harmonious whole. The two perceptions of the ground plan are simply two mutually exclusive endeavours to cope with this traumatic antagonism, to heal its wound via the imposition of a balanced symbolic structure. Is it necessary to add that it is exactly the same with respect to sexual difference: 'masculine' and 'feminine' are like the two configurations of houses in the Lévi-Straussian village? And in order to dispel the illusion that our 'developed' universe is not dominated by the same logic, suffice it to recall the splitting of our political space into Left and Right: a Leftist and a Rightist behave exactly like members of the opposite subgroups in the Lévi-Straussian village. They not only occupy different places within the political space; each of them perceives the very disposition of the political space differently – a Leftist as the field that is inherently split by some fundamental antagonism; a Rightist as the organic unity of a Community disturbed only by foreign intruders.

However, Lévi-Strauss makes a further crucial point here: since the two subgroups none the less form one and the same tribe, living in the same village, this identity somehow has to be symbolically inscribed – how, if the entire symbolic articulation, all social institutions, of the tribe are not neutral, but are overdetermined by the fundamental and constitutive antagonistic split? By what Lévi-Strauss ingeniously calls the 'zero-institution', a kind of institutional counterpart to the famous *mana*, the empty signifier with no determinate meaning, since it signifies only the presence of meaning as such, in opposition to its absence: a specific institution which has no positive, determinate function – its only function is the purely negative one of signalling the presence and actuality of social institution as such, in opposition to its absence, to pre-social chaos. It is the reference to such a zero-institution that enables all members of the tribe to experience themselves as such, as members of the same tribe. Is not this zero-institution, then, *ideology* at its purest, that is, the direct embodiment of the ideological function of providing a neutral all-encompassing space in which social antagonism is obliterated, in which all members of society can recognize themselves? And is not the struggle for *hegemony* precisely the struggle over how this zero-institution will be overdetermined, coloured by some particular signification?

To provide a concrete example: is not the modern notion of *nation* such a zero-institution that emerged with the dissolution of social links grounded in direct family or traditional symbolic matrixes, that is, when, with the onslaught of modernization, social institutions were less and less grounded in naturalized tradition and more and more experienced as a matter of 'contract'?[35] Of special importance here is the fact that national identity is experienced as at least minimally 'natural', as a belonging grounded in 'blood and soil', and, as such, opposed to 'artificial' belonging to social institutions proper (state, profession . . .): premodern institutions functioned as 'naturalized' symbolic entities (as institutions grounded in unquestionable traditions), and the moment institutions were conceived as social artefacts, the need arose for a 'naturalized' zero-institution that would serve as their neutral common ground.

And – back to sexual difference – I am tempted to risk the hypothesis that, perhaps, the same logic of zero-institution should be applied not only to the *unity* of a society, but also to its *antagonistic split*: what if sexual difference is ultimately a kind of *zero-institution of the social split within humankind*, the naturalized minimal zero-difference, a split which, prior to signalling any determinate social difference, signals this difference as such? The struggle for hegemony is then, again, the struggle over how this zero-difference will be overdetermined by other particular social differences.

So it is important that in both cases – apropos of nation as well as apropos of sexual difference – we stick to the Hegelian logic of 'positing the presuppositions': neither nation nor sexual difference is the immediate/natural presupposition later perlaborated/'mediated' by the work of culture[36] – they are both (presup)posed (retroactively posited) by the very 'cultural' process of symbolization.

V

To conclude, let me tackle Butler's critique of Mladen Dolar's critical reading of the Althusserian problematic of interpellation as constitutive of the subject;[37] this critique is an excellent summary of what deconstructionism finds unacceptable in Lacan. According to Dolar, the emergence of the subject cannot be conceived as a direct effect of the individual's recognizing him or herself in ideological interpellation: the subject emerges as correlative to some traumatic objectal remainder, to some excess which, precisely, cannot be 'subjectivized', integrated into the symbolic space. Dolar's key thesis is thus: 'for Althusser, the subject is what makes ideology work; for psychoanalysis, the subject emerges where ideology fails'.[38] In short, far from emerging as the outcome of interpellation, the subject emerges only when and in so far as interpellation liminally *fails*. Not only does the subject never fully recognize itself in the interpellative call: its resistance to interpellation (to the symbolic identity provided by interpellation) *is* the subject. In psychoanalytic terms, this failure of interpellation is what *hysteria* is about; for this reason, the subject *as such* is, in a way, hysterical. That is to say: what is hysteria if not the stance of the permanent questioning of one's symbolic identity, of the identity conferred on me by the big Other: 'You say I am (a mother, a whore, a teacher . . .), but *am I really what you say I am? What is in me that makes me what you say I am?*' From here, Dolar moves on to a double criticism of Althusser: first, Althusser does not take into account this objectal remainder/excess that resists symbolization; secondly, in his insistence on the 'material' status of Ideological State Apparatuses (ISAs), Althusser misrecognizes the 'ideal' status of the symbolic order itself as the ultimate Institution.

In her response, Butler accuses Dolar of Cartesian idealism: identifying materiality with 'actual' ISAs and their ritual practices, she describes the remainder that resists as *ideal*, as a part of inner psychic reality that cannot be reduced to an effect of interpellatory rituals. (Here, Butler pays the price of overhastily translating Dolar's position into philosophical terms he does *not* use – for instance, in this rather astounding passage: 'Theological resistance to materialism is exemplified in Dolar's explicit defense of Lacan's Cartesian inheritance, his insistence upon the pure ideality of the soul . . .'[39] *where* does either Dolar or Lacan 'explicitly defend' the pure ideality of the soul?[40]) It would therefore appear that Dolar, under the guise of insisting on the Real *qua material* remainder, repeats against Althusser the classic *Idealist* gesture of insisting on how the inner (self-)experience of subjectivity

cannot be reduced to an effect of external material practices and/or rituals: in the final analysis, the Lacanian '*objet petit a*' *qua* real turns out to
be the codename for an ideal psychic object beyond reach of material
practices. . . . Furthermore, Butler also accuses Dolar of idealizing the
big Other, that is, of endorsing the (Lacanian) shift from material ISAs
and their rituals to the notion of an immaterial/ideal symbolic order.

As for this last notion, the (im)materiality of the big Other, Dolar's
point is thoroughly materialist: he does not claim that an ideal quasi-
Platonic 'big Other' actually exists (as a Lacanian, he is well aware that
il n'y a pas de grand Autre); he merely claims that, in order for interpellation
(interpellative recognition) to occur, material practices and/or rituals of
real social institutions (schools, laws . . .) do not suffice, that is, the subject has to *presuppose* the symbolic Institution, an ideal structure of
differences.[41] This 'ideal' function of the 'big Other' *qua* ego ideal (as
opposed to *ideal ego*) can also be discerned through the notion of *interpassivity*, of transposing on to the Other – not my activity, but my very
passive experience.[42] Let us recall the proverbial crippled adolescent
who, unable to compete in basketball, identifies himself with a famous
player he watches on the television screen, imagines himself in his place,
acting 'through' him, getting satisfaction from his triumphs while sitting
alone at home in front of the screen – examples like this abound in conservative cultural criticism, with its complaint that in our era, people,
instead of engaging in direct social activity, prefer to remain impassive
consumers (of sex, of sport . . .), achieving satisfaction through imaginary identification with the other, their ideal ego, observed on screen.
What Lacan is aiming at with the ego ideal (the point of symbolic identification), however, as opposed to ideal ego (the point or figure of
imaginary identification), is the exact opposite: what about the basketball
player himself? What if he can shine in the game only in so far as he
imagines himself being exposed to some – ultimately fantasized –
Other's gaze, seeing himself being seen by that gaze, imagining the way
his brilliant game is fascinating that gaze? This third gaze – the point
from which I see myself as likeable, in the guise of my ideal ego – is the
ego ideal, the point of my symbolic identification, and it is here that we
encounter the structure of interpassivity: I can be active (shining on the
basketball court) only in so far as I identify with another impassive gaze

for which I am doing it, that is, only in so far as I transpose on to another the passive experience of being fascinated by what I am doing, in so far as I imagine myself *appearing* to this Other who registers my acts in the symbolic network. So interpassivity is not simply a symmetrical reversal of 'interactivity' (in the sense, described above, of being active through (our identification with) another): it gives birth to a 'reflexive' structure in which the gaze is redoubled, in which I 'see myself being seen as likeable'. (And incidentally, in the same sense, exhibitionism – being exposed to the Other's gaze – is not simply a symmetrical reversal of voyeurism, but the original constellation that supports its two subspecies, exhibitionism proper and voyeurism: even in voyeurism, it is never just me and the object I am spying on, a third gaze is always-already there: the gaze which sees me seeing the object. So – to put it in Hegelian terms – exhibitionism is its own subspecies – it has two species, voyeurism as well as exhibitionism itself in its 'oppositional determination'.)

When Dolar speaks of the 'remainder', however, this is not the ideal big Other, but precisely the *small* other, the 'bone in the throat' that resists symbolic idealization. Or – with regard to the opposition between the Inner and the External – the remainder of which Dolar speaks (*objet petit a*) is precisely not internal/ideal, but extimate, thoroughly contingent, a foreign body at my very heart, decentring the subject. In short, far from being an ideal–immaterial–internal object opposed to externality, the 'remainder' of which Dolar speaks is the remainder of contingent *externality* that persists within every move of internalization/idealization, and subverts the clear line of division between 'inner' and 'outer'. In somewhat simplistic Hegelian terms, *objet petit a* is the remainder that can never be 'sublated [*aufgehoben*]' in the movement of symbolization. So not only is this remainder not an 'inner' object irreducible to external materiality – it is precisely the irreducible trace of externality in the very midst of 'internality', its condition of impossibility (a foreign body preventing the subject's full constitution) which is simultaneously its condition of possibility. The 'materiality' of this remainder is that of the *trauma* which resists symbolization. So what one should do here in order not to miss Lacan's point is to reject the equivalence between 'materiality' and so-called 'external reality': *objet petit a*, of course, is not 'material' in the sense of an object within 'external reality', but it is 'material' in the sense of an impenetrable/dense stain within the 'ideal' sphere of psychic life itself. True *materialism* does not consist in the simple operation of reducing inner psychic experience to an effect of the processes taking place in 'external reality' – what one should do, in addition, is to isolate a 'material' traumatic kernel/remainder at the very heart of 'psychic life' itself.

Butler's misunderstanding emerges at its most radical apropos of the relationship between ritual and belief. When Althusser refers to Pascal's 'Act as if you believe, pray, kneel down, and belief will come by itself', he is not merely making the simple behaviourist assertion of the dependence of inner belief on external social interaction; what he proposes is, rather, an intricate reflective mechanism of retroactive 'autopoietic' causality, of how 'external' ritual performatively generates its own ideological foundation: kneel down, *and you shall believe that you knelt down because of your belief* – that your kneeling was the effect/expression of your inner belief.[43] So: when Dolar insist that, in order to kneel down and follow the ritual, the subject already has to believe, does he not thereby miss Althusser's point by getting caught in the archetypal ideological vicious circle (in order for the process of subjectivization to take place, the subject *already has to be there*)? When Butler reads Dolar's point about belief as if it implies this vicious circle, she counters it with a reference to Wittgenstein:

> Wittgenstein remarks, 'We speak, we utter words, and only later get a sense of their life'. Anticipation of such sense governs the 'empty' ritual that is speech, and ensures its iterability. In this sense, then, we must neither first believe before we kneel nor know the sense of words before we speak. On the contrary, both are performed 'on faith' that sense will arrive in and through articulation itself – an anticipation that is not thereby governed by a guarantee of noematic satisfaction.[44]

But is not the point of the Lacanian notion of the retroactive temporality of meaning, of signified as the circular effect of the signifier's chain, and so on, precisely that meaning always comes 'later', that the notion of 'always-already there' is the true imaginary illusion-misrecognition?

The belief which has to be there when we perform a ritual is precisely an 'empty' belief, the belief at work when we perform acts '*on faith*' – this belief, this trust that, *later*, sense will emerge, is precisely the *presupposition* of which Dolar, following Lacan, speaks. (It is with reference to this gap that forever separates these *two* beliefs – the first, 'empty', belief at work when we engage in a symbolic process 'on faith', and the full belief in a Cause – that one should also read Kierkegaard's famous insistence on how we, Christians, never simply believe, but ultimately *believe only in order to believe*.[45]) This act of faith which makes us kneel (or, more generally, engage in a symbolic process) is what Derrida means when he speaks of the 'primordial Yes!' that constitutes the minimal engagement; it is what Lacan means when he interprets the Freudian *Bejahung* as the primordial acceptance of the symbolic order – the opposite is not *Verneinung* (since *Verneinung* denies an element which was already inscribed in the symbolic order), but the more primordial *Verwerfung*, refusal to participate. So, in short, this primordial 'Yes!' is proven in a negative way by the fact that there *are* subjects who do not say 'Yes!', but 'No!' – so-called psychotics who, precisely, *refuse* to engage in the symbolic process.

Underlying all these misunderstandings is the fundamental difference in how we conceive the notion of *subject*. Dolar criticizes Althusser not for 'eliding the dimension of subjectivity'[46] (that is, 'the lived and imaginary experience of the subject',[47]) but precisely for the opposite: for conceiving the subject as imaginary, as an effect of imaginary *reconnaissance/méconnaissance*. In short, Lacan's answer to the question asked (and answered in a negative way) by such different philosophers as Althusser and Derrida – 'Can the gap, the opening, the Void which precedes the gesture of subjectivization, still be called "subject"?' – is an emphatic 'Yes!' – for Lacan, the subject prior to subjectivization is not some Idealist pseudo-Cartesian self-presence preceding material interpellatory practices and apparatuses, but the very gap in the structure that the imaginary (mis)recognition in the interpellatory Call endeavours to fill in. We can also see here how this notion of the subject is strictly correlative to the notion of the 'barred' symbolic structure, of the structure traversed by the antagonistic split of an impossibility that can never be fully symbolized.[48] In short, the intimate link between *subject* and *failure* lies not in the fact that 'external' material social rituals and/or practices forever fail to reach the subject's innermost kernel, to represent it adequately – that some internality, some internal object irreducible to the externality of social practices (as Butler reads Dolar), always remains – but, on the contrary, in the fact that the 'subject' itself is *nothing but* the failure of symbolization, of its own symbolic representation – the subject is nothing 'beyond' this failure, it emerges through this failure, and the *objet petit a* is merely a positivization/embodiment of this failure.

VI

This notion of the subject as the 'answer of the Real' finally allows me to confront Butler's standard criticism of the relationship between the Real and the Symbolic in Lacan: the determination of the Real as that which resists symbolization is itself a symbolic determination, that is, the very gesture of excluding something from the Symbolic, of positing it as beyond the prohibitive Limit (as the Sacred, Untouchable), is a symbolic gesture (a gesture of symbolic exclusion) *par excellence* . . . . In contrast to this, however, one should insist on how the Lacanian Real is strictly *internal* to the Symbolic: it is nothing but its inherent limitation, the impossibility of the Symbolic fully to 'become itself'. As we have already emphasized, the Real of sexual difference does not mean that we have a fixed set of symbolic oppositions defining masculine and feminine 'roles', so that all subjects who do not fit into one of these two slots are excluded/rejected into the 'impossible Real'; it means precisely that every attempt at its symbolization fails – that sexual difference cannot be adequately translated into a set of symbolic oppositions. However, to avoid a further misunderstanding: the fact that sexual difference cannot be translated into a set of symbolic oppositions in no way implies that it is 'real' in the sense of some pre-existing external substantial Entity beyond the grasp of symbolization: precisely as real, sexual difference is *absolutely internal* to the Symbolic – it is its point of inherent failure.

It is in fact Laclau's notion of antagonism that can exemplify the Real: just as sexual difference can articulate itself only in the guise of the series of (failed) attempts to transpose it into symbolic oppositions, so the antagonism (between Society itself and the non-Social) is not simply external to the differences that are internal to the social structure, since, as we have already seen, it can articulate itself only in the guise of a difference (by mapping itself on to a difference) between elements of social space.[49] If the Real were to be directly external to the Symbolic, then Society definitely *would* exist: for something to exist, it has to be defined by its external limit, and the Real would have served as this externality guaranteeing the inherent consistency of Society. (This is what anti-Semitism does by way of 'reifying' the inherent deadlock–impossibility–antagonism of the Social in the external figure of the Jew – the Jew is the ultimate guarantee that society exists. What happens in the passage from the position of strict class struggle to Fascist anti-Semitism is not just a simple replacement of one figure of the enemy [the bourgeoisie, the ruling class] with another [the Jews], but the shift from the logic of antagonism which makes Society impossible to the logic of external Enemy which guarantees Society's consistency.) The paradox, therefore, is that Butler is, in a way, right: yes, the Real *is* in fact internal/inherent to the Symbolic, not its external limit, but *for that very reason*, it cannot be symbolized. In other words, the paradox is that the Real as external, excluded from the Symbolic, is in fact a symbolic determination – what eludes symbolization is precisely the Real as the *inherent point of failure* of symbolization.[50]

Precisely because of this internality of the Real to the Symbolic, it *is* possible to touch the Real through the Symbolic – that is the whole point of Lacan's notion of psychoanalytic treatment; this is what the Lacanian notion of the psychoanalytic *act* is about – the act as a gesture which, by definition, touches the dimension of some impossible Real. This notion of the act must be conceived of against the background of the distinction between the mere endeavour to 'solve a variety of partial problems' within a given field and the more radical gesture of subverting the very structuring principle of this field. An act does not simply occur *within* the given horizon of what appears to be 'possible' – it redefines the very contours of what is possible (an act accomplishes what, within the given symbolic universe, appears to be 'impossible', yet it changes its conditions so that it creates retroactively the conditions of its own possibility). So when we are reproached by an opponent for doing something unacceptable, an act occurs when we no longer defend ourselves by accepting the underlying premiss that we hitherto shared with the opponent; in contrast, we fully accept the reproach, changing the very terrain that made it unacceptable – an act occurs when our answer to the reproach is 'Yes, *that* it is precisely what I am doing!'

In film, a modest, not quite appropriate recent example would be Kevin Kline's blurting out 'I'm gay' instead of 'Yes!' during the wedding ceremony in *In and Out*: openly admitting the truth that he is gay, and thus surprising not only us, the spectators, but even himself.[51] In a series of recent (commercial) films, we find the same surprising radical gesture. In *Speed*, when the hero (Keanu Reeves) is confronting the terrorist black-mailer partner who holds his partner at gunpoint, he shoots not the blackmailer , but *his own partner* in the leg – this apparently senseless act momentarily shocks the blackmailer, who lets go of the hostage and runs away. . . . In *Ransom*, when the media tycoon (Mel Gibson) goes on television to answer the kidnappers request for two million dollars as a ransom for his son, he surprises everyone by saying that he will offer two million dollars to anyone who will give him any information about the kidnappers, and announces that he will pursue them to the end, with all his resources, if they do not release his son immediately. This radical ges-ture stuns not only the kidnappers – immediately after accomplishing it, Gibson himself almost breaks down, aware of the risk he is courting. . . . And finally, the supreme case: when, in the flashback scene from *The Usual Suspects*, the mysterious Keyser Soeze (Kevin Stacey) returns home and finds his wife and small daughter held at gunpoint by the members of a rival mob, he resorts to the radical gesture of shooting his wife and daughter themselves dead – this act enables him mercilessly to pursue members of the rival gang, their families, parents, friends, killing them all. . . .

What these three gestures have in common is that, in a situation of the forced choice, the subject makes the 'crazy', impossible choice of, in a way, *striking at himself*, at what is most precious to himself. This act, far from amounting to a case of impotent aggressivity turned on oneself, rather changes the co-ordinates of the situation in which the subject finds himself: by cutting himself loose from the precious object through whose possession the enemy kept him in check, the subject gains the space of free action. Is not such a radical gesture of 'striking at oneself' constitutive of subjectivity as such? Did not Lacan himself accomplish a similar act of 'shooting at himself' when, in 1979, he dissolved the *École freudienne de Paris*, his *agalma*, his own organization, the very space of his collective life? Yet he was well aware that only such a 'self-destructive' act could clear the terrain for a new beginning.

In the domain of politics proper, most of today's Left succumbs to ideological blackmail by the Right in accepting its basic premisses ('the era of the welfare state, with its unlimited spending, is over', etc.) – ultimately, this is what the celebrated 'Third Way' of today's social democracy is about. In such conditions, an authentic act would be to counter the Rightist agitation apropos of some 'radical' measure ('You want the impossible; this will lead to catastrophe, to more state intervention . . .') not by defending ourselves by saying that this is not what we mean, that we are no longer the old Socialists, that the proposed measures will not increase the state budget, that they will even render state expenditure more 'effective' and give a boost to investment, and so on and so forth, but by a resounding 'Yes, that is *precisely* what we want!'.[52] Although Clinton's presidency epitomizes the Third Way of today's (ex-) Left succumbing to Rightist ideological blackmail, his healthcare reform programme would none the less amount to a kind of *act*, at least in today's conditions, since it would be based on the rejection of the hegemonic notions of the need to curtail Big State expenditure and administration – in a way, it would 'do the impossible'. No wonder, then, that it failed: its failure – perhaps the only significant, albeit negative, *event* of Clinton's presidency – bears witness to the material force of the ideological notion of 'free choice'. That is to say: although the great majority of so-called 'ordinary people' were not properly acquainted with the reform programme, the medical lobby (twice as strong as the infamous defence lobby!) succeeded in imposing on the public the fundamental idea that with universal healthcare, free choice (in matters concerning medicine) would be somehow threatened – against this purely fictional reference to 'free choice', any enumeration of 'hard facts' (in Canada, healthcare is less expensive and more effective, with no less free choice, etc.) proved ineffectual.

As for the subject's (agent's) identity: in an authentic act, I do not simply express/actualize my inner nature – rather, I redefine myself, the very core of my identity. To evoke Butler's often-repeated example of a subject who has a deep homosexual 'passionate attachment', yet is unable openly to acknowledge it, to make it part of his symbolic identity:[53] in an authentic sexual act, the subject would have to change the way he relates to his homosexual 'passionate attachment' – not only in the sense of 'coming out', of fully identifying himself as gay. An act does not only shift the limit that divides our identity into the acknowledged and the disavowed part more in the direction of the disavowed part, it does not only make us to accept as 'possible' our innermost disavowed 'impossible' fantasies: it transforms the very coordinates of the disavowed phantasmic foundation of our being. An act does not merely redraw the contours of our public symbolic identity, it also transforms the spectral dimension that sustains this identity, the undead ghosts that haunt the living subject, the secret history of traumatic fantasies transmitted 'between the lines', through the lacks and distortions of the explicit symbolic texture of his or her identity.

Now I can also answer the obvious counter-argument to this Lacanian notion of the act: if we define an act solely by the fact that its sudden emergence surprises/transforms its agent itself and, simultaneously, that it retroactively changes its conditions of (im)possibility, is not Nazism, then, an act *par excellence*? Did Hitler not 'do the impossible', changing the entire field of what was considered 'acceptable' in the liberal democratic universe? Did not a respectable middle-class *petit bourgeois* who, as a guard in a concentration camp, tortured Jews, also accomplish what was considered impossible, in his previous 'decent' existence and acknowledge his 'passionate attachment' to sadistic torture? It is here that the notion of 'traversing the fantasy', and – on a different level – of transforming the constellation that generates social symptoms becomes crucial. An authentic act disturbs the underlying fantasy, attacking it from the point of 'social symptom' (let us recall that Lacan attributed the invention of the notion of symptom to Marx!). The so-called 'Nazi revolution', with its disavowal/displacement of the fundamental social antagonism ('class struggle' that divides the social edifice from within) – with its projection/externalization of the cause of social antagonisms into the figure of the Jew, and the consequent reassertion of the corporatist notion of society as an organic Whole – clearly *avoids* confrontation with social antagonism: the 'Nazi revolution' is *the* exemplary case of a pseudo-change, of a frenetic activity in the course of which many things did change – 'something was going on all the time' – so that, precisely, something – that which *really matters* – would *not* change; so that things would fundamentally 'remain the same'.

In short, an authentic act is not simply external with regard to the hegemonic symbolic field disturbed by it: an act is an act only *with regard to* some symbolic field, as an intervention into it. That is to say: a symbolic field is always and by definition in itself 'decentred', structured around a central void/impossibility (a personal life-narrative, say, is a *bricolage* of ultimately failed attempts to come to terms with some trauma; a social edifice is an ultimately failed attempt to displace/obfuscate its constitutive antagonism); and an act disturbs the symbolic field into which it intervenes not out of nowhere, but precisely *from the standpoint of this inherent impossibility, stumbling block, which is its hidden, disavowed structuring principle*. In contrast to this authentic act which intervenes in the constitutive void, point of failure – or what Alain Badiou has called the 'symptomal torsion' of a given constellation[54] – the inauthentic act legitimizes itself through reference to the point of substantial fullness of a given constellation (on the political terrain: Race, True Religion, Nation . . .): it aims precisely at obliterating the last traces of the 'symptomal torsion' which disturbs the balance of that constellation.

One palpable political consequence of this notion of the act that has to intervene at the 'symptomal torsion' of the structure (and also a proof that our position does not involve 'economic essentialism') is that in each concrete constellation, there is *one* touchy nodal point of contention which decides where one 'truly stands'. For example, in the recent struggle of the so-called 'democratic opposition' in Serbia against the Milošević regime, the truly touchy topic is the stance towards the Albanian majority in Kosovo: the great majority of the 'democratic opposition' unconditionally endorse Milošević's anti-Albanian nationalist agenda, even accusing him of making compromises with the West and 'betraying' Serb national interests in Kosovo. In the course of the student demonstrations against Milošević's Socialist Party falsification of the election results in the winter of 1996, the Western media which closely followed events, and praised the revived democratic spirit in

Serbia, rarely mentioned the fact that one of the demonstrators' regular slogans against the special police was 'Instead of kicking us, go to Kosovo and kick out the Albanians!'. So – and this is my point – it is theoretically as well as politically wrong to claim that, in today's Serbia, 'anti-Albanian nationalism' is simply one among the 'floating signifiers' that can be appropriated either by Milošević's power bloc or by the opposition: the moment one endorses it, no matter how much one 'reinscribes it into the democratic chain of equivalences', one already accepts the terrain as defined by Milošević, one – as it were – is already 'playing his game'. In today's Serbia, the absolute *sine qua non* of an authentic political act would thus be to reject absolutely the ideologico-political topos of the Albanian threat in Kosovo.

Psychoanalysis is aware of a whole series of 'false acts': psychotic-paranoiac violent *passage à l'acte*, hysterical acting out, obsessional self-hindering, perverse self-instrumentalization – all these acts are not simply wrong according to some external standards, they are *immanently wrong*, since they can be properly grasped only as reactions to some disavowed trauma that they displace, repress, and so on. What we are tempted to say is that the Nazi anti-Semitic violence was 'false' in the same way: all the shattering impact of this large-scale frenetic activity was fundamentally 'misdirected', it was a kind of gigantic *passage à l'acte* betraying an inability to confront the real kernel of the trauma (the social antagonism). So what we are claiming is that anti-Semitic violence, say, is not only 'factually wrong' (Jews are 'not really like that', exploiting us and organizing a universal plot) and/or 'morally wrong' (unacceptable in terms of elementary standards of decency, etc.), but also 'untrue' in the sense of an inauthenticity which is simultaneously epistemological and ethical, just as an obsessional who reacts to his disavowed sexual fixations by engaging in compulsive defence rituals acts in an inauthentic way. Lacan claimed that even if the patient's wife is really sleeping around with other men, the patient's jealousy is still to be treated as a pathological condition; in a homologous way, even if rich Jews 'really' exploited German workers, seduced their daughters, dominated the popular press, and so on, *anti-Semitism is still an emphatically 'untrue', pathological ideological condition* – why? What makes it pathological is the *disavowed subjective libidinal investment* in the figure of the Jew – the way social antagonism is displaced-obliterated by being 'projected' into the figure of the Jew.[55]

So – back to the obvious counter-argument to the Lacanian notion of the act: this second feature (for a gesture to count as an act, it must 'traverse the fantasy') is not simply a further, additional criterion, to be added to the first ('doing the impossible', retroactively rewriting its own conditions): if this second criterion is not fulfilled, the first is not really met either – that is to say, we are not actually 'doing the impossible', traversing the fantasy towards the Real.

*

The problem of today's philosophico-political scene is ultimately best expressed by Lenin's old question 'What is to be done?' – how do we reassert, on the political terrain, the proper dimension of the act? The main form of the resistance against the act today is a kind of unwritten *Denkverbot* (prohibition to think) similar to the infamous *Berufsverbot* (prohibition to be employed by any state institution) from the late 1960s in Germany – the moment one shows a minimal sign of engaging in political projects that aim seriously to change the existing order, the answer is immediately: 'Benevolent as it is, this will necessarily end in a new Gulag!' The 'return to ethics' in today's political philosophy shamefully exploits the horrors of Gulag or Holocaust as the ultimate bogey for blackmailing us into renouncing all serious radical engagement. In this way, conformist liberal scoundrels can find hypocritical satisfaction in their defence of the existing order: they know there is corruption, exploitation, and so on, but every attempt to change things is denounced as ethically dangerous and unacceptable, recalling the ghosts of Gulag or Holocaust. . . .

And this resistance against the act seems to be shared across a wide spectrum of (officially) opposed philosophical positions. Four philosophers as different as Derrida, Habermas, Rorty and Dennett would probably adopt the same left-of-centre liberal democratic stance in practical political decisions; as for the political conclusions to be drawn from their thought, the difference between their positions is negligible. On the other hand, already our immediate intuition tells us that a philosopher like Heidegger on the one hand, or Badiou on the other, would definitely adopt a different stance. Rorty, who made this perspicacious obervation, concludes from it that philosophical differences do not involve, generate or rely on political differences – politically, they do not really matter. What, however, if philosophical differences *do* matter politically, and if, as a consequence, this *political* congruence between philosophers tells us something crucial about their pertinent *philosophical* stance? What if, in spite of the great passionate public debates between deconstructionists, pragmatists, Habermasians and cognitivists, they none the less share a series of philosophical premises – what if there is an unacknowledged proximity between them? And what if the task today is precisely to break with this terrain of shared premises?

Notes

1. More precisely, the idea, already present in her first book, *Subjects of Desire* (New York: Columbia University Press 1987), of connecting the notion of reflexivity at work in psychoanalysis (the reversal of the regulation of desire into the desire for regulation, etc.) with the reflexivity at work in German Idealism, especially in Hegel.

2. To begin with, one would have to question (or 'deconstruct') the series of preferences accepted by today's deconstructionism as the indisputable background for its endeavour: the preference of difference over sameness, for historical change over order, for openness over closure, for vital dynamics over rigid schemes, for temporal finitude over eternity. . . . For me, these preferences are by no means self-evident.

3. See Slavoj Žižek, *The Ticklish Subject: The Absent Centre of Political Ontology*, London and New York: Verso 1999, especially chs 4 and 5.

4. It is worth mentioning here that the first to formulate the problematic which underlies this notion of hegemony (a One which, within the series of elements, holds the place of the impossible Zero, etc.) was Jacques-Alain Miller, in his 'Suture', intervention at Jacques Lacan's seminar on 24 February 1965, first published in *Cahiers pour l'analyse* 1 (1966): 37–49.

5. Ernesto Laclau, 'The Politics of Rhetoric', intervention at the conference 'Culture and Materiality', University of California, Davis, 23–25 April 1998 (forthcoming 2000).

6. This shift is analogous to the series of shifts that characterize the emergence of modern society as *reflexive* society: we are no longer directly 'born into' our way of life; rather, we have a 'profession', we play certain 'social roles' (all these terms denote an irreducible contingency, the gap between the abstract human subject and its particular way of life); in art, we no longer directly identify certain artistic rules as 'natural',

we become aware of a multitude of historically conditioned 'artistic styles' between which we are free to choose.

7. Let me take Francis Fukuyama's half-forgotten thesis about the End of History with the advent of the global liberal democratic order. The obvious choice seems to be: either one accepts the allegedly Hegelian thesis of the End of History, of the finally found rational form of social life, or one emphasizes that struggles and historical contingency go on, that we are far from any End of History. . . . My point is that neither of the two options is truly Hegelian. One should, of course, reject the naive notion of the End of History in the sense of achieved reconciliation, of the battle already won in principle; however, with today's global capitalist liberal democratic order, with this regime of 'global reflexivity', we *have* reached a qualitative break with all history hitherto; history in a way, *did* reach its end; in a way we actually *do* live in a post-historical society. Such globalized historicism and contingency are the definitive indices of this 'end of history'. So, in a way, we should really say that today, although history is not at its end, the very notion of 'historicity' functions in a different way from before.

8. The opposite case is even more crucial and fateful for the history of Marxist politics: not when the proletariat takes over the (democratic) task left unaccomplished by the 'preceding' class, the bourgeoisie, but when the very revolutionary task of the proletariat itself is taken over by some 'preceding' class – say, by the *peasants* as the very opposite of the proletariat, as the 'substantial' class *par excellence*, as in revolutions from China to Cambodia.

9. Is it not, then, that in today's opposition between the dominant forms of the political Right and Left, what we actually have is what Marco Revelli called 'the two Rights': that the opposition is actually the one between the 'populist' Right (which calls itself 'Right') and the 'technocratic' Right (which calls itself the 'New Left')? The irony is that today, because of its populism, the Right is much closer to articulating the actual ideological stance of (whatever remains of) the traditional working class.

10. Wendy Brown, *States of Injury*, Princeton, NJ: Princeton University Press 1995, p. 60.

11. Ibid., p. 61.

12. Karl Marx, *Grundrisse*, Harmondsworth: Penguin 1972, p. 99.

13. On a more general level – and well beyond the scope of this essay – one should again today make thematic the status of *(material) production* as opposed to participation in symbolic exchange (it is the merit of Fredric Jameson that he insists on this point again and again). For two philosophers as different as Heidegger and Badiou, material production is not the site of 'authentic' Truth-Event (as are politics, philosophy, art...); deconstructionists usually start with the statement that production is also part of the discursive regime, not outside the domain of symbolic culture – and then go on to ignore it and focus on culture. . . . Is not this 'repression' of production reflected within the sphere of production itself, in the guise of the division between the virtual/symbolic site of 'creative' planning–programming and its execution, its material realization, carried out more and more in Third World sweatshops, from Indonesia or Brazil to China? This division – on the one hand, pure 'frictionless' planning, carried

out on research 'campuses' or in 'abstract' glass-covered corporate high-rises; on the other, the 'invisible' dirty execution, taken into account by the planners mostly in the guise of 'environmental costs', etc. – is more and more radical today – the two sides are often even geographically separated by thousands of miles.

14. On this spectacle of pseudo-production, see Susan Willis, *A Primer for Daily Life*, New York: Routledge 1991, pp. 17–18.

15. Am I not thereby getting close to Richard Rorty's recent attack on 'radical' Cultural Studies elitism (see Richard Rorty, *Achieving Our Country*, Cambridge, MA: Harvard University Press 1998)? The difference none the less is that Rorty seems to advocate the Left's participation in the political process *as it is* in the USA, in the mode of resuscitating the progressive Democratic agenda of the 1950s and early 1960s (getting involved in elections, putting pressure on Congress . . .), not 'doing the impossible', that is, aiming at the transformation of the very basic co-ordinates of social life. As such, Rorty's (political, not philosophical) 'engaged pragmatism' is ultimately the complementary *reverse* of the 'radical' Cultural Studies stance, which abhors actual participation in the political process as an inadmissible compromise: these are two sides of the same deadlock.

16. Brown, *States of Injury*, p. 14.

17. Ibid., p. 60. In a more general way, political 'extremism' or 'excessive radicalism' should always be read as a phenomenon of ideologico-political *displacement*: as an index of its opposite, of a limitation, of a refusal actually to 'go to the end'. What was the Jacobins' recourse to radical 'terror' if not a kind of hysterical acting out bearing witness to their inability to disturb the very fundamentals of economic order (private property, etc.)? And does not the same go even for the so-called 'excesses' of Political Correctness? Do they also not betray the retreat from disturbing the actual (economic, etc.) causes of racism and sexism?

18. An example of this suspension of class is the fact, noticed by Badiou (see Alain Badiou, *L'abrégé du métapolitique*, Paris: Éditions du Seuil 1998, pp. 136–7) that in today's critical and political discourse, the term 'worker' has disappeared from the vocabulary, substituted and/or obliterated by 'immigrants [immigrant workers: Algerians in France, Turks in Germany, Mexicans in the USA]'. In this way, the *class* problematic of workers' exploitation is transformed into the *multiculturalist* problematic of racism, intolerance, etc. – and the multiculturalist liberals' excessive investment in protecting immigrants' ethnic, etc., rights clearly derives its energy from the 'repressed' class dimension.

19. Jacob Torfing, *New Theories of Discourse*, Oxford: Blackwell 1999, p. 36.

20. Ibid., p. 38.

21. Ibid., p. 304.

22. Brown, *States of Injury.*, p. 14.

23. In other words, 'concrete universality' means that every definition is ultimately *circular*, forced to include/repeat the term to be defined among the elements providing its definition. In this precise sense, all great progressive materialist definitions are circular, from Lacan's 'definition' of the signifier ('a signifier is what represents the subject

for the chain of all other signifiers') up to the (implicit) revolutionary definition of man ('man is what is to be crushed, stamped on, mercilessly worked over, in order to produce a new man'). In both cases, we have the tension between the series of 'ordinary' elements ('ordinary' signifiers, 'ordinary' men as the 'material' of history) and the exceptional 'empty' element (the 'unary' Master-Signifier, the socialist 'New Man', which is also at first an empty place to be filled up with positive content through revolutionary turmoil). In an authentic revolution, there is no a priori positive determination of this New Man – that is, a revolution is not legitimized by the positive notion of what Man's essence, 'alienated' in present conditions and to be realized through the revolutionary process, is: the only legitimization of a revolution is negative, a will to break with the Past. So, in both cases, the subject is the 'vanishing mediator' between these two levels, that is, this twisted/curved tautological structure in which a subspecies is included, counted, in the species as its own element, is the very structure of subjectivity. (In the case of 'man', the revolutionary subject – Party – is the 'vanishing mediator' between 'normal' corrupted men and the emerging New Man: it represents the New Man for the series of 'ordinary' man.)

24. As such, concrete universality is linked to the notion of symbolic *reduplicatio*, of the minimal gap between a 'real' feature and its symbolic inscription. Let us take the opposition between a rich man and a poor man: the moment we are dealing with *reduplicatio*, it is no longer enough to say that the species of man can be subdivided into two subspecies, the rich and the poor, those with money and those without it – it is quite meaningful to say that there are also 'rich men without money' and 'poor men with money', that is, people who, in terms of their symbolic status, are identified as 'rich', yet are broke, have lost their fortune; and people who are identified as 'poor' in terms of their symbolic status yet have unexpectedly struck it rich. The species of 'rich men' can be thus subdivided into rich men *with* money and rich men *without* money, that is, the notion of 'rich men' in a way includes itself as its own species. Along the same lines, is it not true that in the patriarchal symbolic universe, 'woman' is not simply one of the two subspecies of humankind, but 'a *man* without a penis'? More precisely, one would have to introduce here the distinction between phallus and penis, because phallus *qua* signifier is precisely the symbolic *reduplicatio* of penis, so that in a way (and this is Lacan's notion of symbolic castration), *the very presence of the penis indicates the absence of the phallus* – man has it (the penis), and is not it (the phallus), while woman who does not have it (the penis), *is* it (the phallus). So, in the male version of castration, the subject *loses, is deprived of, what he never possessed in the first place* (in perfect opposition to *love* which, according to Lacan, means *giving what one does not have*). Perhaps this also shows us the way – one of the ways – to redeem Freud's notion of *Penisneid*: what if this unfortunate 'penis envy' is to be conceived as a *male* category, what if it designates the fact that the penis a man actually has is never *that*, the *phallus*, that it is always deficient with regard to it (and this gap can also express itself in the typical male phantasmic notion that there always is at least one *other* man whose penis 'really is the phallus', who really embodies full potency)?

25. I draw here on Glyn Daly's paper 'Ideology and its Paradoxes' (forthcoming in *The Journal of Political Ideologies*).

26. I elaborated the logic of this 'obscene supplement of power' in detail in Chapter 1 of *The Plague of Fantasies*, London and New York: Verso 1997.

27. I draw here on Peter Pfaller, 'Der Ernst der Arbeit ist vom Spiel gelernt', in *Work and Culture*, Klagenfurt: Ritter Verlag 1998, pp. 29–36.

28. Christa Wolf, *The Quest for Christa T.*, New York: Farrar, Straus & Giroux 1970, p. 55.

29. In a strictly symmetrical way, the Soviet literary critics were right in pointing out that John le Carré's great spy novels – in depicting the Cold War struggle in all its moral ambiguity, with Western agents like Smiley, full of doubts and incertitudes, often horrified at the manipulations they were forced to effect – were much more potent literary legitimizations of Western anti-Communist democracy than vulgar anti-Communist spy thrillers in the mode of Ian Fleming's James Bond series.

30. This is also why *Gender Trouble* is by far Butler's 'greatest hit', and *Hegemony and Socialist Strategy* (co-authored with Chantal Mouffe) Laclau's 'greatest hit': on top of their timely and perspicacious intervention into the theoretical scene, both books were identified with a specific *political* practice, serving as its legitimization and/or inspiration – *Gender Trouble* with the anti-identitarian turn of queer politics towards the practice of performative displacement of the ruling codes (cross-dressing, etc.); *Hegemony* with the 'enchainment' of the series of particular (feminist, anti-racist, ecological . . .) progressive struggles as opposed to the standard leftist domination of the economic struggle. (Judith Butler, *Gender Trouble: Feminism and the Subversion of Identity*, New York: Routledge 1990; Ernesto Laclau and Chantal Mouffe, *Hegemony and Socialist Strategy: Towards a Radical Democratic Politics*, London and New York: Verso 1985.)

31. And, along the same lines, is not the opposition between the impossible actualization of the fullness of Society and the pragmatic solving of partial problems – rather than being a non-historical a priori – also the expression of a precise historical moment of the so-called 'breakdown of large historico-ideological narratives'?

32. This gap that forever separates the Real of an antagonism from (its translation into) a symbolic opposition becomes obvious in a surplus that emerges apropos of every such translation. For example, the moment we translate class antagonism into the opposition of classes *qua* positive, existing social groups (bourgeoisie versus working class), there is always, for structural reasons, a surplus, a third element which does not 'fit' this opposition (*lumpenproletariat*, etc.). And of course, it is the same with sexual difference *qua* real: this, precisely, means that there is always, for structural reasons, a surplus of 'perverse' excesses over 'masculine' and 'feminine' as two opposed symbolic identities. One is even tempted to say that the symbolic/structural articulation of the Real of an antagonism is always a *triad*; today, for example, class antagonism appears, within the edifice of social difference, as the triad of 'upper class' (the managerial, political and intellectual elite), 'middle class', and the non-integrated 'lower class' (immigrant workers, the homeless . . .).

33. At least, if by 'Kantianism' we understand the standard notion of it; there is another Kant to be rediscovered today, the Kant of Lacan – see Alenka Zupančič, *Ethics of the Real. Kant, Lacan*, London and New York: Verso 1999.

34. Claude Lévi-Strauss, 'Do Dual Organizations Exist?', in *Structural Anthropology* (New York: Basic Books 1963), pp. 131–63; the drawings are on pages 133–4.

35. See Rastko Močnik, 'Das "Subjekt, dem unterstellt wird zu glauben" und die Nation als eine Null-Institution', in *Denk-Prozesse nach Althusser*, ed. H. Boke, Hamburg: Argument Verlag 1994.

36. To this misperception correspond two evolutionist notions: the notion that all 'artificial' social *links* gradually develop out of their natural foundation, the direct ethnic or blood relation; and the concomitant notion that all 'artificial' forms of social *division* and exploitation are ultimately grounded in and gradually develop out of their natural foundation, the difference between the sexes.

37. See Judith Butler, *The Psychic Life of Power: Theories in Subjection*, Stanford, CA: Stanford University Press 1997, pp. 120–29. Mladen Dolar's 'Beyond Interpellation' was published in *Qui Parle* 6, no. 2 (Spring–Summer 1993): 73-96. For a Lacanian reading of Althusser similar (and indebted) to Dolar's, see chs 2 and 5 of Slavoj Žižek, *The Sublime Object of Ideology*, London and New York: Verso 1989.

38. Dolar, 'Beyond Interpellation', p. 76.

39. Butler, *The Psychic Life of Power*, p. 127.

40. On Dolar's precise formulation of the relationship between the Lacanian subject and the Cartesian *cogito*, see Mladen Dolar, 'Cogito as the Subject of the Unconscious', in Slavoj Žižek, ed., *Cogito and the Unconscious*, Durham, NC: Duke University Press 1998.

41. The Lacanian 'big Other' does not designate merely the explicit symbolic rules regulating social interaction, but also the intricate cobweb of *unwritten* 'implicit' rules. Suffice it to mention Roger Ebert's *The Little Book of Hollywood Clichés* (London: Virgin 1995), which contains hundreds of stereotypes and obligatory scenes, from the famous 'Fruit Cart' rule (during any chase scene involving a foreign or ethnic locale, a fruit cart will be overturned, and an angry pedlar will run into the middle of the street to shake his fist at the hero's departing vehicle) to more refined cases of the 'Thanks, but No Thanks!' rule (when two people have just had a heart-to-heart conversation, as Person A starts to leave the room, Person B says (tentatively): 'Bob [or whatever A's name is]?' A pauses, turns, and says 'Yes?' B then says: 'Thanks') or of the 'Grocery Bag' rule (whenever a scared, cynical woman who does not want to fall in love again is pursued by a suitor who wants to tear down her wall of loneliness, she will go grocery shopping; the bags will then always break and the fruit and vegetables spill everywhere – either to symbolize the mess her life is in, and/or so that the suitor can help her pick up the pieces of her life, not only her potatoes and apples). This is what the 'big Other' *qua* the symbolic substance of our lives is: this set of unwritten rules which in fact regulate our actions. However, the spectral supplement to the symbolic Law aims at something more radical: at an obscene narrative kernel that has to be 'repressed' in order to remain operative.

42. On this notion, see Chapter 3 of Žižek, *The Plague of Fantasies*.

43. This point was made clearly by Isolde Charim in her intervention 'Dressur und Verneinung' at the colloquium *Der Althusser-Effekt*, Vienna, 17–20 March 1994.

44. Butler, *The Psychic Life of Power*, p. 124.

45. Furthermore, as I have already demonstrated elsewhere (see Chapter 4 of Slavoj Žižek, *Tarrying with the Negative*, Durham, NC: Duke University Press 1993), belief (in an ideological Cause) is also always a reflexive belief, a second-degree belief in the precise sense of minimal 'intersubjectivity': it is never a direct belief, but a belief in belief: when I say 'I still believe in Communism', what I ultimately mean is 'I believe that I am not alone, that the Communist idea is still alive, that there are still people who believe in it'. The notion of belief thus inherently involves the notion of a 'subject supposed to believe', of another subject in whose belief I believe.

46. Butler, *The Psychic Life of Power*, p. 120.

47. Ibid., p. 122.

48. As to this notion of the subject, see Chapter 1 of Žižek, *Tarrying with the Negative*. Incidentally, the most consistent and ingenious defence of Althusser against Dolar's (as well as my) Lacanian criticism was elaborated by Robert Pfaller, for whom the distance experienced towards interpellation is the very form of ideological mis-recognition: this apparent failure of interpellation, its self-relating disavowal – the fact that I, the subject, experience the innermost kernel of my being as something which is not 'merely that' (the materiality of rituals and apparatuses), *is the ultimate proof of its success*: of the fact that the 'effect-of-subject' really took place. And, in so far as the Lacanian term for this innermost kernel of my being is *objet petit a*, it is justifiable to claim that this *objet petit a*, the secret treasure, the *agalma*, is the *sublime object of ideology* – the feeling that there is 'something in me more than myself' which cannot be reduced to any of my external symbolic determinations – that is, to what I am for others. Is this feeling of an unfathomable and inexpressible 'depth' of my personal-ity, this 'inner distance' towards what I am for others, the exemplary form of the *imaginary* distance towards the symbolic apparatus? That is the crucial dimension of the ideological *effet-sujet*: not in my direct identification with the symbolic mandate (such a direct identification is potentially psychotic; it turns me into a 'shallow mechanical doll', not into a 'living person'), but in my experience of the kernel of my Self as something which pre-exists the process of interpellation, as subjectivity *prior* to interpellation. The anti-ideological gesture *par excellence* is therefore the act of 'sub-jective destitution' by means of which I *renounce* the treasure in myself and fully admit my dependence on the externality of symbolic apparatuses – that is to say, fully assume the fact that my very self-experience of a subject who was already there prior to the external process of interpellation is a retroactive misrecognition brought about by the very process of interpellation. See Robert Pfaller, 'Negation and Its Reliabilities', in Žižek, ed., *Cogito and the Unconscious*.

49. As the reader may have noticed, my manipulative strategy in this essay is to play one of my partners against the other – what are friends for, if not to be manipulated in this way? I (implicitly) rely on Butler in my defence of Hegel against Laclau (let us not forget that Butler vindicated even Hegelian Absolute Knowledge, that ultimate *bête noire* of anti-Hegelians: see her brilliant intervention 'Commentary on Joseph Flay's "Hegel, Derrida, and Bataille's Laughter"', in William Desmond, ed., *Hegel and His*

Critics, Albany, NY: SUNY Press 1989, pp. 174–8), and now on Laclau's notion of antagonism in order to defend the Lacanian Real against Butler's criticism.

50. For the Lacanian *cognoscenti*, it is clear that I am referring here to his 'formulas of sexuation': the Real as external is the exception that grounds symbolic universality, while the Real in the strict Lacanian sense – that is, as inherent to the Symbolic – is the elusive, entirely non-substantial point of failure that makes the Symbolic forever 'non-all'. On these 'formulas of sexuation', see Jacques Lacan, *Le Séminaire, livre XX: Encore*, Paris: Éditions du Seuil 1975, chs VI, VII.

51. However, the film turns into social *kitsch* by staging the easy conversion of the small-town community from horror at the fact that the teacher of their children is gay into tolerant solidarity with him – in a mocking imitation of Rancièreian metaphoric universalization, they all proclaim: 'We are gay!'.

52. When the status quo cynics accuse alleged 'revolutionaries' of believing that 'everything is possible', that one can 'change everything', what they really mean is that *nothing at all is really possible*, that we cannot *really* change anything, since we are basically condemned to the world the way it is.

53.
> Many people feel that who they are as egos in the world, whatever imaginary centres they have, would be radically dissolved were they to engage in homo-sexual relations. They would rather die than engage in homosexual relations. For these people homosexuality represents the prospect of the psychotic dis-solution of the subject. (Judith Butler's interview with Peter Osborne, in *A Critical Sense*, ed. Peter Osborne, London: Routledge 1966, p. 120)

54. See Alain Badiou, *L'être et l'événement*, Paris: Éditions du Seuil 1988, p. 25.

55. And is this not strictly analogous to False Memory Syndrome? What is prob-lematic here is not only the fact that 'memories' unearthed through the suggestive help of the all-too-willing therapist are often revealed to be fake and fantasized – the point, rather, is that *even if they are factually true* (that is, even if the child was actually molested by a parent or a close relative), *they are 'false'*, since they allow the subject to assume the neutral position of a passive victim of external injurious circumstances, obliterating the crucial question of his or her *own libidinal investment* in what happened to him or her.

Competing Universalities

Judith Butler

According to the protocol that Ernesto Laclau, Slavoj Žižek, and I accepted prior to writing these sections of the book, we did not know in advance what the first contributions of the other authors would be at the time that we wrote our own. I presumed that Žižek would raise the question of the status of sexual difference, so I decided to dedicate a good portion of this second essay to that topic. But what surprised me about his contribution was its convergence with my own on the problem of formalism, and I think that much of what I have laid out in the first contribution here constitutes something of a reply, *avant la lettre*, to his suggestion that I am perhaps a closet formalist after all. This is made all the more interesting by his suggestion, Hegelian-style, that I am also a historicist. I believe the Lacanian group that writes in Žižekian vein is the only group of scholars who have called me a historicist, and I am delighted by the improbability of this appellation. Things become more difficult to negotiate, however, when I am also labelled a 'deconstructionist'. This is a term that no one who practises deconstructive criticism has ever used, one which turns a variable practice of reading into an ideological identity (note that one does not use the derogatory '*Lacaniste*' to describe someone of Lacanian persuasion). Rather than accept or refuse these various labels – or, indeed, ask whether what they name is really me – I will try to take a different tack in offering a reply to the many interesting points that Žižek raises.[1]

Hegemony's trace

I think that Žižek and I are in agreement on the point that we both make, in different ways, concerning how the exclusion of certain contents from any given version of universality is itself responsible for the production of universality in its empty and formal vein. I take it that we both derive this point from Hegel, and that it is imperative to understand how specific mechanisms of exclusion produce, as it were, the effect of formalism at the level of universality. Indeed, so far our contributions have produced an unwitting comedy of formalisms in which Žižek and I trade the accusation, and Laclau offers a spirited defence of the term. As for my own position, the formalism that characterizes universality, as I argued in my previous piece, is always in some ways marred by a trace or remainder which gives the lie to the formalism itself. I am in partial agreement with Žižek when he writes: 'the ultimate question is: which specific content has to be excluded so that the very *empty form* of universality emerges as the "battlefield" for hegemony?' (SŽ, p. 110). Indeed, I would suggest that there may be yet another set of questions beyond this 'ultimate' one (though probably not itself ultimate): how does the empty form of universality that emerges under such conditions provide evidence for the very exclusions by which it is wrought? In what ways do the incoherences of universality emerge in political discourse to offer a refracted view of what both limits and mobilizes that discourse? What form of political hermeneutics is needed to read such moments in the articulation of formal universality?

Žižek, however, makes another point – shrewdly citing Wendy Brown to this effect – that the battle for hegemony which takes place through the unfolding discourse of universality generally fails to take into account the 'background' of capitalism that makes it possible. Arguing that class has become unspeakable for Laclau, he wonders, with Brown, whether the struggle over the articulation of identity-positions within the political field renaturalizes capitalism as an inadvertent consequence. Indeed, Žižek offers us three different 'levels' of analysis, employing architectonic metaphors to make his point: two furnished by Lacan, and one taken from Marx. The struggle over hegemony takes place against a background of capitalism, and capitalism, understood as a historically specific set of economic relations, is identified as both the condition and occluded background of hegemonic struggle. Similarly, in explaining how Lacan becomes patched into this framework, he tells us:

> One should . . . distinguish between two levels: the hegemonic struggle for which particular content will hegemonize the empty universal notion; and the more fundamental impossibility that renders the Universal empty, and thus a terrain for hegemonic struggle. (SŽ, p. 111)

In explaining this more fundamental level, he remarks that 'every version of historicism relies on a minimal "ahistorical" formal framework defining the terrain within which the open and endless game of contingent inclusions/exclusions, substitutions, renegotiations, displacements, and so on, takes place' (SŽ, p. 111). Implicit to this distinction is the equation of historicism with contingency and with particularity. What is 'historical' are the specific and changeable struggles; what is non-historical is the frame within which they operate. And yet, if hegemony consists in part in challenging the frame to permit intelligible political formations previously foreclosed, and if its futural promise depends precisely on the revisability of that frame, then it makes no sense to safeguard that frame from the realm of the historical. Moreover, if we construe the historical in terms of the contingent and political formations in question, then we restrict the very meaning of the historical to a form of positivism. That the frame of intelligibility has its own historicity requires not only that we rethink the frame as historical, but that we rethink the meaning of history beyond both positivism and teleology, and towards a notion of a politically salient and shifting set of epistemes.

In one of his arguments, then, Žižek suggests paradoxically that neither Laclau nor I historicize the problem of hegemony sufficiently, and that we are closet formalists (even Kantians), by virtue of this failure to thematize capitalism sufficiently as the necessary background for hegemonic struggle. And in a separate argument, he refers to a different sort of background that is elided in my discussion – one which is more fundamental and ahistorical, one that he will subsequently describe as the constitutive lack which, in his terms, is the subject and which, as a lack, conditions the possibility of hegemonic struggle. There are, then, actually three 'levels' to this architectonic, if we take Žižek at his word. And yet, depending on the context in which he is arguing, it appears that two of them are primary conditions for hegemony: the one, historicist, is capitalism; the other, formalist, is the subject as lack. There is no discussion here that gives us an idea of how to understand these two primary conditions in relation to one another: is one more primary than the other? Do they constitute different sorts of primacies? How are we to understand capitalism working in conjunction with the subject as lack to produce something like the co-conditions of hegemonic struggle? I believe it is not enough to distinguish these as 'levels' of analysis, since it is unclear that the subject is not, for instance, from the start, structured by certain general features of capitalism, or that capitalism does not produce certain quandaries for the unconscious and, indeed, the psychic subject more generally. Indeed, if a theory of capital and a theory of the psyche are not to be thought together, what does that imply about the division of intellectual labour that takes place first under the mantle of Lacan and then under the mantle of Marx, shifts brilliantly between the paradigms, announces them all as necessary, but never quite gets around to asking how they might be thought – or rethought – together?

This is not to say that they do not appear together, for sometimes we receive an example from the social world that is said to illustrate a psychic process. But Lacan emerges time and again in Žižek's theory at the limit of the theory of capital. This is seen perhaps most ingeniously in his reading of Althusser and Lacan together in *The Sublime Object of Ideology*.[2] The interpellation of subjects performed by the institutional apparatus of the state works to the extent that an 'excess' is posited that surpasses the social parameters of interpellation itself, a surplus within the field of reality that cannot be directly assimilated into the terms of reality. Here one might understand this excess in various ways: as another effort to sublimate the traumatic, as an effort to set a psychic limit to the field of social reality, or as an effort to indicate, without capturing it, what remains ineffable in the subject, the ineffability of the unconscious which is at once the condition and limit of the subject itself. This seems to be what Žižek is approaching through different means above when he refers to the subject's 'constitutive lack'. His resistance to what he calls 'historicism' consists in refusing any account given by social construction that might render this fundamental lack as an effect of certain social conditions, an effect which is misnamed through metalepsis by those who would understand it as the cause or ground of any and all sociality. So it would also refuse any sort of critical view which maintains that the lack which a certain kind of psychoanalysis understands as 'fundamental' to the subject is, in fact, rendered fundamental and constitutive as a way of obscuring its historically contingent origins.

For the sake of argument, and in order to render this 'debate' perhaps a bit more subtle, let us assume that this last position, which I have described as 'critical', is not precisely my view. But let us also concede that it has important affinities with the view I do hold: one which accepts, with Žižek and Laclau, that psychoanalysis has a crucial role to play in any theory of the subject. As I hope to make clear, I agree with the notion that every subject emerges on the condition of foreclosure, but do not share the conviction that these foreclosures are prior to the social, or explicable through recourse to anachronistic structuralist accounts of kinship. Whereas I believe that the Lacanian view and my own would agree on the point that such foreclosures can be considered 'internal' to the social as its founding moment of exclusion or preemption, the disagreement would emerge over whether either castration or the incest taboo can or ought to operate as the name that designates these various operations.

Žižek proposes that we distinguish between levels of analysis, claiming that one level – one that appears to be closer to the surface, if not superficial – finds contingency and substitutability within a certain historical horizon (here, importantly, history carries at least two meanings: contingency and the enabling horizon within which it appears). He is clearly referring to Laclau and Mouffe's notion of the chain of equivalence, the possibility of new and contingent identity-formations within the contemporary political field, and the capacity of each to make its claims with reference to the others in the service of an expanding democratic field. The other level – which, he claims, is 'more fundamental' – is an 'exclusion/foreclosure that *grounds this very horizon*' (SŽ, p. 108, Žižek's capitalization). He warns both Laclau and me against 'conflat[ing] two levels, the endless political struggle of/for inclusions/exclusions *within* a given field . . . and a more fundamental exclusion which sustains this very field' (SŽ, p. 108). On the one hand, the historical horizon appears to exist on a different level from the more fundamental one, one which pertains to the traumatic lack in or of the subject. On the other hand, it is clear that this second level, the more fundamental one, is tied to the first by being both its ground and its limit. Thus, the second level is not exactly exterior to the first, which means that they cannot, strictly speaking, be conceived as separable 'levels' at all, for the historical horizon surely 'is' its ground, whether or not that ground appears within the horizon that it occasions and 'sustains'.

Elsewhere he cautions against understanding this fundamental level, the level at which the subject's lack is operative, as external to social reality: 'the Lacanian Real is strictly *internal* to the Symbolic' (SŽ, p. 120). And we can see that the relation that Žižek offers by way of the heuristic of 'levels' or 'planes' does not quite hold up, and that topography itself is unsettled by the complex set of claims he wants to make. The topographies Žižek offers as a way of clarifying his position must fall apart if his position is to be rightly understood. But that is perhaps only a marginally interesting point.

This point assumes greater importance, however, as we attempt to rethink the relationship between the psychic and the social. This seems important first of all when we consider the generalized theory that accounts for subject-formation through a traumatic inauguration. This trauma is, strictly speaking, prior to any social and historical reality, and it constitutes the horizon of intelligibility for the subject. This trauma is constitutive of all subjects, even though it will be interpreted retroactively by individual subjects in various ways. This trauma, linked conceptually to the lack, is in turn linked to both the scene of castration and the incest taboo. These are terms that are routed through the structuralist account of kinship, and although they function here to delimit a trauma and a lack which form the constitutive rupture of social reality, they are themselves framed by a very specific theory of sociality, one that understands the symbolic order to establish a social contract of sorts. Thus, when Žižek writes in *Enjoy Your Symptom!*[3] of the lack that inaugurates and defines – negatively – human social reality, he posits a transcultural structure to social reality that presupposes a sociality based in fictive and idealized kinship positions that presume the heterosexual family as constituting the defining social bond for all humans:

> the fundamental insight behind the notions of the Oedipus Complex, incest prohibition, symbolic castration, the advent of the Name of the Father, etc., is that a certain 'sacrificial situation' defines the very status of man *qua* 'parlêtre,' 'being of language' . . . what is the entire psycho-analytic theory of 'socialization,' of the emergence of the subject from the encounter of a presymbolic life substance of 'enjoyment' and the symbolic order, if not the description of a sacrificial situation which, far from being exceptional, is the story of everyone and as such *constitutive*? This constitutive character means that the 'social contract,' the inclusion of the subject in the symbolic community, has the structure of a *forced choice*. . . . (p. 74)

Žižek's discussion seeks to underscore the sacrificial situation that inaugurates subject-formation, and yet in his discussion he posits an equivalence between the symbolic community and the social contract, even as the social contract is appropriately ironized through inclusive quotation marks.[4] On the next page he makes clear the continuing relevance of the Lévi-Straussian schema for his thinking on originary lack: 'women become an object of exchange and distribution only after the "mother thing" is posited as prohibited' (p. 75). The choice, for the – presumptively male – subject, is thus 'le père ou pire' (the father or worse). I do not mean in these pages to take issue with the theory of kinship and the symbolic at work here, although I do so in more general terms in my book on Antigone.[5] I wish only to point out that the very theoretical postulation of the originary trauma presupposes the structuralist theory of kinship and sociality – one which is highly contested by anthropology and sociology alike, and which has diminished relevance for new family formations throughout the globe. Foucault was right to question whether late modern social forms could be defined by systems of kinship, and the anthropologist David Schneider has shown in compelling terms how kinship has been artificially constructed by ethnographers hoping to secure a transcultural understanding of heterosexuality and biological reproduction as the points of reference for kinship organization.[6] Similarly, Pierre Clastres has offered an important set of studies which show the very partial operation of kinship relations in defining the social contract and the social bond – studies which have brought into question the very equivalence of idealized kinship, symbolic community, and social contract that conditions Žižek's theorization of primary lack.[7]

Thus it is not enough to say that a primary rupture inaugurates and destabilizes social reality and the domain of sociality itself, if that rupture can be thought only in terms of a very particular and highly contestable presumption about sociality and the symbolic order.

This problem, as I understand it, is related to the 'quasi-transcendental' status that Žižek attributes to sexual difference. If he is right, then sexual difference, in its most fundamental aspect, is outside the struggle for hegemony even as he claims with great clarity that its traumatic and non-symbolizable status *occasions* the concrete struggles over what its meaning should be. I gather that sexual difference is distinguished from other struggles within hegemony precisely because those other struggles – 'class' and 'nation', for instance – do not simultaneously name a fundamental and traumatic difference *and* a concrete, contingent historical identity. Both 'class' and 'nation' appear within the field of the symbolizable horizon on the occasion of this more fundamental lack, but one would not be tempted, as one is with the example of sexual difference, to call that fundamental lack 'class' or 'nation'. Thus, sexual difference occupies a distinctive position within the chain of signifiers, one that both occasions the chain and is one link in the chain. How are we to think the vacillation between these two meanings, and are they always distinct, given that the transcendental is the ground, and occasions a sustaining condition for what is called the historical?

The doubling of sexual difference

There are surely some feminists who would agree with the primacy given to sexual difference in such a view, but I am not one of them. The formulation casts sexual difference in the first instance as more fundamental than other kinds of differences, and it gives it a structural status, whether transcendental in the garden-variety or 'quasi-' mode, which purports to be significantly different from the concrete formulations it receives within the horizon of historical meaning. When the claim is made that sexual difference at this most fundamental level is merely formal (Shepherdson[8]) or empty (Žižek), we are in the same quandary as we were in with ostensibly formal concepts such as universality: is it fundamentally formal, or does it *become* formal, become available to a formalization on the condition that certain kinds of exclusions are performed which enable that very formalization in its putatively transcendental mode?

This becomes an important consideration when we recognize that the spheres of 'ideality' which Žižek attributes to the symbolic order – the structures that govern symbolizability – are also structural features of the analysis, not contingent norms that have become rarefied as psychic ideals. Sexual difference is, thus, in his view, (1) non-symbolizable; (2) the occasion for contesting interpretations of what it is; (3) symbolizable in ideal terms, where the ideality of the ideal carries with it the original non-symbolizability of sexual difference itself. Here again the disagreement seems inevitable. Do we want to affirm that there is an ideal big Other, or an ideal small other, which is more fundamental than any of its social formulations? Or do we want to question whether any ideality that pertains to sexual difference is ever not constituted by actively reproduced gender norms that pass their ideality off as essential to a pre-social and ineffable sexual difference?

Of course, the reply from even my most progressive Lacanian friends is that I have no need to worry about this unnamable sexual difference that we nevertheless name, since it has no content but is purely formal, forever empty. But here I would refer back to the point made so trenchantly by Hegel against Kantian formalisms: the empty and formal structure is established precisely through the not fully successful sublimation of content as form. It is not adequate to claim that the formal structure of sexual difference is first and foremost without content, but that it comes to be 'filled in' with content by a subsequent and anterior act. That formulation not only sustains a fully external relation between form and content, but works to impede the reading that might show us how certain kinds of formalisms are generated by a process of abstraction that is never fully free from the remainder of the content it refuses. The formal character of this originary, pre-social sexual difference in its ostensible emptiness is *accomplished* precisely through the reification by which a certain idealized and necessary dimorphism takes hold. The trace or remainder which formalism needs to erase, but which is the sign of its foundation in that which is anterior to itself, often operates as the clue to its unravelling. The fact that claims such as 'cultural intelligibility requires sexual difference' or 'there is no culture without sexual difference' circulate within the Lacanian discourse intimates something of the constraining normativity that fuels this transcendental turn, a normativity secured from criticism precisely because it officially announces itself as prior to and untainted by any given social operation of sexual difference. If Žižek can write, as he does: 'the ultimate question is: which specific content has to be excluded so that the very *empty form* of universality emerges as the "battlefield" for hegemony?' (SŽ, p. 110), then he can certainly entertain the question: 'which specific content has to be excluded so that the very *empty form* of sexual difference emerges as a battlefield for hegemony?'

Of course, as with any purely speculative position, one might well ask: who posits the original and final ineffability of sexual difference, and what aims does such a positing achieve? This most unverifiable of concepts is offered as the condition of verifiability itself, and we are faced with a choice between an uncritical theological affirmation or a critical social inquiry: do we accept this description of the fundamental ground of intelligibility, or do we begin to ask what kinds of foreclosures such a positing achieves, and at what expense?

If we were to accept this position, we could argue that sexual difference has a transcendental status even when sexed bodies emerge that do not fit squarely within ideal gender dimorphism. We could nevertheless explain intersexuality by claiming that the ideal is still there, but the bodies in question – contingent, historically formed – do not conform to the ideal, and it is their nonconformity that is the essential relation to the ideal at hand. It would not matter whether sexual difference is instantiated in living, biological bodies, for the ineffability and non-symbolizability of this most hallowed of differences would depend on no instantiation to be true. Or, indeed, we could, in trying to think about transsexuality, follow the pathologizing discourse of Catherine Millot,[9] who insists upon the primacy and persistence of sexual difference in the face of those lives which suffer under that ideality and seek to transform the fixity of that belief. Or take the extraordinarily regressive political claims made by Sylviane Agacinski, Irène Thèry and Françoise Héritier in relation to contemporary French efforts to extend legally sanctioned alliances to non-married individuals.[10] Agacinski notes that precisely because no culture can emerge without the presumption of sexual difference (as its ground and condition and occasion), such legislation must be opposed, because it is at war with the fundamental presuppositions of culture itself. Héritier makes the same argument from the perspective of Lévi-Straussian anthropology, arguing that efforts to counter nature in this regard will produce psychotic consequences.[11] Indeed, this claim was made so successfully that the version of the law that finally won approval in the French National Assembly explicitly denies the rights of gays and lesbians to adopt, fearing that the children produced and raised under such circumstances, counter to nature and culture alike, would be led into psychosis.

Héritier cited the notion of the 'symbolic' that underlies all cultural intelligibility in the work of Lévi-Strauss. And Jacques-Alain Miller also joined in, writing that whereas it is certain that homosexuals should be granted acknowledgement of their relationships, it would not be possible to extend marriage-like legal arrangements to them, for the principle of fidelity for any conjugal pair is secured by the 'the feminine presence', and gay men apparently lack this crucial anchor in their relationships.[12]

One might well argue that these various political positions which make use of the doctrine of sexual difference – some of which are derived from Lévi-Strauss, and some from Lacan – are inappropriate applications of the theory; and that if sexual difference were safeguarded as a truly empty and formal difference, it could not be identified with any of its given social formulations.

But we have seen above how difficult it is, even on the conceptual level, to keep the transcendental and the social apart. For even if the claim is that sexual difference cannot be identified with any of its concrete formulations or, indeed, its 'contents', then it is equally impossible to claim that it is radically extricable from any of them as well. Here we see something of the consequences of the vacillating status of the term. It is supposed to be (quasi-)transcendental, belonging to a 'level' other than the social and symbolizable, yet if it grounds and sustains the historical and social formulations of sexual difference, it is their very condition and part of their very definition. Indeed, it is the non-symbolizable condition of symbolizability, according to those who accept this view.

My point, however, is that to be the transcendental condition of possibility for any given formulation of sexual difference is also to be, precisely, the *sine qua non* of all those formulations, the condition without which they cannot come into intelligibility. The 'quasi-' that precedes the transcendental is meant to ameliorate the harshness of this effect, but it also sidesteps the question: what sense of transcendental is in use here? In the Kantian vein, 'transcendental' can mean: the condition without which nothing can appear. But it can also mean: the regulatory and constitutive conditions of the appearance of any given object. The latter sense is the one in which the condition is not external to the object it occasions, but is its constitutive condition and the principle of its development and appearance. *The transcendental thus offers the criterial conditions that constrain the emergence of the thematizable.* And if this transcendental field is not considered to have a historicity – that is, is not considered to be a shifting episteme which might be altered and revised over time – it is unclear to me what place it can fruitfully have for an account of hegemony that seeks to sustain and promote a more radically democratic formulation of sex and sexual difference.

If sexual difference enjoys this quasi-transcendental status, then all the concrete formulations of sexual difference (second-order forms of sexual difference) not only implicitly refer back to the more originary formulation but are, in their very expression, constrained by this non-thematizable normative condition. Thus, sexual difference in the more originary sense operates as a radically incontestable principle or criterion that establishes intelligibility through foreclosure or, indeed, through pathologization or, indeed, through active political disenfranchisement. As non-thematizable, it is immune from critical examination, yet it is necessary and essential: a truly felicitous instrument of power. If it is a 'condition' of intelligibility, then there will be certain forms that threaten

intelligibility, threaten the possibility of a viable life within the sociohis-
torical world. Sexual difference thus functions not merely as a ground
but as a defining condition that must be instituted and safeguarded
against attempts to undermine it (intersexuality, transsexuality, lesbian
and gay partnership, to name but a few).

Hence it is not merely a poor use of Lacan or of the symbolic order
when intellectuals argue against non-normative sexual practices on the
grounds that they are inimical to the conditions of culture itself.
Precisely because the transcendental does not and cannot keep its separate place as a more fundamental 'level', precisely because sexual
difference as transcendental ground must not only take shape within the
horizon of intelligibility but structure and limit that horizon as well, it
functions actively and normatively to constrain what will and will not
count as an intelligible alternative within culture. Thus, as a transcendental claim, sexual difference should be rigorously opposed by anyone
who wants to guard against a theory that would prescribe in advance
what kinds of sexual arrangements will and will not be permitted in
intelligible culture. The inevitable vacillation between the transcendental and social functioning of the term makes its prescriptive function
inevitable.

Foreclosures

My disagreement with this position is clear, but that does not mean that
I dispute the value of psychoanalysis or, indeed, some forms of Lacanian
reading. It is true that I oppose uses of the Oedipus complex that assume
a bi-gendered parental structure and fail to think critically about the
family. I also oppose ways of thinking about the incest taboo that fail to
consider the concomitant taboo on homosexuality which makes it legible and which, almost invariably, mandates heterosexuality as its
solution. I would even agree that no subject emerges without certain
foreclosures, but would reject the presumption that those constituting
foreclosures, even traumas, have a universal structure that happened to
be described perfectly from the vantage point of Lévi-Strauss or Lacan.
Indeed, the most interesting difference between Žižek and myself is

probably on the status of originary foreclosure. I would suggest that those foreclosures are not secondarily social, but that foreclosure is a way in which variable social prohibitions work. They do not merely prohibit objects once they appear, but they constrain in advance the kinds of objects that can and do appear within the horizon of desire. Precisely because I am committed to a hegemonic transformation of this horizon, I continue to regard this horizon as a historically variable schema or episteme, one that is transformed by the emergence of the non-representable within its terms, one that is compelled to reorientate itself by virtue of the radical challenges to its transcendentality presented by 'impossible' figures at the borders and fissures of its surface.

The value of psychoanalysis is also, clearly, to be found in a consideration of how identification and its failures are crucial to the thinking of hegemony. I believe that Laclau, Žižek and I agree on this point. The salience of psychoanalysis comes into view when we consider how it is that those who are oppressed by certain operations of power also come to be invested in that oppression, and how, in fact, their very self-definition becomes bound up with the terms by which they are regulated, marginalized, or erased from the sphere of cultural life. In some ways, this is the age-old problem of identifying with the oppressor, but it takes a different turn once we consider that identifications may be multiple, that one can identify with various positions within a single scene, and that no identification is reducible to identity (this last being another point on which I believe Žižek, Laclau and I can agree). It is always tricky territory to suggest that one might actually identify with the position of the figure that one opposes because the fear, justifiably, is that the person who seeks to understand the psychic investment in one's own oppression will conclude that oppression is generated in the minds of the oppressed, or that the psyche trumps all other conditions as the cause of one's own oppression. Indeed, sometimes the fear of these last two consequences keeps us from even posing the question of what the attachment might be to oppressive social conditions and, more particularly, oppressive definitions of the subject.

Why any of us stay in situations that are manifestly inimical to our interests, and why our collective interests are so difficult to know – or, indeed, to remember – is not easy to determine. It seems clear, however,

that we will not begin to determine it without the assistance of a psychoanalytic perspective. Clarifying the terms of self-preservation seems
to me crucial for anyone who seeks to galvanize a minority rejection of
the status quo. And like most subjects who set out with purposes in
mind, and find ourselves achieving other aims than those we intend, it
seems imperative to understand the limits on transparent self-understanding, especially when it comes to those identifications by which we
are mobilized and which, frankly, we would rather not avow.
Identification is unstable: it can be an unconscious effort to approximate
an ideal which one consciously loathes, or to repudiate on an unconscious level an identification which one explicitly champions. It can
thereby produce a bind of paralysis for those who cannot, for whatever
reason, interrogate this region of their investments. It can become even
more complicated, however, when the very political flag that one waves
compels an identification and investment that lead one into a situation
of being exploited or domesticated through regulation. For the question
is not simply what an individual can figure out about his or her psyche
and its investments (that would make clinical psychoanalysis into the
endpoint of politics), but to investigate what kinds of identifications are
made possible, are fostered and compelled, within a given political field,
and how certain forms of instability are opened up within that political
field by virtue of the process of identification itself. If the interpellation
of the shiny, new gay citizen requires a desire to be included within the
ranks of the military and to exchange marital vows under the blessing of
the state, then the dissonance opened up by this very interpellation
opens up in turn the possibility of breaking apart the pieces of this suddenly conglomerated identity. It works against the congealment of
identity into a taken-for-granted set of interlocking positions and, by
underscoring the failure of identification, permits for a different sort of
hegemonic formation to emerge. It does this, however, only ideally, for
there is no guarantee that a widespread sense of that dissonance will
take hold and take form as the politicization of gay people in the direction of a more radical agenda.

    In this sense, the very categories that are politically available for iden-
tification restrict in advance the play of hegemony, dissonance and
rearticulation. It is not simply that a psyche invests in its oppression, but

that the very terms that bring the subject into political viability orchestrate the trajectory of identification and become, with luck, the site for a disidentificatory resistance. I believe that this formulation fairly approximates a view that is commonly held by my co-authors here.

In the intersection of Foucault and Freud, I have sought to provide a theory of agency that takes into account the double workings of social power and psychic reality. And this project, partially undertaken in *The Psychic Life of Power*,[13] is motivated by the inadequacy of the Foucauldian theory of the subject to the extent that it relies upon either a behaviourist motion of mechanically reproduced behaviour or a sociological notion of 'internalization' which does not appreciate the instabilities that inhere in identificatory practices.

The fantasy in the norm

In a Foucauldian perspective, one question is whether the very regime of power that seeks to regulate the subject does so by providing a principle of self-definition for the subject. If it does, and subjectivation is bound up with subjection in this way, then it will not do to invoke a notion of the subject as the ground of agency, since the subject is itself produced through operations of power that delimit in advance what the aims and expanse of agency will be. It does not follow from this insight, however, that we are all always-already trapped, and that there is no point of resistance to regulation or to the form of subjection that regulation takes. What it does mean, however, is that we ought not to think that by embracing the subject as a ground of agency, we will have countered the effects of regulatory power. The analysis of psychic life becomes crucial here, because the social norms that work on the subject to produce its desires and restrict its operation do not operate unilaterally. They are not simply imposed and internalized in a given form. Indeed, no norm can operate on a subject without the activation of fantasy and, more specifically, the phantasmatic attachment to ideals that are at once social and psychic. Psychoanalysis enters Foucauldian analysis precisely at the point where one wishes to understand the phantasmatic dimension of social norms. But I would caution against understanding fantasy as something which occurs 'on one level' and social interpellation as something that takes place 'on another level'. These architectonic moves do not answer the question of the interrelation between the two processes or, indeed, how social normativity is not finally thinkable outside the psychic reality which is the instrument and source of its continuing effectivity. Norms are not only embodied, as Bourdieu has argued, but embodiment is itself a mode of interpretation, not always conscious, which subjects normativity itself to an iterable temporality. Norms are not static entities, but incorporated and interpreted features of existence that are sustained by the idealizations furnished by fantasy.

Whereas Žižek insists that at the heart of psychic life one finds a 'traumatic kernel/remainder' which he describes alternately as material and ideal, the materiality to which he refers, however, has nothing to do with material relations. This traumatic kernel is not composed of social relations but functions as a limit-point of sociality, figured according to metaphors of materiality – that is to say, kernels and stains – but neither apparent nor legible outside of these figurations and not, strictly speaking, ideal, since it is not conceptualizable, and functions, indeed, as the limit of conceptualization as well. I wonder whether a Wittgensteinian approach to this question might simplify matters. We can agree that there is a limit to conceptualization and to any given formulation of sociality, and that we encounter this limit at various liminal and spectral moments in experience. But why are we then compelled to give a technical name to this limit, 'the Real', and to make the further claim that the subject is constituted by this foreclosure? The use of the technical nomenclature opens up more problems than it solves. On the one hand, we are to accept that 'the Real' means nothing other than the constitutive limit of the subject; yet on the other hand, why is it that any effort to refer to the constitutive limit of the subject in ways that do not use that nomenclature are considered a failure to understand its proper operation? Are we using the categories to understand the phenomena, or marshalling the phenomena to shore up the categories 'in the name of the Father', if you will? Similarly, we can try to accept the watered-down notion of the symbolic as separable from normative kinship, but why is there all that talk about the place of the Father and the Phallus? One can, through definitional *fiat*, proclaim that the symbolic commits one to no particular notion of kinship or perhaps, more generally, to a fully empty and generalized conception of kinship, but then it is hard to know why the 'positions' in this symbolic always revolve around an idealized notion of heterosexual parenting. Just as Jungians never did supply a satisfactory answer for why the term 'feminine' was used when anyone of any gender could be the bearer of that principle, so Lacanians are hard-pressed to justify the recirculation of patriarchal kin positions as the capitalized 'Law' at the same time as they attempt to define such socially saturated terms in ways that immunize them from all sociality or, worse, render them as the pre-social (quasi-)transcendental condition of sociality as such. The fact that my friends Slavoj and Ernesto claim that the term 'Phallus' can be definitionally separated from phallogocentrism constitutes a neologistic accomplishment before which I am in awe. I fear that their statement rhetorically refutes its own propositional content, but I shall say no more.

Whereas I accept the psychoanalytic postulate, eschewed by some prevalent forms of ego psychology, that the subject comes into being on the basis of foreclosure (Laplanche), I do not understand this foreclosure as the vanishing point of sociality. Although it might be inevitable that individuation requires a foreclosure that produces the unconscious, a remainder, it seems equally inevitable that the unconscious is not pre-social, but *a certain mode in which the unspeakably social endures*. The unconscious is not a psychic reality purified of social content that subsequently constitutes a necessary gap in the domain of conscious, social life. *The unconscious is also an ongoing psychic condition in which norms are registered in both normalizing and non-normalizing ways, the postulated site of their fortification, their undoing and their perversion, the unpredictable trajectory of their appropriation in identifications and disavowals that are not always consciously or deliberately performed*. The foreclosures that found – and destabilize – the subject are articulated through trajectories of power, regulatory ideals which constrain what will and will not be a person, which tend to separate the person from the animal, to distinguish between two sexes, to craft identification in the direction of an 'inevitable' heterosexuality and ideal morphologies of gender, and can also produce the material for tenacious identifications and disavowals in relation to racial, national and class identities that are very often difficult to 'argue' with or against.

Psychoanalysis cannot conduct an analysis of psychic reality that presumes the autonomy of that sphere unless it is willing to naturalize the forms of social power that produce the effect of that autonomy. Power emerges in and as the formation of the subject: to separate the subject-generating function of foreclosure from the realm of productive power is to disavow the way in which social meanings become interpreted as part of the very action of unconscious psychic processes. Moreover, if the ideals of personhood that govern self-definition on preconscious and unconscious levels are themselves produced through foreclosures of various kinds, then the panic, terror, trauma, anger, passion, and desire that emerge in relation to such ideals cannot be understood without reference to their social formulations. This is not to say that social forms of power produce subjects as their simple effects, nor is it to claim that norms are internalized as psychic reality along behaviourist lines. It is to emphasize, however, the way that social norms are variously lived as psychic reality, suggesting that key psychic states such as melancholia or mania, paranoia and fetishism, not only assume specific forms under certain social conditions, but have no underlying essence other than the specific forms they assume. The specificity of the psyche does not imply its autonomy.

The prospect of engaging in sexual relations that might invite social condemnation can be read in any number of ways, but there is no way to dispute the operation of the social norm in the fantasy. Of course, the norm does not always operate in the same way: it may be that the sexual practice is desired precisely because of the opprobrium it promises, and that the opprobrium is sought because it promises, psychically, to restore a lost object, a parental figure, or indeed a figure of the law, and to restore a connection through the scene of punishment (much of melancholia is based upon this self-vanquishing wish). Or it may be that the sexual practice is desired precisely because it acts as a defence against another sort of sexual practice that is feared or disavowed, and that the entire drama of desire and anticipated condemnation operates to deflect from another, more painful psychic consequence. In any of these cases, the norm operates to structure the fantasy, but it is also, as it were, put to use in variable ways by the psyche. Thus, the norm structures the fantasy, but does not determine it; the fantasy makes use of the norm, but does not create it.

If that sexual practice turned out to be, say, anal penetration, and the person who lives a vexed relation to it turns out to be a man in some generic sense, then many questions can emerge: is the fantasy to perform or to receive it, to perform and receive it both at once; is the fantasy also operating as a substitute for another fantasy, one which has an unacceptable aggression at its core, or which involves incestuous desire? What figure does the social norm assume within the fantasy, and is the identification with the desire and with the law both at once, so that it is not easy to say where the 'I' might be simply located within the scenography of the fantasy? And if one finds oneself in a debilitated state in relation to this fantasy, suffering paranoia and shame, unable to emerge in public, interact with others, do we not need an explanation for this kind of suffering that takes into account not only the social power of the norm, but the exacerbation of that social power as it enters into and shapes the psychic life of fantasy? Here it would not be possible to postulate the social norm on one side of the analysis, and the fantasy on the other, for the *modus operandi* of the norm is the fantasy, and the very syntax of the fantasy could not be read without an understanding of the lexicon of the social norm. The norm does not simply enter into the life of sexuality, as if norm and sexuality were separable: the norm is sexualized and sexualizing, and sexuality is itself constituted, though not determined, on its basis. In this sense, the body must enter into the theorization of norm and fantasy, since it is precisely the site where the desire for the norm takes shape, and the norm cultivates desire and fantasy in the service of its own naturalization.

One Lacanian temptation is to claim that the law figured in the fantasy is the Law in some capitalized sense, and that the small appearance indexes the operation of the larger one. This is the moment in which the theory of psychoanalysis becomes a theological project. And although theology has its place, and ought not to be dismissed, it is perhaps important to acknowledge that this is a credo of faith. To the extent that we mime the gestures of genuflection that structure this practice of knowledge, we do perhaps come to believe in them, and our faith becomes an effect of this mimetic practice. We could, with Žižek, claim that a primordial faith preconditions the gestures of genuflection we make, but I would suggest that all that is necessary to start on this theological venture is the desire for theology itself, one that not all of us share. Indeed, what seems more poignant here for psychoanalysis as both theory and clinical practice is to see what transformations social norms undergo as they assume various forms within the psyche, what specific forms of suffering they induce, what clues for relief they also, inadvertently, give.

Or let us consider various forms of self-mutilation that have the apparent aim of marring or even destroying the body of the subject. If the subject is a woman, and she takes responsibility for a seduction that lured her father away from her mother (and her mother away from her), or took her brother away from her sister (and both away from her), then it may be that the mutilation serves as an attempt to annihilate the body which she understands as the source of her guilt and her loss. But it may also be that she does not seek to annihilate the body, but only to scar it, to leave the marks for all to see, and so to communicate a sign, perform the corporeal equivalent to a confessional and a supplication. Yet these marks may not be readable to those for whom they are (ambivalently) intended, and so the body communicates the signs that it also fails to communicate, and the 'symptom' at hand is one of a body dedicated to an illegible confession. If we abstract too quickly from this scene, and decide that there is something about the big Other operating here, something quasi-transcendental or a priori that is generalizable to all subjects, we have found a way to avoid the rather messy psychic and social entanglement that presents itself in this example. The effort to generalize into the a priori conditions of the scene takes a short cut to a kind of universalizing claim that tends to dismiss or devalue the power of social norms as they operate in the scene: the incest taboo, the nuclear family, the operation of guilt in women to thwart the putatively aggressive consequences of their desire, women's bodies as mutilated signs (an unwitting playing out of the Lévi-Straussian identification of women with circulating signs in *The Elementary Structures of Kinship*).

Žižek has in part made his mark in contemporary critical studies by taking Lacan out of the realm of pure theory, showing how Lacan can be understood through popular culture, and how popular culture conversely indexes the theory of Lacan. Žižek's work is full of rich examples from popular culture and various kinds of ideologies and their complicated 'jokes', but these examples serve to illustrate various principles of psychic reality without ever clarifying the relation between the social example and the psychic principle. Although the social examples serve as the occasions for insights into the structures of psychic reality, we are not given to understand whether the social is any more than a lens for understanding a psychic reality that is anterior to itself. The examples function in a mode of allegory that presumes the separability of the illustrative example from the content it seeks to illuminate. Thus, this relation of separation recapitulates the architectonic tropes of two levels that we have seen before. If this kind of separation between the psychic and the social is not appropriately called Cartesian, I would be glad to find another term to describe the dualism at work here.

This extended discussion does not yet make clear the place of psychoanalysis for a broader conception of politics. Žižek has contributed immeasurably to this project by showing us how disidentification operates in ideological interpellation, how the failure of interpellation to capture its object with its defining mark is the very condition for a contest about its meanings, inaugurating a dynamic essential to hegemony itself. It seems clear that any effort to order the subject through a performative capture whereby the subject becomes synonymous with the name it is called is bound to fail. Why it is bound to fail remains an open question. We could say that every subject has a complexity that no single name can capture, and so refute a certain form of nominalism. Or we could say that there is in every subject something that cannot be named, no matter how complicated and variegated the naming process becomes (I believe that this is Žižek's point). Or we could think a bit more closely about the name, in the service of what kind of regulatory apparatus it works, whether it works alone, whether in order to 'work' at all it requires an iteration that introduces the possibility of failure at every interval. It is important to remember, however, that interpellation does not always operate through the name: this silence might be meant for you. And the discursive means by which subjects are ordered fails not only because of an extra-discursive something that resists assimilation into discourse, but because discourse has many more aims and effects than those that are actually intended by its users. As an instrument of non-intentional effects, discourse can produce the possibility of identities that it means to foreclose. Indeed, the articulation of foreclosure is the first moment of its potential undoing, for the articulation can become rearticulated and countered once it is launched into a discursive trajectory, unmoored from the intentions by which it is animated.

In the case of foreclosure, where certain possibilities are ruled out so that cultural intelligibility can be instituted, giving discursive form to the foreclosure can be an inaugurating moment of its destabilization. The unspeakable speaks, or the speakable speaks the unspeakable into silence, but these speech acts are recorded in speech, and speech becomes something else by virtue of having been broken open by the unspeakable. Psychoanalysis enters here to the extent that it insists upon the efficacy of unintended meaning in discourse. And although Foucault failed to see his affinity with psychoanalysis, he clearly understood that the 'inadvertent consequences' produced by discursive practices not fully controlled by intention have disruptive and transformative effects. In this sense, psychoanalysis helps us to understand the contingency and risk intrinsic to political practice – that certain kinds of aims which are deliberately intended can become subverted by other operations of power to effect consequences that we do not endorse (e.g. the feminist anti-pornography movement in the USA saw its cause taken up by right-wing Republicans, to the dismay of – we hope – some of them). Conversely, attacks by one's enemies can paradoxically boost one's position (one hopes), especially when the broader public has no desire to identify with the manifest aggression represented by their tactics. This does not mean that we ought not to delineate goals and devise strategies, and just wait for our foes to shoot themselves in their various feet. Of course, we should devise and justify political plans on a collective basis. But this will not mean that we would be naive in relation to power to think that the institution of goals (the triumphs of the civil rights movement) will not be appropriated by its opponents (California's civil rights initiative) to dismantle those accomplishments (the decimation of affirmative action).

Conditions of possibility for politics – and then some

The possibilities of these reversals and the feared prospect of a full co-optation by existing institutions of power keep many a critical intellectual from engaging in activist politics. The fear is that one will have to accept certain notions which one wants to subject to critical scrutiny. Can one embrace a notion of 'rights' even as the discourse tends to localize and obscure the broader workings of power, even as it often involves accepting certain premises of humanism that a critical perspective would question? Can one accept the very postulate of 'universality', so central to the rhetoric of democratic claims to enfranchisement? The demand for 'inclusion' when the very constitution of the polity ought to be brought into question? Can one call into question the way in which the political field is organized, and have such a questioning accepted as part of the process of self-reflection that is central to a radical democratic enterprise? Conversely, can a critical intellectual use the very terms that she subjects to criticism, accepting the pre-theoretical force of their deployment in contexts where they are urgently needed?

It seems important to be able to move as intellectuals between the kinds of questions that predominate these pages, in which the conditions of possibility for the political are debated, and the struggles that constitute the present life of hegemonic struggle: the development and universalization of various new social movements, the concrete workings of coalitional efforts and, especially, those alliances that tend to cross-cut identitarian politics. It would be a mistake to think that these efforts might be grouped together under a single rubric, understood as 'the particular' or 'the historically contingent', while intellectuals then turn to more fundamental issues that are understood to be clearly marked off from the play of present politics. I am not suggesting that my interlocutors are guilty of such moves. Laclau's work, especially his edited volume *The Making of Political Identities*,[14] takes on this question explicitly. And Žižek has also emerged as one of the central critics of the political situation in the Balkans, more generally, and is engaged, more locally, in the political life of Slovenia in various ways. Moreover, it seems that the very notion of hegemony to which we are all more or

less committed demands a way of thinking about social movements
precisely as they come to make a universalizing claim, precisely when
they emerge within the historical horizon as the promise of democratization itself. But I would caution that establishing the conditions of
possibility for such movements is not the same as engaging with their
internal and overlapping logics, the specific ways in which they appropriate the key terms of democracy, and directing the fate of those
terms as a consequence of that appropriation.

The lesbian and gay movement, which in some quarters has
extended to include a broad range of sexual minorities, has faced a
number of questions regarding its own assimilation to existing norms in
recent years. Whereas some clamoured for inclusion in the US military,
others sought to reformulate a critique of the military and question the
value of being included there. Similarly, whereas throughout some
areas of Europe (especially France and Holland) and the USA some
activists have sought to extend the institution of marriage to non-
heterosexual partners, others have sustained an active critique of the
institution of marriage, questioning whether state recognition of
monogamous partners will in the end delegitimate sexual freedom for
a number of sexual minorities. One might say that the advances that
are sought by mainstream liberal activists (inclusion in the military and
in marriage) are an extension of democracy and a hegemonic advance
to the extent that lesbian and gay people are making the claim to be
treated as equal to other citizens with respect to these obligations and
entitlements, and that the prospect of their inclusion in these institutions is a sign that they are at present carrying the universalizing
promise of hegemony itself. But this would not be a salutary conclusion,
for the enstatement of these questionable rights and obligations for
some lesbians and gays establishes norms of legitimation that work to
remarginalize others and foreclose possibilities for sexual freedom
which have also been long-standing goals of the movement. The naturalization of the military–marriage goal for gay politics also
marginalizes those for whom one or the other of these institutions is
anathema, if not inimical. Indeed, those who oppose both institutions
would find that the way in which they are represented by the
'advance of democracy' is a violation of their most central, political

commitments. So how would we understand the operation of hegemony in this highly conflicted situation?

First of all, it seems clear that the political aim is to mobilize against an identification of marriage or military rights with the universalizing promise of the gay movement, the sign that lesbians and gays are becoming human according to universally accepted postulates. If marriage and the military are to remain contested zones, as they surely should, it will be crucial to maintain a political culture of contestation on these and other parallel issues, such as the legitimacy and legality of public zones of sexual exchange, intergenerational sex, adoption outside marriage, increased research and testing for AIDS, and transgender politics. All of these are debated issues, but where can the debate, the contest, take place? *The New York Times* is quick to announce that lesbians and gays have advanced miraculously since Stonewall, and many of the major entertainment figures who 'come out' with great enthusiasm also communicate that the new day has arrived. The Human Rights Campaign, the most well-endowed gay rights organization, steadfastly stands in a patriotic salute before the flag. Given the overwhelming tendency of liberal political culture to regard the assimilation of lesbians and gays into the existing institutions of marriage and the military as a grand success, how does it become possible to keep an open and politically efficacious conflict of interpretations alive?

This is a different question from asking after the conditions of possibility for hegemony and locating them in the pre-social field of the Real. And it will not do simply to say that all these concrete struggles exemplify something more profound, and that our task is to dwell in that profundity. I raise this question not to counterpose the 'concrete' to 'theory', but to ask: what are the specifically theoretical questions raised by these concrete urgencies? In addition to providing an inquiry into the ideal conditions of possibility for hegemony, we also need to think about its conditions of efficacy, how hegemony becomes realizable under present conditions, and to rethink realizability in ways that resist totalitarian conclusions. The open-endedness that is essential to democratization implies that the universal cannot be finally identified with any particular content, and that this incommensurability (for which we do not need the Real) is crucial to the futural possibilities of democratic contestation.

To ask after the new grounds of realizability is not to ask after the 'end' of politics as a static or teleological conclusion: I presume that the point of hegemony on which we might concur is precisely the ideal of a possibility that exceeds every attempt at a final realization, one which gains its vitality precisely from its non-coincidence with any present reality. What makes this non-coincidence vital is its capacity to open up new fields of possibility and, thus, to instil hope where a sense of fatality is always threatening to close down political thinking altogether.

Particular and universal in the practice of translation

This incommensurability is given an elegant formulation in Laclau's work, where it centres on the logical incompatibility of the particular and the universal, and the uses of the logical impossibility of synthesis that goads the hegemonic process. Laclau accounts for the emergence of the concept of hegemony from two sources in Marx: one which assumes that a particular class will become identified with universal goals, and another which assumes that the incommensurability between a particular class and its universalist aspirations will occasion an open-ended process of democratization. The second formulation guides his discussion of Sorel, Trotsky, Hegel and Gramsci, which concludes with the following set of claims:

> If the hegemonic *universalizing* effects are going to irradiate from a *particular* sector in society, they cannot be reduced to the organization of that particularity around its own interests, which will necessarily be corporative. If the hegemony of a *particular* social sector depends for its success on presenting its own aims as those realizing the *universal* aims of the community, it is clear that this identification is not the simple prolongation of an institutional system of domination but that, on the contrary, all expansion of the latter presupposes the success of that articulation between universality and particularity (i.e. a hegemonic victory). (EL, p. 50)

Although the quotation above is offered as support for the centrality of the intellectual function in providing the necessary 'articulation', I offer it here to raise a different sort of question. It is unclear to me that given social sectors or, indeed, given social movements are necessarily particularistic prior to the moment in which they articulate their own aims as the aims of the general community. Indeed, social movements may well constitute communities that operate with notions of universality which bear only a family resemblance to other discursive articulations of universality. In these cases, the problem is not to render the particular as representative of the universal, but to adjudicate among competing notions of universality.

Of course, if we treat universality as a purely logical category – by which I mean that for which a formal and symbolizable formulation is possible – then there can be no competing versions of universality. Yet Laclau would probably agree that the articulation of universality does change over time and changes, in part, precisely by the kinds of claims that are made under its rubric which have not been understood as part of its purview. Such claims expose the contingent limits of universalization, and make us mindful that no ahistorical concept of the universal will work as a gauge for what does or does not belong within its terms. I agree wholeheartedly with Laclau's account of Gramsci: 'the only universality society can achieve is a hegemonic universality – a universality contaminated by particularity' (EL, p. 51). I would suggest, though – and hope to have shown in my first essay for this volume – that Hegel would wholeheartedly agree with this formulation as well. But if various movements speak in the name of what is universally true for all humans, and not only do not agree on the substantive normative issue of what that good is, but also understand their relation to this postulated universal in semantically dissonant discourses, then it seems that one task for the contemporary intellectual is to find out how to navigate, with a critical notion of translation at hand, among these competing kinds of claims on universalization.

But does it make sense to accept as a heuristic point of departure that the political field ought to be divided among those social sectors which make particular, corporatist claims, and a discourse of universality which stipulates the kinds of claims that will be admitted into the process of democratization? We can see how the notion of 'sovereignty', which operated politically in the most recent Balkan war in a variety of

competing ways, could not be subjected to a single lexicographical definition. To do that would have been to miss the political salience of the
category as it was invoked by Slobodan Milošević, by Noam Chomsky,
by the Italian student movement against NATO. It was not used in the
same way by each of these speakers, and yet it functioned in an impas-
sioned way as the Left split between interventionist and pacifist wings.
Indeed, one might understand some of the conflict to be between an
international consensus that the sovereignty of nations is to be pro-
tected against incursion by foreign powers, and another international
consensus that certain forms of murderous injustice must be countered
by the international community precisely by virtue of certain international obligations, more or less codified, that we bear towards one
another, despite nationality. Both make certain kinds of 'universal'
claims, and there does not appear to be any easy way of adjudicating
between these competing universalisms.

Now I would expect that Laclau might say that what remains important for hegemony is to recognize that these are particular claims about
what universality ought to be, and that these particular claims will make
their bid for the status of a universal. What will be important, then, is
how a consensus can be achieved, and which one, if either, will come to
be identical, in a transient fashion, with the universal itself. Laclau might
also distinguish between the process of universalization that characterizes this very struggle and the contingent versions of universality that are
struggling for conceptual domination within the contemporary political
scene. By reserving the term 'universalization' for the active process by
which this contest proceeds, and 'universality' for specific contenders for
the hegemonic claim, this first term exempts itself from being one of the
contenders, and seems to supply a framework within which all contention takes place. It seems clear, however, that even the open-ended
notion of universalization upon which Laclau, Žižek, and I agree is not
fully compatible with other versions of universalization – which are
found in other forms of Marxist theory, some of which Laclau has outlined for us, and in liberal theory (including Habermas's normative view
of the universalization of the unconstrained speech act in which are to
be found principles of reciprocity which form the ideal consensus
towards which any and all contention is said implicitly to strive). Thus,

even the theoretical effort to name and direct the process of universalization will be subject to contention – which is, of course, no reason not
to propose it and to make it as persuasive as possible to accept.

In Laclau's position, the second view which emphasizes the incommensurability between particular and universal implies that 'universal
emancipation is achieved only through its transient identification with
the aims of a particular social sector . . . a *contingent* universality constitutively requiring political mediation and relations of representation'
(EL, p. 51). This last not only necessitates the role of the intellectual as
the mediating link, but specifies that role as one of logical analysis. We
will return to the status of logical relations in a moment, but first I
would like to consider the particular task of mediation that is required.
If hegemony is to work, the particular must come to represent something other than itself. As Laclau begins to specify this problem of
representation in his essay, he makes a turn away from Marxian analysis towards phenomenology, structuralism and poststructuralism as they,
in consonant fashion, distinguish between the signifier and the signified.
Thus, the arbitrary relation that governs signification is equated with the
contingency upon which hegemony depends. The intellectual effort to
bring this contingency into view, to expose what is necessary as contingent, and to mobilize an insight into the political uses of this
contingency assumes the form of a structural analysis of language itself.
And although some would surely argue that this move sacrifices the
materialist tradition of Marxism to a form of linguistic inquiry, Laclau's
point is to show that this problem of representation has been at the
heart of materialism, of the problem of hegemony, and of the articulation of powerful and persuasive resistance to the reified forms that the
political field assumes.

Much of Laclau's argument here rests on the operative assumption
that given social sectors and political formations that have not yet
demonstrated the universalizing effects of their demands are 'particular'.
The political field is divided from the start, it seems, between those
modes of resistance that are particular and those that successfully make
the claim to universality. Those that make the latter claim do not lose
their status as particular, but they do engage in a certain practice of representational incommensurability whereby the particular comes to *stand*

for the universal without becoming identical with it. Thus the particular, which constitutes only one part or sector of the sociopolitical field, nevertheless comes to represent the universal, which means that the possibility for the principles of equality and justice that define the political field within a nominally democratic context seems now to depend upon the actualization of the goals of the 'particular' sector. It is not the case that the particular now postures as the universal, usurping the universal in its name, but that the universal comes to be regarded as insubstantial unless the claims of the particular are included within its purview.

This description surely fits some of the representational dilemmas of movements of political enfranchisement, but there are some political dilemmas of representation that it cannot fully address. For instance, in those cases where the 'universal' loses its empty status and comes to represent an ethnically restrictive conception of community and citizenship (Israel), or becomes equated with certain organizations of kinship (the nuclear, heterosexual family), or with certain racial identifications, then it is not just in the name of the excluded particulars that politicization occurs, but in the name of a different kind of universality. Indeed, it may be that these alternative visions of universality are embedded in so-called particular political formations of resistance to begin with, and that they are no less universal than those that happen to enjoy hegemonic acceptance. The democratic struggle is thus not primarily one of persuasive synecdoche, whereby the particular comes to stand, compellingly, for the whole. Neither is the problem purely a logical one in which, by definition, the particular is excluded from the universal, and this exclusion becomes the condition for the relation of representation that the particular performs in relation to the universal. For if the 'particular' is actually studied in its particularity, it may be that a certain competing version of universality is intrinsic to the particular movement itself. It may be that feminism, for instance, maintains a view of universality that implies forms of sexual egalitarianism which figure women within a new conception of universalization. Or it may be that struggles for racial equality have within them from the start a conception of universal enfranchisement that is inextricable from a strong conception of multicultural community. Or that struggles against sexual and gender discrimination involve promoting new notions of freedom of assembly or freedom of association that are universal in character even as they, by implication, seek to throw off some of the specific shackles under which sexual minorities live, and could, by extension, question the exclusive lock on legitimacy that conventional family structures maintain.

Thus, the question for such movements will not be how to relate a particular claim to one that is universal, where the universal is figured as anterior to the particular, and where the presumption is that a logical incommensurability governs the relation between the two terms. It may be, rather, one of establishing *practices of translation* among competing notions of universality which, despite any apparent logical incompatibility, may nevertheless belong to an overlapping set of social and political aims. Indeed, it seems to me that one of the tasks of the present Left is precisely to see what basis of commonality there might be among existing movements, but to find such a basis without recourse to transcendental claims. One might argue – and Laclau very possibly would – that whatever set of debates or translative projects emerges among divergent aspects of the Left, they will vie for hegemony under the rubric of an empty signifier, and that the particular and substantive claims about universality will finally take place under yet another rubric of universality, one which is radically empty, irreducible to specific content, signifying nothing other than the ongoing debate over its possible meanings. But is such a notion of universality ever as empty as it is posited to be? Or is there a specific form of universality which lays claim to being 'empty'? To quote Žižek again, in the spirit of Hegel: 'the ultimate question is: which specific content has to be excluded so that the very *empty form* of universality emerges as the "battlefield" for hegemony?' And is it truly empty, or does it carry the trace of the excluded in spectral form as an internal disruption of its own formalism? Laclau himself gives support for this view when he writes in his first contribution to this volume: 'A theory of hegemony is not, in that sense, a neutral description of what is going on in the world, but a description whose very condition of possibility is a normative element governing, from the very beginning, whatever apprehension of "facts" as facts there could be' (EL, p. 80).

Laclau and Mouffe have argued that one task for the Left is to establish a chain of equivalence among competing groups, so that each is, by virtue of its own contingent and incomplete articulation, structurally similar to the other, and this structurally common 'lack' becomes the basis for a recognition of a common constitutive condition. It is not clear to me that each of the competing groups on the Left is primarily structured by the lack which is said to be constitutive of identity, since it is not clear to me that all such groups are organized around the concept of identity. A struggle against racism is not necessarily grounded in an identity-based set of claims, though it may have some of those claims as part of its movement. Similarly, a struggle to end homophobia may not be an identitarian project: it may be one that makes claims based on a wide range of sexual practices, rather than identities. What remains difficult to achieve, however, is a strong coalition among minority communities and political formations that is based in a recognition of an overlapping set of goals. Can a translation be made between the struggle against racism, for instance, and the struggle against homophobia, the struggle against the IMF in Second and Third World economies which involves making greater claims to sovereign self-determination among those disenfranchised and gutted state economies and counter-nationalist movements that seek to distinguish self-determination from violent forms of xenophobia and domestic racism?

There are universal claims intrinsic to these particular movements that need to be articulated in the context of a translative project, but the translation will have to be one in which the terms in question are not simply redescribed by a dominant discourse. For the translation to be in the service of the struggle for hegemony, the dominant discourse will have to alter by virtue of admitting the 'foreign' vocabulary into its lexicon. The universalizing effects of the movement for the sexual enfranchisement of sexual minorities will have to involve a rethinking of universality itself, a sundering of the term into its competing semantic operations and the forms of life that they indicate, and a threading together of those competing terms into an unwieldy movement whose 'unity' will be measured by its capacity to sustain, without domesticating, internal differences that keep its own definition in flux. I do believe that, *contra* Žižek, the kinds of translations that are needed politically involve an active engagement with forms of multiculturalism, and that it would be a mistake to reduce the politics of multiculturalism to the politics of particularity. It is better understood, I believe, as a politics of translation in the service of adjudicating and composing a movement of competing and overlapping universalisms.

The practice of logic, the politics of discourse, and legitimating the liminal

I do not believe that the intellectual can be at a radical distance from such movements, although I am not sure I can return to Gramsci's notion of the 'organic' intellectual, much as I respect the contemporary circulation of that model in the work and in the person of Angela Davis. But I am party to it in this respect: I do not think that the role of the intellectual is to take new social movements as objects of intellectual inquiry, and derive from them the logical features of their claim-making exercises, without actually studying the claims themselves to see whether the logic in question suits the phenomena at hand. When we make claims about the conditions of possibility of such movements, and seek to show that they are all constituted in the same way, and base our claims on the nature of language itself, then we no longer need to take those social movements as our objects, for we can restrict ourselves to the theory of language. This is not to say that theories of language are not important to figuring out the representational dilemmas of new social movements. They manifestly are. But it seems important not to assume that the particular challenges for articulation that govern the Left – its very 'conditions of possibility' – are, of necessity, exactly the same as the more generalized challenge of representation posed by structuralist conditions of signification. We become metacommentators on the conditions of possibility of political life without then bothering to see whether the dilemmas we assume to pertain universally are, in fact, at work in the subject we purport to study. It will not do to claim that this *a priori* must be the case, that it follows from a generalized understanding of language that it is the case, because language, since structuralism, has proved to be a more dynamic and complex phenomenon than

Saussure or Husserl could have thought. So neither the generalized understanding of language nor its relation to the objects for which it supplies (some) conditions of possibilities can be taken for granted.

My difference with Laclau on this matter becomes clear, I believe, when we consider the way in which he defines the 'logical' status of his analysis of social relations: 'We are not, of course, talking about formal logic, or even about a general dialectical logic, but about the notion which is implicit in expressions such as "the logic of kinship", "the logic of the market", and so forth' (EL, p. 76). He proceeds to characterize this use of logic as 'a rarefied system of objects, as a "grammar" or cluster of rules which make some combinations and substitutions possible and exclude others' (EL, p. 76). He follows this discussion with a set of claims establishing this logic as synonymous with 'discourse' and 'the symbolic': 'It is what, in our work [Laclau and Mouffe's], we have called "discourse", which broadly coincides with what in Lacanian theory is called the "symbolic"' (EL, pp. 76–7). Acknowledging, however, that social practices cannot be reduced to expressions of the symbolic, he nevertheless seeks to identify the limit of antagonism with the Lacanian notion of the Real. My impression is that this clustering together of logic, grammar, discourse and symbolic elides several issues in the philosophy of language that have significant bearing on the arguments being made on their basis. It seems problematic, for instance, to identify the logic of a social practice with its grammar, if only because grammars work, as Wittgenstein remarked, to produce a set of use-based meanings that no purely logical analysis can uncover. Indeed, the move from the early to the late Wittgenstein is often understood as the turn away from a logical analysis of language to that of the grammar of use. Similarly, the notion of a grammar is not fully coincident with the notion of discourse developed by Foucault and elaborated in Laclau and Mouffe's *Hegemony and Socialist Strategy*. Even for the Foucault of *The Archaeology of Knowledge*, it is unclear whether 'a discourse' can be referred to as a static unity in the same way as a logic or a grammar can be.[15] Moreover, that text also establishes discourse at a significant distance from both the structuralist account of 'language' and the Lacanian symbolic.

Over and against Saussure, Foucault emphasizes the importance of discontinuity and rupture, and offers a critique of transcendentality (although power is not yet fully integrated into his analysis of discourse). In the conclusion to that work, he offers the figure of a structuralist critic, one who believes that all language can be found to have a single, constitutive condition. The voice he lends to this hypothetical structuralist could easily be adapted to that of a Lacanian who offers the 'Real' as the limit to language as such. That critic remarks that he cannot accept the analysis of discourses 'in their succession without referring them to something like a constituent activity', and argues that all specific discourses take their structure and possibility from a more generalized conception of language, 'the language [*langue*] of our knowledge, that language which we are using here and now, the structural discourse itself that enables us to analyse so many other languages [*langages*], that language . . . we regard as irreducible' (p. 201). In defending himself against the accusation that he forsakes the transcendentality of discourse, Foucault serenely accepts the charge:

> You are quite right: I misunderstood the transcendence in discourse. . . . If I suspended all reference to the speaking subject, it was not to discover laws of construction or forms that could be applied in the same way by all speaking subjects, nor was it to give voice to the great universal discourse that is common to all men [*sic*] at a particular period. On the contrary, my aim was to show what the differences consisted of, how it was possible for men, within the same discursive practice, to speak of different objects . . . I wanted . . . to define the positions and functions that the subject could occupy in the diversity of discourse. (p. 200)

Accordingly, the historicity and discontinuity of 'structure' produces the complex semantic field of the political. There is no recourse to a universal language, but neither is there recourse to a single structure or a single lack that underscores all discursive formations. Our exile in heterogeneity is, in this sense, irreversible.

In concluding, then, I would like briefly to address the question, posed by Laclau, whether 'the contingent dimension of politics [can] be thought within a Hegelian mould' (EL, p. 64). I will then turn to the practice of performative contradiction to suggest not only how performativity has been retheorized at some distance from the problem of parody, but also how performativity might be thought against the assimilationist drift in the discourse of universality.

Laclau is clearly right to insist that Hegel referred politics to the state, whereas Gramsci identified the sphere of civil society as most crucial to the process of hegemonic rearticulations. But what Laclau does not consider is the way a theory of cultural intelligibility can be derived from Hegel quite apart from his explicit theory of the state. The sphere of '*Sittlichkeit*' that is formulated in both *The Phenomenology of Spirit* and *The Philosophy of Right* designates the shared set of norms, conventions and values that constitute the cultural horizon in which the subject emerges into self-consciousness – that is, a cultural realm which both constitutes and mediates the subject's relation to itself. I would suggest that this theory offers a separate 'centre of gravity' for Hegel's social analysis, implying as it does that a changeable set of norms constitutes not only the conditions of the subject's self-constitution, but for any and all con- ceptions of personhood according to which the subject comes to understand him- or herself. These norms do not take any 'necessary' forms, for they not only succeed each other in time, but regularly come into crisis encounters which compel their rearticulation. If the thinking of contingency is to take place in relation to Hegel, it would have to be in the context of this theory of *Sittlichkeit*. The fact that there are various forms of recognition, and that the very possibility for recognition is con- ditioned by the existence of a facilitating norm, is a contingent and promising feature of social life, one that struggles for legitimation cannot do without.

Moreover, although Laclau insists on Hegel's panlogicism, it is unclear what he means by this or, indeed, what follows from it. The *Phenomenology*, for instance, operates according to a temporality that is irreducible to teleology. The closure of that text is not the realization of the State or the manifestation of the Idea in history. It is, significantly, a reflection upon the very possibility of beginning, and a gesture towards a conception of infinity which is without beginning or end and, hence, at a crucial distance from teleology. Indeed, the problem of naming that the *Phenomenology* demonstrates is not far from the problem of the name as it emerges in the context of discussions of hegemony. The subject of that text emerges under one name (consciousness, self-consciousness, Spirit, Reason), only to discover that its name must be sacrificed in order to take more fully into account the conditions of its own emergence. It is never clear what final form those conditions must take, and this means that the dynamic process of its own temporalization never achieves closure. Žižek also refuses the reading of Hegel that would assume that all temporalization in his work is in the service of teleological closure. Following the tradition of criticism established by Kojève, he reads Hegel as introducing a problem of time that is fundamentally concerned with the retroactive constitution of the object, the moment in which the object which first appears turns out to have its opposite as its essence, and so becomes subject to an inversion on the condition of a retroactive constitution of its 'truth'. Whereas I appreciate this emphasis in Žižek, I am also compelled to caution against a certain resolution of the Hegelian problematic in an aporia. One thinks one is opposing Fascism, only to find that the identificatory source of one's own opposition is Fascism itself, and that Fascism depends essentially on the kind of resistance one offers. Something comes to light in such examples that makes us mindful of a certain dialectical dependency which prevails between terms of dominance and resistance, but is this illumination of dialectical inversion sufficient? And is it sufficient for a theory of hegemony?

Is it not necessary to make a further Hegelian suggestion: that the configuration within which dominance and resistance collapse into one another needs to be revamped along lines which not only take into account the limitations of the former configuration, but produce a more expansive and more self-critical politics? Can the term 'resistance' be renewed in another form that exceeds the instrumental uses to which Fascism has subjected its predecessors? Can there be a more active subversion of Fascism that remains more difficult to assimilate to the aims of Fascism itself? Central to the possibility of moving beyond the aporetic structure of dialectical inversion is the recognition that historical conditions produce certain forms of binary oppositions. Under what conditions, therefore, does the political field appear (to some) to be structured through the incommensurability of particular and universal? Surely this was the kind of question Marx could have asked, but it is also part of the Hegelian inheritance that he did not repudiate. Similarly, under what conditions does the hegemonic field become ordered according to a different set of principles? Or, more specifically, why does resistance appear in a form that is so easily co-opted by the opposition? What condition would have to be in place before we might be able to think resistance outside of this aporetic bind? Moving towards such a new configuration of resistance is like coming up with a new name to designate the situation in which resistance is reorganized on the basis of its prior failings. There is no guarantee that resistance will work this time, but there is a new configuration organized and sustained by the new name or the old name in reinscription, which not only takes account of its own historicity, but moves forward to a wager on a more effective strategy. The future that the Hegelian operation opens up has no guarantee of necessary success, but it is a future, an open one, related to the infinity that preoccupies Hegel's non-teleological reflections on time, and which surely has some resonance with the open-ended futurity of hegemony on which both my interlocutors here also depend.

In Hegel, the field in which oppositions turn out to have presupposed each other is one that is led into crisis when the practice of nomination becomes so profoundly equivocal that nothing and everything is meant by the name. It is unclear what is resistance, what is Fascism, and the understanding of this equivocation precipitates a crisis of sorts, one which calls for a new organization of the political field itself. This can be called a crisis or a passage of unknowingness, or it can be understood as precisely the kind of collapse that gives rise either to a new nomenclature or to a radical reinscription of the old. The risk here is that the dialectic can work to extend the very terms of dominance to include every aspect of opposition. This is the trope of the monolithic and carnivorous Hegel whose 'Spirit' incorporates every difference into identity. But there is an inverse operation – one which is less well noted in Hegel, but which has its own insurrectionary possibilities. This is the scenario in which the dominant terms come into epistemic crisis, no longer know how to signify and what to include, and where the opposition brings to paralysis the incorporative movement of dominance, laying the ground for the possibility of a new social and political formation. Although it does turn out in *The Philosophy of Right*, for instance, that the national state conditions every other sector of society, including '*die sittliche Welt*', it is equally the case that the legal apparatus of the state gains it efficacy and legitimacy only through being grounded in an extra-legal network of cultural values and norms. The dependency works both ways, and the question that I would like to pursue in closing my contribution is: how can the dependency of the legal dimension of the state on cultural form be mobilized to counter the hegemony of the state itself?

One of the pressing instances of this problem is to be found in the current Euro–American debate on same-sex legal alliances or marriages. It is important to counter the homophobic arguments marshalled against these proposals, and I have indicated above how these arguments work in the French context to deny important legal entitlements to lesbian and gay people. But the most pressing question is whether this ought to be the primary goal of the lesbian and gay movement at the present time, and whether it constitutes a radical step towards greater democratization or an assimilationist politics that mitigates against the movement's claim to be working in the direction of substantive social justice. In the bid to gain rights to marry, the mainstream gay political movement has asked that an existing institution open its doors to same-sex partners, that marriage no longer be restricted to heterosexuals. It has further argued that this move will make the institution of marriage more egalitarian, extending basic rights to more citizens, overcoming arbitrary limits to the process by which such rights are universalized. We might be tempted to applaud, and think that this represents something of the radically universalizing effects of a particular movement. But consider the fact that a critique of this strategy claims that the petition to gain entry into the institution of marriage (or the military) extends the power of the very institution and, in extending that power, exacerbates the distinction between those forms of intimate alliance that are legitimated by the state, and those that are not. This critique further claims that certain kinds of rights and benefits are secured only through establishing marital status, such as the right to adopt (in France, in certain parts of the USA) or the entitlement to a partner's health benefits, or the right to receive inheritance from another individual, or indeed the right to executive medical decision-making or the right to receive the body of one's dead lover from the hospital. These are only some of the legal consequences of marital status; there are, of course, several other kinds of legitimation that are cultural and economic; and the tax code also stipulates some ways in which profitability can be secured more easily through establishing marital status, including the ability to claim dependants in the US. Thus the successful bid to gain access to marriage effectively strengthens marital status as a state-sanctioned condition for the exercise of certain kinds of rights and entitlements; it strengthens the hand of the state in the regulation of human sexual behaviour; and it emboldens the distinction between legitimate and illegitimate forms of partnership and kinship. Moreover, it seeks to reprivatize sexuality, removing it from the public sphere and from the market, domains where its politicization has been very intense.[16]

Thus the bid to gain access to certain kinds of rights and entitlements that are secured by marriage by petitioning for entrance into the institution does not consider the alternative: to ask for a delinking of precisely those rights and entitlements from the institution of marriage itself. We might ask: what form of identification mobilizes the bid for marriage, and what form mobilizes its opposition, and are they radically distinct? In the first case, lesbian and gay people see the opportunity for an identification with the institution of marriage and so, by extension, common community with straight people who inhabit that institution. And with whom do they break alliance? They break alliance with people who are on their own without sexual relationships, single mothers or single fathers, people who have undergone divorce, people who are in relationships that are not marital in kind or in status, other lesbian, gay, and transgender people whose sexual relations are multiple (which does not mean unsafe), whose lives are not monogamous, whose sexuality and desire do not have the conjugal home as their (primary) venue, whose lives are considered less real or less legitimate, who inhabit the more shadowy regions of social reality. The lesbian/gay alliance with these people – and with this condition – is broken by the petition for marriage. Those who seek marriage identify not only with those who have gained the blessing of the state, but with the state itself. Thus the petition not only augments state power, but accepts the state as the necessary venue for democratization itself.

So, the claim to extend the 'right' of marriage to non-heterosexual people may appear at first to be a claim that works to extend existing rights in a more universalizing direction, but to the extent that those universalizing effects are those that emanate from the state legitimation of sexual practice, the claim has the effect of widening the gap between legitimate and illegitimate forms of sexual exchange. Indeed, the only possible route for a radical democratization of legitimating effects would be to relieve marriage of its place as the precondition of legal entitlements of various kinds. This kind of move would actively seek to dismantle the dominant term, and to return to non-state-centred forms of alliance that augment the possibility for multiple forms on the level of culture and civil society. Here it should become clear that I am not, in this instance, arguing for a view of political performativity which holds that it is necessary to occupy the dominant norm in order to produce an internal subversion of its terms. Sometimes it is important to refuse its terms, to let the term itself wither, to starve it of its strength. And there is, I believe, a performativity proper to refusal which, in this instance, insists upon the reiteration of sexuality beyond the dominant terms. What is subject to reiteration is not 'marriage' but sexuality, forms of intimate alliance and exchange, the social basis for the state itself. As increasing numbers of children are born outside marriage, as increasing numbers of households fail to replicate the family norm, as extended kinship systems develop to care for the young, the ill and the aging, the social basis for the state turns out to be more complicated and less unitary than the discourse on the family permits. And the hope would be, from the point of view of performativity, that the discourse would eventually reveal its limited descriptive reach, avowed only as one practice among many that organize human sexual life.

I have been referring to this political dilemma in terms which suggest that what is most important is to make *certain kinds of claims*, but I have not yet explained what it is to make a claim, what form a claim takes, whether it is always verbal, how it is performed. It would be a mistake to imagine that a political claim must always be articulated in language; certainly, media images make claims that are not readily translatable into verbal speech. And lives make claims in all sorts of ways that are not necessarily verbal. There is a phrase in US politics, which has its equivalents elsewhere, which suggests something about the somatic dimension of the political claim. It is the exhortation: 'Put your body on the line'. The line is usually understood to be the police line, the line over which you may not step without the threat of police violence. But it is also the line of human bodies in the plural which make a chain of sorts and which, collectively, exert the physical force of collective strength. It is not easy, as a writer, to put one's body on the line, for the line is usually the line that is written, the one that bears only an indirect trace of the body that is its condition. The struggle to think hegemony anew is not quite possible, however, without inhabiting precisely that line where the norms of legitimacy, increasingly adjudicated by state apparatuses of various kinds, break down, where liminal social existence emerges in the condition of suspended ontology. Those who should ideally be included within any operation of the universal find themselves not only outside its terms but as the very outside without which the universal could not be formulated, living as the trace, the spectral remainder, which does not have a home in the forward march of the universal. This is not even to live as the particular, for the particular is, at least, constituted within the field of the political. It is to live as the unspeakable and the unspoken for, those who form the blurred human background of something called 'the population'. To make a claim on one's own behalf assumes that one speaks the language in which the claim can be made, and speaks it in such a way that the claim can be heard. This differential among languages, as Gayatri Chakravorty Spivak[17] has argued, is the condition of power that governs the global field of language. Who occupies that line between the speakable and the unspeakable, facilitating a translation there that is not the simple augmentation of the power of the dominant? There is nowhere else to stand, but there is no 'ground' there, only a reminder to keep as one's point of reference the dispossessed and the unspeakable, and to move with caution as one tries to make use of power and discourse in ways that do not renaturalize the political vernacular of the state and its status as the primary instrument of legitimating effects. Another universality emerges from the trace that only borders on political legibility: the subject who has not been given the prerogative to be a subject, whose *modus vivendi* is an imposed catachresis. If the spectrally human is to enter into the hegemonic reformulation of universality, a language between languages will have to be found. This will be no metalanguage, nor will it be the condition from which all languages hail. It will be the labour of transaction and translation which belongs to no single site, but is the movement between languages, and has its final destination in this movement itself. Indeed, the task will be not to assimilate the unspeakable into the domain of speakability in order to house it there, within the existing norms of dominance, but to shatter the confidence of dominance, to show how equivocal its claims to universality are, and, from that equivocation, track the break-up of its regime, an opening towards alternative versions of universality that are wrought from the work of translation itself. Such an opening will not only relieve the state of its privileged status as the primary medium through which the universal is articulated, but re-establish as the conditions of articulation itself the human trace that formalism has left behind, the left that is Left.

Notes

1. This exchange follows upon several published exchanges among the three of us. I offered a critique of Žižek's *The Sublime Object of Ideology* in my book *Bodies that Matter* (New York: Routledge 1993), in a chapter entitled 'Arguing with the Real'. I also published a piece entitled 'Postmarxism and Poststructuralism', *Diacritics* 23.4 (Winter 1993) 3-11, in which I review both Ernesto Laclau's *Emancipation(s)* and Drucilla Cornell's *The Philosophy of the Limit*. Ernesto Laclau and I then published an exchange in a journal called *TRANS*.arts.cultures.media 1.1 (Summer 1995), an online journal which also appeared in paperback form; this last exchange has been republished in *Diacritics* 27.1 (Spring 1997).

2. Slavoj Žižek, *The Sublime Object of Ideology*, London and New York: Verso 1989.

3. Slavoj Žižek, *Enjoy Your Symptom!*, New York and London: Routledge 1992.

4. I take it that the reason 'social contract' is ironized through quotation marks is that, strictly speaking, there is no social contract in the same sense as there is no sexual relation – that is, that the relation is a fantasy conditioned and ruptured by an underlying lack.

5. Judith Butler, *Antigone's Claim: Kinship between Life and Death*, New York: Columbia University Press, forthcoming.

6. David Schneider, *A Critique of the Study of Kinship*, Ann Arbor: University of Michigan Press 1984.

7. See Pierre Clastres, *Society Against the State*, trans. Robert Hurley, New York: Zone Books 1987.

8. Charles Shepherdson, *Vital Signs: Nature, Culture, Psychoanalysis*, New York: Routledge 2000.

9. See Catherine Millot, *Horsexe: Essay on Transsexuality*, trans. Kenneth Hylton, Brooklyn, NY: Autonomedia 1990.

10. See Sylviane Agacinski, 'Questions autour de la filiation', le Forum, *Ex Aequo* (July 1998), an interview on her recent book, *Politique des sexes* (Paris: Éditions du Seuil 1998). There she claims not only explicitly that no 'civil pact of solidarity' ought to be accorded to gay people because their relationships are 'private', not 'social', but that heterosexuality constitutes 'une origine mixte . . . qui est naturelle, est aussi un fondement culturel et symbolique' (p. 24). Irène Thèry has made a similar argument in her numerous public presentations against the PACS in France, a legal effort to accord limited legal rights to non-married couples. See Thèry, *Couple, filiation et parenté aujourd'hui* (Paris: Odile Jacob 1998). Héritier has made perhaps the boldest arguments in favour of the symbolic, arguing that heterosexuality is coextensive with the symbolic order, that no culture can emerge without this particular formation of sexual difference as its foundation, and that the PACS and other such efforts seek to undo the foundations of culture itself.

11. For a more general understanding of her view that sexual difference and heterosexual parenting are essential to all culturally viable forms of kinship, see Françoise Héritier, *Masculin/Féminin: La pensée de la différence* (Paris: Odile Jacob 1996). See also her remarks in 'Aucune société n'admet de parenté homosexuelle', *La Croix* (November 1998). I thank Eric Fassin for guiding me through some of this material.

12. See the response supplied by Miller to Éric Laurent's essay 'Normes nouvelles de "l'homosexualité"', in 'L'inconscient homosexuel', *La Cause freudienne: revue de psychanalyse*, p. 37:

> À mon avis, il existe, chez les homosexuels, des liens affectifs de longue durée qui justifient parfaitement, selon des modalités à étudier, leur reconnaissance juridique, si les sujets le souhaitent. Savoir si cela doit s'appeler mariage ou pas est une autre question. Ces liens ne sont pas exactement du même modèle que les liens affectifs hétérosexuels. En particulier, quand ils unissent deux hommes, on ne trouve pas l'exigence de fidélité érotique, sexuelle, introduite pour le couple hétérosexuel par un certain nombre de facteurs – du côté féminin dans un certain registre, dans un autre registre par les exigences du partenaire masculin. (pp. 12–13)

> In my opinion, there are in homosexual relations long-term emotional ties which perfectly justify, in accordance with juridical clauses to be studied, their legal recognition, if the subjects so desire. Whether this ought to be called marriage or not is another question. These ties are not exactly of the same model as heterosexual emotional ties. In particular, when they unite two men, we do not find the demand for erotic, sexual fidelity that is introduced into the heterosexual couple by a certain number of factors – from the feminine side in a certain register; in another register by the demands of the male partner.

13. Judith Butler, *The Psychic Life of Power: Theories in Subjection*, Stanford, CA: Stanford University Press 1997.

14. Ernesto Laclau, ed., *The Making of Political Identities*, London and New York: Verso 1994.

15. For Foucault's critique of grammar, see Michel Foucault, *The Archaeology of Knowledge & The Discourse on Language*, trans. Alan Sheridan, New York: Pantheon Books 1972, pp. 37–39, 60–68, 200–201.

16. See Michael Warner, 'Normal and Normaller', *GLQ* 5.2 (1999); and Janet Halley, 'Recognition, Rights, Regulation, Normalization', unpublished MS. The politicization of sexuality in the public sphere was evidenced in the Stonewall Riots in New York, for instance, where the rights of gay people to congregate had been violated by the New York City Police Department. Violent police action against sexual minorities continues in several countries, including the USA. In Brazil, in August 1998, military policemen tortured, humiliated and drowned two transvestite sex workers. Mexico reports the death of 125 gay people between April 1995 and May 1998. The International Gay and Lesbian Human Rights Commission keeps an active file on the myriad forms of public violence that continues on an international level against lesbians, gays, and transgendered people. The unionization of prostitutes by Coyote and similar organizations has also been crucial for advocating for safe working conditions for sex workers. Communities of sexual minorities whose relations of sexual exchange take place outside of conjugal or semi-conjugal forms run the more general risk of being pathologized and marginalized as marriage assumes the status of a normative ideal within the gay movement.

17. Gayatri Chakravorty Spivak, 'Can the Subaltern Speak?', in *Marxism and the Interpretation of Culture*, ed. Cary Nelson and Lawrence Grossberg, Urbana: University of Illinois Press 1988.

Structure, History
and the Political

Ernesto Laclau

I am very grateful to Judith Butler and Slavoj Žižek for the detailed analyses of my approach that they have provided in answering our original questionnaire. Although I cannot accept many of their criticisms, they have been extremely useful to me in helping me develop some aspects of my own problematic which had not, perhaps, received sufficient emphasis. I think also that our exchanges – even our disagreements – could be helpful in creating a space to think politics in terms of a theoretical vocabulary which – albeit influential in contemporary thought – has so far been conspicuously absent from political analysis. I will devote the first two parts of this essay to replying to Butler and Žižek's criticisms; in the last section I will concentrate on giving a preliminary answer to the questions with which I closed my first intervention in this exchange.

Reply to Butler

I have already explained why I think Butler's objections to incorporating the Lacanian Real into the explanation of hegemonic logics are not valid. As she expands her argument in her new intervention, however, I will return to this question and present my reply in a more comprehensive manner. Butler's basic question is formulated as follows: 'Is the incompleteness of subject-formation that hegemony requires one in

which the subject-in-process is incomplete precisely because it is constituted through exclusions that are politically salient, not structurally static
or foundational? And if this distinction is wrong-headed, how are we to
think those constituting exclusions that are structural and foundational
together with those we take to be politically salient to the movement of
hegemony? . . . Can the ahistorical recourse to the Lacanian bar be reconciled with the strategic question that hegemony poses, or does it stand
as a quasi-transcendental limitation on all possible subject-formation
and, hence, as fundamentally indifferent to the political field it is said to
condition?' (JB, pp. 12–13).

Throughout her text, Butler establishes a set of oppositions between
what she calls the field of structural limitation, on the one hand, and
what she refers to as the 'social', the 'cultural' or the context-dependent.
It is difficult to comment on these distinctions properly because Butler
never defines what she understands by the 'social' or the 'cultural' –
taking them, rather, as self-evident realities to which she points in a
purely referential way. I think, however, that one can safely say that the
distinction is, roughly, for her, that between an aprioristic quasi-transcendental limit, on the one hand, and a field of purely
context-dependent rules and forms of life, on the other, which are historically contingent and escape the determination by that limit. To this
I would have three objections to make:

1.   Butler never explicitly asks herself a question that her whole text is
crying out for: what are the conditions of context-dependency and historicity as such? Or – to cast the argument in a more transcendental
fashion – how has an object to be constituted in order to be truly context-dependent and historical? If Butler had asked herself this
question – which is finally about the ontological constitution of the historical as such – she would have been confronted with two alternatives
which, I suspect, would have been equally unpalatable to her: either she
would have had to assert that historicity as such is a contingent historical construct – and therefore that there are societies which are not
historical and, as a result, fully transcendentally determined (ergo,
Butler's whole project would become self-contradictory) – or she would
have had to provide some ontology of historicity as such, as a result of

which the transcendental-structural dimension would have had to be reintroduced into her analysis. In practice she does not refrain from doing the latter. Thus, for instance, she asserts: 'no assertion of universality takes place apart from a cultural norm, and, given the array of contesting norms that constitute the international field, no assertion can be made without at once requiring a cultural translation' (JB, p. 35). To this one could object, following Butler's method: is the assertion that 'no assertion of universality takes place apart from a cultural norm' a structural limit or a context-dependent assertion, in which case the possibility emerges of societies in which universality *does arise* apart from any cultural norm? Of course, it would be absurd to reason along these lines, but it is important to determine where the absurdity is located. It is, I think, in the fact that, through a hypostasis, a purely negative condition has been turned into a positive one. If I say that the limits to historical variability are to be found in something which can be *positively* determined, I would have set up a transcendental limit which has an ontic determination of its own. But if I say that a negative limit has been set up – something which prevents any positive limit from being fully constituted – no ontic determination is involved. The only thing it is possible to say at that point is that a formal movement of substitutions will take place, without the formal movement being able to determine the actual contents being substituted. Now, is this not the very condition of radical contextualization and historicity? In that case, however, Butler's context-dependency becomes very close to Lacan's Real – which consists precisely in a traumatic core which resists symbolization, has access to the level of representation only through borrowing ontic contents without necessarily being ascribed to any of them. I would add only that the Lacanian Real has an advantage over Butler's context substitution: that while the latter introduces a plurality of contexts in a purely descriptive or enumerative way, Lacan's Real allows us to go deeper into the logic of context transformation.

This point is crucial for the logic of hegemony. I have just said that the sleight of hand on which Butler's argument is based consists in a hypostasis by which a purely negative condition is turned into a positive one – only at that price can one assert the non-historicity of the structural limit. But we could perhaps retain that hypostasis, albeit playing a different game with it from that in which Butler engages. For it is clear that without some positivization of the negative, without some presence of the Real within symbolization, we would have a purely inert negative condition without any discursive effect – and consequently without any possible historical influence. This positivization of the negative is what I have called the production of tendentially empty signifiers, which is the very condition of politics and political change. They are signifiers with no *necessary* attachment to any precise content, signifiers which simply name the positive reverse of an experience of historical limitation: 'justice', as against a feeling of widespread unfairness; 'order', when people are confronted with generalized social disorganization; 'solidarity' in a situation in which antisocial self-interest prevails, and so on. As these terms evoke the impossible fullness of an existing system – they are names of the unconditioned in an entirely conditioned universe – they can be, at different moments, identified with the social or political aims of various and divergent groups. So we argue that: (a) the limit is a purely negative one – it points to the ultimate impossibility of society's self-constitution; (b) as society attempts to reach a fullness which is ultimately going to be denied it, it generates empty signifiers which function discursively as the names of this absent fullness; (c) as these names, precisely because they are empty, are not *per se* attached to any particularistic social or political aim, a hegemonic struggle takes place to produce what will ultimately prove to be contingent or transient attachments. Although the Lacanian Real was not originally an attempt to think hegemonic displacements, I do not see in it anything which goes against the concept of the latter. And especially, I do not see any validity in Butler's claim that the notion of a structural limit – conceived in this way – militates against the notion of historical variation. It is precisely because there is such a structural limit that historical variation becomes possible.

2.   My second objection is linked to the way in which Butler handles the problem of the relations between the abstract and the concrete. She approaches this question through a lengthy discussion of Hegel into which, despite my interest in the matter, I cannot enter here for reasons of space. So I will concentrate my critique on some of the conclusions

that Butler draws from her Hegelian analysis, simply adding that some of my criticisms apply not only to Butler but also to Hegel himself. There are two main remarks I want to make. The first is related to the way in which Butler conflates in her discussion two entirely different language games: 'to apply a rule' and 'to give an example'. I have already dealt with this question in my first essay, and I now want to expand my remarks.

To apply a rule consists on concentrating in the single instance of application, making an abstraction of all other instances. It is in this sense that, since the rule does not have a super-hard transcendentality, Wittgenstein argued convincingly that the instance of application becomes part of the rule itself. But to give an example is exactly the opposite: it is to present a variety of particular cases as equivalent to each other – this is achievable only by making an abstraction of the individuality of the various instances. In my first essay I gave the example of three sentences – one from a Fascist discourse, the second from a Marxist one, and the third coming from feminism – as examples of the agreement between noun and verb in the sentence. Of course the examples, to some extent, constitute the rule, for if an example could be quoted that violates the rule and is nevertheless accepted as legitimate by the native speakers of that language, we would have to conclude that the rule has been wrongly formulated. But without making an abstraction of the ideological content of the sentences, of the instances of their enunciation, and so on, a grammatical description of a language would be impossible. This is a first objection that I want to present to Butler: that her discourse moves within a concept of context which is too undifferentiated, and does not discriminate enough between different levels of efficacy and structural determination within society.

This leads me to my second critical remark. I have said enough for the reader to realize why I find that assertions such as the following are unwarranted: 'If the subject always meets its limit in the selfsame place, then the subject is fundamentally exterior to the history in which it finds itself: there is no historicity to the subject, its limits, its articulability' (JB, p. 13). If the limit means simply the impossibility of the a priori transcendental constitution of any *positive content*, it is difficult to see how this limit could be something different from the very ontological condition of historicity. And the sentence following the one just quoted does not fare any better: 'Moreover, if we accept the notion that all historical struggle is nothing other than a vain effort to displace a founding limit that is structural in status, do we then commit ourselves to a distinction between the historical and the structural domains that subsequently excludes the historical domain from the understanding of opposition?' (JB, p. 13). I do not understand what 'opposition' means in this statement, but its general trend is clear enough: we are condemned to political impotence if the limits are structural. I think that the conclusion to be drawn is exactly the opposite: if the structural limit is conceived as the impossibility of constitution of any aprioristic essence, we can find the source of some hope and some militancy in the fact that politico-hegemonic articulations can always be changed. The elimination of any structural limit would introduce total nihilism into the argument, for we could not say anything concerning the historicity or non-historicity of present-day power structures.

My difficulty with Butler's position lies in the fact that by identifying the 'abstract' with 'structural aprioristic limitation' she subscribes to a notion of the 'concrete' which (a) lacks any principle of structuration, and is more or less equivalent to indeterminate contingent variation; and (b) closes itself to the possibility that abstraction itself is concretely produced, and is at the source of a variety of historical effects. To give just one example: in criticizing my notion of identity, she writes:

> The notion that all identity is posited in a field of differential relations is clear enough, but if these relations are pre-social, or if they constitute a structural level of differentiation which conditions and structures the social but is distinct from it, we have located the universal in yet another domain: in the structural features of any and all languages. . . . Such an approach separates the formal analysis of language from its cultural and social syntax and semantics. . . . Moreover, if we conceive of universality as an 'empty' place, one that is 'filled' by specific contents, and further understand political meanings to be the contents with which the empty place is filled, then we posed an exteriority of politics to language that seems to undo the very concept of political performativity that Laclau espouses. Why should we conceive of universality as an empty 'place'

which awaits its content in an anterior and subsequent event? Is it empty only because it has already disavowed or suppressed the content from which it emerges, and where is the trace of the disavowed in the formal structure that emerges? (JB, p. 34)

This passage, which is crucial in Butler's critique of my work, could be subdivided into three kinds of statements: (a) those which misrepresent what I am saying; (b) those which omit a vital point of my argument; (c) those which make critical claims that contradict one another. Rather than transforming this classification into a formal principle of exposition, however, I will consider various fragments of Butler's argument, which the reader will find no difficulty in assigning to each of those three categories.

(i)   First, Butler introduces her usual war machines – the 'cultural' and the 'social' – without the slightest attempt at defining their meanings, so it is impossible to understand what she is talking about except through some conjecture. My own guess is that if she is opposing the 'cultural' and the 'social' to something which is on the one hand 'universal' and on the other 'structural', one has to conclude that structural determinations are universal, and that they are incommensurable with social and cultural specificity. From this it is not difficult to conclude that Butler is advocating, from the point of view of theoretical analysis, some sort of sociological nihilism. Taken at face value, her assertions would mean that the use of *any* social category describing forms of structural effectivity would be a betrayal of cultural and social specificity. If that were so, the only game in town would be journalistic descriptivism. Of course, she can say that this was not her intention, and that she wanted only to speak out against essentialist, aprioristic notions of structural determination. In that case, however, she would have to answer two questions: (1) where is her own approach to a more differentiated analysis of levels of structural limitation and determination to be found? (2) where does she find that I have *ever* advocated in my work a theory of ahistorical aprioristic structural determination? On the second point, there can be no answer. The theory of hegemony is a theory about the universalizing effects emerging out of socially and culturally specific contexts. On the first point the answer is more nuanced – in fact, there *could* be an answer if Butler managed to go beyond her rigid opposition structural determination/cultural specificity. Any social theory worth the name tries to isolate forms of structural determination which are context-specific in their variation and relative weight, but tries also, however, to build its concepts in such a way that they make social, and historical comparisons possible. Butler's own approach to society at its best moments – her innovative and insightful approach to performativity, where (and I agree with her) there are several points of coincidence with the theory of hegemony – proceeds in that way. I have only to add, in this respect, that one finds it difficult not to turn Butler's weapons against herself, and ask the insidious question: is performativity an empty place to be variously filled in different contexts, or is it context-dependent, so that there were societies where there were not performative actions?

(ii)   From Butler's passage quoted above, we learn with amazement that language is pre-social. In what sense pre-social? Is it a gift of Heaven? Or a product of biology? With some goodwill, however, we could perhaps argue that Butler does not mean *that* – what she has in mind is that, given the kaleidoscopic rhythm of variation and differentiation she attributes to the social, she finds it difficult to anchor the latter in the more stable structures of language which, up to a certain point, cut across cultural and historical differentiations. In that case, however, she has not fully grasped the meaning of our introduction of linguistic categories into social analysis. In my previous contribution to this exchange, I argued that the formalization of the Saussurean model by the Copenhagen and Prague Schools made possible the cutting of the umbilical cord of linguistic categories with the phonic and conceptual substances and, thus, opened the way to a generalized semiology (a science of the operations of signs in society, which Saussure had advocated but failed to constitute). Thus Barthes, in the 1960s, tried to see how linguistic categories such as the distinctions signifier/signified, syntagm/paradigm, and so on, could operate on the level of other social grammars: the alimentary code, the fashion system, furniture, and so forth. Today, of course, we have moved well beyond Barthes, but the possibility of generalizing the use of linguistic categories to various levels of social organization is as valid as it was in the 1960s. It is in this precise sense that many of us have tried to introduce linguistic and rhetorical devices into the study of politics, devices that we have found more promising and fruitful than the alternative approaches available on the market, such as rational choice, structural functionalism, systems theory, and others.

Now, it is true that this generalization of linguistic categories was made possible by the increasing formalism of linguistic analysis and its detachment from the substances which had been the 'material objects' of classical linguistics. Does this mean, however, as Butler suggests, that this approach 'separates the formal analysis of language from its cultural and social syntax and semantics'? Hardly. To come back for a moment to Barthes: when he is applying linguistic categories to his different semio-logical systems, he is not just taking those categories as formal entities which remain selfsame independently of the context of their operation, but as being contaminated and partially deformed by those contexts. Thus, a category such as the signifier has to be partially changed when we move from language as such to the system of fashion, and so on. This contamination of the abstract by the concrete makes the realm of formal categories more a world of 'family resemblances', in the Wittgensteinian sense, than the self-contained formal universe of Butler. At some point, of course, the family resemblances could become too loose and tenuous, and a change of paradigm could become necessary. Now, it is in this sense that we have asked ourselves whether some formal properties of language – conceived in the broad sense specified above – from which the logic of empty signifiers emerges could help in under-standing some emptying logics which we had detected as central operators in political processes. But it was clear to us that each of the case studies did not mechanically apply a formal rule, but contaminated and partially subverted the latter. None of the thinkers who have intro-duced, in their own particular ways, a structural approach into the study of society – not Barthes, nor Foucault, or Lacan and – (given that it is I who am under fire) certainly not myself – conforms to Butler's caricat-ural formalistic determinism. As for her reference to people who have located the universal 'in the structural features of any and all languages',

I would suggest that Butler would have to travel back in time to the *Grammaire* of Port-Royal to find a remotely relevant example.

3.   Butler's exclusionary dualism between abstract formalism and the 'social' makes her unaware of something which is, however, of capital importance for understanding the constitution and workings of the social itself: the processes by which the movement of the concrete itself constitutes the abstract. (That is, an 'abstract' which is not a formal dimension preceding or separated from the concrete, but something to which the concrete itself 'tends': A concrete abstract, if you like.) And it is in these concrete abstracts, not in any a priori formalistic realm, that we find the locus of the universal.

Let us take a couple of examples. The movement of commodities under capitalism does away with their particular individual characteristics to make them equivalent as bearers of value. Here we have an abstraction which directly structures social relations themselves. The *formal* characteristics of commodities are not imposed upon them by any aprioristic formalism, but emerges out of their *concrete* interaction. Now take another example – the discourse on human rights. In order to assert the rights of people *as* human beings, we have to make an abstraction of differences of race, gender, status, and so on. Here again we have abstractions which produce concrete historical effects in so far as they are incarnated in institutions, codes, practices, and so forth.

What we have called the logic of empty signifiers belongs to this type of concrete abstract or universal. The real question is not, as Butler thinks, whether in an atemporal, pre-social place there is an abstract category 'emptiness' that all societies should fill some way or another, but whether concrete societies, out of movements inherent to their very concreteness, tend to generate signifiers which are tendentially empty. In Italy, during the war of liberation against Nazi occupation, the symbols of Garibaldianism and Mazzinianism functioned as general equivalents – as myths in the Sorelian sense – as a language which universalized itself by becoming the surface of inscription of an increasingly large number of social demands. So in this process of universalization these symbols became increasingly synonymous with liberation, justice, autonomy, and so on. The larger the number of social demands that they inscribed within their field of representation, the more they became empty, because they became less and less able exclusively to represent *particular* interests within society. In the end, they became the signifiers of the absent fullness of society, of what was lacking. As we can see, there is a mutual contamination here between the abstract and the concrete, because: (a) which signifiers will fulfil this function of empty universal representation depends on each social or historical context; (b) the *degree* to which this process of emptying takes place is also contextually dependent (less so in highly institutionalized contexts, more so in contexts of 'organic crises', etc.); (c) the very logic of empty signifiers has a genealogy of its own – although its formal *possibility* can be abstractly determined, its historical actualization depends on conditions that are not derivable from that possibility.

I think that if Butler has been unaware of what I have called the concrete abstract or universal, it is a result of her argument being so rooted in the Hegelian way of conceiving the articulation between the abstract and the concrete, which is one not of *contamination* but of *reconciliation*. I think that the perfect balance attempted by a notion such as *Sittlichkeit* utterly excludes the possibility of hegemonic logics. The assertion that Butler does not take into account the question of the 'concrete abstract' is not, however, entirely correct. This question is, in some way, present in her discourse in what she calls 'cultural translations'. This is the aspect of her approach to which I feel closer, and which makes me think that in the end our political positions are not really so far apart, whatever the differences in our theoretical grounding of them.

'Cultural translation' plays a pivotal role in Butler's analysis. In the first place, it allows her to distance herself from the unified character of the Hegelian *Sittlichkeit*. As she asserts:

> Although Hegel clearly understands customary practice, the ethical order and the nation as simple unities, it does not follow that the universality which crosses cultures or emerges out of culturally heterogeneous nations must therefore transcend culture itself. In fact, if Hegel's notion of universality is to prove good under conditions of hybrid cultures and vacillating national boundaries, it will have to become a universality forged through the work of cultural translation. (JB, p. 20)

I find this most convincing. It means that the universal – or the abstract – should not be discarded in the name of historical specificity, but should itself be considered as a specific historical construct. This coincides, almost term by term, with what I have earlier called the 'concrete abstract'. It is for that reason that, as Butler asserts, 'no notion of universality can rest easily within the notion of a single "culture", since the very concept of universality compels an understanding of culture as a relation of exchange and a task of translation' (JB, pp. 24–5).

In the second place, as Butler clearly shows, the fact that the universal always emerges out of a concrete situation means that the traces of particularism will always contaminate the universal. She mentions the case of universalism as an imperialist ideology, but the same could be said of the universalisms of an opposite sign – those of the oppressed. This contamination will always end in hybrids in which particularism and universalism become indissociable. In Butler's words:

> what emerges is a kind of political claim which . . . is neither exclusively universal nor exclusively particular; where, indeed, the particular interests that inhere in certain cultural formations of universality are exposed, and no universal is freed from its contamination by the particular contexts from which it emerges and in which it travels. (JB, p. 40)

I could hardly agree more. This is exactly what, in my own terminology, means that there is no universality which is not a hegemonic universality.

What, however, about the internal structure of the translating operation? Let me say, to start with, that one of the most puzzling aspects of Butler's summary of my approach is the fact that she has omitted to mention the one concept which, in my terminology, is particularly close to her notion of 'translation': that of 'equivalence'. She even identifies the notion of 'difference' in my work with that of 'exclusion' or 'antagonism', which is clearly incorrect, for in my approach, 'difference' means *positive* identity, while all antagonistic reordering of the political space is linked to the category of equivalence. I have tried to distinguish, in the logics constitutive of the social, two kinds of operation: the logic of difference, which institutes *particular* locations within the social spectrum; and the logic of equivalence, which 'universalizes' a certain particularity on the basis of its substitutability with an indefinite number of other particularities – the distinction broadly corresponds, in linguistics, to that between relations of combination and substitution, or between the syntagmatic and the paradigmatic poles. In a populist discourse, for instance, the social space tends to be dichotomized around two syntagmatic positions and the ensemble of identities weaken their differential characters by establishing between themselves an equivalential relation of substitution, while an institutional discourse multiplies the differential-syntagmatic positions and, as a result, reduces the equivalential movements that are possible within a certain social formation.

Now, I think that the internal structure of what Butler calls 'translation' and what I call 'equivalence' is very close indeed. Translation, for her, means the deterritorialization of a certain content by adding something which, being outside the original context of enunciation, universalizes itself by multiplying the positions of enunciation from which that content derives its meaning. A feminist discourse claiming women's rights in the name of human equality does exactly that. Butler gives two examples from Joan Wallach Scott and Paul Gilroy which are particularly clear in this respect. Well, a relation of equivalence, in the sense that I understand it, performs exactly that role. Equivalence does not mean identity – it is a relation in which the differential character of the equivalential terms is still operating there, giving to equivalence its specific features, as opposed to mere 'equation'. But this also entails that the equivalential moment is there anyway, producing its effect, whose name is *universality*. The only status I am prepared to grant to universality is that of being the precipitate of an equivalential operation, which means that the 'universal' is never an independent entity, but only the set of 'names' corresponding to an always finite and reversible relation between particularities. If I prefer the term 'equivalence' to 'translation', it is because the latter (unless it is taken in its etymological sense of *translatio*) retains the teleological nuance of the possibility of a *total* substitution of one term by another. And although we know all about '*traduttore, traditore*', this is still the recognition of the failure – as inevitable as you like – of what was originally intended. The term 'equivalence' does not imply that ambiguity: it is clear from the very beginning that we are not dealing with an operation which tends to collapse difference into identity.

Anyway, whether translation or equivalence, I think that both Butler and I are aiming at something which is intellectually and politically similar. Despite my critical remarks about what I see as serious misreadings of my texts, I cannot avoid the feeling that we are thinking and fighting on the same terrain. I just want to close this section with two questions addressed to Butler: (1) Is there not a certain contradiction – one which is translated into her reading of my texts – between accepting the notion of a contaminated universality, and incorporating the Hegelian dialectics between abstract and concrete which implies a perfect – non-contaminated – adjustment between abstract and concrete? (2) If the concrete always contaminates the abstract, is it not the case that a particular posing itself as the universal, rather than being a special and extreme case that one can confine to Jacobin Terror, becomes a feature of *any* social life, so that antagonism, as we have always maintained, is an ineradicable feature of the social?

Reply to Žižek

I will deal, in the first place, with a set of specific objections to my work to be found in Žižek's essay; then I will move on to the more general question concerning the alternative 'class struggle versus postmodernism' that his text raises. First, I will deal with three types of objections: (1) those linked with the relationship between the necessary failure in constituting society and Kant's notion of a Regulative Idea; (2) those linked with naturalization as a necessary condition of the Political and the double impossibility inherent in the notion of antagonism; (3) those linked with the possibility of historizing historicism itself.

1.   The first objection can be answered quite easily, and in fact I am rather surprised that Žižek has raised it at all. It is related, on the one hand, to the question of the resignation inherent in the notion of an infinite approach and, on the other, to the partial nature of the problems that one can solve in this process of infinite advance. Žižek asks:

> Does this solution not involve the Kantian logic of the infinite approach
> to the impossible Fullness as a kind of 'regulative Idea'? Does it not
> involve the resigned/cynical stance of 'although we know we will fail, we
> should persist in our search' – of an agent which knows that . . . effort
> will necessarily fail, but which none the less accepts the need for this
> global Spectre as a necessary lure to give it the energy to engage in solv-
> ing partial problems? (SŽ, p. 93)

In the past, Žižek knew better than this. He wrote about my approach,
for instance, in terms of the Kantian notion of 'enthusiastic resignation' – which, as he knows very well, does not include a scintilla of
cynicism. Let us consider the two sides of the argument: unachievable
Regulative Idea, and partial nature of the problems to be solved. The
difference between a Kantian-based approach and mine is that for Kant,
the content of the Regulative Idea is given once and for all, from the
very beginning; while in my view, the object of the cathectic investments itself is constantly changing. So there is no linear accumulative
process by which any cynicism about ultimate unachievable ends could
arise. For historical actors engaged in actual struggles, there is no cynical resignation whatsoever: their actual aims are all that constitute the
horizon within which they live and fight. To say that ultimate fullness is
unachievable is by no means to advocate any attitude of fatalism or resignation; it is to say to people: what you are fighting for is everything
there is; your actual struggle is not limited by any preceding necessity. As
for the partial character of the problems to be solved, we should be careful in distinguishing two aspects: on the one hand, the 'ontic' content of
what is actually solved; on the other, the 'ontological' investment which
is made in bringing that solution about . The partial nature of the problems, in this sense, does not mean taking them one by one, and dealing
with them in an administrative way – as in the Saint-Simonian motto
adopted by Marx: from the government of men to the administration of
things – it means that there is always going to be a gap between the content which at some point incarnates society's aspiration to fullness, and
this fullness as such, which has no content of its own. When people in
Eastern Europe after 1989 were galvanized by the virtues of the market,
or when socialists spoke about the socialization of the means of

production, they were thinking of those transformations not as *partial* ways of solving problems of economic management, but as panaceas to bring about a global human emancipation – in that sense they cathected partial historical achievements with a symbolic significance far transcending them. It is only in this sense – to stress the unbridgeable gap between the differential, concrete partial character of the change brought about, and the wider symbolism and expectations without which hegemony and politics would be inconceivable – that I have spoken about solving 'a variety of partial problems'. As the reader can see, this has little to do with the Regulative Idea – which involves no cathectic investment in the concrete, for the content of fullness is given from the very beginning – or with an administrative management of partial problems – because that can be done without any hegemonic investment being involved in their solution. So – no relation between my politics and the theoreticians of the Third Way, of whom I am as critical as Žižek.

2. Žižek writes:

> this justified rejection [by myself] of the fullness of post-revolutionary Society does *not* justify the conclusion that we have to renounce any project of a global social transformation, and limit ourselves to partial problems to be solved: the jump from a critique of the 'metaphysics of presence' to anti-utopian 'reformist' gradualist politics is an illegitimate short circuit. (SŽ, p. 101)

I agree entirely that this short circuit is illegitimate; the only thing I want to add is that it is only Žižek who is jumping into it. We should establish a basic distinction here: it is one thing to say that social and political demands are discrete, in the sense that each of them does not *necessarily* involve the others (so they would be partial); it is quite another thing to say that they can be politically met only through a gradualist process of dealing with them one by one. If, for instance, a relation of equivalence is established between a plurality of social demands, the satisfaction of *any* of them will depend on the construction of a more global social imaginary, whose effects will be far more systemic than anything that mere gradualism could envisage. 'Gradualism', in fact, is the first of the utopias: the belief that there is a neutral administrative centre which can deal with social issues in a non-political way. If we think of major transformations of our societies in the twentieth century, we see that 'partial' reforms, in all cases, were made possible only through significant alterations in the more global social imaginaries – think of the New Deal, the welfare state, and, in more recent years, the discourses of the 'moral majority' and of neoliberalism; but, I would argue, something not so very different could be said of processes whose effects are certainly more global and systemic, such as the Russian Revolution.

The difficulty with Žižek's position – a point to which I will return later – is that he never clearly defines what he understands by the global approach to politics. He opposes partial solutions within a horizon to changes in the horizon as such. I am not opposed to that formulation, provided that we agree about what a horizon is and about the logic of its constitution. Is it a ground of the social? Is it an imaginary construction totalizing a plurality of discrete struggles? Žižek is not precise enough about these matters, and his reference to an author like the young Lukàcs, the quintessence of class reductionism, does little to dispel possible misunderstandings. I will come back in a moment to these more general matters. At this point I want to explain clearly why I do not share Žižek's view that the Political *can be operative only in so far as it "represses" its radically contingent nature, in so far as it undergoes a minimum of "naturalization"*', and the conclusion that *it is also impossible adequately to represent/articulate this very antagonism/negativity that prevents Society from achieving its full ontological realization* (SŽ, p. 100). I do not disagree either with Žižek's analysis of the role of ideological fantasy or with his conclusion that when 'this very *impossibility* is represented in a positive element, inherent impossibility changed into an external obstacle' (SŽ, p. 100). What I would, however, put into question are two things: (a) that the relationship between impossibility and external object is a purely arbitrary one; (b) that impossibility itself can be represented only through a purely arbitrary projection. On the first point, I would argue that although the gap between an event's ability to bring about the fullness of society and its ability to solve a series of partial problems can never be properly bridged, the latter is not simply the result of an arbitrary choice – as the example of the Jew seems to suggest. Tzarism and the apartheid regime were *actual* obstacles to a plurality of democratic reforms and not just arbitrary targets positivizing an inherent impossibility. The fact that they *also* did the latter is what gave the discourses which overthrew those regimes their dimension of horizon – what brought about, beyond a mere addition of partial reforms, a proper overdetermination between them. But – to put it in psychoanalytic terms – the fact that no drive is necessarily attached to an object does not mean that the object is unimportant, or that its choice is entirely arbitrary.

As for the second point, concerning Žižek's assertion of the need for a minimum of naturalization and the impossibility of representing impossibility as such, my response is qualified. In one sense I entirely agree with him. I have insisted in my work, time and again, that an object which is both impossible and necessary can be revealed only through its representation by something different from itself. If that is all the notion of 'naturalization' involves, I would have no quarrel with it. But I am afraid that, for Žižek, there is something else involved, as his examples of the religious community, the Westerns, and so on, suggest. For in the endless play of substitutions that Žižek is describing, one possibility is omitted: that, instead of the impossibility leading to a series of substitutions which attempt to supersede it, it leads to a symbolization of impossibility *as such* as a positive value. This point is important: although positivization is unavoidable, nothing prevents this positivization from symbolizing impossibility as such, rather than concealing it through the illusion of taking us beyond it. No doubt this operation still retains an element of naturalization, because the very fact of giving a name to something which – like the Pascalian zero – is nameless is creating an entity out of something which is clearly no entity at all; but this minimum of naturalization is different from the one that would be involved in equating 'impossibility' with a *positive differential content*. The possibility of this weakened type of naturalization is important for democratic politics, which involves the institutionalization of its own openness and, in that sense, the injunction to identify with its ultimate impossibility.

3. Žižek asks:

> when Butler speaks of the unending political process of renegotiating the
> inclusions/exclusions of the predominant ideological universal notions,
> or when Laclau proposes his model of the unending struggle for hege-
> mony, *the 'universal' status of this very model is problematic*: are they providing
> the *formal* co-ordinates of *every* ideologico-political process, or are they
> simply elaborating the notional structure of *today's* ('postmodern') *specific*
> political practice which is emerging after the retreat of the classical Left?
> They (more often than not, in their explicit formulations) *appear* to do the
> first. (SŽ, p. 106)

As we see, Žižek's argument is a variation on Butler's about transcendental limits and historicism, although ironically, while Butler's charge
was addressed to Žižek's and my own work, Žižek is formulating the
same objection against Butler and myself. I will refrain from joining the
club and making the same criticism – this time against Butler and Žižek.
Most of my answer can be found in my reply to Butler, but let me say a
couple of things about the specific way in which Žižek's argument is formulated. The first thing to say is that I do not accept his sharp
distinction between a transcendental analytic (under which – quite prob-
lematically – he subsumes the Heideggerian existential structure of
social life) and the description of a definite historical condition.
'Hegemony' as a theoretical framework is both at the same time and,
however, none of them. In a first sense, it is the description of some
processes which are particularly visible in the contemporary world. If it
were *only* that, however, it would require another metatheoretical
framework allowing the description of 'hegemony' as the *differentia speci-
fica* of a certain *genus*. But there is no such metatheoretical framework.
Only in contemporary societies is there a generalization of the hegemonic form of politics, but for this reason we can interrogate the past,
and find there inchoate forms of the same processes that are fully visible
today; and, when they did not occur, understand why things were different. Conversely, these differences make the specificity of the present
more visible. Today, for instance, we have a descriptive category for
some processes as 'distribution of income' – a category which did not

exist in the Ancient World. Would it make sense, therefore, to say that in the Ancient World, income was not distributed? Obviously not. But the distribution took place through mechanisms different from ours in the present – mechanisms that we can, however, describe in terms of our system of categories because we are in full possession of the notion of 'distribution of income', a notion which became fully available only when *alternative* forms of distribution became a historical possibility.

What is important is to break with the false alternative 'ahistorical transcendentalism/radical historicism'. This is a false alternative, because its two terms entail each other, and finally assert exactly the same. If I assert radical historicism, it will require some kind of meta-discourse specifying epochal differences which will necessarily have to be transhistorical. If I assert hard transcendentalism, I will have to accept the contingency of an empirical variation which can be grasped only in historicist terms. Only if I fully accept the contingency and historicity of my system of categories, but renounce any attempt to grasp the meaning of its historical variation conceptually, can I start finding a way out of that blind alley. Obviously this solution does not suppress the duality transcendentalism/historicism, but at least it introduces a certain *souplesse*, and multiplies the language games that it is possible to play within it. There is a name for a knowledge which operates under these conditions: it is *finitude*.

Let us now discuss the more general political points Žižek makes in his intervention in this exchange. His discourse is structured around a sharp opposition that he establishes between class struggle and postmodernism – the first concerning the relations of production and, more generally, capitalism; the second the various forms of the contemporary politics of recognition. In spite of the 'yes, please!' of Žižek's title, he is sharply critical of the second, and of what he thinks is an unwise abandonment of the first. I will organize my answer around two basic theses: the first, that I do not think the two types of struggle are as different as Žižek believes; the second, that Žižek structures his discourse around entities – class, class struggle, capitalism – which are largely fetishes dispossessed of any precise meaning. Before starting, however, I want to state that I share with Žižek a real concern about the present state of

social struggles and, more generally, about the way in which the Left
envisages its responsibilities in the contemporary world. I agree with him
that the spread of issue-orientated politics has been accompanied by the
abandonment of more global strategic perspectives, and that this abandonment involves an unconscious acceptance of the dominant logics of
the system. I think, however, that the solutions he proposes to take the
Left out of its present impasse are fundamentally flawed.

Let us start with the Žižekian opposition between class struggle, and
what Žižek calls postmodern identity politics. Are they *essentially* different? Everything depends on the way we conceive class struggle. Where
is the fundamental antagonism at its root located? In *New Reflections on the
Revolution of Our Time*, I have argued that class antagonism is not inherent to capitalist relations of production, but that it takes place between
those relations and the identity of the worker outside them. Various
aspects must be carefully distinguished. First, we have to distinguish the
contradiction between forces and relations of production – which, I
have maintained, is a contradiction without antagonism – from class
struggle – which is an antagonism without contradiction. So if we concentrate on the latter, where is the antagonism located? Certainly not
within the relations of production. The capitalists extract surplus-value
from the workers, but both capital and labour should be conceived of, as
far as the logic of capitalism is concerned, not as actual people but as
economic categories. So if we are going to maintain that class antagonism is inherent to the relations of production, we would have to prove
that from the abstract categories 'capital' and 'wage labour' we can logically derive the antagonism between both – and such a demonstration
is impossible. It does not logically follow from the fact that the surplus-
value is extracted from the worker that the latter will resist such
extraction. So if there is going to be antagonism, its source cannot be
internal to the capitalist relations of production, but has to be sought in
something that the worker is outside those relations, something which is
threatened by them: the fact that below a certain level of wages the
worker cannot live a decent life, and so on. Now, unless we are confronted with a situation of extreme exploitation, the worker's attitude
vis-à-vis capitalism will depend entirely on how his or her *identity* is constituted – as socialists knew a long time ago, when they were confronted

by reformist tendencies in the trade-union movement. There is nothing in the worker's demands which is *intrinsically* anti-capitalist.

Could we perhaps say that these demands have priority over those of other groups because they are closer to the economy, and thus at the heart of the functioning of the capitalist system? This argument does not fare any better. Marxists have known for a long time that capitalism is a world system, structured as an imperialist chain, so crises at one point in the system create dislocations at many other points. This means that many sectors are threatened by the capitalist logic, and that the resulting antagonisms are not necessarily related to particular locations in the relations of production. As a result, the notion of class struggle is totally insufficient to explain the identity of the agents involved in anti-capitalist struggles. It is simply the remainder of an old-fashioned conception which saw in an assumed general proletarianization of society the emergence of the future burier of capitalism.

The notion of 'combined and uneven development' had already pointed out the emergence of complex, non-orthodox political identities as the agencies of revolutionary change in the contemporary world, and the phenomena of globalization have accentuated this tendency. So my answer to Žižek's dichotomy between class struggle and identity politics is that class struggle is just one species of identity politics, and one which is becoming less and less important in the world in which we live.

What, however, about his critique of multiculturalism, which maintains that the specific demands of different groups can be absorbed one by one by the dominant system and, in this way, help to consolidate it? This is only too true, but does it not happen in exactly the same way with the demands of the workers? In so far as a system is able to absorb the demands of the subordinated groups in a 'transformist' way – to use the Gramscian expression – that system will enjoy good health. The crucial point is that there is no special location within a system which enjoys an a priori privilege in an anti-systemic struggle. I do not think that multicultural struggles *per se* constitute a revolutionary subject, any more than the working class does. But this does not lead me to oppose their demands either. Just as I support trade-union demands in spite of the fact that they can, in principle, be satisfied within capitalism, I support demands of multicultural groups and other issue-orientated groups without thinking that they are announcing the end of capitalist domination. What worries Žižek – and I share his concern – is that the proliferation of particularisms not linked by any more global emancipatory discourse could lead not only to the preservation of the status quo but also to a more pronounced swing to the Right. This is a legitimate preoccupation, but the way to answer it is not to resuscitate an entity – class struggle – which does not have any precise meaning in the contemporary world.

Apart from this global dichotomy, which has little substance, Žižek could be criticized for introducing into his discourse a set of categories which, taken literally, either have no precise meaning, or the little they have goes against what I would have thought is the main tendency of Žižek's thought. Most of these terms come from the Marxist tradition, and Žižek uses them in a rather acritical way. Something in his work that I find rather surprising is the fact that despite his professed Marxism, he pays no attention whatsoever to the intellectual history of Marxism, in which several of the categories he uses have been refined, displaced, or – to encapsulate it in one term – deconstructed. All Žižek's Marxist concepts, examples and discussions come either from the texts of Marx himself, or from the Russian Revolution. There is no reference to Gramsci, virtually none to Trotsky, and as far as I know not a single reference to Austro-Marxism, where many of the issues which are attracting the attention of contemporary socialism were discussed for the first time. Let me give a few examples.

Ideology

Žižek writes:

> the ruling ideology, in order to be operative, has to incorporate a series of features in which the exploited/dominated majority will be able to recognize its authentic longings. In short, every hegemonic universality has to incorporate *at least two* particular contents: the 'authentic' popular content and its 'distortion' by the relations of domination and exploitation. (*The Ticklish Subject*, p. 184)

This is a most surprising statement coming from a Lacanian, for it is intelligible only if one accepts a notion of 'false consciousness' *à la* Lukács which is totally incompatible with the Freudian discovery of the unconscious, let alone the theory of hegemony. For the dominant and exploitative groups do not distort the popular content any more than the most revolutionary of the socialist discourses: they simply articulate it in a different way. The fact that one prefers one type of articulation rather than another does not mean that one is teleologically 'true', while the other can be dismissed as 'distortion'. If that were so, the hegemonic struggle would have been won before it started.

Class

I have already referred to this point. Let me simply add that Žižek speaks of a 'silent suspension of class analysis' as a kind of 'disavowal'. It is difficult to comment on this, because in this respect Žižek's reference to classes is just a succession of dogmatic assertions without the slightest effort to explain the centrality of the category of class for the understanding of contemporary societies. One cannot avoid the feeling that the notion of class is brought into Žižek's analysis as a sort of *deus ex machina* to play the role of the good guy against the multicultural devils. The only feature of 'classes' which emerges from Žižek's text is that classes, in some way, are constituted and struggle at the level of the 'system', while all the other struggles and identities would be intra-systemic. The reason for this is not analysed – and it would indeed be a very difficult proposition to defend without introducing some crude version of the base/superstructure model. I think that this is what Žižek ultimately does, and it is a new example of the way in which his discourse is schizophrenically split between a highly sophisticated Lacanian analysis and an insufficiently deconstructed traditional Marxism.

Capitalism

Žižek takes a patently anti-capitalist stance, and asserts that the proponents of postmodernism 'as a rule, leave out of sight the resignation at its heart – the acceptance of capitalism as "the only game in town", the renunciation of any real attempt to overcome the existing capitalist liberal regime' (SŽ, p. 95). The difficulty with assertions like this is that they mean absolutely nothing. I understand what Marx meant by overcoming the capitalist regime, because he made it quite explicit several times. I also understand what Lenin or Trotsky meant for the same reason. But in the work of Žižek that expression means nothing – unless he has a secret strategic plan of which he is very careful not to inform anybody. Should we understand that he wants to impose the dictatorship of the proletariat? Or does he want to socialize the means of production and abolish market mechanisms? And what is his political strategy to achieve these rather peculiar aims? What is the alternative model of society that he is postulating? Without at least the beginning of an answer to these questions, his anti-capitalism is mere empty talk.

But perhaps Žižek has something more reasonable in mind: for instance, the overcoming of the prevalent neoliberal economic model and the introduction of state regulation and democratic control of the economy, so that the worst effects of globalization are avoided. If that is what he means by anti-capitalism, I would certainly agree with him, but so would most of the 'postmodernists' against whom his polemic is addressed. It is certainly true that a mainly cultural Left has not paid enough attention to the economic issues since the welfare state model disintegrated. But in order to start doing so, it is necessary to take into account the structural changes in capitalism over the last thirty years and its social effects, some of which have been the disappearance of the peasantry, the drastic fall in numbers of the working class, and the emergence of a social stratification quite different from that on which Marxist class analysis was based.

To conclude: I think that Žižek's political thought suffers from a certain 'combined and uneven development'. While his Lacanian tools, together with his insight, have allowed him to make considerable advances in the understanding of ideological processes in contemporary societies, his strictly political thought has not advanced at the same pace, and remains fixed in very traditional categories. But this unevenness is the law of intellectual work. I remember that the late Michel Pêcheux said that the great encounter of the twentieth century never took place: Freud and Lenin discussing the Saussurean notion of 'value' in a coach on the Orient Express decorated by the Futurists.

Dialectics of emancipation

I will devote this last section to a preliminary attempt to answer some questions about the destiny of the universal in our society. Butler, Žižek and I are all concerned with the elaboration of an emancipatory discourse which does not dissolve into mere particularism but keeps a universal dimension alive. We achieve this, however, in somewhat different ways: while Žižek attempts to determine a systemic level which would 'totalize' social relations and would be universal in and for itself, both Butler and I tend to elaborate a notion of universality which would be the result of some form of interaction between particularities – hence Butler's notion of 'cultural translations' and my notion of 'equivalence'. I will try, in what follows, to expand on the consequences for 'emancipation' of the category of 'equivalence', using as a frame of reference the four dimensions of hegemony that I discussed in my previous essay:

1) Unevenness of power is constitutive.
2) There is hegemony only if the dichotomy universality/particularity is superseded; universality exists only if it is incarnated in – and subverts – some particularity but, conversely, no particularity can become political without also becoming the locus of universalizing effects.
3) Hegemony requires the production of tendentially empty signifiers which, while maintaining the incommensurability between universal and particulars, enables the latter to take up the representation of the former.
4) The terrain in which hegemony expands is that of a generalization of the relations of representation as condition of the constitution of the social order.

1. This first dimension stresses universality's dependency on particularity. The reasons are clear. Let us remember Marx's model of *political* emancipation. The condition for a particular group to present its aims as those of the community at large was the presence of another sector which is perceived as a general crime. This is a first dimension of power inherent in the universalist emancipatory project: the very condition of universality presupposes a radical exclusion. There is,

however, another dimension of power: the ability of a group to assume a function of universal representation presupposes that it is in a better position than other groups to assume this role, so that power is unevenly distributed between various organisms and social sectors. These two dimensions of power – unevenness and exclusion – presuppose a dependency of universality on particularity: there is no universality which operates as pure universality, there is only the relative universalization created by expanding a chain of equivalences around a central particularistic core. The Gramscian notion of 'war of position' expresses exactly that: the transition from a corporative to a hegemonic class presupposes not the abandonment of the particular aims constitutive of the hegemonic sector, but the universalization of them on the basis of the equivalential relation they establish with other subordinated sectors of society. This means that power is the condition of emancipation – there is no way of emancipating a constellation of social forces except by creating a new power around a hegemonic centre.

This, however, creates an apparent difficulty: is it not the case that the opposite is true, that emancipation involves the elimination of power? Only if we are thinking of an emancipation which is total and attains a universality that is not dependent on particularities – as in the case of Marx's 'human' emancipation. The latter, however, for reasons discussed above, is impossible. But I would go further: I would argue that the contamination of emancipation by power is not an unavoidable empirical imperfection to which we have to accommodate, but involves a higher human ideal than a universality representing a totally reconciled human essence, because a fully reconciled society, a transparent society, would be entirely free in the sense of self-determination, but that full realization of freedom would be equivalent to the death of freedom, for all possibility of dissent would have been eliminated from it. Social division, antagonism and its necessary consequence – power – are the true conditions of a freedom which does not eliminate particularity.

If we now consider the emancipatory potential of present-day societies from the viewpoint of this first dimension, we find a political landscape that we contemplate with mixed feelings. On the one hand we have an increasing proliferation of issue-orientated, multicultural and particularistic demands that create the potential – but only the potential – for more expanded chains of equivalence than in the past and, as a result, the possibility of more democratic societies. This is an aspect to which both Butler and I are particularly sensitive. On the other hand, however, we are living at a time in which the great emancipatory narratives of the past are in sharp decline, and as a result of this decline there are no easily available universalizing discourses which could perform the equivalential function. This is the danger of which Žižek, quite rightly, warns us: that particularisms remain pure particularisms and, in that way, become absorbed by the dominant system. The main task of the Left, as I see things today, is the construction of languages providing that element of universality which makes possible the establishment of equivalential links.

2.   If the first dimension of hegemony stresses the moment of the universal's subordination to the particular, this second dimension emphasizes the universalizing effects which are necessary if there is going to be politics at all. Let us again consider Žižek's warning about the dangers of pure particularism. The more particularized a demand, the easier it is to satisfy it and integrate it into the system; while if the demand is equivalent to a variety of other demands, no partial victory will be considered as anything other than an episode in a protracted war of position. I remember that during my years of activism in the student movement in Argentina, the division between Right and Left in the student body became evident in terms of attitudes towards concrete demands (hours when the library was going to be open, the price of tickets in the students' restaurant, etc.). For some, a mobilization which attained its immediate aims should finish there, while for those of us who were more militant, the question was how to keep the mobilization going, which was possible only in so far as we had historical aims – aims that we knew the system could not satisfy. In some sense our worst enemies were those university administrators who offered concrete solutions to the problems we were posing – not, obviously, in the sense that we dismissed these solutions, but in that the important thing, for us, was to see those partial victories as mere episodes in a protracted war of position tending towards more global aims.

The central point is that for a certain demand, subject position, identity, and so on, to become political means that it is *something other* than

itself, living its own particularity as a moment or link in a chain of equivalences that transcends and, in this way, universalizes it. Food riots in
France had taken place following a remarkably similar pattern since the
Middle Ages; but it was only when they broke their local particularism
and became a link in the more universalistic discourse of the *philosophes*
that they became a force for systemic change. That is my basic quarrel
with the category 'class struggle': it tends to anchor the moment of
struggle and antagonism in the sectorial identity of a group, while any
meaningful struggle transcends any sectorial identity and becomes a
complexly articulated 'collective will'. In that sense a truly political
mobilization, even if it is conducted mainly by workers, is never simply
a 'working-class struggle'. Here again we find the basic political dilemma
of our age: will the proliferation of new social actors lead to the enlargement of the equivalential chains which will enable the emergence of
stronger collective wills; or will they dissolve into mere particularism,
making it easier for the system to integrate and subordinate them?

3.   What, however, about the structure of the equivalential discourses
which would enable the emergence of new collective wills? If the equivalential chains extend to a wide variety of concrete demands, so that the
ground of the equivalence cannot be found in the specificity of any
one of them, it is clear that the resulting collective will will find its
anchoring point on the level of the social imaginary, and the core of that
social imaginary is what we have called empty signifiers. It is the empty
character of these anchoring points that truly universalizes a discourse,
making it the surface of inscription of a plurality of demands beyond
their particularities. And, as an emancipatory discourse presupposes the
aggregation of a plurality of discrete demands, we can say that there is
no true emancipation except in a discourse whose anchoring terms
remain empty. It is not necessary that the term does not have a precise
meaning, in as much as there is a gap between its concrete content and
the set of equivalential meanings associated with it. *Front Populaire* designated an alliance of political forces, but in the political climate of the
France of the 1930s it raised a wide variety of social hopes that far
exceeded its actual political reality.

   It is important to point out that these social imaginaries organized around some empty signifiers represent, in my view, the limit of socially attainable universalization. There is no universality, as we have seen, except through an equivalence between particularities, and such equivalences are always contingent and context-dependent. Any step beyond this limit would necessarily fall into a historical teleology, with the result that universality, which should be considered as a horizon, would become a ground. I want to stress above all the function of surfaces of inscription that these horizons exercise. Once they become the generalized language of social change, any new demand will be constructed as one more link in the equivalential chain embraced by those horizons. They become, in this sense, powerful instruments in the displacement of the relations of force in society. Conversely, their decline is linked to their decreasing ability to embrace social demands, which recognize themselves less and less in the political language provided by that horizon.

The crisis of the Left, from this point of view, can be seen as a result of the decline of the two horizons which had traditionally structured its discourse: communism and, in the West, the welfare state. Since the beginning of the 1970s it is the Right which has been hegemonic: neoliberalism and the moral majority, for instance, have become the main surfaces of inscription and representation. The Right's hegemonic ability is evident in the fact that even social democratic parties have tended to accept its premisses as a new and unchallengeable 'common sense'. The Left, for its part, finding its own social imaginaries shattered and without any expansive force, has tended to retreat into the defence of merely specific causes. But there is no hegemony which can be grounded in this purely defensive strategy. This should be the main battlefield in the years to come. Let us state it bluntly: there will be no renaissance of the Left without the construction of a new social imaginary.

4.   Finally, representation. From its critique by Rousseau to the Marxian assertion that the liberation of the workers will be the deed of the workers themselves, the idea of representation has been considered with considerable suspicion by emancipatory discourses. Without representation, however, there is no hegemony. If a particular sector has to incarnate the universal aims of the community, representation is essentially inherent to the hegemonic link. However, is representation really a

second best, something to which we have to resign ourselves because the fullness of society is not immediately given, but has to be labouriously constructed through a system of mediations?

Here we can put forward a similar argument to the one we put forward in relation to 'power'. Why is a relation of representation necessary in the first place? As I have argued in other works, because at a certain point decisions are going to be taken which affect the interests of somebody who is materially absent from it. And, as I have also argued, representation is always a double movement from represented to representative and from representative to represented – this latter movement again allowing us to see the emergence of a process of universalization. The task of a representative in Parliament, for instance, does not simply consist in transmitting the wishes of those he represents; he will have to elaborate a new discourse which convinces the other Members – by, for instance, arguing that the interests of the people in his constituency are compatible with the national interest, and so on. In this way he inscribes those interests within a more universal discourse and, in so far as his discourse also becomes that of the people of his constituency, they also are able to universalize their experience. The relation of representation thus becomes a vehicle of universalization and, as universalization is a precondition of emancipation, it can also become a road to the latter. In the conditions of interconnection which exist in a globalized world, it is only through relations of representation that universality is achievable.

In this section I have tried to point to some of the language games which a hegemonic logic makes it possible to play with categories such as 'power', 'representation' and 'emptiness'. But, obviously, many more games are possible. I see as a main task of political theory to develop these language games and thus to promote the expansion of political imagination. We should – this time politically – help to let the fly out of the bottle.

Da Capo senza Fine
Slavoj Žižek

When Gilles Deleuze tries to account for the crucial shift in the history of cinema from *image-mouvement* to *image-temps*, he makes a seemingly naive and brutal reference to 'real history', to the traumatic impact of World War II (which was felt from Italian neorealism to American *film noir*). This reference is fully consistent with Deleuze's general anti-Cartesian thrust: a thought never begins spontaneously, out of itself, with its inherent principles – what provokes us to think is always a traumatic encounter with some external Real which brutally imposes itself on us, shattering our established ways of thinking. As such, a true thought is always decentred: one does not think spontaneously, one is *forced* to think.

This Deleuzian argument was the first association that came to my mind after reading Butler's and Laclau's introductory contributions to our debate: for me, at least, the authentic effect of their interventions lay in the fact that they hit me as a violent encounter that shattered my self-complacency – even while I continue to disagree with their criticisms, I had to reformulate my position in a new way. No wonder, then, that my reaction to their interventions oscillated between two extremes: either it seemed to me as if there was a simple misunderstanding to be clarified, or it seemed that there was a radical incompatibility between our respective positions, with no middle ground in between. In short, this oscillation indicates that, in our differences, we are dealing with some *Real*: the gap that separates the three of us is impossible to define in a neutral way – that is to say, the very formulation of how we differ already involves 'taking sides'. Consequently, my main concern in this second intervention will be to accomplish at least a part of this impossible task of *reiterating the differences*.

Butler: historicism and the Real

It seems to me that several of Butler's and Laclau's criticisms of my work were already answered either in my first contribution (which, of course, was at that point unknown to the other two participants) or by the third contributor – I have specifically in mind here Butler's standard argument against the Lacanian Real as an ahistorical quasi-transcendental bar: this criticism is dealt with in detail in my and Laclau's first contributions; see the following keys passage from Laclau, which I fully endorse:

> This is the point Butler's argument is really missing: if the representation of the Real was a representation of something entirely *outside* the symbolic, this representation of the unrepresentable *as unrepresentable* would amount, indeed, to full inclusion. . . . But if what is represented is an *internal* limit of the process of representation as such, the relationship between internality and externality is subverted: the Real becomes a name for the very failure of the Symbolic in achieving its own fullness. (EL, p. 68)

The opposition between an ahistorical bar of the Real and thoroughly contingent historicity is therefore a false one: *it is the very 'ahistorical' bar as the internal limit of the process of symbolization that sustains the space of historicity*. That, in my view, is the fundamental misunderstanding: in Laclau's terms, Butler systematically (mis)reads *antagonism* (which is impossible–real) as (symbolic) *difference/opposition*; in the case, for instance, of the Lacanian sexual difference as real (as that which, precisely, *resists* symbolization), she systematically interprets it as the firm, unchangeable *symbolic* set of oppositions defining the (heterosexual) identity of each of the two sexes.[1] In her first intervention in the present dialogue, this misunderstanding is clearly discernible in the following passage:

A particular identity becomes an identity by virtue of its relative location in an open system of differential relations. In other words, an identity is constituted through its difference from a limitless set of other identities. That difference is specified in the course of Laclau's exposition as a relation of *exclusion* and/or *antagonism*. Laclau's point of reference here is Saussure rather than Hegel . . . the 'incompleteness' of each and every identity is a direct result of its differential emergence: no particular identity can emerge without presuming and enacting the exclusion of others, and this constitutive exclusion or antagonism is the shared and equal condition of all identity-constitution. (JB, pp. 30–31)

It is my contention that, in contrast to this claim, one should assert that antagonism is precisely *not* the Saussurean differential relation where the identity (of a signifier) is nothing but a fascicle of differences; as Laclau puts it in very precise terms, what is missing in the Saussurean differentiality is *the 'reflective' overlapping of internal and external difference*: the difference, for example, which separates woman from man is 'antagonistic' in so far as it simultaneously 'bars' the woman from within, preventing her from achieving full self-identity (in contrast to a pure differential relationship, where the opposition to man defines woman's identity). In other words, the notion of antagonism involves a kind of metadifference: the two antagonistic poles differ in the very way in which they define or perceive the difference that separates them (for a Leftist, the gap that separates him from a Rightist is not the same as *this same gap* perceived from the Rightist's point of view). Or – to put it in yet another way – the overlapping of internal and external difference means that, in the differential field of signifiers, there is always at least one 'signifier without a signified' which has no (determinate) meaning, since it simply stands for the presence of meaning *as such* – and Laclau's notion of 'hegemony' describes precisely the process by means of which the void of the signified of this signifier is filled in by some contingent particular/determinate meaning which, in the case of successful hegemony, starts to function as the stand-in for meaning 'as such'.

The consequences of this misreading are far-reaching: if we conflate the real of an antagonism with symbolic difference(s), then we regress to an *empiricist* problematic – something to which, I think, Butler comes dangerously close in the following passage:

> No doubt it makes a difference whether one understands the invariable incompleteness of the subject in terms of the limits designated by the Real, considered as the point where self-representation founders and fails, or as the inability of the social category to capture the mobility and complexity of persons. (JB, pp. 29–30)

To this, I am tempted to reply that it certainly *does* make a difference: to reduce the structural incompleteness to 'the inability of the social category to capture the mobility and complexity of persons' is to reduce it to the *empiricist* problematic of how ideological categories are too fixed and, as such, are never able to capture the complexity of social reality – that is, to rely on the empiricist opposition between the infinite wealth of reality and the abstract poverty of the categories by means of which we try to grasp reality. Furthermore, does Butler not court the same empiricist problematic when she asserts how '[t]he claim to universality always takes place in a given syntax, through a certain set of cultural conventions in a recognizable venue' (JB, p. 35)? The consequence of this assertion, of course, is that translation (from one to another cultural context, with its given syntax) is crucial for a liberating notion of universality:

> Without translation, the very concept of universality cannot cross the linguistic borders it claims, in principle, to be able to cross . . . without translation, the only way the assertion of universality can cross a border is through a colonial and expansionistic logic. (JB, p. 35)

Against these assertions, I am tempted to claim that, on the contrary, *the concept of universality emerges as the consequence of the fact that each particular culture is precisely* never *and for* a priori *reasons simply particular, but has always-already* in itself *'crossed the linguistic borders it claims'*. In short, while Butler emphasizes that there is no universality without translation, I am tempted to claim that, today, it is crucial to emphasize the *opposite* aspect: *there is no* particularity *without translation*. This means that the alternative 'either the direct imposition of Western human rights as universal or the patient work of translation' is ultimately a false one: the work of translation has *always-already begun*; linguistic borders are *always-already crossed* – that is to say, every assertion of particular identity always-already involves a disavowed reference to universality. Or, to put it in Laclau's terms: *prior to being the neutral link or common thread between a series of particular entities, the "universal" is the name of a gap that forever prevents the particular itself from achieving its (self-)identity.*

There is another shift of emphasis in Butler's notion of universality – a shift with even more directly discernible political consequences, one which concerns the relationship between universality and exclusion. When Butler claims that 'abstraction cannot remain rigorously abstract without exhibiting something of what it must exclude in order to constitute itself as abstraction' (JB, p. 19), she conceives of this exclusion as the exclusion of those who are oppressed (underprivileged) in existing power relations, as is patently the case in the following quote:

> The 'will' that is officially represented by the government is thus haunted by a 'will' that is excluded from the representative function. Thus the government is established on the basis of a paranoid economy in which it must repeatedly establish its one claim to universality by erasing all remnants of those wills it excludes from the domain of representation. (JB, p. 22)

Here, again, I think it is crucial also to emphasize the *opposite* aspect: what universality excludes is not primarily the underprivileged Other whose status is reduced, constrained, and so on, but *its own* permanent founding gesture – a set of unwritten, unacknowledged rules and practices which, while publicly disavowed, are none the less the ultimate support of the existing power edifice. The public power edifice is haunted also by its own disavowed particular obscene underside, by the particular practices which *break its own public rule* – in short, by its 'inherent transgression'.

In *The Siege*, a recent terror thriller, as a response to Muslim terrorists exploding bombs and killing people all over Manhattan, a right-wing US general (played by Bruce Willis) imposes a state of emergency on New

York: tanks roll in, all Arab men of combat age are isolated in stadia, and so on. At the end, the good FBI agent (played, of course, by Denzel Washington) outsmarts the crazy general; his main argument is that such terrorist methods are bad – if we fight fundamentalist violence in this way, then even if we gain a military victory, the enemy has in a way truly won, because we lose what we were defending (democracy) . . . . The falsity of this film is that it first revives all the nasty fantasies a good liberal harbours and secretly enjoys in the depths of his 'privacy', then redeems us from enjoying them by firmly condemning such proce-dures – in a way, we are allowed to have our cake and eat it: to engage in racist fantasizing while maintaining our good liberal conscience. In this sense, *The Siege* stages the phantasmic 'inherent transgression' of the tolerant liberal. And the *political* consequence I draw from this notion of 'inherent transgression' is that one has to abandon the idea that power operates in the mode of identification (one becomes the subject of power by recognizing oneself in its interpellation, by assuming the sym-bolic place imposed on us by it), so that the privileged form of resistance to power should involve a politics of disidentification. A minimum of disidentification is a priori necessary if power is to function – not only in the empiricist sense that 'power can never fully succeed in its attempt to totalize the field', and so on, but in a much more radical sense: power can reproduce itself only through some form of self-distance, by relying on the obscene disavowed rules and practices that are in conflict with its public norms.

To avoid a misunderstanding: I am well aware that Butler herself comes very close to this logic of inherent transgression – this, in my view, is what her notion of disavowed 'passionate attachments' as the con-cealed support of power is ultimately about. Let me elaborate this crucial point via Martha Nussbaum's critique of Butler in *The New Republic*.[2] According to Nussbaum, Butler conceives of Power as an all-embracing and all-powerful edifice that is ultimately impervious to the subject's intervention: any organized individual or collective attempt radically to change the power edifice is doomed to failure; it is caught in advance in the web of Power, so the only thing a subject can do is to play perverse marginal eroticizing games. . . . Here Nussbaum completely misses Butler's point: it is not the subject who, unable to undermine or transform the power edifice effectively, resorts to perverse games of eroticization – it is *the power apparatus itself* which, in order to reproduce itself, has to have recourse to obscene eroticization and phantasmic investment. The disavowed eroticization of the very power-mechanisms that serve to control sexuality is the only way for these mechanisms actually to 'grasp' the subject, to be accepted or 'internalized' by it. So Butler's point is that the 'perverse' sexualization/eroticization of power is *already there* as its disavowed obscene underside, and – to put it in somewhat simplified terms – the goal of her political interventions is precisely to elaborate strategies that would enable subjects to *undermine* the hold of this eroticization over them.

In what, then, does our difference consist? Let me approach this key point via another key criticism from Butler: her point that I describe only the paradoxical *mechanisms* of ideology, the way an ideological edifice *reproduces* itself (the reversal that characterizes the effect of *point de capiton*, the 'inherent transgression', etc.), without elaborating how one can 'disturb' (resignify, displace, turn against themselves) these mechanisms; I show:

> how power compels us to consent to that which constrains us, and how our very sense of freedom or resistance can be the dissimulated instrument of dominance. But what remains less clear to me is how one moves beyond such a dialectical reversal or impasse to something new. How would the new be produced from an analysis of the social field that remains restricted to inversions, aporias and reversals that work regardless of time and place? (JB, p. 29)

In *The Psychic Life of Power*, Butler makes the same point apropos of Lacan himself:

> The [Lacanian] imaginary [resistance] thwarts the efficacy of the symbolic law but cannot turn back upon the law, demanding or effecting its reformulation. In this sense, psychic resistance thwarts the law in its effects, but cannot redirect the law or its effects. Resistance is thus located in a domain that is virtually powerless to alter the law that it opposes. Hence, psychic resistance presumes the continuation of the law in its

anterior, symbolic form and, in that sense, contributes to its status quo. In such a view, resistance appears doomed to perpetual defeat.

In contrast, Foucault formulates resistance as an effect of the very power that it is said to oppose. . . . For Foucault, the symbolic produces the possibility of its own subversions, and these subversions are unanticipated effects of symbolic interpellations.[3]

My response to this is triple. First, on the level of exegesis, Foucault is much more ambivalent on this point: his thesis on the immanence of resistance to power can also be read as asserting that every resistance is caught in advance in the game of the power it opposes. Second, my notion of 'inherent transgression', far from playing another variation on this theme (resistance reproduces that to which it resists), makes the power edifice even *more* vulnerable: in so far as power relies on its 'inherent transgression', then – sometimes, at least – *overidentifying* with the explicit power discourse – *ignoring* this inherent obscene underside and simply taking the power discourse at its (public) word, acting as if it really means what it explicitly says (and promises) – can be the most effective way of disturbing its smooth functioning. Third, and most important: far from constraining the subject to a resistance doomed to perpetual defeat, Lacan allows for a much more radical subjective intervention than Butler: what the Lacanian notion of 'act' aims at is not a mere displacement/resignification of the symbolic co-ordinates that confer on the subject his or her identity, but the radical transformation of the very universal structuring 'principle' of the existing symbolic order. Or – to put it in more psychoanalytic terms – the Lacanian act, in its dimension of 'traversing the fundamental fantasy' aims radically to disturb the very 'passionate attachment' that forms, for Butler, the ultimately ineluctable background of the process of resignification. So, far from being more 'radical' in the sense of thorough historicization, Butler is in fact very close to the Lacan of the early 1950s, who found his ultimate expression in the *rapport de Rome* on 'The Function and the Field of Speech and Language in Psychoanalysis' (1953) – to the Lacan of the permanent process of retroactive historicization or resymbolization of social reality; to the Lacan who emphasized again and again how there is no directly accessible 'raw' reality, how what we perceive as 'reality' is overdetermined by the symbolic texture within which it appears.

Along these lines, Lacan triumphantly rewrites the Freudian 'stages' (oral, anal, phallic . . .) not as biologically determined stages in libidinal evolution, but as different modes of the dialecticial *subjectivization* of the child's position within the network of his or her family: what matters in, say, the anal stage is not the function of defecation as such, but the subjective stance it involves (complying with the Other's demand to do it in an orderly way, asserting one's defiance and/or self-control . . .). What is crucial here is that it is *this* Lacan of radical and unlimited resignification who is at the same time the Lacan of the paternal Law (Name-of-the-Father) as the unquestionable horizon of the subject's integration into the symbolic order. Consequently, the shift from this early 'Lacan of unlimited resignification' to the later 'Lacan of the Real' is not the shift from the unconstrained play of resignification towards the assertion of some ahistorical limit of the process of symbolization: *it is the very focus on the notion of Real as impossible that reveals the ultimate contingency, fragility (and thus changeability) of every symbolic constellation that pretends to serve as the a priori horizon of the process of symbolization.*

No wonder Lacan's shift of focus towards the Real is strictly correlative to the devaluation of the paternal function (and of the central place of the Oedipus complex itself) – to the introduction of the notion that paternal authority is ultimately an imposture, one among the possible 'sinthoms' which allow us temporarily to stabilize and co-ordinate the inconsistent/nonexistent 'big Other'. So Lacan's point in unearthing the 'ahistorical' limit of historicization/resignification is thus not that we have to accept this limit in a resigned way, but that every historical figuration of this limit is itself contingent and, as such, susceptible to a radical overhaul. So my basic answer to Butler – no doubt paradoxical for those who have been fully involved in recent debates – is that, with all the talk about Lacan's clinging to an ahistorical bar, and so on, *it is Butler herself who, on a more radical level, is not historicist enough*: it is Butler who limits the subject's intervention to multiple resignifications/displacements of the basic 'passionate attachment', which therefore persists as the very limit/condition of subjectivity. Consequently, I am tempted to *supplement* Butler's series in her rhetorical question quoted above: 'How would the new be produced from an analysis of the social field that remains restricted to inversions, aporias, reversals, *and performative displacements or resignifications* . . .?'[4]

It is crucial to get the precise idea of what Butler is claiming here: her notion is that since ideological universality (the space of interpellation), in order to reproduce itself and retain its hold, has to rely on its repeated assumption by the subject, this repetition is not only the passive assuming of the same mandate, but opens up the space of re-formation, resignification, displacement – it is possible to resignify/displace the 'symbolic substance' which predetermines my identity, but not totally to overhaul it, since a total exit would involve the psychotic loss of my symbolic identity. This resignification can work even in the extreme case of injurious interpellations: they determine me, I cannot get rid of them, they are the condition of my symbolic being/identity; rejecting them *tout court* would bring about psychosis; but what I can do is resignify/displace them, mockingly assume them: 'the possibilities of resignification will rework and unsettle the passionate attachment to subjection without which subject-formation – and re-formation – cannot succeed'.[5]

My aim is not to deny that such a practice of resignification can be very effective in the ideological struggle for hegemony – does not the success of *The X-Files* provide an excellent illustration of this? What happens in this series is precisely that the standard formula of alien threat and invasion is 'resignified', reset in a different context. Not only does the content of this threat offer a quasi-encyclopaedic 'multiculturalist' combination of all possible myths and folklores (from Eastern European vampires and werewolves to Navajo spectral monsters); what is even more crucial is the setting of these apparitions: derelict suburbs, half-abandoned country houses or lonely forests, most of them in a North of the USA (no doubt conditioned by the fact that, for economic reasons, most of the exteriors are shot in Canada) – the privileged sites of the threat are the outcasts of our society, from Native Americans and illegal Latino immigrants to the homeless and junkies in our cities. Furthermore, the government itself is systematically presented as an ominous network, penetrated by secret organizations which deny their existence, ambiguously collaborating with the aliens . . . .

There is, however, a limit to this process of resignification, and the Lacanian name for this limit, of course, is precisely the *Real*. How does this Real operate in language? In 'Pretending', J.L. Austin evokes a neat example of how pretending to be vulgar can itself become vulgar:[6] when I am with people who have rigid standards of behaviour, I pretend to be vulgar and, as part of a social joke, start to use obscene language or refer to obscene content. My pretending to be vulgar will in fact be vulgar – this collapse of the distinction between pretending and being is the unmistakable signal that my speech has touched some Real. That is to say: apropos of what kind of speech acts does the distance between pretending and being (or, rather, actually doing it) collapse? Apropos of speech acts which aim at the other in the Real of his or her being: hate speech, aggressive humiliation, and so on. In such cases, no amount of disguising it with the semblance of a joke or irony can prevent it from having a hurtful effect – we touch the Real when the efficiency of such symbolic markers of distance is suspended.

And my point is that in so far as we conceive of the politico-ideological resignification in the terms of the struggle for hegemony, today's Real which sets a limit to resignification is Capital: the smooth functioning of Capital is that which remains the same, that which 'always returns to its place', in the unconstrained struggle for hegemony. Is this not demonstrated by the fact that Butler, as well as Laclau, in their criticism of the old 'essentialist' Marxism, none the less silently *accept* a set of premises: they *never* question the fundamentals of the capitalist market economy and the liberal-democratic political regime; they *never* envisage the possibility of a completely *different* economico-political regime. In this way, they *fully participate* in the abandonment of these questions by the 'postmodern' Left: all the changes they propose are changes *within* this economico-political regime.

Laclau: dialectics and contingency

I have a suspicion that the philosophical aspect of this political disagreement between Butler and Laclau on the one side and me on the other finds its expression in our different stances towards the notion of 'essentialism'. Butler and Laclau rely fully on the opposition *essentialism/contingency*; they both conceive of 'progress' (if this term is still defensible) as the gradual passage from 'essentialism' to the more and more radical assertion of contingency. I, however, find the notion of 'essentialism' problematic, in so far as it tends to condense three different levels of resistance to total fluidity: the imaginary 'essence' (the firm shape, *Gestalt*, which persists through the incessant flux of change); the One of the Master-Signifier (the *empty signifier* that serves as the container for the shifting significations: we are all for 'democracy', although the content of this term changes as a result of hegemonic struggles), and the debilitating Sameness of the Real (the trauma that resists its symbolization and, as such, triggers the very repetitive process of symbolization). Is not Butler's criticism of Lacan the exemplary case of how the term 'essentialism' implies the progressive reduction of the latter to the former level: first, the Sameness of the Real is reduced to a 'fixed' symbolic determination (Butler's point that sexual difference as real equals a firm set of heterosexual normative symbolic determinations); then, the symbolic itself is reduced to the imaginary (her thesis that the Lacanian 'symbolic' is ultimately nothing but the coagulated, 'reified', imaginary flux).

The problem with 'essentialism' is thus that this critical designation shares the fatal weakness of the standard procedure of philosophical rejection. The first step in this procedure is the negative gesture of totalizing the field to be rejected, designating it as a single and distinctive field, against which one then asserts the positive alternative – the question to be asked is the one about the hidden limitation of this critical totalization of the Whole that one endeavours to undermine. What is problematic in Kantian ethics is not its formalism as such but, rather, the fact that, prior to Kant's assertion of the autonomous formal moral Law, he has to reject every other foundation of ethics as 'pathological', relating to some contingent, ultimately empirical notion of the Good – what is problematic is this reduction of all previous ethics to the utilitarian notion of the Good as pathological, serving our pleasure . . . (against this, Sade, as the truth of Kant, asserts precisely the paradoxical possibility of a pathological-contingent attitude which works *against* one's well-being, finding satisfaction in this self-blockage – is not the point of the Freudian death drive that one can also suspend the rule of utilitarian egotism on 'pathological' grounds?).

In much the same way, is not Derrida's 'metaphysics of presence' silently dominated/hegemonized by Husserl's subjectivity as the pure auto-affection/self-presence of the conscious subject, so that when Derrida talks about 'metaphysics of presence', he is always essentially referring to the *Husserlian* subject present-to-itself? The problem with sweeping philosophical oppositions (all the others against me and possibly my predecessors) therefore lies in the problematic totalization of all other options under one and the same global label – the multitude thus totalized is always secretly 'hegemonized' by one of its particular species; in the same way, the Derridan notion of the 'metaphysics of presence' is secretly hegemonized by Husserl, so that Derrida in effect reads Plato and all the others *through* Husserl. And it is my contention that the same goes for the critical notion of 'essentialism'. Let us take the case of capitalism itself: against the proponents of the critique of global capitalism, of the 'logic of Capital', Laclau argues that capitalism is an inconsistent composite of heterogeneous features which were combined as the result of a contingent historical constellation, not a homogeneous Totality obeying a common underlying Logic.

My answer to this is the reference to the Hegelian logic of the retroactive reversal of contingency into necessity: of course capitalism emerged from a contingent combination of historical conditions; of course it gave birth to a series of phenomena (political democracy, concern for human rights, etc.) which can be 'resignified', rehegemonized, inscribed into a non-capitalist context. However, capitalism retroactively 'posited its own presuppositions', and reinscribed its contingent/external circumstances into an all-encompassing logic that can be generated from an elementary conceptual matrix (the 'contradiction' involved in the act of commodity exchange, etc.). In a proper dialectical analysis, the 'necessity' of a totality does not preclude its contingent origins and the heterogeneous nature of its constituents – these are, precisely, its *presuppositions* which are then posited, retroactively totalized, by the emergence of dialectical totality. Furthermore, I am tempted to claim that Laclau's critique would have been much more appropriate with regard to the very notion of 'radical democracy', to which Laclau and Mouffe regularly refer in the *singular*: does this notion not actually cover a series of heterogeneous phenomena for which it is problematic to claim that they belong to the same genus: from the feminist, ecological, etc. struggle in developed countries to the Third World resistance to the neoliberal New World Order?

Where, then, do I locate my difference with Laclau? Here, the above-mentioned oscillation between 'mere terminological misunderstandings' and 'radical incompatibility' is even stronger. Let me first deal with some points which may seem to concern mere terminological or factual misunderstandings, as is the case with Laclau's critical remark about my advocacy of the Cartesian *cogito*. With regard to my reference to the 'forgotten obverse, the excessive, unacknowledged kernel of the *cogito*, which is far from the pacifying image of the transparent self', Laclau's claim is that I deprive the *cogito* of its Cartesian content and Lacanize the tradition of modernity, 'like calling oneself a fully fledged Platonist while rejecting the theory of forms' (EL, p. 73). To this criticism I am first tempted to respond, in a naive factual way, that my position is by no means as 'eccentric' as it may sound: there is a long tradition within Cartesian studies of demonstrating that a gap forever separates the *cogito* itself from the *res cogitans*: that the self-transparent 'thinking substance [*res cogitans*]' is secondary, that it already obfuscates a certain abyss or excess that is the founding gesture of *cogito* – was it not Derrida himself who, in his '*Cogito* and the History of Madness', highlighted this moment of excessive madness constitutive of *cogito*?[7] So when Laclau refers approvingly to Kierkegaard's notion of decision ('As Kierkegaard – quoted by Derrida – said: "the moment of the decision is the moment of madness". And as I would add [which Derrida wouldn't]: this is the moment of the subject before subjectivation' [EL, p. 79], I – while, of course, fully endorsing his approval – would insist that this 'moment of madness' can be conceptualized only within the space opened up by the 'empty', 'non-substantial' Cartesian subject.

Furthermore, I claim that democracy itself – what Claude Lefort called the 'democratic invention'[8] can also emerge only within the Cartesian space. The democratic legacy of the 'abstract' Cartesian *cogito* can best be discerned apropos of the pseudo-'feminist' argument for a more prominent role for women in public and political life: their role should be more prominent since, for natural or historical reasons, their predominant stance is less individualistic, competitive, domination-orientated, and more co-operative and compassionate . . . The Cartesian democratic lesson here is that *the moment one accepts the terms of such a discussion, one already concedes defeat and also accepts the pre-democratic 'meritocratic' principle*: there should be more women in public life not because of any particular positive female psychosocial properties, but on account of the simple democratic-egalitarian principle (what Balibar called *égalib-erté*):[9] women have the right to a more prominent role in public decision-making *simply because they constitute half the population*, not on account of any of their specific properties.

Leaving aside the question of how to read Kant (I also think there is an aspect of Kant that is totally obliterated by the standard academic image of him[10]), let me go on to a further difference between Laclau and me which may also appear to be grounded in a simple terminological and/or factual misunderstanding, albeit already in a more ambiguous and problematic way. This difference is clearly discernible in Laclau's criticism that in my reading of Hegel I do not take into account Hegel's panlogicism, that is, the fact that Hegel's philosophy forms a closed *system* which *radically reduces contingency*, since the passage from one position to the next is always, by definition *necessary*:

> accepting entirely that the Absolute Spirit has no positive content of its own, and is just the succession of all dialectical transitions, of its impossibility of establishing a final overlapping between the universal and the particular – are these transitions *contingent* or *necessary*? If the latter, the characterization of the whole Hegelian *project* (as opposed to what he actually did) as panlogicist can hardly be avoided. (EL, p. 60)

For me, Laclau's opposition is all too crude, and misses the (already mentioned) key feature of Hegelian dialectics: the ultimate mystery of what Hegel calls 'positing the presuppositions' is the mystery of how contingency *retroactively* 'sublates' itself into necessity – how, through historical repetition, an initially contingent occurrence is 'transubstantiated' into the expression of a necessity: in short, the mystery of how, through 'autopoietic' self-organization, order emerges out of chaos.[11] Here Hegel is to be read 'with Freud': in Freud also, a contingent feature (say, a traumatic sexual encounter) is elevated into a 'necessity', that is to say, into the structuring principle, into the central point of reference around which the subject's entire life revolves.

The second aspect of Laclau's critique of my reading of Hegel is that

I do not sufficiently take into account the gap between the Hegelian
project in its fundamental dialectical principle and what Hegel actually
accomplishes: Hegel's theoretical *practice* often differs from his 'official'
self-understanding – in what he does, he often relies on (disavowed)
rhetoricity, contingent tropes, and so on. To this, I am tempted to answer
that *the split Laclau is talking about is already discernible in the very fundamental
Hegelian project itself,* which is thoroughly ambiguous. Let me simply mention what may appear to be Hegel's utmost 'logocentric' notion, namely,
the notion of *totality*: one should bear in mind that this notion does not
designate simply a total mediation accessible to a global subject but,
rather, its exact opposite, best exemplified by the dialectic of the
Beautiful Soul: 'totality' is encountered at its purest in the negative experience of falsity and breakdown, when the subject assumes the position
of a judge exempt from what he is passing a judgement on (the position
of a multiculturalist critic of Western cultural imperialism, of the
Western pacifist liberal horrified at the ethnic violence in fundamentalist countries) – here the message of 'totality' is simply: 'No, you are
involved in the system you pretend to reject; purity is the most perfidious
form of cheating.' . . . So, far from being correlative to the Universal
Subject, 'totality' is *really experienced* and 'actually exists' precisely in the
negative shock of failure, of paying the price for forgetting to include
oneself in the situation into which one intervenes. Furthermore, I think
that here we are not dealing with a simple case of misreading Hegel: the
fact that Laclau tends to reduce the properly Hegelian dialectic of necessity and contingency to the simplified standard notion of contingency as
the external/empirical mode of appearance of a 'deeper' underlying
Necessity indicates some *inherent* inconsistency in his theoretical edifice,
an inconsistency in the relationship between the descriptive and the
normative – here is Laclau's answer to my criticism on this point:

> I have been confronted many times with one or other version of the fol-
> lowing question: if hegemony involves a decision taken in a radically
> contingent terrain, what are the grounds for deciding one way or the
> other? Žižek, for instance, observes: 'Laclau's notion of hegemony
> describes the universal mechanism of ideological "cement" which
> binds any social body together, a notion that can analyse all possible

sociopolitical orders, from Fascism to liberal democracy; on the other hand, Laclau none the less advocates a determinate political option, "radical democracy".' I do not think this is a valid objection. It is grounded in a strict distinction between the descriptive and the normative which is ultimately derivative from the Kantian separation between pure and practical Reason. But this is, precisely, a distinction which should be eroded: there is no such strict separation between fact and value. A value-orientated practical activity will be confronted with problems, facilities, resistances, and so on, which it will discursively construct as 'facts' – facts, however, which could have emerged in their facticity only from within such activity. (EL, pp. 79–80)

I think two levels are confounded here. I fully endorse Laclau's argument against the strict distinction between the descriptive and the normative – in fact, I myself refer to a similar example of how the Nazis' 'description' of the social situation in which they intervene (degeneration, the Jewish plot, a crisis of values . . .) already depends on the practical 'solution' they propose. In Hegelese, it is not only, as Marx put it, that '[m]en make their own history; but they do not make it just as they please; they do not make it under circumstances chosen by themselves, but under circumstances directly encountered, given and transmitted from the past';[12] it is also that these circumstances or 'presuppositions' are themselves always-already 'posited' by the practical context of our intervention in them. In this sense, I fully endorse Laclau's point that 'the question: "If the decision is contingent, what are the grounds for choosing this option rather than a different one?", is not relevant' (EL, p. 85): there are no ultimate 'objective' grounds for a decision, since these grounds are always-already retroactively constructed from the horizon of a decision. (I myself often use the example of religion here: one does not become a Christian when one is convinced by reason of the truth of Christianity; rather, only when one is a Christian can one *really* understand in what sense Christianity is true.) My point, however, is precisely that *it is Laclau's theory of hegemony itself which relies on an unreflected gap between the descriptive and the normative*, in so far as it functions as a neutral conceptual tool for accounting for *every* ideological formation, including Fascist populism (one of Laclau's favourite examples). Of course, Laclau would have answered here that the universal theory of hegemony is not simply neutral, since it already involves the practical stance of 'radical democracy'; but again, my answer would be that, precisely, I do not see in what specifically *inherent* way the very universal notion of 'hegemony' is linked to a particular ethico-political choice. And – as I have already argued in my first contribution to this debate – I think the key to this ambiguity is the unresolved question of the *historicity of the assertion of historicism/contingency itself* in Laclau's (as well as Butler's) theoretical edifice.

Against historicism

So much for answering concrete criticisms. Let me now focus on clarifying a couple of more general points that emerged during our dialogue. First, the issue of radical historicism (in the sense of asserting radical contingency) versus Kant (i.e. the Kantian theme of a formal a priori that provides an ahistorical frame for every possible contingent content). Since deconstructionism is often perceived as overlapping with historicism (to 'deconstruct' a universal notion means, among other things, to show how the notion in question is in fact grounded in a specific historical context which qualifies its universality with a series of exclusions and/or exceptions), it is crucial to distinguish the strict deconstructionist stance from the historicist stance which pervades today's Cultural Studies. Cultural Studies, as a rule, involves the stance of cognitive suspension characteristic of historicist relativism: cinema theorists in Cultural Studies, for instance, no longer ask basic questions like 'What is the nature of cinematic perception?', they simply tend to reduce such questions to the historicist reflection upon conditions in which certain notions emerged as the result of historically specific power relations. In other words, we are dealing with the historicist abandonment of the very question of the inherent 'truth-value' of a theory under consideration: when a typical Cultural Studies theorist deals with a philosophical or psychoanalytic edifice, the analysis focuses exclusively on unearthing its hidden patriarchal, Eurocentric, identitarian, etc., 'bias', without even asking the naive but none the less necessary question: OK, but what *is* the structure of the universe? How *does* the human psyche 'really' work? Such questions are not even taken seriously in Cultural Studies, since – in a typical rhetorical move – Cultural Studies denounces the very attempt to draw a clear line of distinction between, say, true science and pre-scientific mythology, as part of the Eurocentric procedure of impos- ing its own hegemony by means of the exclusionary discursive strategy of devaluing the Other as not-yet-scientific . . . . In this way, we end up arranging and analysing science proper, premodern 'wisdom', and other forms of knowledge as different discursive formations evaluated not with regard to their inherent truth-value but with regard to their sociopolitical status and impact (a native 'holistic' wisdom can thus be considered much more 'progressive' than the 'mechanistic' Western sci- ence responsible for the forms of modern domination). The problem with such a procedure of historicist relativism is that it continues to rely on a set of silent (non-thematized) ontological and epistemological pre- suppositions on the nature of human knowledge and reality: usually a proto-Nietzschean notion that knowledge is not only embedded in but also generated by a complex set of discursive strategies of power (re)pro- duction, and so on.

Does this mean, however, that the only alternatives to cultural his- toricist relativism are either naive empiricism or the old-fashioned metaphysical TOE (Theory of Everything)? Here, precisely, decon- struction at its best involves a much more nuanced position. As Derrida argues so cogently in 'White Mythology', it is not sufficient to claim that 'all concepts are metaphors', that there is no pure epistemological cut, since the umbilical cord connecting abstract concepts with everyday metaphors is irreducible. First, the point is not simply that 'all concepts are metaphors', but that the very difference between a concept and a metaphor is always minimally metaphorical, relying on some metaphor. Even more important is the opposite conclusion: the very reduction of a concept to a bundle of metaphors already has to rely on some implicit *philosophical (conceptual)* determination of the difference between concept and metaphor – that is to say, on the very opposition it tries to under- mine.[13] We are thus forever caught in a vicious cycle: true, it is impossible to adopt a philosophical stance which is free of the con- straints of everyday naive lifeworld attitudes and notions; however, although it is *impossible*, this philosophical stance is simultaneously *unavoidable*. (Derrida makes the same point apropos of the well-known historicist thesis that the entire Aristotelian ontology based on the ten modes of being is an effect/expression of Greek grammar: the problem is that *this reduction of ontology (of ontological categories) to an effect of grammar presupposes a certain notion (categorical determination) of the relationship between grammar and ontological concepts which is itself already metaphysical-Greek.*[14])

We should always bear in mind this delicate Derridan stance on account of which he avoids the twin pitfalls of naive realism as well as of direct philosophical foundationalism: a 'philosophical foundation' to our experience is *impossible*, yet *necessary* – although all that we perceive, understand, articulate, is, of course, overdetermined by a horizon of pre-understanding, this horizon itself remains ultimately impenetrable. Derrida is thus a kind of metatranscendentalist, in search of the conditions of possibility of philosophical discourse itself – if we miss this precise point, that Derrida undermines philosophical discourse *from within*, we reduce 'deconstruction' to just one more naive historicist relativism. Thus Derrida's position here is the opposite of that of Foucault who, in answer to a criticism that he spoke from a position whose possibility is not accounted for within the framework of his theory, retorted cheerfully: 'These kinds of questions do not concern me: they belong to the police discourse with its files constructing the subject's identity!'

In other words, the ultimate lesson of deconstruction seems to be that one cannot postpone the *ontological* question *ad infinitum*. That is to say: what is deeply symptomatic in Derrida is his oscillation between, on the one hand, the hyper-self-reflective approach which denounces the question of 'how things really are' in advance, and limits itself to third-level deconstructive comments on the inconsistencies of philosopher B's reading of philosopher A, and, on the other, direct 'ontological' assertions about how *differance* and archi-trace designate the structure of all living things and are, as such, already operative in animal nature. One should not miss the paradoxical interconnection of these two levels here: the very feature which forever prevents us from grasping our intended object directly (the fact that our grasping is always refracted, 'mediated', by a decentred otherness) is the feature which connects us with the basic proto-ontological structure of the universe. . . .

So deconstructionism involves two prohibitions: it prohibits the 'naive' empiricist approach (let us examine the material in question carefully, then generalize hypotheses about it . . .), as well as global non-historical metaphysical theses about the origin and structure of the universe. And it is interesting to note how the recent cognitivist backlash against deconstructionist Cultural Studies violates precisely these two prohibitions. On the one hand, cognitivism rehabilitates the empiricist freshness of approaching and examining the object of research without the background of a global theory (at last one can study a film or a group of films without having to possess a global theory of Subject and Ideology . . . .). On the other hand, what indicates the recent rise of quantum physics popularizers and other proponents of the so-called Third Culture if not a violent and aggressive rehabilitation of the most fundamental metaphysical questions (what is the origin and the putative end of the universe, etc.)? The explicit goal of people like Stephen Hawking is a version of TOE: the endeavour to discover a basic formula of the structure of our universe that one could print and wear on a T-shirt (or, for a human being, the genome that identifies what I objectively am). So, in clear contrast to the strict Cultural Studies prohibition of direct 'ontological' questions, the proponents of Third Culture approach the most fundamental 'metaphysical' issues (the ultimate constituents of reality; the origins and end of the universe; the nature of consciousness; how life emerged; etc.) undaunted – as if the old dream – which died with the demise of Hegelianism – of a broad synthesis of metaphysics and science, the dream of a global theory of *all* grounded in exact scientific insights, is coming alive again. . . .

On a different level, this circular mutual implication which is characteristic of deconstructionism proper is also discernible in political philosophy. Hannah Arendt[15] articulated refined distinctions between power, authority and violence: Power proper is at work neither in organizations run by direct non-political authority (by an order of command that does not rely on politically grounded authority: the Army, the Church, the school) nor in the case of the direct reign of violence (terror). Here, however, it is crucial to insist that the relationship between political power and pre-political violence is one of mutual implication: not only is (political) power always-already at the root of every apparently 'non-political' relationship of violence; violence itself is the necessary supplement of power. That is to say: it is true that the accepted violence and direct relationship of subordination in the Army, the Church, the family, and other 'non-political' social forms is in itself the 'reification' of a certain ethico-*political* struggle and decision – the job of a critical analysis should be to discern the hidden *political* process that sustains all these 'non-' or 'pre-political' relationships. In human society, the political is the englobing structuring principle, so that every neutralization of some partial content as 'non-political' is a political gesture *par excellence*. At the same time, however, a certain excess of non-political violence is the necessary supplement to power: power always has to rely on an obscene stain of violence – that is to say, political space is never 'pure', it always involves some kind of reliance on 'pre-political' violence.

The relationship between these two implications is *asymmetrical*: the first mode of implication (every violence is political, grounded in a political decision) indicates the overall symbolic overdetermination of social reality (we never attain the zero-level of pure violence; violence is always mediated by the eminently symbolic relationship of power), while the second mode of implication indicates the excess of the Real in every symbolic edifice. Similarly, the two deconstructionist prohibitions/implications are not symmetrical either: the fact that we can never leave behind the conceptual background (that in all deconstruction of the Conceptual we rely on some notion of the opposition between concept and metaphor) indicates the irreducible symbolic overdetermination, while the fact that all concepts remain grounded in metaphors indicates the irreducible excess of some Real.

This double prohibition that defines deconstructionism bears clear and unambiguous witness to its Kantian transcendental philosophical origins (which, to avoid misunderstanding, is *not* meant as a criticism here): is not the same double prohibition (on the one hand, the notion of the transcendental constitution of reality involves the loss of a direct naive empiricist approach to reality; on the other, it involves the prohibition of metaphysics, that is, of the all-encompassing world-view that provides the noumenal structure of the Whole universe) characteristic of Kant's philosophical revolution? In other words, one should always bear in mind that Kant, far from simply expressing a belief in the constitutive power of the (transcendental) subject, introduces the notion of the transcendental dimension in order to answer the fundamental and irresolvable deadlock of human existence: a human being strives compulsively towards a global notion of truth, of a universal and necessary cognition, yet this cognition is simultaneously forever inaccessible to him. For this reason, Kant was undoubtedly the first philosopher who, in his notion of 'transcendental illusion', implicitly outlined a *theory* of the structural necessity of ghosts: 'ghosts' ('undead' entities in general) are apparitions which are constructed in order to fill in this gap between necessity and impossibility which is constitutive of the human condition.[16]

'Concrete universality'

A further substantial clarification is needed with regard to Butler's criticism that I present an abstract/decontextualized matrix or logic of ideology/domination, and use concrete cases only as examples and/or illustrations of this formal matrix – her claim is that, by doing this, I secretly *Kantianize* Hegel, introducing the pre-Hegelian gap between the universal formal matrix and its contingent historical content/illustrations. This confronts us with the difficult philosophical issue of the properly dialectical relationship between universality and particularity – with the Hegelian notion of 'concrete universality'. Although Hegel was Althusser's *bête noire*, it is my contention that Hegelian 'concrete universality' is uncannily close to what Althusser called the *articulation* of an overdetermined totality. Perhaps the most appropriate way to tackle this problem is via the notion of *suture* which, in the last few years, has undeservedly gone out of fashion.

One should begin by dispelling the key misunderstanding: suture does not stand for the idea that traces of the production process, its gaps, its mechanisms, are obliterated, so that the product can appear as a naturalized organic whole. In a first approach, one could define suture as the structurally necessary *short circuit* between different levels. So, of course, suture involves the overcoming of the crude distinction between different levels – in cinema studies, the inherent formal analysis of style, narrative analysis, research into the economic conditions of the studio system of production, and so on. However, suture must be distinguished from the otherwise very productive and interesting new historicist probing into the contingent particular set of conditions which gave birth to some well-known stylistic innovation: often, such an innovation occurred as a creative invention to resolve some very common deadlock concerning the economic limitations of cinema production.

The first association in cinema studies here, of course, is Val Lewton's stylistic revolution in horror films: the universe of his *Cat People* and *Seventh Victim* simply belongs to a different planet compared with the universe of, say, *Frankenstein* or *Dracula* – and, as we know, Lewton's procedure of only hinting at the presence of Evil in everyday reality in the guise of dark shadows or strange sounds, never directly showing it, was prompted by the financial limitations of B-productions.[17] Similarly, the greatest post-World War II revolution in opera staging, that of Bayreuth in the early 1950s, which replaced bombastic stage costumes with a bare stage and singers dressed only in pseudo-Greek tunics, the main effects being achieved by strong lighting, was an inventive solution conditioned by financial crisis: Bayreuth was practically broke, so it couldn't afford rich staging and costumes; by a stroke of luck, some large electrical concern offered them strong searchlights. . . . Such explanations, however, insightful and interesting as they are, do not yet undermine (or – to use the old-fashioned term – 'deconstruct') the notion of the inherent evolution of stylistic procedures, that is, the standard formalist narrative of the autonomous growth of artistic styles – these external conditions leave the internal logic intact, just as, if a scientist tells me that my passionate love is actually brought about by neuronal or biochemical processes, this knowledge in no way undermines or affects my passionate (self-)experience. Even if we go a step further, and endeavour to discern global correspondences between different levels of the phenomenon of cinema (how a certain narrative structure relies on a certain set of ideological presuppositions, and finds its optimal expression in a determinate set of formal procedures of montage, framing of shots, etc., like the standard notion of classic Hollywood involving the ideology of American individualism, the linear narrative closure, the shot/reverse-shot procedure, etc.), we do not yet reach the level of suture.

What, then, is still missing? The dialectical notion of *reflexivity* might be of some help here: to put it in Laclau's terms, 'suture' means that external difference is always an internal one, that the external limitation of a field of phenomena always reflects itself within this field, as its inherent impossibility fully to become itself. To take a harrowing example from philosophy: Étienne Balibar demonstrated convincingly how Althusser, in his last theoretical writings in the years just prior to his mental collapse with its well-known tragic results, systematically endeavoured to destroy his previous 'standard' propositions – these writings are sustained by a kind of philosophical death-drive, by a will to obliterate, to undo, one's previous achievements (like the epistemological cut, etc.).[18] If, however, we account for this 'will to self-obliteration' in the simple terms of the unfortunate theoretical effects of a personal pathology – of the destructive turn which finally found its outlet in the murderous assault on his wife – we *miss the point*: true as it may be on the level of biographical facts, this external causality is of no interest whatsoever if we do not succeed in interpreting it as an external shock that set in motion some inherent tension already at work within Althusser's philosophical edifice itself. In other words, Althusser's self-destructive turn ultimately had to be accounted for in the terms of his philosophy itself. . . .

We can see how, in this precise sense, suture is the exact opposite of the illusory self-enclosed totality that successfully erases the decentred traces of its production process: suture means that, precisely, such self-enclosure is a priori impossible, that the excluded externality always leaves its traces – or, to put it in standard Freudian terms, that there is no repression (from the scene of phenomenal self-experience) without the return of the repressed. More precisely, in order to produce the effect of self-enclosure, one must add to the series an excessive element which 'sutures' it precisely in so far as it does not belong to the series, but stands out as an exception, like the proverbial 'filler' in classificatory systems, a category which poses as one among the species of a genus, although it is actually just a negative container, a catch-all for everything that does not fit the species articulated from the inherent principle of the genus (the 'Asiatic mode of production' in Marxism).

As for cinema, this, again, means that one cannot simply distinguish different levels – say, the narrative line from the formal procedures of shot/counter-shot, tracking and crane shots, and so on – and then establish structural correspondences between them, that is, determine how certain narrative modes entail – or at least privilege – certain formal procedures. We attain the level of suture only when, in a unique short circuit, we conceive of a certain formal procedure not as expressing a certain aspect of the (narrative) content, but as marking/signalling the part of content that is excluded from the explicit narrative line, so that *if we want to reconstruct 'all' the narrative content, we must reach beyond the explicit narrative content as such, and include some formal features which act as the stand-in for the 'repressed' aspect of the content.*

To take a well-known elementary example from the analysis of melodramas: the emotional excess that cannot express itself directly in the narrative line finds its outlet in ridiculously sentimental musical accompaniment, or in some other formal features. An excellent example is the way Claude Berri's *Jean de Florette* and *Manon des Sources* displace Marcel Pagnol's original film (and his own later novelization of it) on which they are based. Pagnol's original retains the traces of 'authentic' French provincial community life, in which people's acts follow old, quasi-pagan religious patterns; while Berri's films fail in their effort to recapture the spirit of this closed premodern community. Unexpectedly, however, the inherent obverse of Pagnol's universe is the theatricality of the action and the element of ironic distance and comicality, while Berri's films, although they are shot more 'realistically', emphasize destiny (the musical leitmotiv is based on Verdi's *La forza del destino*), and a melodramatic excess whose hystericality often borders on the ridiculous (like the scene in which, after the rain passes over his field, the desperate Jean cries and berates Heaven).[19] So, paradoxically, the closed ritualized premodern community implies theatrical comicality and irony, while the modern 'realistic' rendering involves Fate and melodramatic excess. . . . In this respect, Berri's films are the opposite of Lars von Trier's *Breaking the Waves*: in both cases, we are dealing with the tension between form and content; in *Breaking the Waves*, however, the excess is located in the content (and the subdued pseudo-documentary form brings out the excessive content); while in Berri, *the excess in the form obfuscates and thus brings home, the flaw in content, the impossibility of realizing the pure classical tragedy of destiny today.*

The ultimate *philosophical* example here is that of the subjective versus objective dimension: subjective perception–awareness–activity versus objective socio-economic or physiological mechanisms. A dialectical theory intervenes with a double short circuit: objectivity relies on a subjective surplus-gesture; subjectivity relies on *objet petit a*, the paradoxical object which is the subject's counterpoint. This is what Lacan is aiming at in his persistent reference to torus and other variations on the Moebius-band-like structures in which the relationship between inside and outside is inverted: if we want to grasp the minimal structure of subjectivity, the clear-cut opposition between inner subjective experience and outer objective reality is not sufficient – there is an excess on both sides. On the one hand, we should accept the lesson of Kant's transcendental idealism: out of the confused multitude of impressions, *objective* reality emerges through the intervention of the *subject's* transcendental act. Kant does not deny the distinction between the multitude of subjective impressions and objective reality; his point is merely that this very distinction results from the intervention of a *subjective* gesture of transcendental constitution. Similarly, Lacan's 'Master-Signifier' is the 'subjective' signifying feature which sustains the very 'objective' symbolic structure: if we abstract this subjective excess from the objective symbolic order, the very objectivity of this order disintegrates. On the other hand, the Lacanian *objet petit a* is the exact opposite of the Master-Signifier: not the subjective supplement which sustains the objective order, but the objective supplement which sustains subjectivity in its contrast to the subjectless objective order: *objet petit a* is that 'bone in the throat', that disturbing stain which forever blurs our picture of reality – it is the *object* on account of which 'objective reality' is forever inaccessible to the subject.[20]

This already brings us to the next feature, that of *universality and its exception*. The properly dialectical procedure, practised by Hegel as well as by Freud in his great case studies, can be best described as a direct jump from the singular to the universal, bypassing the mid-level of particularity:

> In its dialectic of a clinical case, psychoanalysis is a field in which the singular and the universal coincide without passing through the particular.

This is not common in philosophy, with the exception, perhaps, of certain Hegelian moments.[21]

When Freud deals with a case of claustrophobia, he always embarks on a search for some *singular* traumatic experience which is at the root of this phobia: the fear of closed spaces in general is grounded in an experience of . . . . Here, Freud's procedure is to be distinguished from the Jungian search for archetypes: the root is not a paradigmatic universal traumatic experience (like the proverbial horror of being enclosed in the mother's womb), but some singular experience linked to a closed space in a wholly contingent, external way – what if the subject witnessed some traumatic scene (which could also have taken place elsewhere) *in a closed space*? Even more 'magic' is the opposite situation, when, in his case analyses, Freud, as a rule, makes the direct leap from a close dissection of a singular case (like that of the Wolf Man or of the fantasy 'A child is being beaten') to the universal assertion of what 'fantasy (masochism, etc.) "as such" is'.

From the standpoint of empiricist cognitivism, of course, such a short circuit immediately gives rise to a host of critical questions: how can Freud be so sure that he has picked on a truly representative example? Should we not at least compare this case with a representative sample of other, different cases, and so verify the universality of the concept in question? The dialectical counter-argument is that such careful empirical generalization never brings us to a true universality – why not? Because *all particular examples of a certain universality do not entertain the same relationship towards their universality*: each of them struggles with this universality, displaces it, and so on, in a specific way, and the great art of dialectical analysis consists in being able to pick out the exceptional singular case which allows us to formulate the universality 'as such'.[22] Just as Marx articulated the universal logic of the historical development of humanity on the basis of his analysis of capitalism as the excessive (imbalanced) system of production (for Marx, capitalism is a contingent monstrous formation whose very 'normal' state is permanent dislocation, a kind of 'freak of history', a social system caught in the vicious superego cycle of incessant expansion – yet precisely as such, it is the 'truth' of the entire previous 'normal' history), Freud was

able to formulate the universal logic of the Oedipal mode of socialization through identification with the paternal Law precisely because
he lived in exceptional times in which Oedipus was already in a state of
crisis.[23]

The basic rule of dialectics, therefore, is: whenever we are offered a
simple enumeration of subspecies of a universal species, we should
always look for the exception to the series. In contrast to this properly
dialectical direct mix of a special case and sweeping generalizations
(like the detailed analysis of a scene from a *noir* melodrama, from which
one directly draws general conclusions on feminine subjectivity and the
gaze in the patriarchal order), today's cognitivist antidialecticians insist
on clear theoretical classifications and gradual generalizations based
on careful empirical research. They distinguish transcultural universal
features (part of our evolutionary heritage and the psychic structure of
human beings) from features that are specific to particular cultures and
periods – that is to say, they operate in terms of a simple pyramid rising
from natural or other trans-cultural universal features to more and
more specific characteristics which depend on localized contexts. The
elementary dialectical counter-argument here is that the very relationship between transcultural universals and culture-specific features is not
an ahistorical constant, but historically overdetermined: the very notion
of a transcultural Universal means different things in different cultures.
The procedure of comparing different cultures and isolating or identifying their common features is never a neutral procedure, but
presupposes some specific viewpoint – while one can claim, say, that all
cultures recognize some kind of difference between subjective imagination and reality, things as they exist out there, this assertion still begs
the question of what 'objective reality' means in different cultures.
When a European says: 'Ghosts don't really exist', while a Native
American says that he communicates with them, and that they therefore
do really exist, does 'really' mean the same thing for both of them? Is
not our notion of 'really existing' (which relies on the opposition
between Is and Ought, between Being and Values, etc.) specific to
modernity?

Noir as a Hegelian concept

Of course, today's cognitive semantics no longer advocates the simplistic logic of empirical generalization, of classification into genuses
through the identification of common features; rather, it emphasizes
how terms that designate species display a kind of 'radial' structure of
intricate family resemblances, without any unambiguous feature to unify
all the members of a species (recall the difficulties in elaborating a definition of *noir* that would in fact include all the films we 'intuitively'
perceive as *noir*). This, however, is not yet what a properly dialectical
notion of the universal amounts to. To demonstrate this limitation of the
preconceptual historicist account, let us take an exercise in cinema
theory historicism at its best: Marc Vernet's rejection of the very concept
of *film noir*.[24]

In a detailed analysis, Vernet demonstrates that all the main features
that constitute the common definition of *film noir* ('expressionist'
chiaroscuro lightning and oblique camera angles, the paranoiac universe of the hardboiled novel, with corruption elevated to a cosmic
metaphysical feature embodied in the *femme fatale*, etc.), as well as the
explanation for them (the threat the social impact of World War II
posed to the patriarchal phallic regime, etc.) are simply false. What
Vernet does apropos of *noir* is something similar to what the late François
Furet did with the French Revolution in historiography: he turns an
Event into a non-Event, a false hypostasis that involves a series of misrecognitions of the complex concrete historical situation. *Film noir* is not
a category of the history of Hollywood cinema, but a category of the
criticism and history of cinema that could have emerged only in France,
for the French gaze immediately after World War II, including all the
limitations and misrecognitions of such a gaze (the ignorance of what
went on before in Hollywood, the tension of the ideological situation in
France itself in the aftermath of the war, etc.).

This explanation reaches its apogee when we take into account the
fact that poststructuralist deconstructionism (which serves as the standard theoretical foundation of the Anglo-Saxon analysis of *film noir*)
has, in a way, exactly the same status as *film noir* according to Vernet: just
as American *noir* does not exist (in itself, in America), since it was

invented for and by the French gaze, one should also emphasize that poststructuralist deconstructionism does not exist (in itself, in France), since it was invented in the USA, for and by the American academic gaze, with all its constitutive limitations. (The prefix *post* in 'poststructuralism' is thus a reflexive determination in the strict Hegelian sense of the term: although it seems to designate the property of its object – the change, the cut, in the French intellectual orientation – it actually involves a reference to the gaze of the subject perceiving it: 'post' means things that went on in French theory after the American (or German) gaze had perceived them, while 'structuralism' *tout court* designates French theory 'in itself', before it was noted by the foreign gaze. 'Poststructuralism' is structuralism from the moment it was noted by the foreign gaze.)

In short, an entity like 'poststructuralist deconstructionism' (the term itself is not used in France) comes into existence only for a gaze that is unaware of the details of the philosophical scene in France: this gaze brings together authors (Derrida, Deleuze, Foucault, Lyotard . . .) who are simply not perceived as part of the same *épistème* in France, just as the concept of *film noir* posits a unity which did not exist 'in itself'. And just as the French gaze, ignorant of the ideological tradition of American individualist anti-combo populism, misperceived through the existentialist lenses the heroic cynical-pessimistic fatalist stance of the *noir* hero as a socially critical attitude, the American perception inscribed the French authors into the field of radical cultural criticism, and thus attributed to them a feminist, etc., critical social stance for the most part absent in France itself.[25] Just as *film noir* is not a category of American cinema, but primarily a category of French cinema criticism and (later) of the historiography of cinema, 'poststructuralist deconstructionist' is not a category of French philosophy, but primarily a category of the American (mis)reception of the French authors designated as such. So, when we are reading what is arguably the paradigmatic example and topic of (cinema) deconstructionist theory, a feminist analysis of the way the *femme fatale* in *film noir* symbolizes ambivalent male reaction to the threat to the patriarchal 'phallic order', we actually have a nonexistent theoretical position analysing a nonexistent cinematic genre. . . .

Is such a conclusion really unavoidable, however, even if we concede
that, on the level of data, Vernet is right? Although Vernet actually
undermines a lot of the standard *noir* theory (for example, the rather
crude notion that the *noir* universe stands for the paranoiac male reaction to the threat to the 'phallic regime' embodied in the *femme fatale*),
the enigma that remains is the mysterious efficiency and persistence of
the notion of *noir*: the more Vernet is right on the level of facts, the
more enigmatic and inexplicable becomes the extraordinary strength
and longevity of this 'illusory' notion of *noir*, the notion that has
haunted our imagination for decades. What, then, if *film noir* is none
the less a *concept* in the strict Hegelian sense: something that cannot
simply be explained, accounted for, in terms of historical circumstances, conditions and reactions, but acts as a structuring principle
that displays a dynamics of its own – *film noir* is a real concept, a unique
vision of the universe that combines the multitude of elements into
what Althusser would have called an *articulation*.[26] So, once we have
ascertained that the notion of *noir* does not fit the empirical multitude
of *noir* films, instead of rejecting this notion, we should risk the notorious Hegelian rejoinder 'So much the worse for reality!' – more
precisely, we should engage in the dialectic between a universal notion
and its reality, in which the very gap between the two sets in motion the
simultaneous transformation of reality, and of the notion itself. It is
because real films never fit their notion that they are constantly changing, and this change imperceptibly transforms the very notion, the
standard by means of which they are measured: we pass from the
hardboiled-detective *noir* (the Hammett–Chandler formula) to the 'per-
secuted innocent bystander' *noir* (the Cornell Woolrich formula), and
thence to the 'naive sucker caught up in a crime' *noir* (the James Cain
formula), and so on.

The situation here is in a way similar to that of Christianity: of
course, almost all its elements were already there in the Dead Sea
Scrolls; most of the key Christian notions are clear cases of what
Stephen Jay Gould would have called 'exaptations',[27] retroactive rein-
scriptions which misperceive and falsify the original impact of a notion,
and so forth; but none the less, this is not enough to explain the Event of
Christianity. The concept of *noir* is therefore extremely productive not

only for the analysis of films, but even as a tool to help us retroactively cast a new light on previous classic works of art; in this vein, implicitly applying Marx's old idea that the anatomy of man is the key to the anatomy of the monkey, Elisabeth Bronfen uses the co-ordinates of the *noir* universe to throw a new light on Wagner's *Tristan* as the ultimate *noir* opera.[28] A further example of how *noir* enables us to 'deliver' Wagner's operas retroactively are his long retrospective monologues, that ultimate horror of impatient spectators – do not these long narratives call for a *noir* flashback to illustrate them?

Perhaps, however, as we have already insinuated, Wagner is a Hitchcockian *avant la lettre* rather than a *noir* composer: not only is the ring from his *Ring* the ultimate MacGuffin; much more interesting is the whole of Act I of *Die Walküre*, especially the long orchestral passage in the middle which constitutes a true Wagnerian counterpart to the great party sequence in Hitchcock's *Notorious*, with its intricate exchange of glances: three minutes without a singing voice, only orchestral music that accompanies and organizes a complex exchange of glances between the three subjects (the love couple of Sieglinde and Siegmund and their common enemy, Sieglinde's brutal husband Hunding) and the fourth element, the object, the magic sword Nothung deeply embedded in a gigantic trunk that occupies centre stage. In his famous Bayreuth centenary staging of the *Ring* (1975–79), Patrice Chéreau solved the problem of how to stage this rather static scene with an intricate, sometimes almost ridiculous ballet of the three characters moving around and exchanging their respective places (first Hunding between Siegmund and Sieglinde, then Sieglinde stepping over to Siegmund and both confronting Hunding, etc.), as if the role of the third, disturbing element is being displaced from one actor to another (first Siegmund, then Hunding). I am tempted to claim that this exquisite ballet – which almost reminds us of the famous boxing scene in Chaplin's *City Lights*, with its interplay between the two boxers and the referee – desperately endeavours to compensate us for the fact that no subjective shots are feasible on the theatrical stage: were this three-minute scene to be filmed like the party scene from *Notorious*, with a well-synchronized exchange of establishing shots, objective close-ups and subjective shots, Wagner's music would find its appropriate visual counterpart – an exemplary case of Wagnerian scenes which, as Michel Chion put it, should be read today in a kind of *futur antérieur*, since 'they seem retrospectively to call for the cinema to correct them'.[29] This interpretative procedure is the very opposite of teleology: teleology relies on a linear evolutionary logic in which the lower stage already contains *in nuce* the seeds of the higher stage, so that evolution is simply the unfolding of some underlying essential potential, while here, the lower (or, rather, previous) stage becomes readable only retroactively, in so far as it is itself ontologically 'incomplete', a set of traces without meaning, and thus open to later reappropriations.

We are therefore tempted to designate the two foreign misrecognizing Gazes whose oblique point of view was constitutive of their respective objects (*film noir*, 'poststructuralist deconstructionism') as precisely the two exemplary cases of the so-called 'drama of false appearances':[30] the hero and/or heroine are/is placed in a compromising situation, either over their sexual behaviour or because of a crime; their actions are observed by a character who sees things in the wrong way, reading illicit implications into their innocent behaviour; at the end, of course, the misunderstanding is clarified, and the hero or heroine is absolved of any wrongdoing. The point, however, is that through this game of false appearance, *a censored thought is allowed to be articulated*: the spectator can imagine the hero or heroine enacting forbidden wishes, but escape any penalty, since he or she knows that despite the false appearances, nothing has happened: they are innocent. The twisted imagination of the onlooker who misreads innocent signs or coincidences is the stand-in for the spectator's 'pleasurably aberrant viewing':[31] this is what Lacan had in mind when he claimed that truth has the structure of a fiction – the very suspension of literal truth opens up the way for the articulation of libidinal truth. This situation was beautifully illustrated in Ted Tetzlaff's *The Window*, in which a small boy actually witnesses a crime, although nobody believes him and his parents even force him to apologize to the murderers for the false rumours he is spreading about them. . . .[32]

However, it is Lillian Hellman's play *The Children's Hour*, twice filmed (both times directed by William Wyler), which offers perhaps the clearest, almost laboratory-type example of this 'drama of false appearances'. As is well known, the first version (*These Three* [1936]), provided the occasion for one of the great Goldwynisms: when Sam Goldwyn, the producer, was warned that the film takes place among lesbians, he supposedly replied: 'That's OK, we'll turn them into Americans!' What actually happened then was that the alleged lesbian affair around which the story pivots was in fact turned into a standard heterosexual affair. The film takes place in a posh private school for girls run by two friends, the austere and domineering Martha and the warm and affectionate Karen, who is in love with Joe, the local doctor. When Mary Tilford, a vicious pre-teen pupil, is censured for a misdeed by Martha, she retaliates by telling her grandmother that late one evening she saw Joe and Martha (not Karen, his fiancée) 'carrying on' in a bedroom near the students' quarters. The grandmother believes her, especially after this lie is corroborated by Rosalie, a weak girl terrorized by Mary, so she removes Mary from the school, and advises all the other parents to do the same. The truth eventually comes out, but the damage has been done: the school is closed, Joe loses his post at the hospital, and even the friendship between Karen and Martha comes to an end after Karen admits that she, too, has her suspicions about Martha and Joe. Joe leaves the country for a job in Vienna, where Karen later joins him. . . . The second version (1961) is a faithful rendition of the play: when Mary retaliates, she tells her grandmother that she has seen Martha and Karen kissing, embracing and whispering, implying that she does not fully understand what she was witnessing, just that it must have been something 'unnatural'. After all the parents withdraw their children from the school, and the two women find themselves alone in the large building, Martha realizes that she does actually love Karen in more than just a sisterly fashion – unable to bear the guilt she feels, she hangs herself. Mary's lie is finally exposed, but it is far too late now: in the final scene, Karen leaves Martha's funeral and walks proudly past Mary's grandmother, Joe, and all the other townspeople who were gulled by Mary's lies. . . .

The story revolves around the evil onlooker (Mary) who, through her lie, unwittingly realizes the adult's unconscious desire: the paradox, of course, is that prior to Mary's accusation, Martha was not aware of her lesbian longings – it is only this external accusation that makes her

aware of a disavowed part of herself. The 'drama of false appearances' thus realizes its truth: the evil onlooker's 'pleasurably aberrant
viewing' externalizes the repressed aspect of the falsely accused subject. The interesting point is that although, in the second version, the
censorship distortion is corrected, the first version is, as a rule, considered far superior to its 1961 remake, mainly because it is full of
repressed eroticism: not the eroticism between Martha and Joe, but the
eroticism between Martha and Karen – although the girl's accusation
concerns the alleged affair between Martha and Joe, Martha is
attached to Karen in a much more passionate way than Joe, with his
rather conventional straight love . . . . The key to the 'drama of false
appearances' is therefore that, in it, less overlaps with more. On the one
hand, the standard procedure of censorship is not to show the (prohibited) event (murder, sex act) directly, but in the way it is reflected in
the witnesses; on the other hand, this deprivation opens up a space to
be filled in by phantasmic projections – that is to say, it is possible that
the gaze which does not see what is actually going on clearly sees *more*,
not *less*.

Similarly, the notion of *noir* (or of 'poststructuralist deconstructionism', for that matter), although it results from a limited foreign
perspective, perceives in its object a potential which is invisible to those
who are directly engaged in it. That is the ultimate dialectical paradox of
truth and falsity: sometimes, the aberrant view which misreads a situation from its limited perspective can, by virtue of this very limitation,
perceive the 'repressed' potential of the observed constellation. It is true
that, if we submit productions usually designated as *noir* to a close historical analysis, the very concept of *film noir* loses its consistency, and
disintegrates; paradoxically, however, we should none the less insist that
Truth is on the level of the spectral (false) appearance of *noir*, not in
detailed historical knowledge. The effectiveness of this concept of *noir* is
that which today enables us immediately to identify as *noir* the short
scene from *Lady in the Lake*, the simple line of a dialogue in which the
detective answers the question 'But why did he kill her? Didn't he love
her?' with a straight 'That is reason enough to kill'.

Furthermore, sometimes the external misperception exerts a productive influence on the misperceived 'original' itself, forcing it to

become aware of its own 'repressed' truth (arguably, the French notion of *noir*, although it is the result of misperception, exerted a strong influence on American film-making). Is not the supreme example of this productivity of the external misperception the American reception of Derrida? Did it not – although it clearly *was* a misperception – exert a retroactive productive influence on Derrida himself, forcing him to confront ethico-political issues more directly? Was not the American reception of Derrida in this sense a kind of *pharmakon*, a supplement to the 'original' Derrida himself – a poisonous stain–fake, distorting the original and at the same time keeping it alive? In short, would Derrida still be so much 'alive' if we were to subtract from his work its American misperception?

From alienation to separation

After this clarification of 'concrete universality', I can finally answer Butler's criticism of Kantian formalism: her notion that Lacan hyposta-sizes the symbolic order into an ahistorical fixed system of rules which predetermine the scope of the subject's intervention, so that the subject is a priori unable actually to resist the symbolic order, or to change it radically. So what is the Lacanian 'big Other' as the 'decentred' symbolic order? A seemingly eccentric definition from Hegel's philosophy of nature (that of a plant as an animal with its intestines outside its body[33]) offers, perhaps the most succinct description of what the subject's 'decentrement' is about.

Let us again approach this via *Die Walküre*, in which Wotan, the supreme god, is split between his respect for the sacred link of marriage (advocated by his wife Fricka) and his admiration for the power of free love (advocated by his beloved rebellious daughter Brünnhilde); when the brave Siegmund, after escaping with the beautiful Sieglinde, wife of the cruel Hunding, has to confront Hunding in a duel, Brünnhilde violates Wotan's explicit order (to let Siegmund be killed). In defence of her disobedience, Brünnhilde claims that by trying to help Siegmund, she has actually carried out Wotan's own disavowed true will – in a way she is nothing but this 'repressed' part of Wotan, a part he had to renounce when he decided to yield to Fricka's pressure . . . . In a Jungian reading, one could thus claim that Fricka and Brünnhilde (as well as other lesser gods who surround Wotan) merely externalize different libidinal components of his personality: Fricka, as the defender of the orderly family life, stands for his superego, while Brünnhilde, with her passionate advocacy of free love, stands for Wotan's unconstrained love passion.

For Lacan, however, it is already going too far to say that Fricka and Brünnhilde 'externalize' different components of Wotan's psyche: the subject's decentrement is original and constitutive; 'I' am from the very outset 'outside myself', a *bricolage* of external components – Wotan does not merely 'project' his superego in Fricka, Fricka *is* his superego, just as Hegel claims that a plant is an animal that has its intestines outside its body, in the form of its roots embedded in the earth. So – if a plant is an animal with its intestines exterior to itself, and if, in consequence, an animal is a plant with its roots *within* itself, then a human being is biologically an animal, but spiritually a plant, in need of firm roots – is not the *symbolic order* a kind of spiritual intestines of the human animal outside its Self: the spiritual Substance of my being, the roots from which I draw my spiritual food, are outside myself, embodied in the decentred symbolic order? This fact that, spiritually, man remains an animal, rooted in an external substance, accounts for the impossible New Age dream of turning man into a true *spiritual* animal, floating freely in spiritual space, without any need for substantial roots outside himself.

So what is decentrement? When Woody Allen made a series of public appearances before journalists in the wake of his scandalous separation from Mia Farrow, he acted in 'real life' exactly like neurotic and insecure male characters in his films. So should we conclude that 'he put himself in his films', the main male characters in his films are half-concealed self-portraits? No – the conclusion to be drawn is exactly the opposite: in 'real life', Woody Allen identified with and copied a certain model that he elaborates in his films – that is to say, it is 'real life' that imitates symbolic patterns expressed at their purest in art. However, the 'big Other' is not simply the decentred symbolic 'substance'; the further crucial feature is that this 'substance' is, in its turn, again subjectivized, experienced as the 'subject supposed to know', the Other of the (forever split, hysterical) subject, the guarantee of the consistency of the field of Knowledge. As such, the 'subject supposed to know' is often embodied in a concrete individual, not only God himself (the paradoxical function of God *qua* big Other from Descartes through Hobbes and Newton, and so on, up to Einstein is precisely to guarantee the *materialist* mechanism of Nature – God is the ultimate guarantee that nature 'does not play at dice', but obeys its own laws), but even some quasi-empirical figure; let us recall this well-known passage from Heidegger:

> Recently I got a second invitation to teach at the University of Berlin. On that occasion I left Freiburg and withdrew to the cabin. I listened to what the mountains and the forest and the farmlands were saying, and I went to see an old friend of mine, a 75–year-old farmer. He had read about the call to Berlin in the newspaper. What would he say? Slowly he fixed the sure gaze of his clear eyes on mine, and keeping his mouth tightly shut, he thoughtfully put his faithful hand on my shoulder. Ever so slightly he shook his head. That meant: absolutely no.[34]

Here we have it all: the uncorrupted/experienced old farmer as the subject supposed to know who, with his barely perceptible gesture, a prolongation of the whisper of 'the mountains and the forest', provides the definitive answer. . . . On a different level, did not a reference to the judgement of an authentic member of the working class play the same role in some versions of Marxism–Leninism? And is it not true that even today, multiculturalist 'politically correct' discourse attributes the same authentic stance of the one 'supposed to know' to some privileged (African-American, gay . . .) figure of the Other?

Even deprived of this supposed knowledge, the quasi-empirical embodiment of the big Other is a person elevated into the ideal Witness to whom one speaks and whom one endeavours to fascinate – is not this function of the big Other discernible in a strange feature of the majority of James Bond films: after the Big Criminal captures Bond, instead of killing Bond immediately, he keeps him alive, and even gives him a kind of quick inspection tour of his enterprise, explaining the big coup he is planning to execute in the next hour? It is, of course, this very need for a Witness to whom the operation should be explained that costs the Big Criminal dearly: this delay gives Bond the chance to spot a weakness in his enemy and strike back at the last minute (or sometimes even the last second).

This big Other as the point of transference is central to the very definition of the psychoanalytic notion of interpretation. Freud's introductory example in his *Interpretation of Dreams* is the reading of his own dream about Irma's injection dream – what is the ultimate meaning of this dream? Freud himself focuses on the dream-thought, on his 'superficial' (fully conscious) wish to obliterate his responsibility for the failure of his treatment of Irma; in Lacanian terms, this wish clearly belongs to the domain of the *Imaginary*. Furthermore, Freud provides some hints about the *Real* in this dream: the unconscious desire of the dream is that of Freud himself as the 'primordial father' who wants to possess all the three women who appear in the dream. In his early *Seminar II*, Lacan proposes a purely *symbolic* reading: the ultimate meaning of this dream is simply that *there is a meaning*, that there is a formula (of trimethylamine) which guarantees the presence and consistency of meaning.[35] However, some recently published documents[36] clearly establish that the true focus of this dream was the *transferential* desire to save Fliess – Freud's close friend and collaborator who, at that time, was for him the 'subject supposed to know' – from his responsibility and guilt: it was Fliess who botched up Irma's nose operation, and the dream's desire is to exculpate not the dreamer (Freud himself), but the dreamer's big Other, that is, to demonstrate that the transferential Other wasn't responsible for the medical failure, that he wasn't deficient in knowledge.

The Lacanian big Other *qua* the symbolic order is thus the ultimate guarantor of Truth towards which no external distance is ever possible: even when we deceive, and precisely *in order to* deceive successfully, the trust in the big Other is already there. When the symbolic trust is in effect lost, the subject assumes the attitude of a radical sceptic – as Stanley Cavell has pointed out, the sceptic wants his big Other to establish the connection between his claims to knowledge and the objects upon which these claims are to fall in a way which would occur without the knower's intervention, that is, in a state of suspension of the knower's absorption in the work he knows. The knowledge the sceptic would fully acknowledge is a kind of impossible/real knowledge, a knowledge involving no subjective position, no engagement in the Other of the symbolic pact, a knowledge without a knower.[37] In other words, the sceptic suspends the dimension of the big Other, of the symbolic pact and engagement, the domain within which the knower always-already dwells, and which provides the background of our relating to the world and thus, in a way constitutes this world, since what we experience as world is always-already embedded in a concrete lifeworld experience of myself as an engaged agent. The sceptic wants 'proof' that my words actually refer to objects in the world, yet he first suspends the big Other, the horizon of the symbolic pact which regulates this reference and cannot be 'proven', since it grounds in advance the very logic of possible proofs.[38]

This dimension of the 'big Other' is that of the constitutive *alienation* of the subject in the symbolic order: the big Other pulls the strings; the subject does not speak, he 'is spoken' by the symbolic structure. In short, this 'big Other' is the name for the social Substance, for all that on account of which the subject never fully dominates the effects of his acts – on account of which the final outcome of his activity is always something other than what he aimed at or anticipated.[39] It is crucial here, however, to note that in the key chapters of *Seminar XI*, Lacan struggles to delineate the operation that follows alienation and is in a sense its counterpoint, that of *separation*: alienation *in* the big Other is followed by the separation *from* the big Other. Separation takes place when the subject realizes how the big Other is in itself inconsistent, purely virtual, 'barred', deprived of the Thing – and fantasy is an attempt to fill out this lack *of the Other, not of the subject*: to (re)constitute the consistency of the big Other. For that reason, fantasy and paranoia are inextricably linked: at its most elementary, paranoia is a belief in an 'Other of the Other', in another Other who, hidden behind the Other of the explicit social texture, programmes (what appears to us as) the unforeseen effects of social life, and thus guarantees its consistency: beneath the chaos of the market, the degradation of morals, and so on, is the purposeful strategy of the Jewish plot . . . This paranoiac stance has acquired a further boost with today's digitalization of our daily lives: when our entire (social) existence is progressively externalized–materialized in the big Other of the computer network, it is easy to imagine an evil programmer erasing our digital identity, and thus depriving us of our social existence, turning us into non-persons.

Perhaps the ultimate literary example of the shift from alienation to separation occurs in Kafka's writings. On the one hand, Kafka's universe is that of extreme alienation: the subject is confronted with an impervious Other whose machinery functions in an entirely 'irrational' way, as if the chain that links causes and effects has broken down – the only stance the subject can assume towards this Other (of the Court, of the Castle bureaucracy) is that of impotent fascination. No wonder Kafka's universe is that of universal–formal guilt independent of any concrete content and act of the subject who perceives himself as guilty. However, the final twist of the paradigmatic Kafkaesque story, the parable on the Door of the Law from *The Trial*, pinpoints precisely what is false in such a self-perception: the subject failed to include himself in the scene, that is, to take into account how he was not merely an innocent bystander of the spectacle of the Law, since 'the Door was there only for him'. The dialectical paradox is that since the subject's *exclusion* from the fascinating spectacle of the big Other elevated the big Other into an all-powerful transcendent agency that generates an a priori guilt, it is the very *inclusion* into the observed scene that allows the subject to achieve *separation* from the big Other – to experience his subjective position as correlative to the big Other's inconsistency/impotence/lack: in separation, the subject experiences how his own lack with regard to the big Other is already the lack that affects the big Other itself (or, to quote Hegel's immortal formulation again, in separation I experience how the impenetrable secret *of* the Ancient Egyptians were already secrets *for* the Egyptians themselves).

This reference to separation allows me to counter the criticism according to which there is in Lacan a secret longing for the 'strong' symbolic order/prohibition threatened by today's narcissistic disintegration: does Lacan really envisage as the only solution to the recent deadlock the reassertion of some fundamental symbolic prohibition/Law? Is this really the only alternative to the postmodern global psychotization of social life? It is true that the Lacan of the 1940s and 1950s does contain elements of such conservative cultural criticism; his constant effort from the 1960s onwards, however, is to break *out* of this framework, to expose the *fraud* of paternal authority (rejecting also the Pascalian cynical solution that one should obey the Power even if one knows of its false/illegal origins). Furthermore, this reference to separation also allows us to answer Butler's point that the Lacanian big Other, the symbolic order, forms a kind of Kantian a priori which cannot be undermined by the subject's intervention, since every resistance to it is doomed to perpetual defeat: the big Other is unassailable only in so far as the subject entertains towards it a relationship of alienation, while separation precisely opens up the way for such an intervention.

In terms of affects, the difference between alienation and separation equals the difference between *guilt* and *anxiety*: the subject experiences guilt before the big Other, while anxiety is a sign that the Other itself is lacking, impotent – in short, *guilt masks anxiety*. In psychoanalysis, guilt is therefore a category which ultimately *deceives* – no less than its opposite, innocence. Despite its shocking and obviously 'unjust' character, even the paradigmatic Stalinist remark apropos of the victims of political trials ('The more they proclaim their innocence, the more guilty they are!') therefore contains a grain of truth: the ex-Party cadres wrongfully condemned as 'traitors' *were* guilty in a way, although not, of course, of the crimes of which they were explicitly accused – their true guilt was a kind of metaguilt; that is, it lay in the way they themselves participated in the creation of the system which rejected them, so that on some level, at least, their condemnation meant that they got from the system their own message in its inverted-true form. Their guilt resided in their very assertion of innocence which means that they thought more about their insignificant individual fate than about the larger historical interests of the Party (which needed their sacrifice) – what made them guilty was this form of abstract individuality which underlay their stubborn assertion of innocence. They were thus caught in a strange forced choice: if they admitted their guilt, they were guilty; if they insisted on their innocence, they were, in a way, even more guilty. On the other hand, this example of the accused in the Stalinist show-trial clearly expresses the tension between guilt and anxiety: the Party leaders needed the accused's confession of *guilt* in order to avoid the unbearable *anxiety* of having to admit that 'the big Other does not exist', that the historical Necessity of the Progress to Communism is an inconsistent phantasmic fake.

And perhaps, in so far as the ultimate name for the decentred symbolic place that overdetermines my speech is the Freudian 'unconscious', I am even tempted to risk a kind of rehabilitation of *consciousness*: if, in psychoanalysis, guilt is ultimately unconscious (not only in the sense that the subject is unaware of his or her guilt, but also in the sense that he or she, while experiencing the pressure of guilt, is unaware of what he or she is guilty of), what then if anxiety, as the counterpoint of guilt, should be linked to consciousness? The status of consciousness is much more enigmatic than it may appear: the more its marginal and ephemeral character is emphasized, the more the question forces itself upon us: What *is* it, then? To what *does* self-awareness amount? The more Lacan denigrates its function, the more inscrutable it becomes.

Perhaps a key is provided by Freud's notion that the unconscious knows of no death: what if, at its most radical, 'consciousness' *is* the awareness of one's finitude and mortality? So Badiou (who reduces the awareness of one's mortality to the animal dimension of human beings) is wrong here: there is nothing 'animal' about finitude and mortality – only 'conscious' beings are actually finite and mortal, that is, only they *relate* to their finitude 'as such'. Awareness of one's own mortality is not one among many aspects of self-awareness, but its very zero-level: in an analogy to Kant's notion that each consciousness of an object involves self-consciousness, each awareness involves an implicit (self-)awareness of one's own mortality and finitude. This awareness is then disavowed by the subject's unconscious disbelief in his or her mortality, so that the elementary model of 'I know very well, but . . .' is perhaps the very model of self-awareness: 'I know very well that I am mortal, but nevertheless . . . (I do not accept it; I unconsciously believe in my immortality, since I cannot envisage my own death)'.[40]

The usual psychiatrist's complaint is that the patient often accepts some traumatic fact on a purely intellectual level, while continuing to reject it emotionally, acting and behaving as if this fact were nonexistent. What, however, if such a gap is *constitutive* of my (self-) consciousness, not just its secondary distortion? What if consciousness *means* that I am aware of some fact whose full affective impact is suspended? What if, in consequence, I can *never* consciously 'fully assume' the place of my unconscious belief, of my fundamental fantasy (of my 'primordial attachment', to use Butler's term)? In so far as, for Freud, anxiety is the 'universal affect' that signals the primordial repression of (the minimal distance from) the scene of incestuous *jouissance*, consciousness, in effect, equals anxiety. So when Butler asks the rhetorical question –

> Why should we conceive of universality as an empty 'place' which awaits its content in an anterior and subsequent event? Is it empty only because it has already disavowed or suppressed the content from which it emerges, and where is the trace of the disavowed in the formal structure that emerges? (JB, p. 34)

– I fully endorse her implicit stance. My answer (apart from rejecting the inappropriate use of the term 'disavowal', which has another precise meaning in psychoanalysis) is: Lacan's 'primordial repression' of *das Ding* (of the pre-symbolic incestuous Real Thing) is precisely that which creates universality as an empty place; and the 'trace of the disavowed in the formal structure that emerges' is what Lacan calls *objet petit a*, the remainder of the *jouissance* within the symbolic order. This very necessity of the primordial repression shows clearly why one should distinguish between the exclusion of the Real that *opens up* the empty place of the universal and the subsequent hegemonic struggles of different particular contents to *occupy* this empty place. And here I am even tempted to read Butler against herself – say, against her sympathetic recapitulation of Laclau: 'Inevitable as it is that a political organization will posit the possible filling of that [empty place of the universal] as an ideal, it is equally inevitable that it will fail to do so' (JB, p. 32). It is in endorsing this logic of the ideal to be endlessly approximated that I see the under-lying *Kantianism* of both Butler and Laclau.

Here, I think, it is crucial to defend the key *Hegelian* insight directed against the Kantian position of the universal a priori frame distorted by empirical 'pathological' conditions, in all its versions, including the Habermasian universal communicational a priori: it is not enough to posit a universal formal criterion and then to agree that, owing to contingent empirical distortions, reality will never fully rise to its level. The question is, rather: how, through what violent operation of exclusion/repression, does this universal frame itself emerge? With regard to the notion of hegemony, this means that it is not enough to assert the gap between the empty universal signifier and the particular signifiers that endeavour to fill its void – the question to be raised is, again, how, through what operation of exclusion, does this void itself emerge?

For Lacan, this preceding loss (the loss of *das Ding*, what Freud called the 'primordial repression') is not the loss of a determinate object (say, the renunciation of the same-sex libidinal partner), but the loss which paradoxically *precedes* any lost object, so that each positive object that is elevated to the place of the Thing (Lacan's definition of sublimation) in a way *gives body to the loss*. What this means is that that the Lacanian Real, the bar of impossibility it stands for, does not primarily cross the subject, but *the big Other itself*, the socio-symbolic 'substance' that confronts the subject and in which the subject is embedded. In other words, far from signalling any kind of closure which constrains the scope of the subject's intervention in advance, the bar of the Real is Lacan's way of asserting the terrifying abyss of the subject's ultimate and radical *freedom*, the freedom whose space is sustained by the Other's inconsistency and lack. So – to conclude with Kierkegaard, to whom Laclau refers: 'the moment of decision is the moment of madness' precisely in so far as there is no big Other to provide the ultimate guarantee, the ontological cover for the subject's decision.

Notes

1. Perhaps the best way to condense the difference between me and Butler would be to emphasize that I am tempted to exchange the order of words in the titles of her two books: there is *body trouble* because *gender (sexual difference) matters* – to be sure, sexual difference is not a fact of biology, but neither is it a social construction – rather, it designates a traumatic cut which disturbs the smooth functioning of the body. What

makes it traumatic is not the violent imposition of the heterosexual norm, but the very violence of the cultural 'transubstantiation' of the biological body through its sexuation.

2. See Martha Nussbaum, 'The Professor of Parody', *The New Republic*, 22 February 1999: 13–18.

3. Judith Butler, *The Psychic Life of Power*, Stanford, CA: Stanford University Press 1997, pp. 98–9.

4. For a more detailed consideration of this point, see Chapter 5 of Slavoj Žižek, *The Ticklish Subject: The Absent Centre of Political Ontology*, London and New York: Verso 1999.

5. Butler, *The Psychic Life of Power*, p. 105.

6. See John L. Austin, 'Pretending', in *Philosophical Papers*, Oxford: Oxford University Press 1979.

7. See Jacques Derrida, *Speech and Phenomena*, Evanston, IL: Northwestern University Press 1973.

8. See Claude Lefort, *The Political Forms of Modern Society*, Cambridge, MA: MIT Press 1986.

9. See Étienne Balibar, *Race, Nation, Class*, London and New York: Verso 1995.

10. On this other aspect of Kant, see Alenka Župančic, *Ethics of the Real: Kant*, London and New York: Verso 1999.

11. I have dealt in more detail with this dialectical reversal of contingency into necessity in *The Sublime Object of Ideology* (London and New York: Verso 1989) and in *For They Know Not What They Do* (London and New York: Verso 1991).

12. Karl Marx, 'The Eighteenth Brumaire of Louis Bonaparte', in Karl Marx and Friedrich Engels, *Collected Works*, London: Lawrence & Wishart 1955, vol. 2, p. 103.

13. See Jacques Derrida, 'La mythologie blanche', in *Poétique* 5 (1971), pp. 1–52.

14. See Jacques Derrida, 'Le supplément de la copule', in *Marges de la philosophie*, Paris: Éditions de Minuit 1972.

15. See Chapter 2 of Hannah Arendt, *On Violence*, New York: Harcourt Brace 1970.

16. For a more detailed development of this point, see Chapter 3 of Slavoj Žižek, *Tarrying with the Negative*, Durham, NC: Duke University Press 1993.

17. This procedure was not restricted to horror movies – like the famous scene of the murder of the little girl in *The Leopard Man* – but also worked in Westerns: in Lewton's last production, *Apache Drums* (1951), Indians lay siege to a group of white people trapped in a church – we never see the scene from the outside, the action takes place inside, only occasionally do we catch a glimpse of an Indian through a narrow window, otherwise we hear only the raiders shouting and shooting.

18. See Étienne Balibar, *Écrits pour Althusser*, Paris: Éditions la Découverte 1991, p. 78.

19. See Phil Powrie, *French Cinema in the 1980s*, Oxford: Clarendon Press 1977, pp. 50–61.

20. The ultimate example of this convoluted exchange of places between the

subjective and the objective is, of course, that of the *gaze* itself – crucial to the Lacanian notion of gaze is that it involves the reversal of the relationship between subject and object: as Lacan puts it in *Four Fundamental Concepts of Psycho-Analysis* (London: Tavistock 1979), there is an antinomy between the eye and the gaze – the gaze is on the side of the object, it stands for the blind spot in the field of the visible from which the picture itself photographs the spectator. No wonder, then, that anti-Lacanian cognitivist cinema theorists speak of the 'missing gaze', complaining that the Lacanian Gaze is a mythical entity that is nowhere to be found in the actuality of the spectator's experience.

Along the same lines, in her unpublished 'Antigone, the Guardian of Criminal Being', Joan Copjec asserts the proto-transcendental status of partial objects (gaze, voice, breast...): they are the 'conditions of possibility' of their organs-counterparts. The gaze is the condition of possibility of the eye, that is, of our seeing something in the world (we see something only in so far as an X eludes our eye and 'returns the gaze'); the voice is the condition of possibility of our hearing something; and so on. These partial *objets petit a* are neither subjective nor objective, since they embody the short circuit between the two dimensions: they function as the objective 'bone in the throat' that sustains subjectivity.

21. François Regnault, *Conférences d'esthétique lacanienne*, Paris: Agalma 1997, p. 6.

22. For example, apropos of the theme of the *double*, one should avoid at any price the standard deconstructionist globalization, that is, the flattening of this term by means of which everything becomes an example of an uncanny redoubling of the One (woman is the double of man, writing the double of voice . . .), and insist that the problematic of the double is grounded in a specific historical moment of Romanticism (E.T.A. Hoffmann, Edgar Allan Poe).

23. Paul Theroux devotes a chapter of *The Great Railway Bazaar* (Harmondsworth: Penguin 1975) to Vietnam in 1974, after the peace agreement and the withdrawal of the US Army, and before the Communist victory. In this in-between time, a couple of hundred of US soldiers stayed there as deserters, officially and legally nonexistent, living in slum shacks with their Vietnamese wives, smuggling or engaging in crime. . . . These strange *individual* figures offer the appropriate starting point for the presentation of the *global* social situation of Vietnam in the early 1970s: if we start from them, we can gradually unravel the complex *totality* of Vietnamese society.

24. See Marc Vernet, '*Film Noir* on the Edge of Doom', in Joan Copjec, ed., *Shades of Noir*, London and New York: Verso 1993.

25. Typically, French 'poststructuralist' authors are often, together with the representatives of the Frankfurt School, labeled as part of 'critical theory' – a classification which is unthinkable in France.

26. See Louis Althusser, 'L'objet du Capital', in Louis Althusser, Étienne Balibar and Roger Establet, *Lire le Capital*, vol. II, Paris: François Maspero 1965.

27. See Stephen Jay Gould and Richard Lewontin, 'The Spandrels of San Marco and the Panglossian Paradigm', *Proceedings of the Royal Society*, vol. B205 (1979): pp. 581–98.

28. See Elisabeth Bronfen, '*Noir* Wagner', in Renata Salecl, ed., *Sexuation*, Durham, NC: Duke University Press 2000.

29. Michel Chion, *La musique au cinéma*, Paris: Fayard 1995, p. 256.

30. On this notion, see Martha Wolfenstein and Nathan Leites, *Movies: A Psychological Study*, Glencoe, IL: The Free Press 1950.

31. Richard Maltby, '"A Brief Romantic Interlude": Dick and Jane go to 3½ Seconds of the Classic Hollywood Cinema', in David Bordwell and Noel Carroll, eds, *Post-Theory*, Madison: University of Wisconsin Press 1996, p. 455.

32. What we are dealing with here, of course, is the structure of the *perplexed gaze* as generative of fantasy and sexuation (see Chapter 5 of Žižek, *The Ticklish Subject*). This structure provides the general foundation of the pleasure involved in the act of seeing: there would be no cinema viewer finding pleasure in observing the screen if the very fundamental structure of subjectivity were not characterized by this impassive fascinated and perplexed gaze.

33. See G.W.F. Hegel, *Enzyklopädie der philosophischen Wissenschaften*, Hamburg: Felix Meiner Verlag 1959, para. 348.

34. Martin Heidegger, 'Why We Remain in the Provinces' (7 March 1934), quoted from Berel Lang, *Heidegger's Silence*, Ithaca, NY: Cornell University Press 1996, p. 31.

35. See Chapter 14 of *The Seminar of Jacques Lacan, Book II: The Ego in Freud's Theory and in the Technique of Psychoanalysis*, New York: Norton 1991.

36. See Lisa Appignanesi and John Forrester, *Freud's Women*, Cambridge: Cambridge University Press 1995.

37. Stanley Cavell, *The Claim of Reason*, New York: Oxford University Press 1979, pp. 351–2.

38. One can also see here in what precise sense the sceptic's position is inherently *sadistic*: the sceptic who finds enjoyment in demonstrating the inconsistency of his Other's claims shifts the split nature of subjectivity on to the Other – it is always the Other who is caught out in inconsistencies.

39. A short book by Yitta Halberstam and Judith Leventhal, *Small Miracles: Extraordinary Coincidences from Everyday Life* (Holbrook, MA: Adams Media Corporation 1997), provides an excellent illustration of how this dimension of the 'big Other' – the 'deeper' meaning beneath coincidences – is mobilized in today's popular ideology. It consists of a series of stories like the one about a young boy in a concentration camp who once saw, through the barbed wire, a girl pass by. The next day, the girl, who noticed his wistful gaze, passed by again and threw him an apple. This was repeated over several days. After the war, in 1957, the boy, who survived the camp and was now a successful manager, was set up on a blind date. When they talked about their past lives, the woman, who was of German origin, told him that she remembered a young boy in a camp to whom she threw apples – so his date was his very saviour from the war! They immediately got married and lived happily ever after. . . .This belief that such coincidences deliver a message from some Higher Power is the zero-form of the supposition of the big Other.

40. The point of decentrement is thus not simply that our belief is forever

postponed, displaced, that it never occurs as such; on the contrary, it is that we are dealing with *a belief we cannot get rid of*, a belief which returns more and more strongly, and finally asserts itself in the readiness actually to kill oneself, obeying the order of a castrated leader. So, belief is thus *real*: impossible (forever postponed/displaced) and, simultaneously, necessary, unavoidable. This excessive belief is our specifically 'post-modern', form of inherent transgression. Contrary to appearances, in our allegedly cynical and reflective times it is more difficult than ever to be a true atheist.

Dynamic Conclusions

Judith Butler

This volume runs a certain risk, since it is not clear which of two projects it seeks to fulfill. One the one hand, it is an occasion for some practitioners of theory with convergent commitments to think together about the status of the political domain; on the other hand, it is an occasion on which each practitioner defends his or her position against the criticisms of the others, offers his or her own criticisms, distinguishes his or her position. There appears to be no easy way to resolve this tension, so perhaps the interesting question will become: is the irresolution that the text performs a particularly productive one? And how will we know whether or not it is productive?

One clear benefit of such an exchange is that it not only raises the question of the status of theory within a radical democratic project, but suggests that 'theory' itself is not a monolithic term. It would be too bad, I think, if our efforts devolved into a point-by-point rejoinder to criticisms (although that kind of discussion does have the advantage of offering specifications of the positions at hand), while the status of universality, contingency and hegemony somehow fell by the wayside.

In my view, an understanding of radicalism, whether conceived as political or theoretical or both, requires an inquiry into the presuppositions of its own enterprise. In the case of theory, this radical interrogation must take as its object the transcendental form that theory sometimes takes. One might think that to ask, radically, after presuppositions is of necessity to enter into a transcendental activity, asking about the generalized conditions of possibility according to which the field of knowable objects is constituted. But it seems to me that even this pre-supposition must be questioned, and that the form of this question ought not to be taken for granted. Although it has been said many times by now, it probably bears repeating: to question a form of activity or a conceptual terrain is not to banish or censor it; it is, for the duration, to suspend its ordinary play in order to ask after its constitution. I take it that this was the phenomenological transcription of Kant to be found in Husserl's notion of the *epoché*, and that it provided the important back-drop for Derrida's own procedure of 'placing a concept under erasure'. I would only add, in the spirit of more recent forms of affirmative deconstruction, that a concept can be put under erasure *and* played at the same time; that there is no reason, for instance, not to continue to interrogate and to use the concept of 'universality'. There is, however, a hope that the critical interrogation of the term will condition a more effective use of it, especially considering the criticisms of its spurious for-mulations that have been rehearsed with great justification in recent years in postcolonial, feminist, and cultural studies.

The commitment to radical interrogation means that there is no moment in which politics requires the cessation of theory, for that would be the moment in which politics posits certain premises as off-limits to interrogation – indeed, where it actively embraces the dogmatic as the condition of its own possibility. This would also be the moment in which such a politics sacrifices its claim to be critical, insisting on its own self-paralysis, paradoxically, as the condition of its own forward movement.

Clearly, the fear of political paralysis is precisely what prompts the anti-theoretical animus in certain activist circles. Paradoxically, such positions require the paralysis of critical reflection in order to avoid the prospect of paralysis on the level of action. In other words, those who fear the retarding effects of theory do not want to think too hard about what it is they are doing, what kind of discourse they are using; for if they think too hard about what it is they are doing, they fear that they will no longer do it. In such instances, is it the fear that thinking will have no end, that it will never cease to coil back upon itself in infinite move-ments of circularity, and that limitless thinking will then have pre-empted action as the paradigmatic political gesture? If this is the fear, then it seems to rest upon the belief that critical reflection *precedes* political action – that the former sets out the plan for the latter, and the latter somehow follows the blueprint established by the former. In other words, political action would then presuppose that thinking has already happened, that it is finished – that action is precisely not thinking, unthinking, that which happens when thinking has become the past.

Even in Aristotle's earliest extant writings, he insisted that *phronesis* includes both theoretical and practical forms of wisdom (see the *Protrepticus* and the *Eudemian Ethics*). In the *Nicomachean Ethics*, he does distinguish between *sophia*, understood as theoretical wisdom, and *phronesis*, understood as practical wisdom, even as they combine in the notion of an overall 'intellectual virtue'. In Book VI of that text, he separates thought and action, but this seems to be true only from one perspective. He writes: 'As the saying goes, the action that follows deliberation should be quick, but deliberation should be slow'.[1] Aristotle reviews several ways of knowing in this context, distinguishing, for instance, *synesis* (understanding what another says) from *gnome* (good sense or insight), and concludes that theoretical wisdom is not the same as practical wisdom: theoretical wisdom produces happiness and practical wisdom produces virtue. To the extent that virtue is 'guided by right reason' or, indeed, 'united with right reason' (p. 171), it is inextricably bound up with practical wisdom. He is also clear that not all aspects of practical wisdom become manifest as right action; some are related only to 'the virtue of a part of our soul' (p. 172). Yet practical wisdom does have 'an important bearing on action' (ibid.), since it will be impossible to make a right choice without it. Indeed, choice or action that is unmoored from practical wisdom will, by definition, lack virtue.

'Virtue', in Aristotle's sense, is that which determines what the end of action should be, and practical wisdom is that which orientates our judgement and our action towards doing what is right. Action is not divorced from the knowledge by which it is conditioned, but is composed of that knowledge, and is the mobilization of knowledge as conduct. Indeed, the 'habitus' that Aristotle attributes to the person who cultivates the practice of moral deliberation is one which implies that knowledge is embodied at the moment of action.

When Aristotle claims that 'theoretical wisdom' is not ordered by practical wisdom, he means not only that each form of wisdom pursues different ends (happiness, for theoretical wisdom; virtue, for practical wisdom), but that theoretical wisdom must have a certain measure of autonomy from practical wisdom. To the extent that theoretical wisdom seeks true knowledge of the fundamental principles of reality, and constitutes the science of things 'as they really are', it is engaged in the practice of metaphysical reflection. Aristotle is thus clear that 'theoretical wisdom is not the same as politics' (p. 156). In explaining why we consider that philosophers such as Anaxagoras and Thales have theoretical rather than practical wisdom, he claims: 'they do not know what is advantageous to them . . . they know extraordinary, wonderful, difficult, and superhuman things', but their knowledge is called 'useless because the good they are seeking is not human' (p. 157). Whereas practical wisdom is distinguished by 'deliberation', theoretical wisdom lacks this quality. It is not orientated towards action or, indeed, towards any good attainable by action.

I provide this excursus into Aristotle in order to pose the question of what kind of knowledge we are pursuing here. Ernesto Laclau and Chantal Mouffe have named the Verso series in which this text appears 'phronesis', and this suggests that whatever theoretical work is provided under that rubric will have action as its implicit end. It seems important to note that Aristotle leaves us with a certain ambiguity: with the notion of practical wisdom, he introduces a kind of knowledge without which right political action is impossible. But with intellectual wisdom, he safeguards a certain kind of intellectual inquiry from the constraints imposed upon thought by the implicit or explicit reference to deliberation and action. Which kind of inquiry do we offer here? And does our own writing get caught up in this difficulty, re-elaborating its irresolution in contemporary terms? Do we perhaps know 'extraordinary, wonderful, difficult, and superhuman things', but are they, finally, useless? Moreover, is 'use' the standard by which to judge theory's value to politics?

In the foreword to his dissertation 'To Make the World Philosophical',[2] Marx notes that the very distinction between the philosophical, as a domain of pure thought, and the world, as that which is concrete and actualized, must be read symptomatically as a split produced by the conditions of the modern world. With a certain amount of naive enthusiasm, he writes against this division, announcing its collapse as both a psychological necessity and a political accomplishment: 'It is a psychological law that the theoretical mind, once liberated in itself, turns into practical energy . . . the *practice* of philosophy is itself *theoretical*' (p. 9). By insisting that philosophy, even in its most 'theoretical' aspects, is a practice, and that that practice is theoretical, he at once returns theory to the sphere of action, and recasts action as an embodiment – or habituated form – of knowledge. Specifying the notion of 'critique' and 'reflection' in this early piece of writing, Marx clarifies that philosophy seeks to realize itself, to make the world adequate to its own idea, and that its 'realization is also its loss' (p. 10). For philosophy to realize itself would be for philosophy to lose its ideality, and that loss would constitute the death of philosophy itself. Thus, for philosophy to realize its own goals would be for philosophy to undo itself *as* philosophy. That to which philosophy is opposed is, on the one hand, the 'world' which stands over and against it, as the realized stands to the unrealized. On the other hand, this very 'world' is philosophy in its not-yet-realized form. It is, we might say, a realization that remains at a distance from the realization that philosophy seeks to be. This distance is the condition of criticality itself, an incommensurability which provides the ground for theory as a reflective and critical exercise.

Although it seems difficult to accept the implicitly teleological view proffered by Marx according to which the idea is realized as the world once its independent status as an idea is overcome, it seems important to remember the doubling of positions that Marx describes for reflective consciousness here: 'These individual self-consciousnesses always carry a double-edged demand, one edge turned against the world, the other against philosophy itself'. He continues: 'what in the thing itself appears as a relationship inverted in itself, appears in these self-consciousnesses as a double one, *a demand and an action contradicting each other*' (p. 10; emphasis added). To gain critical distance on the world in its givenness, there is a demand for philosophy, the demand of criticality itself to refuse the given as the extent of the possible. And yet, to remake the world according to the idea that philosophy affords requires the dissolution of philosophy itself that is simultaneous with its realization.

Our contemporary situation is, however, even more confounded, since the value of 'realization' has itself come into crisis. Marx's call for the realization of the ideal of radical equality, for instance, or the egalitarian distribution of wealth, was taken up by some Marxist states as a justification for imposing on populations certain kinds of economic plans that not only fortified the state as a centralized agency of regulation and control, but undercut basic principles of democracy. The call to action can be understood precisely as this drive to realize the ideal. The effort to retrieve and re-elaborate a radical democratic theory for our time therefore demands a critical relationship to 'realization' itself: how ought such ideals to be realized, if they are to be realized? Through what means, and at what price? Do these ideals justify any and all means of implementation? To what extent has Marxism re-encountered the paradox of the Terror that we considered in the context of Hegel's writing: how is it that the implementation or 'realization' of the concept involves, or even requires, a certain violent imposition? What is the violence involved in the realization of the ideal? Moreover, what happens to our sense of futurity, and the futurity which is essential to democracy itself, understood as an open-ended process, one whose 'closure' would be its death, whose realization – to re-cite Marx – would be its loss?

So, it seems that the commitment to a conception of democracy which is futural, which remains unconstrained by teleology, and which is not commensurate with any of its 'realizations' requires a different demand, one which defers realization permanently. Paradoxically – but significantly for the notion of hegemony elaborated in these pages, and inaugurated by Laclau and Mouffe's *Hegemony and Socialist Strategy* – democracy is secured precisely through its resistance to realization.

Now this may be a moment in which a self-defined activist ceases to read these pages, but I think that this insight is, in fact, part of the very practice of activism itself. This last formulation does not mean that there are no moments or events or institutional occasions in which goals are achieved, but only that whatever goals are achieved (and they are, they are), democracy itself remains unachieved – that particular policy and legislative victories do not exhaust the practice of democracy, and that it is essential to this practice to remain, in some permanent way, unrealizable. This valorization of unrealizability can be found in several contemporary thinkers whose political sensibility is crafted in part from the resources of poststructuralism, and I have offered my critical questions about it in a separate essay.[3] One can see this argued in various ways by Drucilla Cornell, Homi Bhabha, Jacques Derrida, Gayatri Chakravorty Spivak, William Connolly and Jean-Luc Nancy, not to mention my interlocutors in this volume.

Although I have argued that 'unrealizability' as a value can register and fortify a certain form of political pessimism, I return to it now to make a different point. I gather that the reason for preserving the ideality of democracy, its resistance to a full or final realization, is precisely to ward off its dissolution. Yet, even though I believe that Laclau, Žižek and I agree on this most fundamental of points, we differ on how that ideality is to be understood, through what language or logic it is to be conceptualized. Moreover, what it means to function as a 'critical' intellectual involves maintaining a certain distance not – as Marx would have it – between the ideality of philosophy and the actuality of the world, but between the ideality of the ideal and the givenness of any of its modes of instantiation.

It is my view that no a priori account of this incommensurability is going to suffice, since the a priori as a heuristic point of departure will have to come under radical scrutiny if it is not to function as a dogmatic moment in theory construction. This does not mean that I am unwilling to take certain notions for granted in order to proceed with an analysis. But even if one deploys the 'a priori' under erasure, as it were, it is no longer functioning as an epistemological foundation. It is operating as a repeatable figure, a linguistic citation, one that takes the foundational use of the term as a circulating trope within a discourse. Indeed, I would not recommend a hypercriticality that puts every word in such discussions into quotation marks. On the contrary: it seems important sometimes to let certain signifiers stand, assume a status of givenness, at a certain moment of analysis, if only to see how they work as they are put to use in the context of a reading, especially when they have become forbidden territory within a dominant discourse. This willingness to let the signifier congeal at the moment of use is not the same as putting that same signifier off-limits. The 'social' is surely one such term in my analysis. The fact that I agree to use the term does not mean that I take it as a 'given', but only to insist upon its importance. Laclau seems to think that I have fallen asleep on the job, but I assure my reader that my vigilance is still at work! The 'social' as a sphere has its history (see Poovey) and its enduring controversies, especially in the tensions that exist, for instance, between social theory and sociology, between the social and the cultural (see Yanagisako) and the social and the structural (see Clastres).[4] To insist upon the term is not to engage in a sociologism that presumes the foundational status of social causalities. On the contrary, I insist upon it here because it seems that the term now signifies something of a superseded past. The formalist account of the *a priori* structures of political articulation tend either to figure the 'social' as its prehistory or to deploy the 'social' as anecdote and example for the pre-social structure it articulates. Indeed, one might argue that formalism provokes a return of the 'social' precisely by virtue of its simultaneous exclusion and subordination within formalist theory itself.[5] It is not that in using the term I am guilty of treating it as a given or, indeed, in a 'purely referential way', but that the term itself has become synonymous with 'the given', a lexicographical habit within poststructuralism that calls for critical attention.

The category of the 'social' reintroduces a conception of language as a practice, a conception of language in relation to power and, hence, a theory of discourse. It also allows for a critical relation to the formalist dimension of linguistic analysis, asking what suppressions and exclusions make formalism possible (a question that Marx was very keen to ask). Moreover, it offers a perspective on embodiment, suggesting that knowledge, to the extent that it is embodied as habitus (Bourdieu),[6] represents a sphere of performativity that no analysis of political articulation can do without. Indeed, if one is interested in understanding the politics of gender, the embodied performativity of social norms will emerge as one of the central sites of political contestation. This is not a view of the social that is settled, but it does represent a series of politically consequential sites of analysis that no purely formalist account of the empty sign will be able to address in adequate terms.

Moreover, if we take the point proffered by Wittgenstein that 'logic' is not mimetically reproduced in the language we use – that the logically enumerated picture of the world does not correspond to the grammar of language, but, on the contrary, that grammar induces logic itself – it becomes necessary to return logical relations to the linguistic practices by which they are engendered. Thus, even if Laclau is able to establish something logically contradictory about my position, he remains within the unexamined sphere of logical relations, separating logic from linguistic practice, and so failing to engage the fundamental terms of disagreement between us.

Although Laclau engages at length in a discursive disputation of my criticism, I think it is best not to respond on a point-by-point basis. I think that his description of my criticism as part of a 'war machine' attributes to me a certain aggression which I do not mean to embody, and I think that as a result, much of what he produces by way of argument is more war tactic than clear argument. It is, I believe, nonsensical to claim, for instance, that I do not see a value in the 'positivization of negation'. My view on the place of the unspeakable and unrepresentable within the social and discursive field refutes that. Neither have I ever claimed that language is pre-social. And I certainly agree with the claim that the analysis of what constitutes a context is an important and necessary question. I do not think contexts are 'given', and I have argued against that in my work for more than a decade. So I hope I will be forgiven if I fail, as I endeavour to do, to respond to criticisms that are more exuberant than philosophically sound.

What I do hope to do, however, is to insist that we do have an important debate among us about to how to grasp the dynamism of hegemonic rearticulation. I openly worry about the degradation of the 'social', and I think that if the linguistic turn in politics that we each represent becomes a formalist turn, we will be repeating mistakes that predate Wittgenstein's *Philosophical Investigations*. I agree, for instance, that one of the key questions to be asked is 'whether concrete societies, out of movements inherent to their very concreteness, tend to generate signifiers which are tendentially empty' (EL, p. 191); but Laclau and I disagree on how best to think that 'emptiness'. For him, it is a generalized 'emptiness' which can be derived from a theory of the sign. I am less certain that the sign ought to be the unit of analysis, and ask whether the sign must itself be resituated within discursive practices. Moreover, I understand the negative along different lines, and return to Hegel to think negativity as part of the problem of historicity.

My thought in my first contribution here was to rely on Hegel to call into question this kind of formalism, but Žižek rejoins that Hegel shows us how theorization itself is prompted by 'something' which cannot be fully grasped within the terms of theory, and he proceeds to offer the 'Real' as the way to refer to this motivating 'X'. Thus his view produces a quandary for me, for it is unclear how best to include Hegel in the task which we share. The interesting irony is that for Žižek, the turn to Hegel offers a theory of reflexivity that is transcendental in its scope, even as transcendentality now indicates, through the figure of *extimité*, a radical gap or fissure within its structure. So it seems important to recognize that this is not traditional transcendentality at work in Žižek's theory. If formalism is disrupted by a radical gap or fissure within its structure, is this a gap or negation that remains in a relation to that which is fissured by its presence? In other words, is this a determinate negation of some sort, one which is defined by precisely what it negates? Or is it – as I think Žižek would insist – an indeterminate negation, an originary power of negation, one might say, which forms the condition and constitutive 'principle' of every object constituted within its field? To read this negativity as indeterminate, as I believe the doctrine of the Real requires, is thus quite different from reading it as determinate. The latter view alone lets us ask why and how certain kinds of unspeakabilities structure the discourses that they do. I fear that my interlocutors will consider this an 'economy-class' interpretation, but it seems important to be able to ask after the foreclosed and unspeakable as the asystematic condition of a particular operation of discourse. This seems especially true of formal discourses which refuse to acknowledge their grounding in non-formalizable practices.[7]

But perhaps the political project of hegemony has diverged over time. I still wonder how one might proceed with a radical interrogation of what Laclau terms 'new social movements', and I would be reluctant to identify that task with a transcendental analysis of the a priori conditions of political articulation itself (across all time and place). It still seems to me to be quite difficult to read social movements; what interpretative practice is necessary, especially when those movements may not be indisputably new, when there is a question of whether they share a structure, and how any common structure or common constituting condition *can be known*? From what vantage point does that common condition come into view, if it does, and what role does the vantage point play in framing and constituting the interpretative object in question? This becomes a crucial question, it seems, when one seeks to determine whether a 'lack' at the heart of all identificatory processes constitutes the common condition – importantly, a loss of foundation – for all identity projects (and, by implication, whether all 'new' social movements can be adequately read as identity movements), or whether the interpretative practice by which 'lack' is consistently attributed to such movements as their non-foundationalist condition is *itself* the common condition of their constitution. The question itself reveals a hermeneutic dimension to the task of reading social movements that cannot, it seems, be avoided. The theory that attributes the lack to the movement itself becomes the condition of the attributed lack, so it becomes necessary to adjudicate what belongs to the performative function of theory, and what belongs, as it were, to the object itself.

Here it seems to me that the theorist must engage in a certain reflexive inquiry about the positioning from which the description emerges. For if we are to claim that all new social movements are structured by a lack which is the condition of identification itself, we have to give some grounds for making this claim. This is made especially difficult by the apparent fact that a 'lack' does not appear in any way that submits to conventional empirical analysis, and that one must be trained to read in certain ways to appreciate how what cannot appear nevertheless structures the field of appearance. Moreover, since 'structure' is also not obvious to the naked eye, even under the most highly bracketed of conditions, something other than confident positing has to take place. The claim to structure would also seem not to be inferential in any usual sense. After all, the process by which Laclau and Mouffe proceeded in their influential *Hegemony and Socialist Strategy* was not to analyse social movements in their specificity and then to derive certain common elements about them on the basis of a prior empirical study. Similarly – if not more emphatically – Žižek's procedure is to show how certain contemporary political formations, utterances, slogans, and claims are illustrative of a logic that exceeds the instances of their exemplification. The particular political instance reflects a structure that is prior to

politics itself, or – perhaps more appropriately – constitutes the transcendental condition of the political field. I trust that it is fair to say that
one function of theory for both Laclau and Žižek (and, at least, for the
earlier scholarship of Chantal Mouffe) is to lay out the a priori conditions for political articulation itself. And whereas I question this
particular mobilization of Kant for this purpose, I do not therefore
claim that the proper point of departure is a posteriori. The Kantian
alternatives, I would suggest, do not need to frame the discussion here.[8]

I am not suggesting that these analyses ought to have begun with the
givenness of the empirical, since I am in agreement with them that any
effort at empirical description takes place within a theoretically delimited
sphere, and that empirical analysis in general cannot offer a persuasive
explanation of its own constitution as a field of inquiry. In this sense, I
agree that theory operates on the very level at which the object of inquiry
is defined and delimited, and that there is no givenness of the object
which is not given within an interpretative field – given to theory, as it
were, as the condition of its own appearance and legibility. Indeed, my
task here is to suggest that the formulation of this debate would be profoundly misguided were we to conclude that the analysis of hegemony
begins either with an empirical description or with a transcendental one.
This way of polarizing the debate is both unnecessary and restrictive, and
it would, most importantly, reproduce a binary that excludes the critical
deployment of theory in ways that refuse precisely both alternatives.
Indeed, we might read the state of debate in which the a priori is consistently counterposed to the a posteriori as a symptom to be read, one that
suggests something about the foreclosure of the conceptual field, its
restriction to tired binary oppositions, one that is ready for a new opening.

This problem emerges again in Žižek's second contribution, when he
voices his concern that a rejection of the category of the Real necessarily culminates in empiricism. I take the point – put forward by Žižek and
Laclau alike – that it does not do justice to their positions to contrast an
ahistorical account of the symbolic to a historicized notion of discourse;
but I am not fully convinced that the way to undermine that opposition
is through positing the ahistorical as the internal condition of the historical. Žižek writes: 'The opposition between an ahistorical bar of the
Real and thoroughly contingent historicity is . . . a false one: *it is the very*

"ahistorical" bar as the internal limit of the process of symbolization that sustains the space of historicity' (SŽ, p. 214). Perhaps I should not take the figure of a 'space' of historicity too literally, but it does seem striking that the figure selected to present temporality would be one that contains and denies it. Moreover, it seems that the opposition is not precisely overcome, but installed as the internal (invariant) feature of any and all historicization. Thus, in this view, at the heart or in the kernel of all historicity is the ahistorical.

Žižek offers two other dialectical inversions of a set of oppositions that he understands me to have made, and it seems worthwhile to consider them both, since what will probably appear is the distance between and proximity of our positions. In the first instance, he claims that the concept of universality *'emerges as the consequence of the fact that each particular culture is precisely* never *and for* a priori *reasons simply particular, but has always-already* in itself *"crossed the linguistic borders it claims"* ' (SŽ, p. 216). I would agree with this proposition in the following sense: there is no self-identity to any particular culture, and any culture which is fenced off from others under the name of cultural autonomy is subverted in part by the crossing of cultures that happens at its border, if not elsewhere. So yes, every particular culture has always-already crossed over the border into another one, and this very crossing is essential to (and subversive of) any conception of particular culture. And although I am glad to make this formulation in universal terms ('every culture . . .'), I am less sure that the universality is secured for a priori reasons. Nothing about the kinds of translations and contaminations that happen as part of the very project of cultural autonomy can be specified prior to an analysis of the forms they actually take. Indeed, one anthropological worry that I have is that if such claims can be made on an a priori level (who has access to that level, and what constitutes the authority of the one who claims to describe that level?), the analysis renders superfluous any actual reading of cultural translations in process. We do not need to know anything about what they are, since we have already determined them on an ostensibly more 'fundamental' level. By prioritizing that fundamental level over any analysis of specific practice, we also privilege a certain philosophical vantage point (not Marx's) over any and all cultural analysis.

The second problem with the Žižekian formulation as I understand it is that it drains the normative force from translation as a political task. If translation, in his words, 'always-already' takes place, does that mean that any political recommendation for it to take place, and to take place in non-imperialist terms, is a redundancy? It may be another false opposition to contrast the sphere of the always-already to that of political accomplishment, but if it is, we still need to be able to think the two perspectives together. *In other words, given that cultural purity is undone in advance by a contamination that it cannot expel, how can this impurity be mobilized for political purposes in order to produce an explicit politics of cultural impurity?* My belief is that the apparent oppositions between formalism and historicism that emerge in this debate will be better served if we can begin to ask these sorts of questions, questions that bring us back to the problem of how to chart a course of action without sacrificing the value of theory.

Similarly, Žižek differentiates the two of us on the matter of power. He claims that I consider the power-driven formulation of universality as based upon the exclusion of those who remain unrepresented by its terms. He counters this by proposing that the 'other' of universality is 'its *own* permanent founding gesture' (SŽ, p. 217). A few paragraphs later, he clarifies: 'power can reproduce itself only through some form of self-distance, by relying on the obscene disavowed rules and practices that are in conflict with its public norms' (SŽ, p. 218). Here Žižek offers one of those paradigmatic moments in which the dialectical inversion he exposes ends in a closed, negative dialectic. Power which seems to be opposed to the obscene is itself fundamentally reliant on that obscene, and finally *is* the obscene. The problem with his counterposition, as I understand it, is this: he does not return to the problem of the unrepresented within the field of representation, and so his response produces the appearance that this serious political problem simply does not interest him. Secondly, the version of the dialectic he offers, while it is very compelling and no doubt partially true, nevertheless remains within a use of the dialectic that opens up to no future, one that remains closed, a logic of inversion which expands the identity of power to embrace its opposite, but does not explode that identity into something new. Significantly, when he later claims that I am 'caught in the game of power that [I] oppose' (SŽ, p. 220), he does not consider that such complicity is, for me, the condition of agency rather than its destruction.

Both Žižek and Laclau point out the limits of resignification as political strategy, and I think it is no doubt right to claim that resignification cannot be the only political strategy. Luckily, I do not believe I ever claimed that! But Žižek's reproach to both Laclau and to me is that 'today's Real which sets a limit to resignification is Capital' (SŽ, p. 223). I think this is a peculiar way to use the notion of the 'Real', unless of course he is claiming that 'Capital' has become unspeakable within the discourses that Laclau and I use. But if he is saying that 'Capital' represents the limit of our discourse: then he is – forgive the 'logical' point here – confirming my very theory about the absences that structure discourse, that they are defined in relation to the discourse itself, and that they are not derivable in every instance from an ahistorical 'bar' that gives us every historicized field. Setting his Butlerian use of the 'Real' aside, however, Žižek makes a good point: that a critique of the market economy is not found in these pages. But he himself does not provide one. Why is this?

My sense is that our work is commonly motivated by a desire for a more radically restructured world, one which would have economic equality and political enfranchisement imagined in much more radical ways than they currently are. The question, though, that remains to be posed for us, I believe, is how we will make the translations between the philosophical commentary on the field of politics and the reimagining of political life. This is surely the kind of question which will render productive and dynamic the opposition between formalism and historicism, between the ostensibly a priori and the a posteriori. One might reply that any notion of economic equality will rely on a more generalized understanding of equality, and that that is part of what is interrogated by this kind of work. Or one might reply that any notion of a future of radically transformed economic relations will rely on a notion of futurity, and futurity is part of what is being attended to here. But such responses go only part of the distance in answering the question that is posed. For what happens to the notion of equality when it becomes economic equality? And what happens to the notion of the future when it becomes an economic future? We ought not simply to 'plug in' the economic as the particular field whose conditions of possibility can be thought out on an a priori level. It may also be that the very sphere of the economic needs to be rethought genealogically. Its separation from the cultural, for instance, by structuralist legacies within anthropology might need to be rethought against those who claim that the very separation of those spheres is a consequence of capital itself.

Žižek's stand against historicism is not always easy for me to follow, perhaps because the circulation of the term has specific meanings in the academic setting in which I work, meanings that are perhaps not the same as those that pertain to his situation. He allies deconstruction, historicism and Cultural Studies – a move which conservative intellectuals in the USA, such as Lynne Cheney and Roger Kimball, are wont to make. Over and against these enterprises, he reasserts the value of philosophy. He regards the former practices as dedicated to the project of exposing the contingent conditions of production under which various cultural forms are produced, and he understands this inquiry into the genealogy of production as substituting for or, indeed, effacing the more fundamental inquiry into the ontology and truth-value of the form itself. I am not sure that I accept this distinction, or that it is applicable to the array of academic work that Žižek seeks to describe. 'The hyper-self-reflective approach', he writes, 'denounces . . . the question of "how things really are" in advance' (SŽ, p. 232), and Žižek clearly laments this loss, announcing his continuing commitment to understanding something about the structure of the universe.

If the 'truth' of how things are must be presented in some way – if truth, indeed, never appears outside a presentation – then it seems to follow that there is no way to dissociate truth from the rhetoricity that makes it possible. Indeed, this is nowhere more emphatically demonstrated than in Žižek's own work. Consider the use of assertion, of formulas, of anecdote, of dialectical demonstration. These are not ornamental 'extras' that simply convey a truth whose truth-value is separable from its rhetorical delivery. The rhetoric also builds the truth that it purports to reveal, and this metaleptic function of his discourse works most efficiently when it remains undisclosed, when the 'transparency' of representation is most dramatically produced. To make this claim is not to say that there is no truth, or that the truth is a trick or an effect of the rhetorical ploy, but only that we are fundamentally dependent on language to say and understand what is true, and that the truth of what is said (or represented in any number of ways) is not separable from the saying. Žižek defines deconstruction in the light of its own ostensible prohibitions, as if the concepts it interrogates become unspeakable by virtue of their deconstruction. Here, it seems, he overlooks the now prevalent circulation of 'affirmative deconstruction', elaborated in different ways by Derrida, Spivak, and Agamben. There are conditions of discourse under which certain concepts emerge, and their capacity for iteration across contexts is itself the condition for an affirmative reinscription. Thus, we can ask: what can the 'human' mean within a theory that is ostensibly anti-humanist? Indeed, we can – and must – ask: what can the human mean within post-humanism? And surely Derrida would not cease to ask the question of truth, though whatever 'truth' is to be will not be separable from the 'question' by which it appears. This is not to say that there is no truth, but only that whatever it will be, it will be presented in some way, perhaps through elision or silence, but there precisely as something to be read.

Similarly, any effort to present as persuasive the a priori conditions of politicization will rely on modes of persuasion that invariably make a different claim from the one in whose service they were enlisted. A structure is being described, set forth as the truth, announced as the way things really are, illustrated as to its workings, developed in readings of films, jokes, and historical anecdotes. The truth which is delivered through such rhetorical means will be contaminated by the means itself, so that it will not actually appear as a transparent reality, and language will not be the empty vessel through which it is conveyed. Language will not only build the truth that it conveys, but it will also convey a different truth from the one that was intended, and this will be a truth about language, its unsurpassability in politics.

Notes

1. Aristotle, *Nicomachean Ethics*, trans. Martin Ostwald, Indianapolis, IN: Babbs-Merrill 1962, p. 162.

2. In *The Marx–Engels Reader*, ed. Robert Tucker, New York: Norton 1978, pp. 9–11.

3. See Judith Butler, 'Poststructuralism and Postmarxism', *Diacritics* 23.4 (Winter 1993): 3–11.

4. See Mary Poovey, *A History of the Modern Fact: Problems of Knowledge in the Sciences of Wealth and Society*, Chicago: University of Chicago Press 1998; Sylvia Junko Yanagisako, *Transforming the Past: Tradition and Kinship Among Japanese Americans*, Stanford, CA: Stanford University Press 1985, pp. 1–26; Pierre Clastres, *Society Against the State*, trans. Robert Hurley, New York: Zone Books 1987.

5. One can see the beginnings of this problem in Lévi-Strauss's discussion of the incest taboo, an argument that Derrida takes up in 'Structure, Sign, and Play in the Discourse of the Human Sciences', in *Writing and Difference*, trans. Alan Bass, Chicago: University of Chicago Press 1978, pp. 278–94 (esp. pp. 282–4). Lévi-Strauss argues that the incest taboo is neither pre-cultural nor cultural, but it denotes a mechanism that regularly transforms the pre-cultural into the cultural. To the extent that the incest taboo is 'structural', it is therefore not part of the contingent cultural or social organizations that it informs, although it cannot be easily located in a pre-cultural space or time.

6. Pierre Bourdieu, *The Logic of Practice*, trans. Richard Nice, Stanford, CA: Stanford University Press 1990.

7. See Charles Taylor, 'To Follow a Rule . . .', in *Bourdieu: A Critical Reader*, ed. Richard Shusterman, London: Basil Blackwell 1999, pp. 29–44.

8. I do see an important place for Kantian analysis in the critical interrogation of freedom, and think that it is most usefully clarified in the *Critique of Judgement* rather than in the explicitly moral treatises. I am indebted to Drucilla Cornell for showing me my affinities with Kant's theory of freedom in this way. See Drucilla Cornell, 'Response to Brenkman', *Critical Inquiry* 25.1 (Fall 1999).

Constructing Universality

Ernesto Laclau

A surprising feature of our exchanges in this book is that despite some serious disagreements – which have not, however, prevented the discovery of important coincidences – no stable frontier separating our overall positions has emerged. This is because neither disagreements nor coincidences have added up consistently, making possible some sort of permanent alliance between some of us. I have found myself allied with Žižek against Butler in the defence of Lacanian theory; with Butler against Žižek in the defence of deconstruction; while Butler and Žižek have found themselves allies against me in the defence of Hegel. I would say that, paradoxically, this impasse in the formation of alliances is one of the main achievements of our dialogue – not only because the practice of a respectful exchange between people holding different opinions is, to say the least, an endangered species in today's intellectual climate, but also because the construction of a common terrain or problematic *in spite of* individual disagreements is always a greater intellectual achievement than building up a dogmatically unified 'orthodox' discourse.

I want to devote this third and last intervention to the expansion of certain theoretical categories which I have introduced in my previous two essays, so that some of their inherent dimensions are more thoroughly explored. In the process of doing so I will be able to make more precise my differences with my two interlocutors and, in some cases, partially to incorporate their analyses into my theoretical framework. Before

that, however, I would like to comment on some new criticisms of my
work that they have made in their second interventions.

Stating the differences

On the question of the Real in Lacan, I have made my stance clear in my
previous two interventions, and I have hardly anything to add. Since
Butler has not really replied to the precise objections to her argument that
I have presented in my first essay, but has simply restated her original position, I do not think there is much basis for any further discussion. We
simply have to agree to disagree. There are, however, other aspects of her
second essay on which I would like to pursue the matter further.

1.   Logic, grammar, discourse and the symbolic

Butler, admittedly, wrote her piece before she had read my second contribution, where I have clarified several of the issues she raises in her new
essay. Let me, anyway, answer, point by point, the different stages of her
argument.

(a)   Logic. Butler writes:

My difference with Laclau on this matter becomes clear, I believe, when
we consider the way in which he defines the 'logical' status of his analysis of social relations. He writes: 'we are not, of course, talking about
formal logic, or even about a general dialectical logic, but about the
notion which is implicit in expressions such as "the logic of kinship", the
"logic of the market", etc.' . . . My impression is that this clustering
together of logic, grammar, discourse and symbolic elides several issues in
the philosophy of language that have significant bearing on the arguments being made on their basis. It is problematic, for instance, to identify
the logic of a social practice with its grammar, if only because grammars
work, as Wittgenstein remarked, to produce a set of use-based meanings
that no purely logical analysis can uncover. Indeed, the move from the
early to the late Wittgenstein is often understood as the turn away from a
logical analysis of language to that of the grammar of use. (JB, p. 170)

The reference to Wittgenstein in this passage is misplaced. Furthermore: Butler's argument can be refuted merely by carefully reading the passage of my text that she is quoting. When Wittgenstein, in his early work, talked about 'logic', he meant the logical analysis of propositions as carried out by Frege and Russell – that is, he was concerned with the logical foundations of any possible language, a project he later repudiated. Now, this is exactly the demarcation that my text tries to establish: it dismisses the very idea of a general logic which would establish the foundation of any possible language and insists, on the contrary, that logics are context-dependent – the market, kinship, and so on depending on the language game in which one is engaged. As Wittgenstein asserts in the *Philosophical Investigations*:

> We are talking about the spatial and temporal phenomenon of language, not about some non-spatial, non-temporal phantasm. . . . But we talk about it as we do about the piece in chess when we are stating the rules of the game, not describing their physical properties. The question 'What is a word really?' is analogous to 'What is a piece in chess?'.[1]

Well, the rules of the game in chess are what I call the logic of chess-playing. They are purely internal to that particular language game, and do not depend on any aprioristic foundation. In political terms, it means that any hegemonic formation has its own internal logic, which is nothing more than the ensemble of language games which it is possible to play within it.

(b)   Grammars, logics and discourse.
Butler's misreading of my text opens the possibility, however, of making more precise the distinction between the four terms which, in her view, I have used indistinctly (logic, grammar, discourse and the symbolic). Let us put aside, to start with, the 'symbolic', which is a Lacanian term, not one of mine, and whose use by me amounts to no more than a 'cultural translation'. I understand by 'grammar' the set of rules governing a particular 'language game' (the set of rules defining what chess-playing is, in Wittgenstein's example). By 'logic', on the contrary, I understand the type of relations between entities that makes possible the actual

operation of that system of rules. While the grammar merely enounces what the rules of a particular language game are, the logic answers to a different kind of question: how entities have to be to make those rules possible. Psychoanalytic categories such as 'projection' or 'introjection', for instance, presuppose processes whose logic is different from those that operate in the physical or biological world. When François Jacob, in his writings on theoretical biology, speaks of 'la logique du vivant', he is using the term 'logic' exactly in the same sense that I am attributing to it. To put it another way: while 'grammar' is always ontic, 'logic' is ontological. And what about 'discourse'? As Butler knows very well – it is a point on which she has very much insisted, and I fully agree with that insistence – the rules governing particular language games do not exhaust the social actions operative in the process of their implementation. Rules are bent or transformed when they are implemented. The Derridan notion of 'iteration', the Wittgensteinian notion of 'applying a rule' – even Butler's notion of 'parodic performances' – presuppose the possibility of this bending or transformation. Without this possibility, hegemonic displacements would be impossible. The ensemble of the rules, plus those actions which implement/distort/subvert them is what we call 'discourse' and when we are referring not to particular language games but to the interaction/articulation between a plurality of them – what Wittgenstein calls 'form of life' – we speak of a 'discursive formation'. As we can see, the types of internal coherence required from a grammar and from a discursive formation are different. A *system* of rules tends ideally to be *systematic*. The fact that this systematic ideal is unattainable – for there will always be what in Lacanian language we call the 'kinks in the symbolic order' – does not rule out the fact that, as a regulative idea, the ideal of systematicity is, in a grammar, fully operative. In a discursive formation this systematicity is absent even as a regulative idea, because it has to include within itself antagonisms and hegemonic rearticulations which subvert the rules and bend them in contradictory directions. The coherence that a discursive formation can have is only a *hegemonic* coherence and it is, indeed, on the level of the discursive formations that hegemonic logics are fully operative.

(c) Foucault.

Butler writes: 'the notion of a grammar is not fully coincident with the notion of discourse developed by Foucault and elaborated in Laclau and Mouffe's *Hegemony and Socialist Strategy*' (JB, p. 170). This is a factual mistake. The notion of 'discourse' that Mouffe and I elaborated in that book is very different from the one presented by Foucault – based as the latter is on a distinction between the discursive and the non-discursive which we reject – and we have explicitly criticized Foucault on that count. Moreover, the work of Foucault has had only a very limited influence on my own approach, and I feel towards it only a very qualified sympathy. As for Butler's remark that 'it is unclear whether "a discourse" can be referred to as a static unity in the same way that a logic or a grammar can be' (JB, p. 170), I entirely agree with her – I think that the distinctions I have introduced in the paragraph above make my position on this matter clear enough. Finally, Butler asserts that for Foucault, '[t]here is no recourse to a single structure or a single lack that underscores all discursive formations. Our exile in heterogeneity is, in this sense, irreversible' (JB, p. 171).

Whether it is an accurate description of Foucault's position or not, I cannot accept this last statement without some qualifications. Let us leave aside Butler's interpretation of Lacan's position, on which I will not comment again. The whole problem revolves around how we are going to conceive this 'exile in heterogeneity'. If this means that our viewpoint does not have a 'super-hard transcendentality', and cannot legislate *sub specie aeternitatis*, I would have no quarrel with it. But I suspect that for Butler it *does* have a different meaning: namely, that it is not possible to state any principle or rule whose tentative validity extends beyond a certain cultural context. Now, if that is what is meant, I think the statement concerning the 'exile' is wrong – in the first place, because neither Foucault, nor Butler – nor, indeed, any theoretician worth the name – can operate without some categories wider than those which apply to a particular context. When Foucault, in *The Archaeology of Knowledge*, talks about objects, enunciative modalities, concepts, strategies, and so on, he is clearly not limiting the area of validity of those categories to a particular cultural context. I think what is being confused here is the contingency and context-dependency of the speaker's position of enunciation, on the one hand, and the range of applicability he attributes to his categories on the other (a range which could perfectly well be 'universal'). But in the second place, for reasons I have suggested in my previous essay, such a sharp contextualization of the range of validity of the statements would be self-defeating for Butler, because in that case she would have to specify contexts, something she can do only through a metacontextual discourse which would have to have transcendental aprioristic validity. The alternative for historicism is clear: either we historicize the place of enunciation – which says nothing about the degree of 'universality' attributed to the statements – or we legislate about that degree – something which can be done only by transcendentalizing the position of enunciation. I think that my historicism is more consequent than Butler's.

2. Intellectuals

Butler, after quoting me to the effect that a contingent universality constitutively requires political mediation and relations of representation, adds that (for me) '[t]his last not only necessitates the role of the intellectual as a mediating link, but specifies that role as one of logical analysis'. Later she adds:

> I do not believe that the intellectual can be at a radical distance from such movements, although I am not sure I can return to Gramsci's notion of the 'organic intellectual', much as I respect the contemporary circulation of that model in the work and in the person of Angela Davis. But I am party to it in this respect. I do not think that the role of the intellectual is to take new social movements as objects of intellectual inquiry, and derive from them the logical features of their claim-making exercises, without actually studying the claims themselves to see whether the logic in question suit the phenomena at hand. (JB, p. 169)

This passage not only shows an astonishing misunderstanding of my position, but also suggests that Butler has not really grasped the meaning of 'organic intellectual' in Gramsci.

Let us start with Gramsci. For him, an 'organic intellectual' was anything but a logical analyst of concepts. It was somebody engaged in the practice of articulation as the essential component in the construction of the hegemony of a group – union organizers, technicians of different sorts, journalists, and others were, for Gramsci, organic intellectuals, and he counterposed them to the traditional 'great' intellectuals. The question of the status of intellectuals had been very much discussed in the Second International, especially in Austro–Marxism, where Adler wrote a book on *Socialism and the Intellectuals* which broke with the sociologism of Kautsky on this matter and advanced positions which, to some extent, anticipated Gramsci. The problem they mostly addressed was the following: socialism did not emerge spontaneously from the working class, but had to be introduced there by the socialist intellectuals (remember Marx: philosophy finds its material weapons in the proletariat, and the proletariat finds its spiritual weapons in philosophy). The main theoretical difficulty was this: how to keep a (working-)class perspective, given that most socialist intellectuals came from the petty bourgeoisie? The question of the intellectuals was, in fact, one of the first – together with nationalism – in which class reductionism found its limits within Marxist theorization. The situation was not, however, overdramatic, because most Marxists expected the formation of the revolutionary subject to be the result of the inexorable laws of capitalist development, and so the intellectual/ideological mediation, though certainly not negligible, was conceived of as rather limited in its area of possible effects. But for Gramsci, the situation was altogether different. For him, the construction of a hegemonic collective will depends on political initiatives that are not the necessary effect of any infrastructural laws of movement. In that sense, the scope of the contingent political construction was greatly widened. This on the one hand increased, as a result, the role of the intellectual function in the construction of hegemony; on the other, it led to the impossibility of restricting that function to the group or caste with which the intellectuals had traditionally been identified. This widened conception of the intellectual – which, as I have said, now comprised people such as union organizers, technicians, journalists and others, to whom we could easily add today other groups like social workers, film-makers, consciousness-raising groups, etc. – Gramsci called 'organic intellectuals'.

It is this widened notion of the intellectual role in the construction of hegemony that I had in mind when I wrote about a contingent universality which requires political mediation and relations of representation. Of course I never wrote anything so ludicrous as that the role of this intellectual mediation is one of logical analysis. I actually challenge my friend Judith to find in my work a single sentence in which I assert something which remotely approaches such absurdity. How I conceive my political role as a philosopher is a different matter. The characterization of my approach in this field as 'logical analysis of concepts' – which would transform me into some sort of logical positivist – would also be a misrepresentation, but it is true that in my work I have dealt extensively with the rhetorical and discursive devices through which contingently articulated social relations become 'naturalized' in order to legitimize relations of power. This task is, of course, far away from a mere logical analysis of concepts in the analytic philosophical tradition, and I am prepared to defend its intellectual and political relevance. I would even ask: is it not also a central component of Judith Butler's intellectual project?

Butler raises several other points in relation to my approach on which I would like to comment, but as these do not involve any misunderstanding on her part, and I see them as highly relevant and interesting – and also quite easy to integrate into my model concerning the relation between universality and particularity – I will address them later, when I discuss the latter.

I move now to those of Žižek's critical points with which I want to take issue.

1.   On horizons

Žižek calls the reader's attention to

> the fact that Butler, as well as Laclau, in their criticism of the old 'essentialist' Marxism, none the less silently *accept* a set of premisses: they *never* put in question the fundamentals of the capitalist market economy and of the liberal democratic political regime; they *never* envisage the possibility of a thoroughly *different* economico-political regime. In this way,

they *fully participate* in the abandonment of these questions by the 'post-modern' Left: all the changes they propose are changes within this economico-political regime. (SŽ, p. 223)

The reader must excuse me for smiling at the naive self-complacence this r-r-revolutionary passage reflects. For if Butler and I are not envisaging 'the possibility of a thoroughly *different* economico-political regime', Žižek is not doing so either. In his previous essay Žižek had told us that he wanted to overthrow capitalism; now we are served notice that he also wants to do away with liberal democratic regimes – to be replaced, it is true, by a thoroughly different regime which he does not have the courtesy of letting us know anything about. One can only guess. Now, apart from capitalist society and the parallelograms of Mr Owen, Žižek *does* actually know a third type of sociopolitical arrangement: the Communist bureaucratic regimes of Eastern Europe under which he lived. Is that what he has in mind? Does he want to replace liberal democracy by a one-party political system, to undermine the division of powers, to impose the censorship of the press? Žižek belongs to a liberal party in Slovenia, and was its presidential candidate in the first elections after the end of communism. Did he tell the Slovenian voters that his aim was to abolish liberal democracy – a regime which was slowly and painfully established after protracted liberalization campaigns in the 1980s, in which Žižek himself was very active? And if what he has in mind is something entirely different, he has the elementary intellectual and political duty to let us know what it is. Hitler and Mussolini also abolished liberal democratic political regimes and replaced them by 'thoroughly different' ones. Only if that explanation is made available will we be able to start talking politics, and abandon the theological terrain. Before that, I cannot even know what Žižek is talking about – and the more this exchange progresses, the more suspicious I become that Žižek himself does not know either.

All this brings me close to the conclusion – which was by no means evident to me when we started this dialogue – that Žižek's thought is not organized around a truly *political* reflection but is, rather, a *psychoanalytic* discourse which draws its examples from the politico-ideological field. In that sense, I agree with Butler when she asserts, apropos of Žižek, that

in his discourse '[t]he examples function in a mode of allegory that presumes the separability of the illustrative example from the content it
seeks to illuminate' (JB, p. 157). It is certainly true that in the process of
doing so Žižek makes a myriad of insightful remarks which throw light
on the structuration of the politico-ideological field – and, a *fortiori*,
show the fruitfulness of psychoanalysis for political thought – but this is
a far cry from the elaboration of a political perspective which, if it is
truly one, has to be centred in a strategic reflection. I can discuss politics
with Butler because she talks about the real world, about strategic problems people encounter in their actual struggles, but with Žižek it is not
possible even to start to do so. The only thing one gets from him are
injunctions to overthrow capitalism or to abolish liberal democracy,
which have no meaning at all. Furthermore, his way of dealing with
Marxist categories consists in inscribing them in a semi-metaphysical
horizon which, if it were accepted – a rather unlikely event – would put
the agenda of the Left back fifty years. Let me give a few examples.

(a) Žižek writes:

> Laclau argues that capitalism is an inconsistent composite of heteroge-
> neous features which were combined as the result of a contingent
> historical constellation, not a homogeneous Totality obeying an under-
> lying common Logic. My answer to this is the reference to the Hegelian
> logic of retroactive reversal of contingency into necessity. . . . [C]apital-
> ism retroactively 'posited its own presuppositions', and reinscribed its
> contingent/external circumstances into an all-encompassing logic that
> can be generated from an elementary conceptual matrix (the 'contra-
> diction' involved in the act of commodity exchange, etc.). In a proper
> dialectical analysis, the 'necessity' of a totality does not preclude its con-
> tingent origins and the heterogeneous nature of its constituents – these
> are, precisely, its *presuppositions* which are then posited, retroactively total-
> ized, by the emergence of dialectical totality. (SŽ, p. 225)

Hegel *dixit*. Well, according to legal practice, no proof is required from
the prosecution when the defendant pleads guilty. Žižek is telling us: (i)
that the degree of totalization the capitalist economy could reach is not

the result of a hegemonic construction articulating a variety of political, economic and ideological dimensions, but a self-generated economic process which simply unfolds the logical consequences deriving from an 'elementary conceptual matrix'; (ii) that, as a result, hegemonic logics are not constitutive of the social, but mere secondary processes taking place within a capitalist framework which is – albeit retroactively – self-grounded. In this way, everything that Marxian and socialist economics has tried to achieve over the last fifty or sixty years – from the Sraffian critique of the labour theory of value, to the analysis of the labour process in capital accumulation, to the study of the role of the state in the latter, to the regulation school – is deleted in one stroke – or, rather, totally ignored – in a return to the nineteenth-century myth of a self-enclosed economic space. And this on the sole basis of a Hegelian aprioristic principle which is supposed to apply to everything in the universe.

(b)   According to Žižek, capitalism is the Real of present-day societies for it is that which always returns. Now, he knows as well as I do what the Lacanian Real is; so he should also be aware that capitalism *cannot* be the Lacanian Real. The Lacanian Real is that which resists symbolization, and shows itself only through its disruptive effects. But capitalism as a set of institutions, practices, and so on can operate only in so far as it is part of the symbolic order. And if, on top of that one thinks – as Žižek does – that capitalism is a self-generated framework proceeding out of an elementary conceptual matrix, it has to be – conceptually – fully graspable and, as a result, a symbolic totality without holes. (The fact that it can cause, like any area of the symbolic, distortive – and so Real – effects over other areas – does not mean that it is, *as such*, the Real.) But, as Žižek knows, there are no symbolic totalities without holes. In that case, capitalism as such is dislocated by the Real, and it is open to contingent hegemonic retotalizations. *Ergo*, it cannot be the *fundamentum inconcussum*, the framework within which hegemonic struggles take place, because – as a totality – it is itself only the result of partial hegemonic stabilizations. So the totality can never be internally generated, for the interior will be essentially contaminated by an ineradicable exteriority. This means that the Hegelian retroactive reversal of contingency into necessity is a totally

inadequate conceptual tool to think the logic of a hegemonic retotaliza-
tion. (This is a good example of the short circuit that takes place
whenever Žižek tries to combine his Lacanianism with his Hegelianism.)

Let us summarize the argument up to this point. At first I was sympathetic to Žižek's insistence on the need for a more global perspective
for the Left. I think, as he does, that for the latter, the pendulum has
moved too much in the direction of an issue-orientated politics and
purely defensive struggles, giving up on strategic thinking on more global
perspectives of change. But the more our discussions progressed, the
more I realized that my sympathy for Žižek's politics was largely the
result of a mirage. These are the main points of discrepancy:

(i)   Žižek thinks that the degree of globality or universality of a struggle depends on its location in the social structure: some struggles,
conceived as 'class struggle' – those of the workers, especially – would
spontaneously and tendentially be more 'universal' in their effects
because they take place at the 'root' of the capitalist system; while
others, more 'cultural' in their aims – such as multiculturalist ones –
would be more prone to particularism and, as a result, easier to integrate
into the present system of domination. For me, this is a spurious distinction. There is no struggle which has inscribed in itself the guarantee
of being the privileged locus of universalistic political effects. Workers'
demands – higher wages, shorter working hours, better conditions in the
workplace, and so on – can, given the appropriate circumstances, be as
easily integrated into the system as those of any other group. Conversely,
given the globalization of capitalism, dislocations could take place which
are at the basis of anti-systemic movements led by groups who are not
directly part of capitalist relations of production. So while for Žižek the
distinction between 'class struggle' and what he calls 'postmodernism' is
fundamental, I tend to blur it.

(ii)   Žižek moves within a new version of the base/superstructure
model. There is a fundamental level on which capitalism proceeds
according to its own logic, undisturbed by external influences, and a
more superficial one where hegemonic articulations take place; the
'base' operates as a framework, putting some sort of a priori limit to

what is historically achievable through mass action. For me, the framework itself results from contingent hegemonic articulations; consequently, the relations between its component elements are essentially unstable and constantly displaced by historical contingent interventions.

(iii) The imagery around the base/superstructure metaphor decisively shapes Žižek's vision of political alternatives. Thus he distinguishes between struggles to change the system and struggles within the system. I do not think that this distinction, posed in those terms, is a valid one. The crucial question is: how systematic is the system? If we conceive this systematicity as the result of endogenous laws of development – as in the case of the retroactive reversal of contingency into necessity – the only alternatives are either that those laws lead, through their operation, to the self-destruction of the system (let us remember the debate, in the Second International, on the mechanic collapse of the system) or to the system's destruction from outside. If, on the contrary, systematicity is seen as a hegemonic construction, historical change is conceivable as a displacement in the relations between elements – some internal and some external to what the system had been. Questions such as the following may be asked: How is it possible to maintain a market economy which is compatible with a high degree of social control of the productive process? What restructuration of the liberal democratic institutions is necessary so that democratic control becomes effective, and does not degenerate into regulation by an all-powerful bureaucracy? How should democratization be conceived so that it makes possible global political effects which are, however, compatible with the social and cultural pluralism existing in a given society? These questions are thinkable within the Gramscian strategy of a war of position, while in Žižek's suggestion of a direct struggle for overthrowing capitalism and abolishing liberal democracy, I can see only a prescription for political quietism and sterility.

2. *The descriptive/normative distinction*

Here I find myself, to a great extent, in agreement with Žižek. I can only subscribe to his assertion that 'there are no ultimate "objective" grounds for a decision, since these grounds are always–already retroactively constructed from the horizon of decision' (SŽ, p. 229). And at the end of his second essay, in a finely argued passage, Žižek shows that 'the Lacanian Real, the bar of impossibility it stands for, does not primarily cross the subject, but *the big Other itself*, the socio-symbolic "substance" that confronts the subject and in which the subject is embedded' (SŽ, p. 258) – to conclude that 'there is no big Other to provide the ultimate guarantee, the ontological cover for the subject's decision'. All this, as I have said, is very well argued and provides new reasons for questioning the very possibility of a pure description. But precisely because I agree so much with Žižek on this point, I find it slightly inconsistent that he charges me with relying '*on an unreflected gap between the descriptive and the normative*, in so far as it [the theory of hegemony] functions as a neutral conceptual tool for accounting for *every* ideological formation' (SŽ, p. 229). If I understand Žižek correctly, he is not arguing that a theory ought not to be purely descriptive: his argument is that a purely descriptive theory is impossible. But then he cannot charge me with doing something which is actually impossible – unless, of course, I had asserted (which I had not) that it is possible, in which case his critique should have taken the form of uncovering the hidden normative grounds of my descriptions. Here I reiterate a similar argument which I made above in relation to a criticism by Butler: there is no reason why a normative stance, which will *anyway* construct facts and include descriptions, could not elaborate more abstract categories, generalizable to a plurality of situations. It is simply a *non sequitur* that the practico-normative roots of the descriptions limit the degree of universality of the categories derivable from them.

  Let us say that, in this respect, *Hegemony and Socialist Strategy* was conceived, as the title itself suggests, as a reflection on *strategy*. The book starts with a consideration of the obstacles that classical Marxist strategy found in the Second International, in the face of developments of the capitalist system which went against Marx's predictions. 'Hegemony' as a new category is presented as a response to these obstacles, and as an attempt to recover the socialist initiative on a changed historical terrain. And 'radical democracy' should be conceived of in the same terms: as describing a political project which rethinks the hegemonic strategy in the new historical conditions of contemporary societies. Of course, once one conceives of one's own project in terms of hegemony, one can also start using the category in a more general sense, as applicable to the practices of different social sectors and historical periods – just as a category such as 'mode of production' could have emerged only in the conditions of modern capitalist production but, once it has done so, there is no logical obstacle to expanding the use of the term to social formations that are very different from capitalism. What is wrong is to think, as Žižek does, that one *starts* from a neutral level of generality and then has *to deduce* from that level one's own political choices – a deduction which would, of course, be impossible. For the same reason, I think that the identical criticism he makes in *The Ticklish Subject* of some other theoreticians – Badiou, Balibar, Foucault, Rancière – is equally ill conceived.

A different criticism, however, which could legitimately be directed at my work is that in the passage from classical Marxism to 'hegemony', and from the latter to 'radical democracy', an enlargement of the addressees of the descriptive/normative project takes place, and that, as a result, a corresponding enlargement of the area of normative argumentation should have followed – while, in my work, this latter enlargement has not sufficiently advanced. In other words, in formulating a political project which addresses the new situation, the descriptive dimension has advanced more rapidly than the normative. I think this is a valid criticism, and I intend to restore the correct balance between the two dimensions in future works. But it is a very different criticism from the one Žižek formulates.

3. Hegel, again

I will be very brief on this point, for I have already elaborated on most of what I have to say, in my first piece. Concerning the 'retroactive reversal of contingency into necessity', I have explained why this move is insufficient to capture the working of hegemonic logics. As for Žižek's assertion that '*the split Laclau is talking about is already discernible in the very fundamental Hegelian project itself*, which is thoroughly ambiguous' (SŽ, p. 228), well . . . I don't know if he is saying something so very different from what I said when, in my first essay, I argued that reason, in

Hegel, is caught in a double movement: on the one hand, it tries to submit to itself the whole world of differences while, on the other, the latter reacts by subverting the workings of reason. In actual fact, Žižek's well-chosen reference to the dialectic of the Beautiful Soul is an excellent example of what I had in mind. The point on which I still disagree with him is that he transforms this ambiguity in the unilateralization of one of its two sides; and also that he does not take sufficiently into account that whenever Hegel makes his project explicit it is always, invariably, the panlogicist side that predominates.[2] Let us just mention – among hundreds of examples which could be quoted – the characterization of the tasks of Philosophy in the first chapter of the *Logic*, in the *Encyclopaedia*.[3]

The same applies to Butler. She argues, in her second piece, that the realm of *Sittlichkeit* should be considered as governed by thoroughly contingent variations, in opposition to the notion of the state. I would like to address two remarks to her. First, she cannot separate, without doing violence to the Hegelian text, the sphere of *Sittlichkeit* from the sphere of the state: they are chained to each other by necessary dialectical links. Second, if it is true that for Hegel, as she asserts, '[t]hese norms [of *Sittlichkeit*] do not take any "necessary" forms, for they not only succeed each other in time, but regularly come into crisis encounters which compel their rearticulation' (JB, p. 172), the succession of cultures is still governed by a necessary dialectic that is fully graspable in 'World History'. As in the case of Žižek, I do not object to the language games that Butler plays around Hegelian categories, so long as it is clear that, in playing them, she is clearly going beyond Hegel.

Deconstructing classes

It is now time to move on to describe the articulation between universality and particularity which is compatible with hegemonic logics. In order to do so, however, I want first to deal with the category of 'class', and with the way in which it has been present in the usual practice of many contemporary discourses. I will refer to two very frequent language games played with the term 'class'.

1.   The first tries to retain the category, while making it compatible with the proliferation of identities linked to the new social movements. The usual practice here is to transform 'class' into one more link in an enumerative chain. Thus we frequently find that when one is arguing about new identities and their specific demands, we find enumerations of the type: 'race, gender, ethnicity, etc., *and* class' – and the 'and' is usually stressed by an intonation of the voice, as if to say: 'Don't forget the old chap'. This satisfies the speaker, because she thinks she has found the square circle between the need to assert new identities and a certain ultimate Marxism that she does not want to abandon entirely. What the speaker does not realize is that what she has enounced is something which is radically incompatible with the Marxist theory of classes. The Marxist notion of 'class' cannot be incorporated into an enumerative chain of identities, simply because it is supposed to be the articulating core around which *all* identity is constituted. What do 'classes' mean when this articulating function is lost, and they become part of a chain embracing a plurality of identities? Differences of wealth? Professional categories? Group belonging in terms of differential geographical areas? It is indeterminate. The term 'class', by becoming part of an enumerative chain, has lost its articulating role without acquiring any new precise meaning. We are dealing with something approaching the status of a 'floating signifier'.

2.   A second strategy in relation to classes (to the working class in this case) consists in asserting what is commonly called the 'enlarged conception of the working class'. I remember a conversation with a well-known American sociologist who told me that Marx's thesis about the increasing proletarianization of society had been verified, because today there are fewer self-employed people than there were in the nineteenth century, and the vast majority of the population receives wages/salaries. To my obvious question – 'In that case, for you, are bank managers members of the working class?' – he answered: 'Well, no, wages should not be higher than a certain level'. To successive similar questions he invariably answered by adding more descriptive sociological features until, in the end, I raised two questions to which he could give no proper answer: (a) how do you know that these sets of

descriptive features come together in some 'actually existing' social agents?; (b) even if you could point to empirical agents who would correspond to the Identikit of the 'working class', is not that very plurality of criteria showing already that the working class today is smaller than it was in the nineteenth century? As we can see, the specification of the criteria required to make the notion of an 'enlarged working class' meaningful undermines that very notion.

We should consider a couple of distinctive features of the two discursive strategies we have just mentioned. The first is that, in both, the notion of 'class' has lost all intuitive content. The classical Marxist concept of 'class' derived its verisimilitude from the fact that it established a correspondence between two levels: a formal structural analysis of the tendencies of capitalist society and of the social agents resulting from them, and an intuitive identification of those agents. Everybody knew who the workers, or the peasants, or the bourgeoisie were. And – Marxists, at least – knew what it meant for the working class to become a 'universal class'. But the very fact that the 'enlarged conception of the working class' discusses *who* the workers are means that the correspondence between the intuitive level and structural analysis no longer obtains. Most damaging: even if the enlarged conception of the working class were correct – which it is not – it would be impossible to derive from it any conclusion concerning 'class politics', for it speaks only about a *virtual* working class, corresponding to no specifiable group. The same for the first strategy: we no longer know what class politics could be if the identity of concrete agents is given by an enumeration of features whose mutual connections are not thought at all.

This leads me to the second and most important feature of the two discursive strategies discussed above. Whatever the shortcomings of the classical Marxist theory of classes, one has to recognize that it never gave up about being a *theory of articulation*. Even in the most naive forms of vulgar Marxism, there was always the attempt to ascribe different features of social agents to different levels of internal efficacy and articulation: the distinction base/superstructure, the triad economic/political/ideological, and so on. The impossibility of containing different and increasingly autonomous contents within the straitjacket of the old frameworks – class, capitalism, and so forth – led, in a first moment, to more complex and subtle mechanisms of articulation, while maintaining the validity of the old articulating entities. Thus the Althusserian School, in the 1960s and 1970s, introduced categories such as determination *in the last instance*, dominant role, relative autonomy, overdetermination, and so on. This was not, however, the end of the process. I think that the last stage in the disintegration of the old frameworks is to be found in enumerating strategies such as the ones we have just mentioned: they give up on articulating logics while maintaining, in some sort of phantasmic role, the old articulating entities. (To enumerate is not to establish any connection between the enumerated entities. Incorporating a formerly articulating entity into an enumeration is one way of depriving it of any meaning. Another is Žižek's: vociferously to proclaim the principle of class struggle, while refusing to say anything about the conditions of its validity.) In some way, we are in a situation similar to the one described by Eric Auerbach[4] apropos the dissolution of the orderly structure of Ciceronian classical language: with the decline of the Roman order, the old institutional distinctions were unable to hegemonize an increasingly chaotic social reality. So the rich hypotactic structures of classical Latin were substituted by an *enumerative* paratactical narrative (et . . . et . . . et) which just added up fragments of a reality that one was no longer able to think in its connections.[5]

It would be a mistake, however, to dismiss these enumerative strategies as simply wrong. They must simply be seen as the first discursive attempts at dealing with those processes, in contemporary societies, which are eroding the relevance of the old framework notions. Let me just mention the most visible of these processes.[6] In the first place, the decline of the working class, over the last thirty to forty years, in the advanced capitalist world, both in absolute numbers and in its structural organization. Its internal splits, its participation in a generalized mass culture – a youth culture, among other things – has seriously eroded the separate working-class identity which was so characteristic of the Fordist era – in Europe, for instance, it had been organized around the red belts of the big industrial cities, which were the centres of a proletarian culture. To this I would have to add the divisions of the workers in terms of nationality – immigrant workers, and so on. Special mention has to be made of the levels of unemployment, which are increasingly putting into question the very notion of 'class' on which Marxism had rested. For Marxism, a *certain* level of unemployment was functional to capitalism in so far as the industrial reserve army was needed for the reconstitution of the level of profits required for capitalist accumulation. But if the level of unemployment goes beyond a certain point, it ceases to be functional to capitalism,[7] and calls into question the identity of the unemployed as a *class* identity. And not only of the unemployed: those who *have* employment can no longer conceive of their identities in relation to an underlying mechanism governing periods of both employment and unemployment. For them, employment becomes a *political* issue, not just the result of a self-regulated *economic* mechanism. So the identities resulting from structural unemployment will be widely open to hegemonic constructions and rearticulations. The same could be said about other structural changes in our societies: the disappearance of the peasantry, which has resulted not in its incorporation into a proletarian mass, as Marx thought, but in the development of an agribusiness which has altered, for the first time in human history, the balance between rural and urban population; the explosion of higher education, which has made students – again, for the first time in history – a sizeable part of the social structure, to be taken into account as far as politics is concerned; the incorporation of women into the labour market, which has been the epicentre of a momentous transformation in gender relations, whose full consequences we are only just starting to glimpse.

The central question, as far as 'class' analysis is concerned, is the following. The unity of a class, for Marxism, should be conceived as a set of subject positions, systematically interlinked so as to constitute a separate identity, and grounded on a core given by the location of the social agent in the relations of production. Such a conception is under threat if: (a) the subject positions lose their systematicity and start decentring instead of reinforcing the identity of the social agent; (b) differential identitary logics cut across class boundaries and tend to constitute identities which do not overlap with class positions; (c) location in the production process loses its centrality in defining the overall identity of social agents. The key point is: have these tendencies become more accentuated in the world of late capitalism, or, on the contrary, have counter-tendencies reinforcing *class* identities been dominant? The question hardly needs to be answered. There are still remainders of full class identities in our world – a mining enclave, some backward peasant areas – but the main line of development works in the opposite direction.

The generalized awareness of this trend is what gives its verisimilitude to those lines of thought that Žižek calls 'postmodernism'. The failure of the post-modern approach, however, is that it has transformed the awareness of the dissolution of class identities, and the disintegration of the classical forms of totalization, into the assertion of an actual dispersion of elements which renders the category of 'articulation' obsolete. In short, it has transformed the *epistemological* failure of classical totalizing discourses into an *ontological* condition of what is going on in our social world. This explains, once again, my differences with Žižek. We both assert the need for an articulating discourse which does not remain on the level of a pure enumeration of discrete identities and demands; but Žižek sees in postmodernism some kind of perverse deviation and, in his search for an articulating, totalizing dimension, goes back to traditional Marxist notions such as 'class struggle' – without in the least engaging in an analysis of the objective historical tendencies undermining them. I, on the contrary, am ready to accept the challenge of postmodernism, and to try to retain the notion of articulating logics, while fully respecting the particularistic tendencies that the postmodern discourse has brought to light. How is this possible? This is the last issue that I want to deal with in the next and final section of this essay.

Collective wills and social totalities

If we are going to succeed in our task, we must be very careful not to ground the articulating logics in anything external to the field of particularities. It has to be an articulation which operates out of the internal logic of the particularities themselves. Conversely, the emergence of the particular as such cannot result from an autonomous, self-induced movement, but has to be conceived of as one of the internal possibilities opened up by the articulating logic. To put it in other terms: universalism (the moment of the articulated totality) and particularism are not two opposed notions, but have to be conceived – to go back for a moment to the metaphor of chess-playing – as the two different moves ('universalizing' and 'particularizing') which shape a hegemonic, articulating totality. So there is no room for conceiving totality as a frame *within which* hegemonic practices operate: the frame itself has to be constituted through hegemonic practices. And such practices are the locus of articulating logics. What, however, is an articulating logic? To explain it I will present, in the first place, a simplified schema which will be made more complex in a second step.

I　Let us take, as our starting point, the example of the formation of a collective will, inspired by Rosa Luxemburg, that we discussed at the beginning of *Hegemony and Socialist Strategy*. Its basic features are:

(a)　In a situation of extreme oppression – the Tsarist regime, for instance – workers start a strike demanding higher wages. The demand is a particular one, but in the context of that repressive regime it is going to be seen as an anti-system activity. So the meaning of that demand is going to be split, from the very beginning, between its own particularity and a more universal dimension.

(b)　It is this potentially more universal dimension that can inspire struggles for different demands in other sectors – students for the relaxation of discipline in educational establishments, liberal politicians for freedom of the press, and so on. Each of these demands is, in its particularity, unrelated to the others; what unites them is that they constitute between themselves a chain of equivalences in so far as all of them are bearers of an anti-system meaning. The presence of a frontier separating the oppressive regime from the rest of society is the very condition of the universalization of the demands via equivalences (in Marx's words: a social sector has to become a general 'crime' for the aims of society as a whole to emerge).

(c)　However, the more extended the chain of equivalences, the more the need for a general equivalent representing the chain as a whole. The means of representation are, however, only the existing particularities. So one of them has to assume the representation of the chain as a whole. This is the strictly hegemonic move: the body of one particularity assumes a function of universal representation.

We can represent this set of relations through the following diagram:

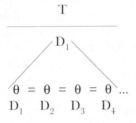

where T stands for Tsarism (in our example); the horizontal line for the frontier separating the oppressive regime from the rest of society; the circles D_1 . . . D_4 for the particular demands, split between a bottom semi-circle representing the particularity of the demand and a top semi-circle representing its anti-system meaning, which is what makes their equivalential relation possible. Finally D_1 above the equivalent circles stands for the general equivalent (it is part of the equivalential chain, but it is also above it).

We have to add one more possibility to this schema: that the oppressive regime engages itself in a hegemonic operation and attempts to absorb transformistically (to use Gramsci's term) some of the oppositional demands. In this way, it can destabilize the frontier that separates it from the rest of society. The way to do this is to break the link between a particular demand and its equivalential relation with all the other demands. If the *logic of equivalence* universalizes the demands by making them all bearers of a meaning which transcends their particularities, the transformistic operation particularizes the demands by neutralizing their equivalential potential. This second logic, which is the strict opposite of the equivalential one is what I call *logic of difference*. (This, incidentally, is the possibility that worries Žižek: that the demands of the new movements become so specific that they could be transformistically integrated into the system, and cease to be the bearers of a more universal, emancipatory meaning.)

All the preceding considerations show clearly why universality, for us, is the universality of an empty signifier: for the only possible universality is the one constructed through an equivalential chain. The more extended this chain is, the less its general equivalent will be attached to any particularistic meaning. This universality, however, is neither formal nor abstract, for the condition of the tendentially empty character of the general equivalent is the increasing extension of a chain of equivalences between particularities. Emptiness, as a result, presupposes the concrete. Both because the general equivalent will be, at the same time, above the chain (as its representative) and inside it, and because the chain will include some equivalences but not others, the universality obtainable through equivalential logics will always be a universality contaminated by particularity. There is not, strictly speaking, a signifier which is truly empty, but one which is only tendentially so.

With these considerations, we have determined three hegemonic operations: the logic of equivalence; its corollary, which is the assumption by a particularity of a function of universal representation; and the logic of difference, which separates the links of the equivalential chains. These three operations are what I have called articulatory logics. I now have to mention – there is space only to mention them – some other dimensions which make this model more complex.

II My previous analysis *presupposed* the presence of a clear-cut frontier separating an oppressive power from the rest of society – although I have already hinted that transformistic strategies can blur or destabilize that frontier. Nevertheless, it is clear that there is no undisturbed chain of equivalences without frontier. What happens, however, if this blurring of the frontiers becomes more general? Also, in what circumstances would that happen? I have mentioned before that the transformistic operation consisted in a particularizing logic based on breaking an equivalential chain. This, however, is only half of the truth; the other half is that the particularized element does not simply remain as purely particular, but enters into a different set of equivalences (those constituting the identity of the dominant powers). So, strictly speaking, the moment of universality is never entirely absent. Butler expresses this very well when she writes:

in those cases where the 'universal' loses its empty status and comes to represent an ethnically restrictive conception of community and citizenship (Israel), or becomes equated with certain organizations of kinship (the nuclear, heterosexual family), or with certain racial identifications, then it is not just in the name of the excluded particulars that politicization occurs, but in the name of a different kind of universality. (JB, p. 166)

This is entirely correct. There is no politics of pure particularity. Even the most particularistic of demands will be made in terms of something transcending it. As, however, the moment of universality will be differently constructed in various discourses, we will have either a struggle between different conceptions of universality, or an extension of the equivalential logics to those very conceptions, so that a wider one is constructed – although we must realize that a remainder of particularity will always be ineradicable. (If we could have an *absolutely* empty signifier, 'universality' would have found its true and final body, and hegemony, as a way of constructing political meanings, would be at an end. 'Total emptiness' and 'total fullness' mean, in fact, exactly the same thing.) The chains of equivalence are *always* disturbed, interrupted by other hegemonic interventions that construct meanings and identities through different equivalential chains. The meaning of the term 'woman', for instance, will be part of different equivalential chains in a feminist discourse and in those of the moral majority. There is an essential unfixity in the meaning attached to some contested signifiers as a result of the operation of a plurality of strategies in the same discursive space. If I have called the general equivalent unifying an undisturbed equivalential chain the *empty signifier*, I will call the one whose emptiness results from the unfixity introduced by a plurality of discourses interrupting each other the *floating signifier*. In practice, both processes overdetermine each other, but it is important to keep the analytic distinction between them. All this means that, as far as I can see, Butler and I are in broad agreement about the interpenetration between universality and particularity in social and political discourses.

I want to conclude with a brief remark concerning the tasks of the

Left, as I see them, in the context of contemporary politics. There is no politics without the creation of political frontiers, but creating such frontiers is more difficult when one cannot rely on stable entities (such as the 'classes' of Marxist discourse) but has to construct through political action the very social entities which have to be emancipated. This, however, is the political challenge of our age. Its contours become more visible if we confront them with the most obvious temptations to elude politics which haunt us: to do away with social division and antagonisms in the name of a conflictless society – the Third Way, the radical centre (there are no right-wing or left-wing economic policies, only good ones, as the inimitable Tony Blair has asserted); to take refuge in exclusively defensive politics, leaving aside any strategic thought about changing today's hegemonic balance of forces; to abandon political struggle altogether and to continue repeating old Marxist formulas which have become empty metaphysical propositions, with little connection with what is actually happening in the world.

There is no future for the Left if it is unable to create an expansive universal discourse, constructed out of, not against, the proliferation of particularisms of the last few decades. A dimension of universality is already operating in the discourses which organize particular demands and an issue-orientated politics, but it is an implicit and undeveloped universality, incapable of proposing itself as a set of symbols able to stir the imagination of vast sectors of the population. The task ahead is to expand those seeds of universality, so that we can have a full social imaginary, capable of competing with the neoliberal consensus which has been the hegemonic horizon of world politics for the last thirty years. It is certainly a difficult task, but it is one which, at least, we can properly formulate. To do so is already to have won a first important battle.

Notes

1. Ludwig Wittgenstein, *Philosophical Investigations*, Oxford: Basil Blackwell 1983, 108, p. 47ᵉ.

2. Butler says that she is not sure what I understand by 'panlogicism'. Let me just say that I use the term in its usual meaning in the literature on Hegel – namely, the project of a presuppositionless philosophy.

3. *The Logic of Hegel*, trans. from *The Encyclopaedia of the Philosophical Sciences* by William Wallace, Oxford: Clarendon Press 1892, ch 1, 'Introduction', pp. 3–29.

4. Erich Auerbach, *Mimesis: The Representation of Reality in Western Literature*, Princeton, NJ: Princeton University Press 1968, chs 3, 4.

5. One could ask oneself why all these intellectual contortions to keep the notion of the centrality of the working class at any cost. It does not require a trained psychoanalyst to discover that the reason is mainly emotional, as the notion of the working class as the emancipatory subject is so deeply rooted in the political imaginary of the Left.

6. See, as a good description of these changes, Eric Hobsbawm, *Age of Extremes: The Short History of the Twentieth Century, 1914–1991*, London: Abacus 1996, ch. 10.

7. This argument was put forward in the 1960s by the Argentinian sociologist José Nun.

Holding the Place

Slavoj Žižek

Butler: the Real and its discontents

Perhaps the ultimate object of contention in our debate is the status of the (Lacanian) Real – so let me begin by reiterating what I perceive to be the core of the problem. Butler's critique relies on the opposition between the (hypostasized, proto-transcendental, pre-historical and pre-social) 'symbolic order', that is, the 'big Other', and 'society' as the field of contingent socio-symbolic struggles: all her main points against Laclau or me can be reduced to this matrix: to the basic criticism that we hypostasize some historically contingent formation (even if it is the Lack itself) into a proto-transcen-dental pre-social formal a priori. For example, when I write 'on the lack that inaugurates and defines, negatively, human social reality', I allegedly posit 'a transcultural structure to social reality that presupposes a sociality based in fictive and idealized kinship positions that presume the heterosexual family as constituting the defining social bond for all humans' (JB, pp. 141–2). If we formulate the dilemma in these terms, then, of course,

> the disagreement seems inevitable. Do we want to affirm that there is an ideal big Other, or an ideal small other, which is more fundamental than any of its social formulations? Or do we want to question whether any ideality that pertains to sexual difference is ever not constituted by actively reproduced gender norms that pass their ideality off as essential to a pre-social and ineffable sexual difference? (JB, p. 144)

This critical line of reasoning, however, only works *if the (Lacanian) Real is silently reduced to a pre-historical a priori symbolic norm*, as is clear from the following formulation: 'The formal character of this originary, pre-social sexual difference in its ostensible emptiness is *accomplished* precisely through the reification by which a certain idealized and necessary dimorphism takes hold' (JB, p. 145). If, then, sexual difference is elevated into an ideal prescriptive norm – if all concrete variations of sexual life are 'constrained by this non-thematizable normative condition' (JB, p. 147), Butler's conclusion is, of course, inevitable: 'as a transcendental claim, sexual difference should be rigorously opposed by anyone who wants to guard against a theory that would prescribe in advance what kinds of sexual arrangements will and will not be permitted in intelligible culture' (JB, p. 148). Butler is, of course, aware how Lacan's *il n'y a pas de rapport sexuel* means that, precisely, any 'actual' sexual relationship is always tainted by failure; however, she interprets this failure as the failure of the contingent historical reality of sexual life fully to actualize the symbolic norm. Consequently, she can claim that, for Lacanians, 'sexual difference has a transcendental status *even when* sexed bodies emerge that do not fit squarely within ideal gender dimorphism'. In this way, I 'could nevertheless explain intersexuality by claiming that *the ideal is still there*, but the bodies in question – contingent, historically formed – do not conform to the ideal' (JB, p. 145; emphasis added).

I am tempted to say that, in order to get close to what Lacan aims at with his *il n'y a pas de rapport sexuel*, one should begin by replacing *even when* in the above quote with *because*: 'sexual difference has a transcendental status *because* sexed bodies emerge that do not fit squarely within ideal gender dimorphism'. That is to say: far from serving as an implicit symbolic norm that reality can never reach, sexual difference as real/impossible means precisely that *there is no such norm*: sexual difference is that 'rock of impossibility' on which every 'formalization' of sexual difference founders. In the sense in which Butler speaks of 'competing universalities', one can thus speak of *competing symbolizations/normativizations of sexual difference*: if sexual difference may be said to be 'formal', it is certainly a strange form – a form whose main result is precisely that it undermines every universal form which attempts to capture it. If one insists on referring to the opposition between the universal and the particular, between the transcendental and the contingent/pathological, then one should say that sexual difference is the paradox of the particular that is more universal than universality itself – a contingent difference, an indivisible remainder of the 'pathological' sphere (in the Kantian sense of the term) which always somehow derails, throws off balance, normative ideality itself. Far from being normative, sexual difference is therefore *pathological* in the most radical sense of the term: a contingent stain that all symbolic fictions of symmetrical kinship positions try in vain to obliterate. Far from constraining the variety of sexual arrangements in advance, the Real of sexual difference is the traumatic cause which sets their contingent proliferation in motion.[1]

This notion of the Real also enables me to answer Butler's criticism that Lacan hypostasizes the 'big Other' into a kind of pre-historical transcendental a priori: when Lacan emphatically asserts that 'there is no big Other [*il n'y a pas de grand Autre*]', his point is precisely that there is no a priori formal structural schema exempt from historical contingencies – there are only contingent, fragile, inconsistent configurations. (Furthermore, far from clinging to paternal symbolic authority, the 'Name-of-the-Father' is for Lacan a *fake*, a *semblance* which conceals this structural inconsistency.) In other words, the claim that the Real is inherent to the Symbolic is strictly equal to the claim that 'there is no big Other': the Lacanian Real is that traumatic 'bone in the throat' that *contaminates* every ideality of the symbolic, rendering it contingent and inconsistent. For this reason, far from being opposed to historicity, the Real is its very 'ahistorical' ground, the a priori of historicity *itself* (here I fully agree with Laclau). We can thus see how the entire *topology* changes from Butler's description of the Real and the 'big Other' as the pre-historical a priori to their actual functioning in Lacan's edifice: in her critical portrait, Butler describes an ideal 'big Other' which persists as a norm, although it is never fully actualized, although the contingencies of history thwart its full imposition; while Lacan's edifice is, rather, centred on the tension between some traumatic 'particular absolute', some kernel which resists symbolization, and the 'competing universalities' (to use Butler's appropriate term) that endeavour in vain to symbolize/normalize it.[2]

The gap between the symbolic a priori Form and history/sociality is utterly foreign to Lacan – that is to say, the 'duality' with which Lacan operates is not the duality of the a priori form/norm, the symbolic Order, and its imperfect historical realization: for Lacan, as well as for Butler, there is *nothing* outside contingent, partial, inconsistent symbolic practices, no 'big Other' that guarantees their ultimate consistency. In contrast to Butler and the historicists, however, Lacan grounds historicity in a different way: not in the simple empirical excess of 'society' over symbolic schemata (here Laclau is right in his criticism of Butler: her notion of society/history as opposed to 'the symbolic' is a direct empiricist reference to an ontologically unexplained positive wealth of reality), but in the resistant kernel *within* the symbolic process itself. The Lacanian Real is thus not simply a technical term for the neutral limit of conceptualization – here, one should be as precise as possible with regard to the relationship between the trauma as real and the domain of socio-symbolic historical practices: the Real is neither pre-social nor a social effect – the point is, rather, that the Social itself is *constituted* by the exclusion of some traumatic Real. What is 'outside the Social' is not some positive a priori symbolic form/norm, merely its negative founding gesture itself.[3]

As a result, when Butler criticizes my alleged inconsistencies, she gets entangled in the results of her own reductive reading of Lacan: she imposes on Lacan the network of classic oppositions (transcendental form versus contingent content; ideal versus material); then, when the object resists and, of course, does not fit this schema, she reads this as the criticized theory's inconsistency (*where*, for instance, do I 'alternately describe [the Real] as material and ideal' (JB, p. 152)?). In the same vein, Butler often uses the obvious fact of co-dependent tension between the two terms as the argument against their conceptual distinction. For example, while I endorse her claim that 'it would not be possible to postulate the social norm on the one side of the analysis, and the fantasy on the other, for the *modus operandi* of the norm is the fantasy, and the very syntax of the fantasy could not be read without an understanding of the lexicon of the social norm' (JB, p. 155), I none the less insist that the formal distinction between these two levels is to be maintained: the social norm (the set of symbolic rules) is sustained by fantasies; it can operate only through this phantasmic support, but the fantasy that sustains it had none the less to be *disavowed*, excluded from the public domain. It is on this level that I find Hannah Arendt's notion of the 'banality of Evil' problematic: to translate it somewhat crudely into Lacanese, Arendt's claim is that the ideal Nazi executor–subject (like Eichmann) was a pure subject of the signifier, an anonymous bureaucratic executor deprived of any passionate bestiality – he accomplished what was asked of or expected from him as a matter of pure routine, without any involvement. My counter-thesis is that, far from functioning in effect as a pure subject of the signifier with no idiosyncratic phantasmic investment, the ideal Nazi subject *did* rely on the passionate bestiality articulated in obscene phantasmic scenarios; these scenarios, however, were not directly subjectively assumed as part of his personal self-experience – they were externalized, materialized in the 'objective' Nazi state ideological apparatus and its functioning.[4]

Perhaps the best way to mark the theoretico-political distance that separates Butler from me is through what I consider her strongest and politically most engaged contribution to our debate: her argumentation apropos of the demand for the legal recognition of gay marriages. While she acknowledges the advantages involved in such a recognition (gay couples get all the entitlements that the 'straight' married couples get; they are integrated into the institution of marriage, and thus recognized as equal to 'straight' couples, etc.), she focuses on the traps of endorsing this demand: in doing so, gays break their alliance (or, to put it in Laclau's terms, exclude themselves from the chain of equivalences) with all those *not* included in the legal form of marriage marriage (single parents, non-monogamous subjects, etc.); furthermore, they strengthen state apparatuses by contributing to their increasing right to regulate private lives. The paradoxical result is thus that the gap between those whose status is legitimized and those who live a shadowy existence is widened: those who remain excluded are even more excluded. Butler's counter-proposal is that instead of endorsing legal form of marriage as the condition of entitlements (inheritance, parenthood, etc.), one should, rather, struggle to *dissociate* these entitlements from the form of marriage: to make them independent of it.

My first general point here is that, with regard to the way the notion

of political universality is elaborated in recent French political philosophy (Rancière, Balibar, Badiou), I perceive the shadowy existence of
those who are condemned to lead a spectral life outside the domain of
the global order, blurred in the background, unmentionable, submerged
in the formless mass of 'population', without even a proper particular
place of their own, in a slightly different way from Butler. I am tempted
to claim that this shadowy existence is *the very site of political universality*: in
politics, universality is asserted when such an agent with no proper
place, 'out of joint', posits itself as the direct embodiment of universality against all those who do have a place within the global order. And
this gesture is at the same time that of subjectivization, since 'subject'
designates by definition an entity that is *not 'substance'*: a dislocated entity,
an entity which lacks its own place within the Whole.

While, of course, I fully support Butler's political aims, my main
apprehension concerns the fact that she conceives state power in the
Foucauldian mode, conceives state power as an agent of control and regulation, inclusion and exclusion; resistance to power is then, of course,
located in the marginal spheres of those who are excluded or half-
excluded from the official power network, leading a shadowy spectral
half-existence, without a proper place within the social space, prevented
from asserting their symbolic identity. Consequently, Butler locates
emancipatory struggle primarily in these marginal agents' resistance
against state regulatory mechanisms, which takes place within civil society. So what is my problem with this framework? What Butler leaves out
of consideration is the way in which *state power itself is split from within and
relies on its own obscene spectral underside*: public state apparatuses are always
supplemented by their shadowy double, by a network of publicly disavowed rituals, unwritten rules, institutions, practices, and so on. Today,
we should not forget that the series of publicly 'invisible' agents leading
a spectral half-existence includes, among others, the entire white
supremacist underground (fundamentalist Christian survivalists in
Montana, neo-Nazis, the remnants of the Ku Klux Klan, etc.). So the
problem is not simply the marginals who lead the spectral half-existence of those excluded by the hegemonic symbolic regime; the problem
is that this regime itself, in order to survive, has to rely on a whole gamut
of mechanisms whose status is spectral, disavowed, excluded from the

public domain. Even the very opposition between state and civil society is thoroughly ambivalent today: no wonder the Moral Majority presents itself (and is in effect organized as) local civil society's resistance against the 'progressive' regulatory interventions of the liberal state.

Although Butler is well aware of the subversive potential of Hegel's notion of 'concrete universality', I am tempted to claim that it is her basic acceptance of the Foucauldian notion of power which explains her failure fully to develop the consequences of the notion of 'concrete universality' for the notion of power, and clearly to locate the split between 'official' universality and its spectral underside within the hegemonic power discourse itself, as its own obscene supplement. So when Butler notes critically that, in my work –

> sexual difference occupies a distinctive position within the chain of signifiers, one that both occasions the chain and is one link in the chain. How are we to think the vacillation between these two meanings, and are they always distinct, given that the transcendental is the ground, and occasions a sustaining condition for what is called the historical? (JB, p. 143)

– my answer is that I fully assume this paradox: it is the basic structural paradox of dialectics, and the *concept* that indicates 'how [we are] to think the vacillation between these two meanings' was proposed long ago by Hegel, and then applied by Marx; it is the concept of 'oppositional determination [*genensätzliche Bestimmung*]' which Hegel introduces in the subchapter on identity in his Greater Logic. In the course of the dialectical process, the universal genus encounters *itself* 'in its oppositional determination', that is, as one of its own species (which is why for Hegel, paradoxically, each genus has ultimately two species: itself and the Species as such). Marx refers to this concept twice: first in the Introduction to the *Grundrisse* manuscript, when he emphasizes the double structural role of production in the articulated totality of production, distribution, exchange, and consumption (production is simultaneously the encompassing universal element, the structuring principle of this totality, *and* one of its particular elements); then in *Capital*, when he posits that, among the multiple species of Capital, the universal genus of Capital 'encounters itself' in finance capital, the immediate embodiment of Capital in general as opposed to particular capitals. What Hegel does with this concept is thus, in my view, strictly analogous to Laclau's notion of antagonistic relationship: the key feature in both cases is that the external difference (constitutive of genus itself) coincides with the internal difference (between the species of the genus). Another way of making the same point is Marx's well-known insistence – again in the Introduction to the *Grundrisse* – that:

> [i]n all forms of society there is one specific kind of production which predominates over the rest, whose relations thus assign rank and influence to the others. It is a general illumination which bathes all the other colours and modifies their particularity. It is a particular ether which determines the specific gravity of every being which has materialized within it.[5]

This overdetermination of universality by part of its content, this short circuit between the universal and particular, is the key feature of Hegelian 'concrete universality', and I am in total agreement with Butler who, it seems to me, also aims at this legacy of 'concrete universality' in her central notion of 'competing universalities': in her insistence on how each particular position, in order to articulate itself, involves the (implicit or explicit) assertion of *its own mode of universality*, she develops a point which I also try repeatedly to make in my own work.

Take the example of religions: it is not enough to say that the genus Religion is divided into a multitude of species ('primitive' animism, pagan polytheism, monotheism, which is then further divided into Judaism, Christianity, Islam . . .); the point, rather, is that *each of these particular species involves its own universal notion of what religion is 'as such', as well as its own view on (how it differs from) other religions.* Christianity is not simply different from Judaism and Islam; within its horizon, the very difference that separates it from the other two 'religions of the Book' appears in a way which is unacceptable for the other two. In other words, when a Christian debates with a Muslim, they do not simply disagree – they disagree about their very disagreement: about what makes the difference between their religions. (And, as I have repeatedly tried to argue, *mutatis mutandis* the same goes for the political difference between Left and Right: they do not simply disagree – the very political opposition between Left and Right appears in a different view perceived from the Left or from the Right.) *This* is Hegel's 'concrete universality': since each particularity involves *its own* universality, its own notion of the Whole and its own part within it, there is no 'neutral' universality that would serve as the medium for these particular positions. Thus Hegelian 'dialectical development' is not a deployment of a particular content within universality but the process by which, in the passage from one particularity to another, *the very universality that encompasses both also changes*: 'concrete universality' designates precisely this 'inner life' of universality itself, this process of passage in the course of which the very universality that aims at encompassing it is caught in it, submitted to transformations.

Laclau: class, hegemony, and the contaminated universal

This brings me to Laclau: in my view, all his critical remarks are ultimately grounded in what I have called his secret Kantianism, in his rejection of the Hegelian legacy of 'concrete universality'. So let me begin with Laclau's counter-argument: the Kantian regulative Idea involves a determinate *positive content* which is given in advance, while the open struggle for hegemony involves no such content. . . . Apart from the fact that the Kantian regulative idea ultimately also designates a purely formal notion of the full realization of Reason, I am tempted to argue that the main 'Kantian' dimension of Laclau lies in his acceptance of the unbridgeable gap between the enthusiasm for the impossible Goal of a political engagement and its more modest realizable content. Laclau himself evokes the example of the collapse of Socialism in Eastern Europe: it was experienced by many of its participants as the moment of sublime enthusiasm, as the promise of global panacea, as an event that would realize freedom and social solidarity, while the results are much more modest – capitalist democracy, with all its impasses, not to mention the rise of nationalist aspirations. My claim is that if we accept such a gap as the *ultimate* horizon of political engagement, does it not leave us

with a choice apropos of such an engagement: either we must blind ourselves to the necessary ultimate failure of our endeavour – regress to
naivety, and let ourselves be caught up in the enthusiasm – or we must
adopt a stance of cynical distance, participating in the game while being
fully aware that the result will be disappointing?[6] Laclau's Kantianism
emerges at its purest when he deals with the relation between emancipation and power. Answering the criticism that if power is inherent to
the emancipatory project, does this not contradict the idea that full
emancipation involves the elimination of power, he argues:

> the contamination of emancipation by power is not an unavoidable
> empirical imperfection to which we have to accommodate, but involves
> a higher human ideal than a universality representing a totally recon-
> ciled human essence, because a fully reconciled society, a transparent
> society, would be entirely free in the sense of self-determination, but that
> full realization of freedom would be equivalent to the death of freedom,
> for all possibility of dissent would have been eliminated from it. Social
> division, antagonism and its necessary consequence – power – are the
> true conditions of a freedom which does not eliminate particularity.
> (EL, p. 208)

Laclau's reasoning is as follows: the ultimate goal of our political
engagement, full emancipation, will never be achieved; emancipation
will remain forever contaminated by power; this contamination, however, is not due only to the fact that our imperfect social reality does not
allow for full emancipation – that is, we are not dealing only with the gap
between ideal and imperfect reality. The very full realization of emancipated society would mean the death of freedom, the establishment of
a closed transparent social space with no opening for a free subjective
intervention – the limitation of human freedom is at the same time its
positive condition . . . . Now, my claim is that this reasoning reproduces
almost verbatim Kant's argumentation, from the *Critique of Practical
Reason*, about the necessary limitation of human cognitive capacities:
God, in his infinite wisdom, limited our cognitive capacities in order to
make us free responsible agents, since, if we were to have direct access to
the noumenal sphere, we would no longer be free, but would turn into

blind automata. Human imperfection is thus, for Kant, the positive condition of freedom.[7] The hidden implication here is the reverse of Kant's
'You can, because you must!', the paradoxical logic of 'You cannot,
because you must not!' – You cannot achieve full emancipation, because
you must not achieve it, that is, because this would mean the end of freedom! I find a similar deadlock in Laclau's answer to my criticism that he
does not account for the historical status of his own theory of hegemony.
Basically I endorse his critical remarks about Butler's assertion of
absolute historicity and context-dependency: Butler avoids the question
of the conditions of context-dependency and historicity – had she asked
this question explicitly:

> she would have been confronted with two alternatives which, [. . .]
> would have been equally unpalatable to her: either she would have had
> to assert that historicity as such is a contingent historical construct – and
> therefore that there are societies which are not historical and, as a result,
> fully transcendentally determined . . . ; or she would have had to provide
> some ontology of historicity as such, as a result of which the transcen-
> dental-structural dimension would have had to be reintroduced into her
> analysis. (EL, pp. 183–4)

I am tempted to claim that this same criticism applies to Laclau himself –
here is his answer to my critique that he does not account for the status of
his theory of hegemony itself (is it a theory of today's specific contingent
historical constellation, so that in Marx's time 'class essentialism' was
adequate, while today we need the full assertion of contingency, or is it a
theory describing a transcendental a priori of historicity?):

> Only in contemporary societies is there a generalization of the hege-
> monic form of politics, but for this reason we can interrogate the past,
> and find there inchoate forms of the same processes that are fully visible
> today; and, when they did not occur, understand why things were dif-
> ferent. (EL, p. 200)

What I find problematic in this solution is that it implicitly endorses the
pseudo-Hegelian evolutionary point of view that I critically evoked in

my first intervention in this debate: although sociopolitical life and its structure were always-already the outcome of hegemonic struggles, it is none the less only today, in our specific historical constellation – in the 'postmodern' universe of globalized contingency – that the radically contingent-hegemonic nature of political processes is finally allowed to 'come/return to itself', to free itself of 'essentialist' baggage. . . . In other words, the real question is: what is the exact status of this 'generalization of the hegemonic form of politics' in contemporary societies? Is it in itself a contingent event, the result of hegemonic struggle, or is it the result of some underlying historical logic which is *not* itself determined by the hegemonic form of politics? My answer here is that this 'generalization of the hegemonic form of politics' is itself dependent on a certain socioeconomic process: it is contemporary global capitalism with its dynamics of 'deterritorialization', which has created the conditions for the demise of 'essentialist' politics and the proliferation of new multiple political subjectivities. So, again, to make myself clear: my point is *not* that the economy (the logic of Capital) is a kind of 'essentialist anchor' that somehow 'limits' hegemonic struggle – on the contrary, it is its *positive condition*; it creates the very background against which 'generalized hegemony' can thrive.[8]

It is along these lines that I am also tempted to address the relationship between 'class struggle' and identity politics. Laclau makes two points here. First: 'class antagonism is not inherent to capitalist relations of production, but [that] it takes place between those relations and the identity of the worker outside them' (EL, p. 202); it emerges only when workers as individuals, not as the mere embodiment of economic categories, for cultural and other reasons, experience their situation as 'unjust', and resist. Furthermore, even if and when workers resist, their demands are not intrinsically anti-capitalist, but can also aim at partial reformist goals that can be satisfied within the capitalist system. As such, 'class struggle is just one species of identity politics, and one which is becoming less and less important in the world in which we live' (EL, p. 203) – the workers' position does not give them any a priori privilege in the anti-systemic struggle.[9]

On the first point, I not only endorse Laclau's anti-objectivist stance; I even think that when he opposes 'objective' relations of production and 'subjective' struggle and resistance, he makes too much of a concession to objectivism. There are no 'objective' relations of production which can *then* involve or not involve the resistance of the individuals caught up in them: the very absence of struggle and resistance – the fact that both sides involved in relations accept them without resistance – *is already the index of the victory of one side in the struggle.* One should not forget that in spite of some occasional 'objectivist' formulations, the reduction of individuals to embodied economic categories (terms of the relations of production) is for Marx not a simple fact, but the result of the process of 'reification', that is, an aspect of the ideological 'mystification' inherent to capitalism. As for Laclau's second point about class struggle being 'just one species of identity politics, one which is becoming less and less important in the world in which we live', one should counter it by the already-mentioned paradox of 'oppositional determination', of the *part* of the chain that sustains its *horizon* itself: class antagonism certainly appears as one in the series of social antagonisms, but it is simultaneously the specific antagonism which 'predominates over the rest, whose relations thus assign rank and influence to the others. It is a general illumination which bathes all the other colours and modifies their particularity'. My example here is, again, the very proliferation of new political subjectivities: this proliferation, which seems to relegate 'class struggle' to a secondary role is the *result* of the 'class struggle' in the context of today's global capitalism, of the advance of so-called 'post-industrial' society. In more general terms, my point of contention with Laclau here is that I do not accept that all elements which enter into hegemonic struggle are in principle equal: in the series of struggles (economic, political, feminist, ecological, ethnic, etc.) there is always *one* which, while it is part of the chain, secretly overdetermines its very horizon.[10] This contamination of the universal by the particular is 'stronger' than the struggle for hegemony (i.e. for which particular content will hegemonize the universality in question): it structures in advance *the very terrain* on which the multitude of particular contents fight for hegemony. Here I agree with Butler: the question is not just which particular content will hegemonize the empty place of universality – the question is, also and above all, which secret privileging and inclusions/exclusions had to occur for this empty place as such to emerge in the first place.

Soyons réalistes, demandons l'impossible!

This brings me, finally, to the Big Question of capitalism itself. Here is Laclau's answer to my claim that the proponents of postmodern politics accept capitalism as 'the only game in town', and renounce any attempt to overcome the existing liberal-capitalist regime:

> The difficulty with assertions like this is that they mean absolutely nothing. . . . Should we understand that [Žižek] wants to impose the dictatorship of the proletariat? Or does he want to socialize the means of production and abolish market mechanisms? And what is his political strategy to achieve these rather peculiar aims? . . . Without at least the beginning of an answer to these questions, [Žižek's] anti-capitalism is mere empty talk. (EL, p. 206)

First, let me emphasize what these lines mean: they mean, in effect, that *today, one cannot even imagine a viable alternative to global capitalism* – the only option for the Left is 'the introduction of state regulation and democratic control of the economy so that the worst effects of globalization are avoided' (EL, p. 206), that is, palliative measures which, while resigning themselves to the course of events, restrict themselves to limiting the damaging effects of the inevitable. Even if this *is* the case, I think one should at least *take note* of the fact that the much-praised postmodern 'proliferation of new political subjectivities', the demise of every 'essentialist' fixation, the assertion of full contingency, occur against the background of a certain silent *renunciation* and *acceptance*: the renunciation of the idea of a global change in the fundamental relations in our society (who still seriously questions capitalism, state and political democracy?) and, consequently, the acceptance of the liberal democratic capitalist framework which *remains the same*, the unquestioned background, in all the dynamic proliferation of the multitude of new subjectivities. In short, Laclau's claim about my anti-capitalism also holds for what he calls the 'democratic control of the economy', and, more generally, for the entire project of 'radical democracy': either it means palliative damage-control measures within the global capitalist framework, or it means *absolutely nothing*.

I am fully aware of what one should call, without any irony, the great achievements of liberal capitalism: probably, never in human history have so many people enjoyed such a degree of freedom and material standard of living as in today's developed Western countries. However, far from accepting the New World Order as an inexorable process which allows only for moderate palliative measures, I continue to think, in the old Marxist vein, that today's capitalism, in its very triumph, is breeding new 'contradictions' which are potentially even more explosive than those of standard industrial capitalism. A series of 'irrationalities' imme- diately comes to mind: the result of the breathtaking growth of productivity in the last few decades is rising unemployment, with the long-term perspective that developed societies will need only 20 per cent of their workforce to reproduce themselves, with the remaining 80 per cent reduced to the status of a surplus from a purely economic point of view; the result of decolonization is that multinationals treat even their own country of origin as just another colony; the result of globalization and the rise of the 'global village' is the ghettoization of whole strata of the population; the result of the much-praised 'disap- pearance of the working class' is the emergence of millions of manual workers labouring in the Third World sweatshops, out of our delicate Western sight . . . The capitalist system is thus approaching its inherent limit and self-cancellation: for the majority of the population, the dream of the virtual 'frictionless capitalism' (Bill Gates) is turning into a night- mare in which the fate of millions is decided in hyper-reflexive speculation on futures.

From the very beginning, capitalist globalization – the emergence of capitalism as the world system – involved its exact opposite: the split, within particular ethnic groups, between those who are included in this globalization and those who are excluded. Today, this split is more rad- ical than ever. On the one hand, we have the so-called 'symbolic class': not only managers and bankers, but also academics, journalists, lawyers, and so on – all those whose domain of work is the virtual symbolic universe. On the other, there are the excluded in all their variations (the permanently unemployed, the homeless, underprivileged ethnic and religious minorities, and so on). In between, there is the notorious 'middle class', passionately attached to the traditional modes of production and ideology (say, a qualified manual worker whose job is threatened), and attacking both extremes, big business and academics as well as the excluded, as 'un-patriotic', 'rootless' deviations. As is always the case with social antagonisms, today's class *antagonism* functions as the intricate interplay between these *three* agents, with shifting strategic alliances: the 'politically correct' symbolic classes defending the excluded against the 'fundamentalist' middle class, and so forth. The split between them is becoming even more radical than traditional class divisions – one is tempted to claim that it is reaching almost ontological proportions, with each group evolving its own 'world-view', its own relation to reality: the 'symbolic class' is individualistic, ecologically sensitive and simultaneously 'postmodern', aware that reality itself is a contingent symbolic formation; the 'middle class' sticks to traditional stable ethics and a belief in 'real life', with which symbolic classes are 'losing touch'; the excluded oscillate between hedonistic nihilism and radical (religious or ethnic) fundamentalism. . . .

Are we not dealing again with the Lacanian triad of Symbolic, Imaginary and Real? Are the excluded not 'real' in the sense of the kernel which resists social integration, and is the 'middle class' not 'imaginary', clinging to the fantasy of society as a harmonious Whole corrupted through moral decay? The main point of this improvised description is that globalization *undermines its own roots*: one can already perceive on the horizon the conflict with the very principle of formal democracy, since, at a certain point, the 'symbolic class' will no longer be able 'democratically' to contain the resistance of the majority.[11] Which way out of this predicament will this class then resort to? Nothing is to be excluded, even up to genetic manipulation to render those who do not fit into globalization more docile . . .

How, then, are we to answer today's predominant consensus according to which the age of ideologies – of grand ideological projects like Socialism or Liberalism – is over, since we have entered the post-ideological era of rational negotiation and decision-making, based upon the neutral insight into economic, ecological, etc. necessities? This consensus can assume different guises, from the neoconservative or Socialist refusal to accept it and consummate the loss of grand ideological projects by means of a proper 'work of mourning' (different attempts to resuscitate global ideological projects) up to the neoliberal opinion according to which the passage from the age of ideologies to the post-ideological era is part of the sad but none the less inexorable process of the maturation of humanity – just as a young man has to learn to accept the loss of grand enthusiastic adolescent plans and enter the everyday adult life of realistic compromises, the collective subject has to learn to accept the withering-away of global utopian ideological projects and the entry into the post-utopian realist era . . . .

The first thing to note about this neoliberal cliché is that the neutral reference to the necessities of the market economy, usually invoked in order to categorize grand ideological projects as unrealistic utopias, is itself to be inserted into the series of great modern utopian projects. That is to say – as Fredric Jameson has pointed out – what characterizes utopia is not a belief in the essential goodness of human nature, or some similar naive notion, but, rather, belief in some global *mechanism* which, applied to the whole of society, will automatically bring about the balanced state of progress and happiness one is longing for – and, in this precise sense, is not *the market* precisely the name for such a mechanism which, properly applied, will bring about the optimal state of society? So, again, the first answer of the Left to those – Leftists themselves – who bemoan the loss of the utopian impetus in our societies should be that this impetus is alive and well – not only in the Rightist 'fundamen-talist' populism which advocates the return to grass-roots democracy, but above all among the advocates of the market economy themselves.[12] The second answer should be a clear line of distinction between utopia and ideology: ideology is not only a utopian project of social transfor-mation with no realistic chance of actualization; no less ideological is the *anti-utopian* stance of those who 'realistically' devalue every global proj-ect of social transformation as 'utopian', that is, as unrealistic dreaming and/or harbouring 'totalitarian' potential – *today's predominant form of ide-ological 'closure' takes the precise form of mental block which prevents us from imagining a fundamental social change, in the interests of an allegedly 'realistic' and 'mature' attitude.*

In his Seminar on the *Ethics of Psychoanalysis*,[13] Lacan developed an opposition between 'knave' and 'fool' as the two intellectual attitudes: the right-wing intellectual is a knave, a conformist who considers the

mere existence of the given order as an argument for it, and mocks the
Left for its 'utopian' plans, which necessarily lead to catastrophe; while
the left-wing intellectual is a fool, a court jester who publicly displays the
lie of the existing order, but in a way which suspends the performative
efficiency of his speech. In the years immediately after the fall of
Socialism, the knave was a neoconservative advocate of the free market
who cruelly rejected all forms of social solidarity as counterproductive
sentimentalism; while the fool was a deconstructionist cultural critic
who, by means of his ludic procedures destined to 'subvert' the existing
order, actually served as its supplement.

Today, however, the relationship between the couple knave–fool and
the political opposition Right/Left is more and more the inversion of the
standard figures of Rightist knave and Leftist fool: are not the Third
Way theoreticians ultimately today's *knaves*, figures who preach cynical
resignation, that is, the necessary failure of every attempt actually to
change something in the basic functioning of global capitalism? And are
not the conservative *fools* – those conservatives whose original modern
model is Pascal and who as it were show the hidden cards of the ruling
ideology, bringing to light its underlying mechanisms which, in order to
remain operative, have to be repressed – far more attractive? Today, in
the face of this Leftist knavery, it is more important than ever to *hold this
utopian place of the global alternative open*, even if it remains empty, living on
borrowed time, awaiting the content to fill it in.

I fully agree with Laclau that after the exhaustion of both the social
democratic welfare state imaginary and the 'really-existing-Socialist'
imaginary, the Left does need a new imaginary (a new mobilizing global
vision). Today, however, the outdatedness of the welfare state and socialist imaginaries is a cliché – the real dilemma is what to do with – how the
Left is to relate to – the predominant *liberal democratic* imaginary. It is my
contention that Laclau's and Mouffe's 'radical democracy' comes all
too close to merely 'radicalizing' this liberal democratic imaginary, while
remaining within its horizon. Laclau, of course, would probably claim
that the point is to treat the democratic imaginary as an 'empty signifier', and to engage in the hegemonic battle with the proponents of the
global capitalist New World Order over what its content will be. Here,
however, I think that Butler is right when she emphasizes that another

way is also open: it is *not* 'necessary to occupy the dominant norm in order to produce an internal subversion of its terms. Sometimes it is important to refuse its terms, to let the term itself wither, to starve it of its strength' (JB, p. 177). This means that the Left has a choice today: either it accepts the predominant liberal democratic horizon (democracy, human rights and freedoms . . .), and engages in a hegemonic battle *within* it, *or it risks the opposite gesture of refusing its very terms, of flatly rejecting today's liberal blackmail that courting any prospect of radical change paves the way for totalitarianism.* It is my firm conviction, my politico-existential premiss, that the old '68 motto *Soyons réalistes, demandons l'impossible!* still holds: it is the advocates of changes and resignifications within the liberal-democratic horizon who are the true utopians in their belief that their efforts will amount to anything more than the cosmetic surgery that will give us capitalism with a human face.

In her second intervention, Butler superbly deploys the reversal that characterizes the Hegelian dialectical process: the aggravated 'contradiction' in which the very differential structure of meaning is collapsing, since every determination immediately turns into its opposite, this 'mad dance', is resolved by the sudden emergence of a new universal determination. The best illustration is provided by the passage from the 'world of self-alienated Spirit' to the Terror of the French Revolution in *The Phenomenology of Spirit*: the pre-Revolutionary 'madness of the musician "who heaped up and mixed together thirty arias, Italian, French, tragic, comic, of every sort; now with a deep bass he descended into hell, then, contracting his throat, he rent the vaults of heaven with a falsetto tone, frantic and soothed, imperious and mocking, by turns" (Diderot, *Nephew of Rameau*)',[14] suddenly turns into its radical opposite: the revolutionary stance pursuing its goal with an inexorable firmness. And my point, of course, is that today's 'mad dance', the dynamic proliferation of multiple shifting identities, also awaits its resolution in a new form of Terror. The only 'realistic' prospect is to ground a new political universality by opting for the *impossible*, fully assuming the place of the exception, with no taboos, no a priori norms ('human rights', 'democracy'), respect for which would prevent us also from 'resignifying' terror, the ruthless exercise of power, the spirit of sacrifice . . . if this radical choice is decried by some bleeding-heart liberals as *Linksfaschismus*, so be it!

Notes

1. Here, of course, I draw on Joan Copjec's path-breaking 'The Euthanasia of Reason', in *Read My Desire*, Cambridge, MA: MIT Press 1995. It is symptomatic that this essay, *the* essay on the philosophical foundations and consequences of the Lacanian notion of sexual difference, is silently passed over in numerous feminist attacks on Lacan.

2. Here, again, we can see how the key to the Lacanian notion of the Real is the overlapping of internal and external difference elaborated exemplarily by Laclau: 'reality' is the external domain that is delineated by the symbolic order, while the Real is an obstacle inherent to the Symbolic, blocking its actualization from within. Butler's standard argument against the Real (that the very line of separation between the Symbolic and the Real is a symbolic gesture *par excellence*) leaves out of consideration this overlapping, which renders the Symbolic inherently inconsistent and fragile.

3. Furthermore, as I have already emphasized in my previous two interventions, Lacan *has* a precise answer to the question of 'which specific content has to be excluded so that the very *empty form* of sexual difference emerges as a battlefield for hegemony': this 'specific content' is what Lacan calls *das Ding*, the impossible–real Thing, or, more specifically, in his *Seminar XI*, 'lamella', that is, libido itself as the undead object, the 'immortal life, or irrepressible life' that 'is subtracted from the living being by virtue of the fact that it is subject to the cycle of sexed reproduction' (Jacques Lacan, *The Four Fundamental Concepts of Psycho-Analysis*, New York: Norton 1977, p. 198).

4. The price Butler pays for this rejection of conceptual distinctions is that she oversimplifies a series of key psychoanalytic insights. For example, her claim that: '[a]lthough it might be inevitable that individuation requires a foreclosure that produces the unconscious, the remainder, it seems equally inevitable that the unconscious is not pre-social, but a certain mode in which the unspeakably social endures' blurs the distinction between the *foreclosure* that generates the traumatic Real and the straight *repression* of some content into the unconscious. What is foreclosed does not persist in the unconscious: the unconscious is the censored part of the subject's discourse; it is a signifying chain that insists on the 'Other Scene' and disturbs the flow of the subject's speech, while the foreclosed Real is an extimate kernel within the unconscious itself.

5. Karl Marx, *Grundrisse*, Harmondsworth: Penguin 1972, p. 107.

6. One should add here that, in historical experience, we often find the opposite gap: an agent introduced a modest measure that aimed merely at solving some particular problem, but then this measure triggered a process of disintegration of the entire social edifice (like Gorbachev's *perestroika*, the aim of which was simply to make Socialism more efficient).

7. In the *Critique of Practical Reason*, Kant endeavoured to answer the question of what would happen to us if we were to gain access to the noumenal domain, to Things in themselves:

instead of the conflict which now the moral disposition has to wage with incli-
nations and in which, after some defeats, moral strength of mind may be
gradually won, God and eternity in their awful majesty would stand unceas-
ingly before our eyes. . . . Thus most actions conforming to the law would be
done from fear, few would be done from hope, none from duty. The moral
worth of actions, on which alone the worth of the person and even of the world
depends in the eyes of supreme wisdom, would not exist at all. The conduct of
man, so long as his nature remained as it is now, would be changed into mere
mechanism, where, as in a puppet show, everything would gesticulate well but
no life would be found in the figures. (Immanuel Kant, *Critique of Practical
Reason*, New York: Macmillan 1956, pp. 152–3)

So, for Kant, direct access to the noumenal domain would deprive us of the very
'spontaneity' which forms the kernel of transcendental freedom: it would turn us into
lifeless automata, or – to put it in today's terms – into 'thinking machines'.

8. To avoid misunderstanding: I am fully aware of the autonomous logic of ideological struggle. According to Richard Dawkins, 'God's utility function' in living nature
is the reproduction of genes; that is to say, genes (DNA) are not a means for the reproduction of living beings, but the other way round: living beings are the means for the
self-reproduction of genes. The same question should be asked apropos of ideology:
what is the 'utility function' of the Ideological State Apparatuses? The materialist
answer is: neither the reproduction of ideology *qua* network of ideas, emotions, etc.,
nor the reproduction of social circumstances legitimized by this ideology, but *the self-
reproduction of the ISA itself*. The 'same' ideology can accommodate to different social
modes; it can change the content of its ideas, etc., just to 'survive' as an ISA. What I
am claiming is that today's capitalism is a kind of global machine that enables a multitude of ideologies, from traditional religions to individualistic hedonism, to 'resignify'
their logic so that they fit its frame – even the teachers of Zen Buddhism like to
emphasizes how the inner peace that comes with the achievement of *satori* enables you
to function more efficiently in the market. . . .

9. Incidentally, my main criticism of identity politics is not its 'particularism' *per se*
but, rather, its partisans' ubiquitous insistence that one's particular position of enunciation legitimizes or even guarantees the authenticity of one's speech: only gays can
speak about homosexuality; only drug addicts about the drug experience, only women
about feminism. . . . Here one should follow Deleuze, who wrote: 'one's own privileged
experiences are bad and reactionary arguments'(*Negotiations*, New York: Columbia
University Press 1995, p. 11): although it may play a limited progressive role in
enabling the victims to assert their subjectivity against the patronizingly sympathetic
liberal discourse *about* them, such 'authentication' by one's direct experience ultimately
undermines the very foundations of emancipatory politics.

10. An example from cinema, again: the ultimate 'trauma' of *Paris Is Burning* – the
film about a group of poor, black Americans who, as part of a parodic show, cross-
dress as upper-class white ladies and mockingly imitate their rituals – is neither race nor
gender identity, but *class*. The point of the film is that, in the three divides subverted by

it (class, race and gender), the class divide, albeit the least 'natural' (i.e. the most 'artificial', contingent, socially conditioned, in contrast to the apparent 'biological' foundation of gender and race), is the most difficult to cross: the only way for the group to cross the class barrier, even in the parodic performance, is to subvert their gender and race identity. . . . (For this point I am indebted to Elisabeth Bronfen, Zurich University.)

11. As the model of an analysis of capitalism close to what I have in mind, see Michael Hardt and Antonio Negri's *Empire* (Cambridge, MA: Harvard University Press 2000), a book which tries to rewrite *The Communist Manifesto* for the twenty-first century. Hardt and Negri describe globalization as an ambiguous 'deterritorialization': triumphant global capitalism has penetrated all pores of social life, down to the most intimate spheres, introducing an unheard-off dynamics which no longer relies on patriarchal and other fixed hierarchical forms of domination, but generates fluid hybrid identities. However, this very dissolution of all substantial social links also lets the genie out of the bottle: it sets free the centrifugal potentials that the capitalist system will no longer be able fully to contain. On account of its very global triumph, the capitalist system is thus more vulnerable than ever today – Marx's old formula still holds: capitalism generates its own gravediggers.

12. The paradox of the US administration's legal action against the monopoly of Microsoft is very pertinent here: does this action not demonstrate how, far from being simply opposed, state regulation and the market are mutually dependent? Left to itself, the market mechanism would lead to the full monopoly of Microsoft, and thus to the self-destruction of competition – it is only through direct state intervention (which, from time to time, orders overlarge companies to break up) that 'free' market competition can be maintained.

13. See Jacques Lacan, *The Ethics of Psychoanalysis*, London: Routledge 1992, pp. 182–3.

14. G.W.F. Hegel, *Phenomenology of Spirit*, Oxford: Oxford University Press 1977, p. 317.